In Memoriam
J.C. Jenkins
1952-1979

As this book was being printed, the author was struck dead by a car on his way to his beloved Sierra. He was returning to his job as Wilderness Ranger in the Golden Trout Wilderness, where he had walked thousands of miles over a period of 7 years gathering material for this superb 2-volume guidebook.

I hope that all who use this book will bring to the mountains the same respect and reverence for them that Jim so fully demonstrated. In doing so, they will be honoring his memory.

Thomas Winnett, President
Wilderness Press

Self-Propelled
in the Southern Sierra

Volume 2: The Great Western Divides

J. C. Jenkins

Wilderness Press
BERKELEY

First edition September 1979
SECOND PRINTING June 1984
Second printing September 1986
Third printing April 1990

Maps by the author (on U.S.G.S. base maps)
Additional map editing by Richard E. Doss
Cover photo by Donald C. Burns
Title page photo by Richard Beach
Photos by the author except as noted
Library of Congress Card Catalog Number 81-70349
International Standard Book Number 0-89997-042-7 (Vol. 2)

Printed in the United States of America
Published by Wilderness Press
        2440 Bancroft Way
        Berkeley, CA 94704
        (415) 843-8080

        Write for free catalog

Acknowledgements

To direct, inform, entertain and inspire—this book could not have come close to achieving these goals without the help of Margaret M. Bell, Barney Buckley, Mike Ellis, Barbara Johnston, John A. Leasure, Clyde Morrison, Bill Ryburn and James R. Shevock of Sequoia National Forest; William Bowen, A. Eugene Fritsche, William I. Gustafson, Phillip S. Kane, Talmage W. Morash and Eugene J. Turner of California State University, Northridge; Richard Burns, John Chew, Paul Fodor, James Howell, Henry Jones, John Palmer and Robert Smith of Sequoia-Kings Canyon National Parks; Jason B. Saleeby of the California Institute of Technology; and also my self-propelled sporting friends Pete Kirchner, Carol and Ruth Moore, Larry L. Norris, John L. Thompson and Dave Wherry. Thanks also to the many people named next to their contributions throughout the text, and to Fred Beckey and The Mountaineers Publications Committee for permitting the quote on page xx. But this book could not have been made at all without the typing, money and love of my parents William and Ruby, nor could it have been done without the patient teaching of my publisher, Thomas Winnett, and so it is to them that this book is dedicated.

Contents

Part 1: Pleasures and Perils

Robert Luthey

Salmon Creek Falls

Chapter One: Pleasures with Pasts

Right here in the little-known Southern Sierra, routes for everyone self-propelled—hikers, backpackers, climbers, cavers, runners, skiers, snowshoers and bicyclists—lead among some of the world's largest, most handsome trees; some of California's largest, and its greatest assortments of, mountain meadows; some of the Sierra Nevada's most alluringly varied waterfall forms and settings; together with some of the range's most outrageous cliffs. Through every season these routes inspire self-propelled travelers from all over the world to make the Southern Sierra the setting for their vacation enjoyment. Besides taking in the place's variety, the pleasures available here include experiencing its vastness. The Southern Sierra has room to give free rein to your historical curiosity or your appetite for exploration and healthy exercise.

Although this book will mainly tell you where these pleasures are likely to be found, you'll probably want to know first whether these "pleasures" will really be pleasures for you. Hence this chapter. Not only will it describe, display, explain and locate representative features that you'll probably want to see; it will also give you a glimmer of the time, physical action and chemical evolution that have brought this beauty within your reach. It's my pleasure to introduce you to the Southern Sierra Nevada of California in hopes that it will call you back again and again to explore it by any means self-propelled!

Displays

The world's largest trees, with their warmly orange bark and their conical or lightning-blunted crowns—the giant sequoias—are here, and almost nowhere else. As a measure of the respect they inspire, some of the first lands to receive US Government protection—a national park and a national forest—are here and both are still named "Sequoia." The four largest, the southernmost and the easternmost, the highest and the lowest individual sequoias that were planted without man's help thrive here in the midst of the world's largest groves of sequoias. Sequoias look ancient, and they are; but exactly how old are they, and where did they come from?

Of the meadows here, 175 are named, many more are nameless, and one—Monache Meadows—is the Sierra's largest. Most of these meadows sport in season an exquisite array of wildflowers, and some of the meadows lie in front of exhilarating panoramas. How did these meadows form? What keeps the forest surrounding them out of them?

Here, Salmon Creek shoots out over an open-book-shaped cliff, strikes the cliff farther down its 240-foot wall and spreads out from there to the base of the wall like a twisted apron. At Marble Falls, the Marble Fork Kaweah River contrasts blue water with sparkling white rock and spills as far as 90 feet at a time in a series of plumes. The South Fork of the Middle Fork Tule River splits at the brink of a box canyon, then falls 40 feet in mirror-image arcs that join at the base. At Tufa Falls, white water spouts from a cave and curtains an arched recess in an orange-streaked cliff. Hidden Falls enters a chasm so narrow that the water's roar can't be heard past the brink. And at the Kern River falls, the most powerful torrents of all strike a ledge and turn cartwheels in their own mist. Viewing these forms of fascinating white water, visitors ask how such falls come to be.

In wondering why, they join those who are stimulated by the sight of towering cliffs and colorful rocks. International climbers are only now discovering that a wealth of challenging walls—many of which have never been climbed—stand here, only a few hours drive from Los Angeles. From the tallest wall, rising 2400 feet to buttress Olancha Peak; to the tallest spires, 1500 feet at the Castle Rocks and The Needles; to the tallest dome face, 1100 feet at Moro Rock, the sheer granitic bedrock creates breathtaking beauty. As if that were not enough, this beauty is itself rivaled by the whites, yellows, reds, blacks, grays, and greens of softer rocks. Dispersed across most of the Southern Sierra, these rocks are concentrated at Moses Mountain and Mineral King. Why are so many different rocks here? How did these differences help form landmarks as striking as these? How did the Southern Sierra acquire so many attractive features?

Origins

The stories behind the Southern Sierra's landscapes, climates, plants and animals spring from common roots: their dependence on one another and the formation of planet Earth. Man's search for the truth about the Earth's past constantly turns up new evidence or suggests new ways of looking at things, so the stories he reconstructs sometimes change swiftly and drastically. Nevertheless, because these stories offer the best understanding available, they add zest to everyone's quest for beauty and refreshment, and they've inspired many who come to be self-propelled in the Southern Sierra to join in the exciting search for the truth about its past.

Actions affecting the earth occur at differing, changing rates and scales, and most of the actions that made the Southern Sierra a place of exceptional beauty have continued

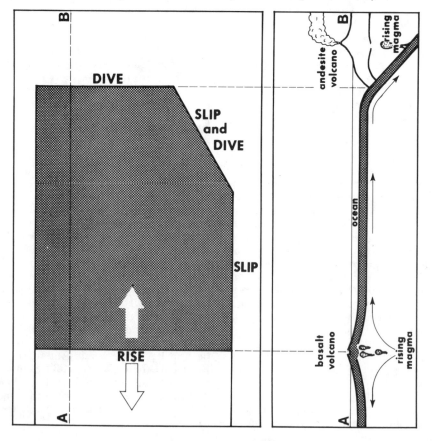

Figure 1: Plate action. Hypothetical plate (surrounded by other plates) viewed from above (left) and viewed in more detail in cross-section A-B (right).

to evolve since the Earth was formed. Only the highlights of their history will be described or depicted here in hopes of whetting your curiosity for the progressively more comprehensive offerings in *California's Changing Landscapes* by Gordon B. Oakeshott and the fascinating *Evolution of the Earth* by Robert H. Dott, Jr., and Roger L. Batten.

On the Shelf

After the earth formed 4.6 billion years ago, it was an unimaginably hot sphere of liquid rock, but that had cooled enough by 4 billion years ago to form a thick outer layer. Split into vast pieces called plates driven by "currents" deep in the molten part of the earth, this layer was ridden by continents that, weighing less than the layer, were buoyed up by the layer in the same way a ship is buoyed up by water. Plates driven apart by these underground "currents" received new crust as molten rock rose through the widening crack between two plates and hardened against the trailing edge of each (as shown in figure 1). Any continent lying over the crack broke along corresponding lines into pieces. While the pieces rode the plates away from each other, the ocean filled the widening gap between them.

That's how the pre-Pacific coast of the North American plate was formed. A supercontinent (composed of pieces that had come together earlier) took 700 million years, from 1450 to 750 million years ago, to break apart along a series of such cracks. Now a line of cliffs reflecting the shape of the spreading zone marked the edge of a new continental shelf offshore from the ancestral North American continent (see figure 2).

Besides supporting reefs formed by algae and other primitive organisms, the shelf stored mineral and metal layers (including silica, calcium, and others) formed when the sea was burdened with more of that chemical than sea water could hold in solution. In addition, debris was washed in and left on the shelf as pre-North America was weathered and worn away. So much junk was left on the shelf that its weight bowed the shelf down. This subsidence corresponded to a rise in eroding pre-North America which, like a boat relieved of weight, rode higher. Because of the rise, even more debris made its

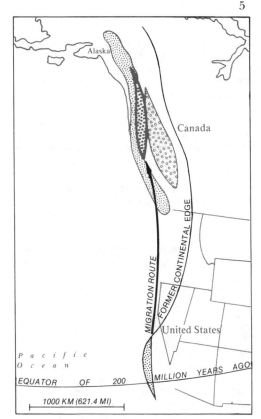

Figure 2: Migrating continental slivers. Since ancestral North America crossed the equator nearly 200 million years ago, part of an early "Sierra" (in black) has moved along faults from the continent to join slivers from elsewhere in making up modern southeastern Alaska (in grey). The continental edge shown in black marks where an ancient supercontinent broke apart 1450-750 million years ago, creating pre-North America.

way to the shelf, including rock grains from 2.5 billion-year-old parts of pre-Canada. These grains had been worn and decayed so much that all that was left of the original rock was tough, pure quartz. As successive layers of rocks on the shelf compressed more and more the layers beneath them, limestone developed from the calcium-saturated reefs, chert formed from millions of organismal skeletons preserved in layers of silica; and sandstone resulted from fused quartz sands.

During the next 400 million years, one of the pre-Pacific plates changed course. This plate was forced deep under its neighboring plate, and its melting completed a cycle that had started when the plates began spreading apart. Long before the diving plate melted completely, superheated liquid rock left it, melted a path through the thick rock above it and erupted onto the ocean floor, forming arc-like chains of island volcanoes. (Japan and the Aleutian Islands are modern examples of island arcs.) By 360 million years ago, the diving plate had jammed the islands against the continental shelf, shoving ocean floor scrapings and old shelf debris over younger layers and creating the Antler belt of scattered offshore islands. This sideways compression folded the layers of debris and deposits.

The remains of these metamorphozed quartzite, limestone and chert layers contribute to the scenic variety in parts of the Sierra Nevada today—especially along Trips 18, 50, 63–66, 79, 84 and 86.

Only 30 million years after the Antler episode of mountain-building began, or 330 million years ago, the continental plate beneath the islands began breaking along new cracks (faults), and the broken plate's pieces moved sideways, up, and down, putting an end to the process of mountain building. Intense weathering of the islands produced clay, which was flushed onto the undersea shelf and left there in layers.

Later physical and chemical action transformed the clay into shale and slate, which guided some canyon-cutting in the Southern Sierra, and which, even today, adds to its local color—see Trips 40 and 53.

Those islands that weren't sunk were worn down, and the undersea shelf on which they stood was again devoted to unstable storage. Then, in what was almost a repeat of the Antler mountain-building episode, the Sonoma Range rose from the sea between 250 and 215 million years ago. The North American plate then broke along a new band of cracks—a band dozens or hundreds of miles wide and thousands of miles long. The continental plate pieces west of the band carried part of the Sonoma Range northward as far as present-day southeastern Alaska. This band or plate junction extended not only far north but also south into the ancestral South Pacific ocean. (The South Pacific area wasn't nearly as far away as "Alaska" was at that time—the North American continent was positioned so that the equator touched the pre-San Diego area.

At the same time the Sonoma Range was being offset, the rubbing of plates along this junction forced chunks of an oceanic plate—including a crust of basalt and part of the iron-rich mantle underneath—to migrate northward from what was then the "South Pacific". While these chunks were crossing the ancestral equator in a shallow part of the ocean, earthquakes tumbled reefs onto them. When the reef-covered chunks, still moving along the ocean floor, passed alongside the Sonoma Range remnants, they were further buried by rubble washed in from the continent. Part of this rubble was sand that came from the area where the Grand Canyon is today.

Before the imported plate chunks could be moved much farther northward, the Pacific plate again began to be forced under the North American continent. The chunks, jammed against a continental shelf just offshore, stuck there. Dead volcanos moved in on the ocean plate, only to be beheaded, mangled beyond recognition and then stuck against the imported chunks, which extended the shelf toward the west. The shelf, expanded, shifted in slices—up, down and sideways—and parts of it, including debris layers or reefs atop it, periodically slid and churned.

The resulting mishmash of rocks contributes to the starkness of today's Yokohl Valley, as seen on Trip 50.

Meanwhile, rather than diving straight down while facing the edge of the continental shelf, the Pacific plate was forced to dive *diagonally*, in both the vertical and horizontal senses of the word. By the time the plate had reached deep into the earth's mantle, friction between the plate and the mantle melted rock, and this ultrahot liquid rock began melting a path through the plate above, changing chemically en route. Some of the explosive liquid erupted both offshore, forming volcanic island arcs, and onshore, sending fiery clouds raining liquid glass racing across the landscape.

A hardened layer of this liquid glass—called "tuff"—can be inspected as you descend into Kern Canyon on Trip 33.

Most of the molten mixture, however, did not erupt. As it cooled deep underneath the coastal Sonoma Range, and that range's successor, the Nevada Range, parts of the mixture grew chemically distinct, crystallizing as gabbro (colored darkest, iron-rich), diorite, granodiorite, quartz monzonite, and alaskite (colored lightest; silica-rich). These rocks formed a thick, durable but relatively brittle westward extension of the North American continental crust.

The Importance of Being Granitic If today's Needles and Castle Rocks (see Trips 41 and 82) had been carved from gabbro

Figure 3: Motion of Earth's Crust east of the San Andreas Fault shows the effect of bulge and break-up—the Sierra Nevada and its Western Divide tilted west while the Kern Plateau rose straight up and the Owens Valley block sank. West of the San Andreas Fault, blocks carried northwest on the Pacific plate jam and warp where forced to turn. Jams like this one absorbed much of the sideways force put on the continent when the ocean plate was pushed underneath it diagonally.

instead of granodiorite and granite, they would not attract climbers and casual sightseers today. Gabbro cracks, weathers and is worn away much more readily than granodiorite or granite, becoming rounded, commonplace features such as Stokes Mountain—Trip 86 in this volume—and Deer Mountain—Trip 85 in volume one. But for rocks of the granitic family to form spires as well as waterfall settings, the arrangement—especially the spacing —of their contraction cracks was almost as important as their hardness. Trip 34 tells how these cracks formed and why they're special.

Though the ocean plate still dove diagonally (starting underground in a trench now buried under the western San Joaquin Valley), a band of faults between the volcanic islands and the continent's shore moved slivers of the continental shelf northward at different speeds. The resulting "traffic jam" used up the sideways force exerted on the continent by the diving plate (see figure 3).

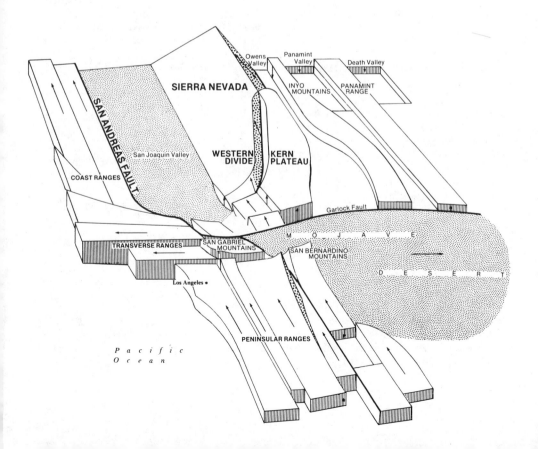

It's a *Good* "Traffic Jam" Today's fault-laced Coast, Transverse and Peninsular ranges are being raised by the same kind of "traffic jam." This one relieves strain on a different plate junction, the San Andreas Fault. So far, this effect has spared Los Angeles the disastrous earthquake that scientists have been expecting for years.

After plate motions changed, close to 80 million years ago, the ocean plate stopped diving here, granitic rocks stopped forming (see figure 3) and, by 40 million years ago, not only had most of the old shelf rocks washed away but the granite beneath them was reduced on its surface to a mildly sloping upland. This ancestral Sierra extended east from a "San Joaquin Valley" coastline into prehistoric Nevada, and although most streams in the "Southern Sierra" flowed southward, a few rivers cut through the range from east to west, draining a lusher "Great Basin" through low, broad valleys.

Today we can see what remains of these valleys at Gomez Meadow—Trip 88 in volume one—and at South Fork Valley—Trip 20 in volume one, and Trip 5 in this book.

Bulge and Breakup

The North American plate first overrode the Pacific spreading zone about 40 million years ago in the Northern California area, and as the point of collision moved southward, the two plates fused. The Pacific plate changed direction and started pulling more and more of California away to the northwest. As the tension grew, western North America bulged up and a nearly continuous belt of faults cut farther and farther southwest through the continent (see figure 3).

The main line of action was the San Andreas Fault Zone, and when it had reached the far edge of the continent—midway down what is now Mexico—about 5 million years ago, a vast chunk of the continent, including the future Los Angeles Metropolitan Area, pulled away, perhaps bound for Alaska. The Pacific coast was being reshaped yet again. (But that's getting ahead of our story.)

Some 35 million years ago, the bulging pre-Sierra cracked intensely at its southern end (near today's Tehachapi Pass) and explosive eruptions with wide-ranging lava flows ensued there for the next 30 million years. The "Southern Sierra" broke into blocks along faults extending north from the main volcanic area, and the Kern Plateau block was an early riser. The prehistoric Kern River, which drained part of the Great Basin, maintained its course, becoming entrenched, while other drainages were beheaded by fault movements. Then the Western Divide block rose (although warping along its western flank made it tilt) and by 4 million years ago the ancestral Kern River had cut through it, too (figure 3 shows block movements).

Despite completion of the new plate junction (the San Andreas Fault) 5 million years ago, the force bowing up the Western U.S. was more effective than ever. Between 4 and 3 million years ago, when the bulge had attained its maximum height in the Southern Sierra area (about 14,500 feet above sea level at Mount Whitney), more lava breached its surface, and the longest flow (of runny basalt) filled 20 miles of deep canyons carved by the Kern and Little Kern rivers (see Trips 34 and 35).

Then the Owens Valley block sank, as much as 4 miles near present-day Lone Pine, creating the Sierra's world-renowned eastern escarpment. (Despite that rock fragments washed in from the new Inyo and Coso mountains and also from the Sierra Nevada have since filled the valley to a depth of 2 miles, it still remains America's deepest.) That's how the ancestral Kern River finally lost its Great Basin drainage, and how its cut-off canyon became a passage vital to Caucasian settlement of California—Walker Pass.

Sources of Changing Sierra Landscapes

EVENT	ACTUAL TIME	PROPORTIONAL TIME
		(100 years = 1 min.)
Earth forms, outer layer splits into rearranging plates	4.6-4 billion years ago	87-76 years ago
Ancient supercontinent breaks apart; break forms edge of undersea shelf of ancestral North America	1450-750 million years ago	28-14 years ago
Shelf-stored debris changes physically, chemically (metamorphism) in Antler and Sonoma mountain-building episodes while the continent's edge is reshaped	360-200 million years ago	6.8-3.8 years ago
Ocean plate forced under continent partly melts, emplacing Sierran granites underground, volcanics on the surface, while rocks in between undergo intense metamorphism	200-80 million years ago	3.8-1.5 years ago
Weathering, flushing exposes, wears down Sierran granites	80-40 million years ago	18½-9¼ months ago
As continental-rim reshaping resumes, Pacific plate captures "Southwest California," causes latest Sierran upheaval and break-up, which culminates as Mount Whitney attains new heights, the Owens Valley block new depths	40-1.5 million years ago	9¼ months-10 days ago

Final Touches

The Big Spreads   Most of the Sierra's meadow acreage—including that of the Sierra's largest meadow—is here in the Southern Sierra. The great rains, snows and consequent glaciers that carved the Sierra north of here rarely got as far south as the Kern Plateau, and also skipped much of the eastern flank of the Western Divide. Vast plateaus remain here as a reminder of what the entire pre-Sierra region was like nearly 40 million years ago. Some relatively small parts of the plateau subsided along faults while, on other parts of the plateau, drainages were blocked by landslides. The resulting lakes, subsequent marshes and ultimate meadows with water-soaked soils demonstrated only one kind of meadow formation locally. Although that kind produced the largest grassland—Monache Meadows (see Volume 1, Trip 64)—another kind made more meadows here.

These meadows (displayed along many trips in this volume), were consequences of the comparatively recent "Little Ice Age" about 150 years ago. They replaced trees that were drowned in soils that had stayed waterlogged too long. Even now, the soil just beneath them is saturated, which keeps the surrounding forest out. This saturation remains in effect until either a prolonged drought occurs or overgrazing lets creeks cut deep in the meadows, making the underground water level sink too far to keep the forest at bay any more. (Fish Creek Meadows became a badlands in just such an aftermath of overgrazing—Trip 34 tells how.)

Giants In The Earth   Ancestors of the giant sequoia dominated the first forests to appear on earth, nearly 300 million years ago. Because of the tree's great resistance to a forest's natural enemies—insects, fungi and fire—it flourished on this continent until 15 million years ago, when the North American plate drifted from the tropical to the temperate latitudes. As yearly precipitation, including summertime rain, decreased, and as temperature changes from day to night became more extreme, the giant sequoia evolved and migrated from the Montana-Idaho region toward the Central California area. Having crossed the bulging western U.S. before it had broken up much, the giant sequoia found a belt on the Sierra's western flank that suited its needs for humidity and an average yearly precipitation approaching 50 inches. When the worldwide climate was warmer and drier, from 8000 to 4000 years ago, the once-continuous sequoia forest of the Sierra Nevada's western flank split into its present groves. Current grove sites reflect the tree's preference for warmer south-facing slopes in the Northern Sierra and sheltered north-facing slopes in the Southern Sierra. (Many trips in this book offer access to these giants.)

Asiatic Indians ground acorns near these sheltering groves before Europeans came and cut over ⅓ of this sequoia habitat (details in Trips 40, 49, 71 and 91). Eventually, even Europeans recognized that dramatic forces had fashioned an irreplaceable resource here, and they set aside much of the Southern Sierra in county parks, state and national forest, national parks, federal recreation lands and designated Wilderness. Now it's yours to enjoy.

Hercules Tree (left center), a giant sequoia in Mountain Home State Forest

Chapter 2: Self-Restraint in the Southern Sierra

The Southern Sierra continues evolving, now under the blades, campfires, lug soles, wastes, chalk, paint and nails of recreationists drawn by the area's beauty but unaware of its delicacy. These scars, this pollution, will probably not endure long enough to show in the range's evolution, but they can spoil the recreation of hundreds or thousands of visitors, some of whom the pollution might sicken, and for some of whom this carelessness could be fatal. Evidence of these consequences remains in the better-known High Sierra, but your care and respect for the Southern Sierra can save both your life and its beauty.

Environmental Protection

Near many forested campsites in the High Sierra, picturesque snags and live trees were stripped or felled for firewood as the supply of dead and down branches was exhausted. To keep such problems from happening here, this book will not guide campers to the firewood. Campers can help by depending on stoves for cooking, making their social, esthetic or warming fires only where dead and down wood is in obvious surplus.

Campfire rings filled with trash, charcoal and charred rocks are still found throughout the High Sierra. Even when some of the campfire debris is cleared away, bare patches of sterilized soil remain, and because the growing season in the "High" and the "Southern" Sierra is short, these scars take a long time to heal. Please heap your coals so that they burn to ash instead of charcoal. Only a blowtorch can properly oxidize foil so that it will disintegrate, and burned plastic is not only still plastic but also a repellent mess, so please put trash in your pack, not in the fire. One can go a step further by learning how to properly clean or erase campfire rings, either as a nominally paid government volunteer (the "Organizational Resources" section tells where to sign up) or as a participant in a club service trip.

Near Mount Whitney, highest of the High Sierra peaks, the disappearance of firewood, the proliferation of campfire rings, the pollution of water sources and the press of too many peakbaggers forced the government to restrict the freedom of would-be climbers with a reservation system, designated camping zones and increased policing. The Southern Sierra has not escaped crowding; quotas determine how many backpackers are allowed to start trips each day in Sequoia National Park, while in the National Forest to the south, reservations are required for staying in one of the Kern River campgrounds. You can help avert the need for further restrictions by choosing those activities and routes that seem less popular today, by starting your trip on a week day, by avoiding all but the remotest country during holiday weekends, and also by putting the other suggestions in this chapter into practice.

Such restrictions are often imposed because trampling causes more and more bare, dusty, muddy or eroded ground to displace wildflowers and other low-lying shrubs. A mere dozen people milling around or hiking single file are enough to start the erosion. Bruised, torn plants grow more slowly, store less energy, produce fewer flowers and seeds and a thinner, more vulnerable crop of seedlings. Signs that hikers have been this way induce more hikers to follow their lead, so more plants are maimed and die; and as their roots decay, topsoil wears away. Silt washes into adjacent streams and lakes, covering the gravel beds that fish need for laying their eggs.

The miniature "Badlands" that once was a campsite and the gash that once was a trail are shunned by campers and walkers, who then create clusters of campsites and multiple parallel paths, each of which further erodes the scenery that visitors come to see. Such problems were evident in 1978 at the lowest of the Mosquito and Franklin lakes and on Farewell Coyote Trail 31E10 near Mineral King. This process can be checked and eventually corrected, and this book is intended to help.

Informed that describing any routes here might lead to unwanted erosion, noise and crowding; endanger rare plants and wildlife; and deprive some visitors of spontaneity and the chance to discover things on their own, I took the following steps to protect the environment described. Damaged trails and campsites were left unmentioned in this book in order to give them time to recover. To spare other campsites the damage that recommendations and popularity bring, capacity ratings alone are offered so readers can find sites large enough for their needs and will not be forced to enlarge them. In the national parks, instead of campsites, widespread zones offering desirable camping were mapped, allowing campers to disperse, further reducing their impact. A variety of alternatives to overpopular activities in overused areas were emphasized. Preliminary, unofficial results from an ongoing National Park Service study of backcountry-visitor travel patterns and impact, published piecemeal in this book, helped determine trip designs in Sequoia-Kings Canyon National Parks. Trips everywhere are described according to the competence of the intended user, giving beginners detailed guidance, and seasoned travelers only a general sense of what to expect. And finally, to insure that this book would truly keep conflicts for readers to a minimum, I had it reviewed for accuracy and objectivity by many, many others who also know and love the Southern Sierra. (As a result, this book earned the endorsement of George H. Stankey, one of the country's most respected researchers of recreational impacts.)

I remembered that in Yosemite Valley, in the central High Sierra, climbers had waited in line to attempt certain routes, and climbers making repeat ascents had found the cracks wider, the flakes less dependable, the holds either smoother or broken off, bolts either pounded or chopped or placed indiscriminately, and caked chalk or paint marring the rock. To help prevent this crowding and to slow this erosion in the Southern Sierra, this book was restricted to describing some enticing Class 3 to 5 routes and to mapping and indexing most other climbing areas, thereby leaving a great many routes for experienced, imaginative, conscientious climbers to pioneer. First ascents received only occasional attention here, for as Fred Beckey wrote, " . . . the climbing adventure is not enhanced by merely getting up, but by keeping the climb a challenge. The dividends should be in the motions of the art, concentration, judgment and technique. Do not use aid on free climbs—leave alone that which you cannot do in good style, for it may diminish the esthetics for others. With the raising of qualitative standards, the rewards are not lost—and neither are the mountains." (*Cascade Alpine Guide*, Seattle: The Mountaineers, 1973.)

But regional degradation cannot be averted without your help. To begin with, you can limit your group to 15 people or less, not just in designated wilderness but wherever you go. You can do your best to avoid the vulnerable shrubbery on narrow stream banks, steep slopes, ridgelines and passes. Before hiking a trail, you can waterproof your boots; for then you will rarely need to leave the tread, even when it is muddy. Should you note any shortcuts or undue erosion, please don't use them; report them promptly to the responsible agency. Never sleep on meadows or other low-lying vegetation; and don't camp within 100 feet of streams, unless you are certain you won't pollute the stream or accelerate bank erosion. More ambitious means to check erosion require expert supervision and include maintaining trails, building and repairing bridges, restoring meadows and installing check dams and other forms of erosion control, either as a government volunteer or as a participant in a club service trip.

One may respond with a little more violence when confronted with unburied human feces (sometimes floating in streams); sudsing cascades; glass, plastic, tin cans and foil excavated from garbage pits by rodents or bears; scattered orange peels and heaps of leftover food allowed to rot near campsites;

and trails littered with worn or useless gear. Although rare in the Southern Sierra, these are the legacy of overcrowding in the High Sierra. "Cat holes" dug well away from streams and potential campsites will penetrate a decomposition layer in the soil, where microorganisms will recycle the feces once they are covered with dirt. Wash in a pot or bucket far removed from the water source, even when using sand or biodegradable soap, and when brushing teeth. There are virtually no trash cans in the Southern Sierra, not even near ranger stations and roads, so always bring a litter bag and pack out the trash yourself. Should you find such wastes in the Southern Sierra, you can arrange to clean them up as a private citizen, a government volunteer or as part of a club service trip.

There is no need to look to the High Sierra for fed or molested "wild" animals; names or other inscriptions on rocks or trees; shot, hacked or stolen signs, tables and benches; overturned toilets, disfigured historical artifacts and defaced cave formations—these recur despite penalties in the Southern Sierra. Should you spot a vandal practicing here, discreetly identify him to authorities. You might arrange to repair what damage you can and help protect the good that remains as a government volunteer or as part of a club service project.

Self-Protection

Theft is increasing at the most accessible roadheads in the High Sierra. Packs have even been stolen while people were sleeping right next to them! Protect your gear when it is not in use by either locking it up out of sight, watching it constantly or having it watched.

Perhaps of all the abuses discussed in these pages, the ultimate one is overreaching. People exceeding their limits concentrate on personal survival, often at the expense of ecological survival. The most personal outcome of such excess in the High Sierra is injury or death; with consequent hardships for family, friends, and other searchers— not to mention the plants they cripple in their desperate haste. To avert this in the Southern Sierra, one should recognize that *a guidebook is no substitute for skills*, and then ac-

quire those skills via the suggestions offered here and the books recommended at the end of this chapter, and also by attending classes and by joining experienced groups in the field.

The most humbling hardships awaiting the unprepared in the Southern Sierra are the numbing chill and dehydrating heat that its climatic extremes deliver (although these extremes are gentle compared to those of the High Sierra). Our bodies are chilled when wind drives cold air or moisture against our skins and sucks away our radiant heat. To save our skins and remain comfortable when savoring the Sierra in winter, we dress and pack for arctic conditions and grow sensitive to wind directions.

Poison oak

Jeff Schaffer

These winds can shift to follow terrain channels, but commonly fit the following patterns. Southwesterly winds, especially those blowing upslope at night, warn us of approaching Pacific storms. So do sudden shifts in wind direction, especially when preceded by the appearance of high, white, lacy clouds and followed by haphazard gusts. Southwesterly winds, responsible for most avalanche-prone cornices, give way as storm fronts pass over to winds from the northwest and north that whip up a few cornices of their own.

But in wind there is always some friction, and when wind stops and air masses stagnate, temperatures plummet and thick ground-fog forms. This "Tule fog" is thickest in the early mornings and evenings of December and January in the San Joaquin Valley, and is deadly because most motorists plow through it at high speed, driving blind. If "Tule fog", rain or snow will hamper your travel, it can be avoided by scrutinizing the satellite photos and listening for warnings broadcast by commercial TV and by the California Highway Patrol. But to avoid the dense, bone-chilling fog that forms mostly at night in protected mountain hollows (where the coldest temperatures lurk) takes experience in on-the-spot weather forecasting. This fog also dissipates reassuringly quickly, usually as soon as the sun heats nearby slopes.

In spring, while the mountain snowpack thaws, while swollen rivers threaten to drown would-be waders and swimmers, while heat again begins to oppress Great Basin deserts, a westerly wind drawn from the coast sometimes howls across Interstate 5 and Tehachapi Summit. At other times, it pushes a cloudbank against the crest of the Greenhorn Mountains and the Western Divide and then soars above the Sierra crest, forming the "Sierra wave," where thin, lenticular clouds glide. These gradually abating winds cool the Sierra while San Joaquin Valley temperatures rise, but summer brings with it a few still days when temperatures everywhere peak over 100°F. In summer the common southeasterly wind that brews afternoon thunderstorms here comes as a relief and a source of great entertainment and peril. Soon the rare heat, occasional windy storms and usual temperateness of Southern Sierran summers yield to sporadic autumn

and winter winds from the north or east. Such winds are called "Santa Anas" in Southern California and "Monos" in this vicinity. Although these winds have occasionally fetched frigid air in the past, they usually give us "shirt-sleeve weather" for as long as they last.

Competent self-propelled travelers also take competing land-users into account when preparing for hazards. Responsible hunters know well the "shoot first—ask questions later" attitude of some "opening-weekend hunters," and avoid them at all costs. So should you. Any ranger or game warden should be able to tell you when the worst days are. Afterward, it is usually safe to venture into the range again wearing a fluorescent cap and other bright clothes.

Although this guide identifies the favorite haunts of motorbikers and "tote-goat" enthusiasts as "cycle-paths" and omits them from the coverage, a few trips do include trails on which such cyclist traffic is legal and moderate, and many trips include trails on which such traffic is legal and light. Always leave the trail and stand well away from it when you hear an approaching cyclist. Hikers angered by cyclists trespassing on trails closed to them should note the license discreetly, report it to the nearest ranger or sheriff, and then be prepared to testify against the offender in court.

Far less of a nuisance to most backpackers and hikers are those few on-trail encounters with pack stock. Although most riders prefer that you stand quietly downslope from the trail, it is always best to ask. Please ensure that future generations will be able to enjoy the same beauty and harmony that you can find today in the Southern Sierra.

Organizational Resources

California Department of Fish and Game

Current hunting and fishing schedules and regulations are available on request during weekdays from 8 a.m. to 5 p.m.

Fresno District Office
1234 East Shaw Avenue
Fresno, CA 93705
209-222-3761

California Department of Forestry

Mountain Home State Forest

Backroad, campground, trail, logging, pest and snow condition reports; campfire permits; current regulations; and free recreation and management literature are available on request. Office hours 8 a.m. to 4:30 p.m.

Forest Manager
P.O. Box 517
Springville, CA 93265
209-539-2855 (winter), 2321 (summer)
Tulare County Emergency Dispatcher
209-734-7477

Fire Departments

KERN COUNTY

Emergency fire and health services anytime.
Bakersfield (headquarters dispatcher)
805-324-6551
Glennville-Posey
Ask Operator for Enterprise 11611
Kernville-Weldon
714-376-2218
Lake Isabella
714-379-2625

TULARE COUNTY

Emergency fire and health services anytime.
Headquarters dispatcher (Visalia)
209-732-5954
Dinuba
209-591-5100
Lemon Cove-Three Rivers
209-597-2418
Lindsay
209-568-2114
Orosi-Cutler
209-528-3031
Porterville-Springville-Camp Nelson
209-784-2750

Sheriff's Department

KERN COUNTY

Snow-tour registration, post-trip checkout; prompted rescues; and law enforcement anytime.

Main Office
1415 Truxton Avenue
Bakersfield, CA 93001
805-327-3392

TULARE COUNTY

Rescues and law enforcement anytime. Snow tour registration and post-trip check-out at the Visalia office for the region north of Mountain Home State Forest (MHSF); at the Porterville Substation for MHSF and points south.

Main Office
County Civic Center
Visalia, CA 93277
209-733-6261

Porterville Substation
379 North 3rd
Porterville, CA 93257
209-784-4573

U.S. Army Corps of Engineers

Emergency fire services; campground, backroad and trail condition reports; campfire permits; current regulations; and free recreation and management literature are available on request.

Lake Isabella Recreation Area
P.O. Box 997
Lake Isabella, CA 93240
714-397-2742

Lake Success Recreation Area
29332 Highway 190
Porterville, CA 93257
209-784-0215

Lake Kaweah Recreation Area
Terminus Project Office
Lemon Cove, CA 93244
209-597-2301

U.S. Forest Service

Sequoia National Forest

Emergency fire and health services; maps (50 cents apiece); backroad, trail, campground, logging, traffic, pest and snow condition reports; campfire and Wilderness permits; current regulations; reservations for selected campgrounds; volunteer aid enlistment (Headquarters only); and free recreation, ecology and management literature are available on request. All offices open weekdays 8 a.m. to 4:30 p.m.

Headquarters
900 West Grand Avenue
Porterville, CA 93257
209-784-1500 (info), 209-781-5780 (fire)

Cannell Meadow District
P.O. Box 6
Kernville, CA 93238
714-376-2294 (info), 2283 or 2218 (fire)

Greenhorn District
800 Truxton Avenue, Room 326
Bakersfield, CA 93301
805-861-4212

Hot Springs District
Route 4 Box 548
California Hot Springs, CA 93207
805-548-6503, (info), 6455 (after-hours emergency)

Hume Lake District
53921 Hwy 245
Miramonte, CA 93641
209-336-2881 (info), 209-875-2591 collect (fire)

Tule River District
32588 Highway 190
Porterville, CA 93257
209-539-2607

Upper Kern Canyon Entrance Station
714-376-6261

U.S. National Park Service

Sequoia-Kings Canyon National Parks

Emergency fire, health and rescue services; law enforcement; maps (free); backroads, trail, campground, pest and snow condition reports; Wilderness permits and trailhead reservations; current regulations; volunteer aid enlistment; and free recreation, ecology and management literature are available on request. All offices are open weekdays, usually from 8 a.m. to 4:30 p.m.

Ash Mountain Headquarters
Three Rivers, CA 93271
209-565-3341 (info), 3444 (fire),
3326 (emergency—anytime)

Grant Grove Ranger Station
Kings Canyon National Park, CA 93633
209-335-2315 (info), 2511 (emergency only—anytime)

*   *   *   *   *

The following private organizations offer education in self-propelled skills and natural history, and sponsor either work parties, recreational trips or educational outings. All activities are open to the general public, although some, such as rock climbing and caving, require specialized skills.

Audubon Society

Fresno chapter
P.O. Box 396
Clovis, CA 93612

Kern County chapter
P.O. Box 3581
Bakersfield, CA 93305

Tulare County chapter
P.O. Box 588
Porterville, CA 93257

Far West Ski Association

Headquarters
3325 Wilshire Blvd.
Los Angeles, CA 90005
213-387-2145

National Speleological Society

Southern California Grotto
c/o Hugh Blanchard
1828 Alpha Avenue
South Pasadena, CA 91030

Sierra Club

Headquarters
530 Bush Street
San Francisco, CA 94104
415-891-8634

Southern California Office
2410 Beverly Blvd.
Los Angeles, CA 90057
213-387-4287

Society of American Foresters

Headquarters
5400 Grosvenor Lane
Bethesda, MD 20014
301-897-8720

Tulare County Historical Society

P.O. Box 295
Visalia, CA 93277

*   *   *   *   *

Part 2: 100 Adventures

Thomas Winnett

Chapter 3: Driving to the Trips by Car

How To Use This Chapter

This chapter differs from its counterpart in *Volume One: The Sierra Crest and The Kern Plateau* because unlike the Kern Plateau, which attracts visitors mainly from Southern California, the great western divides attract recreationists from across the entire state. Although these recreationists converge on the Southern Sierra via quite a few different routes, eventually they all start driving into the range in the same direction on the same roads, the ones that can get them to the start of each trip most quickly. In Volume One, these roads happened to begin in one town, Mojave. Consequently, to reach a roadhead using that book, they read the chapter from the beginning, skipping sections as directed. In this book, however, the shared roads start at a number of separate points, and each shared road is described under chapter subtitles like

Roadheads 56–66: Via Visalia

Look for the appropriate subtitle and start reading from there.

Because many drivers approaching this book's shared roads will pass through either Bakersfield or Fresno, the driving time from both of these towns to the start of each trip appears in the Tripfinder Table at the end of Chapter 4. Supplementing these times, Chapter 3 offers essential directions for the approach from these towns to the start of the shared roads, and it doesn't begin giving mileages until the shared roads begin. From there on, readers will find 2 figures in parenthesis at roadheads and crucial junctions. The entry will look something like this: (2.8, 10.2). The first figure shows how many miles

of route have been covered since the last entry appeared. The second figure shows the sum of the first figures, telling the total distance from the start of a shared route to a particular point that the route is used to reach.

Shared roads, like trees, send out branches progressively farther away from the base. The "trunk" and "branch" roads are described in segments, each describing the route to a roadhead farther away than the last. Each segment begins with the same abbreviation (example: **R2** for Roadhead 2) that identifies that roadhead in the maps in the back of this book. Every segment offers a series of alternative actions to choose between. Often the choice is between stopping at the wrong roadhead and starting to follow directions to the next roadhead. Sometimes you will have the option of skipping ahead in this chapter, and when that occurs, you will be told the best place to start reading—and following directions—again. After this sequence of decisions puts you at the roadhead you had wanted to reach, skip to the description of the trip you have in mind and prepare to go self-propelled!

Because many drivers will reach their roadhead the night before their trip will begin, the nearest opportunities for camping are pointed out. Not everyone will have filled canteens or will have bought everything they need before leaving home, and for those who haven't, this chapter locates the last sources en route.

After you've used this chapter a while, you will be so familiar with the country that you won't have to read more than the segment describing the roadhead you have in mind.

Precautions

Tire chains, handsaw, axe, shovel and an old blanket should be stowed in the trunk of your car. Whenever the roads become sandy, muddy or icy, blocked by blowdowns, gashed by erosion, sloughed away or buried in landslides, such tools will help you cope. On some backroads, weeks can go by with no passersby; if you become trapped there, these tools can be your best, perhaps your only, hope. Your car should also have at least 5 gallons of drinking water, plus extra food and clothes, which could save your life if you get stuck in a remote place.

When parking for a ski or snowshoe tour, don't let your car become snowed in by unexpected storms. Have one member of your party drive it to a lower elevation, or at least within reach of a snowplow-patrolled highway. Except for SNF Road 13S01 from Indian Basin to Hume Lake, forest roads are rarely kept open in winter. Other roads are plowed whenever the need arises. They include the county roads 465Z from Greenhorn Summit to Shirley Meadows, and MTN 107 from Quaking Aspen to the Ponderosa Lodge; and also all state highways and the federally-maintained Generals Highway (but see Trip 95).

To be sure your car will start when you return from the trip, leave the brakes in neutral, chocking the wheels instead, because emergency brakes have been known to freeze tight. But steps taken before you leave home can ensure your safety much better. If your car has a radiator, either buy antifreeze or test the value of your old antifreeze and add some to your radiator's water as directed. Change to a multigrade (10W30 or 10W40) oil. Get a tune-up and maintain your battery. Use gasoline-drying compound to keep ice out of your car's gas line (the compound is stocked by most mountain service stations). And when you finally do arrive at the roadhead, recall that batteries weaken in cold weather and park your car facing downslope; that way, you may be able to start even if the battery's dead.

Make your car unattractive to thieves and vandals by disabling your engine (your mechanic can show you how), hiding everything you leave in the car, closing all windows and locking all doors and compartments.

(Campground fees, Park entrance fees and map prices are 1978 prices and may have changed.)

80 Destinations

Roadheads 1 and 2:
Breckenridge Mountain
Recreation Area

From Los Angeles, drive *Interstate 5* and then *State Freeway 99* northwest to the eastbound *State Freeway 58* exit in Bakersfield. **From Fresno,** drive *Freeway 99* southeast to the *Freeway 58* exit in Bakersfield.

For many trips, Bakersfield is the last source of late-night gas and drinking water. It is also one of the few places near the Southern Sierra where almost any supply or service for self-propelled recreation can be bought.

R1   From State Freeway 99 in Bakersfield (0.0, 0.0), take *State Freeway 58* east and then exit onto *State Highway 184*, signed "Weedpatch Highway" (7.0, 7.0). Turn left (north) here and follow this road past the last reliable water source, located near the last gas stations and stores. Then we bump over railroad tracks to a T intersection (0.5, 7.5) with a liquor store on its northeast corner. Paved *KC Road 218G*, signed "Breckenridge Mountain Road," starts east from here, narrows and soon winds into the foothills. Many bends later, it enters Sequoia National Forest, becomes *SNF Road 28S06* and then traverses a west-facing slope while westward views of Kern Canyon improve. Shortly one reaches a private ranch house on the west at Pine Flat, where the road first encounters pines. Snow often blocks the unplowed road beyond here in winter, so snowshoers and skiers taking Trips 1 and 2 park their cars here at **Roadhead 1** (25.1, 32.6),

and also in nearby turnouts, being careful not to block driveways. You can camp here if you get the ranch owner's permission, but water isn't available.

R2   Drivers on their way to Trip 3 (a hike) take Road 28S06 beyond Pine Flat (0.0, 32.6) when the road is free of snow, and shortly find that its pavement ends upon crossing Lucas Creek. (The rest of the road may be paved by your visit.) One should watch out for the narrower Breckenridge Subdivision roads that peel off to the north and south. (For more detailed guidance, see the description of Trip 1). We presently turn left twice at the north ends (5.6, 38.2), (0.1, 38.3) of a triangle junction with signed SNF Road 28S07, which leads southward to Breckenridge Campground. Then our road descends a ridge of Breckenridge Mountain to Lightners Flat, where we start north along Hobo Ridge on rarely-maintained *SNF Road 28S19* (3.1, 41.4). Drivers of conventional cars might want to park off the road soon, for it shortly becomes rather rough. Then it meets an abandoned though signed link of Remington Ridge Trail 32E51 in a shady swale with parking for several cars, **Roadhead 2** (1.5, 42.9). Beyond here, the road drops swiftly to polluted O'Brien Spring and is only fit for vehicles with 4-wheel drive.

Roadheads 3–15:
Kern Canyon Recreation Area

R3 From Freeway 99 in Bakersfield (0.0, 0.0), *State Highway 178*, initially signed "24th Street," leads east and divides quite soon into 2 wide parallel one-way streets while crossing the downtown commercial district. Then we bear northwest onto the beginning of Freeway 178, which narrows to 2 lanes upon leaving town. Amber lights flashing at the deep V-shaped entrance to lower Kern Canyon warn that the narrow, windy road ahead, which is partly overhung by cliffs, is not cleared of fallen rocks at night. (Watch out!) A few miles up-canyon we enter Sequoia National Forest before passing through Richbar Campground, the last place to camp overnight before taking Trips 4–6. We presently pass the signed north-side turnoff of SNF Road 28S67 to Democrat Hot Springs Resort, then negotiate a few more curves and come to a signed junction (29.3, 29.3) with paved *KC Road 214H*. While drivers bound for Roadheads 4–15 continue forward on Highway 178, those heading for the Mill Creek hike turn right, southeast, onto the winding Kern Canyon Road. Quite soon they cross Mill Creek, then drive 0.3 mile farther to find Mill Creek Trail 31E78 of Trips 4 and

5 beginning near a 3-car turnout, **Roadhead 3** (1.5, 30.8), along the south side of the road. Additional parking spaces can be found near Mill Creek.

R4 *Highway 178* abruptly improves northeast of its junction with Road 214H (0.0, 29.3), becoming wider, smoother and much easier to drive. After a few thousand feet, the improved highway bridges the Kern River and flares to 4-lane width. Now staying well above the river's north bank, our highway soon reaches a junction (6.5, 35.8) with a gated, west-trending road. (If you pass through a huge roadcut, you've gone about 1.5 miles too far.) Trip 6 to Delonegha Creek begins here at **Roadhead 4**. More than 2 dozen cars may be parked on the roadside flat in nearby Lilly Canyon.

R5 The 4-lane segment of *Highway 178* curves farther up Kern Canyon beyond the Lilly Canyon road (0.0, 35.8). Soon the highway bridges the Kern River again and then meets paved *KC Road 477Y*, signed "Borel Road" (2.6, 38.4). Here we part company with drivers speeding toward Roadheads 6–15 on the state highway. While they skip to the R6 description, we take the short county road southeast past the Borel Powerhouse and Canal, and then turn right, southwest, onto paved *KC Road 214H* (0.3, 38.7). Because this winding road demands slow driving, it takes us awhile to get past Hobo Guard Station and Campground ($3/ night) and the nearby resort of Miracle Hot Springs. We presently park at least 1 car in the 10-car lot, **Roadhead 5** (3.8, 42.5), across from the end of signed Remington Ridge Trail 32E51, here disguised as a jeep road. Then we drive the usually traffic-free road further down-canyon to Roadhead 3 (6.4, 48.9), where Trip 5 begins.

R6 Beyond the junction with KC Road 477Y (0.0, 38.4), *Highway 178* crosses the Kern River twice more, becomes a freeway, and then approaches an interchange with State Highway 155. We take the offramp here, then turn northwest onto *Highway 155* (3.3, 41.7). (A substation of the Kern County Sheriff's Department is located a few hundred yards east of here, in the town of Lake Isabella.) Our road winds over a ridge north of the interchange and meets a paved road leading to the headquarters of Lake

Isabella Recreation Area, operated by the U.S. Army Corps of Engineers (USACE). (A visit here to orient yourself to the lake and nearby facilities is especially worthwhile if you plan to camp, swim, hike or bicycle near the shore.) Beyond the headquarters road, Highway 155 leads up past 6 USACE Campgrounds ($3 a night—the last places for Trip 7 climbers to camp and take hot showers) and presently enters the town of Wofford Heights. On the edge of the commercial district (last gas), Highway 155 becomes a 4-lane divided highway signed "Burlando Road" and then abruptly turns west, reverting to 2 lanes and changing its posted name to *"Evans Road"* (6.6, 48.3). We follow it through the turn while drivers heading for Roadhead 15 continue northeast on 4-lane "Burlando Road" and skip to the R15 description. We, meanwhile, check our gas gauges before leaving town because the nearby gas stations are the last ones close to our route. They usually operate only from sunrise to sunset. Afterward, we drive up steep Evans Road, shortly entering Sequoia National Forest. This entrance should alert would-be Bat Rock climbers to watch for an inconspicuous dirt road departing north amid brush at **Roadhead 6** (4.0, 52.3). Parking space is limited to a few scattered one-car turnouts nearby, so large groups may have to meet closer to Wofford Heights and then car-pool up the grade.

R7   The steep upgrade of Highway 155 leads westward from the climber's turnoff (0.0, 52.3) and flares quite soon to 3-lane width, which is maintained for a short stretch. Later we pass through the community of Alta Sierra. West of the village is Greenhorn Mountain County Park, where campground sites ($2 a night) are available from spring through fall. Beyond the park, at Greehorn Summit (3.9, 56.2), the head of the grade, skiers can often find room to park among the snowdrifts off the road to the northeast. Wintertime Trips 8 and 9 begin and Trip 30 ends here at **Roadhead 7.**

R8   Drivers choosing to reach Roadheads 9–14 take SNF Road 23S16 north from Highway 155 (0.0, 56.2,) and skip to the R9 entry, but we turn south onto paved *KC Road 465Z*. Our road is usually plowed to the Shirley Meadows Ski Resort, across from abandoned Shirley Meadows Campground.

Some parking is commonly available between these facilities. Trips 10 and 11 begin here at **Roadhead 8** (2.1, 58.3).

R9   Your road, *SNF Road 23S16* heads north from Greenhorn Summit (0.0, 56.2), and very soon you turn east-southeast onto *SNF Road 25S16* (0.9, 57.1), separating from cars aimed northward at Roadheads 10–14. While those drivers skip to the R10 description, you take a few minutes to drive to a junction with SNF Road 25S20 at Black Mountain Saddle (1.6, 58.7). Once at the saddle, you can find room for half a dozen cars to park among pines at **Roadhead 9**. Trip 12, a hike to Black and Split mountains, gets underway here.

R10   North of the junction (0.0, 57.1) with SNF Road 25S16, we persist in following *Road 23S16* on and alongside the Greenhorn crest, and shortly pass Tiger Flat Campground, where water is available and camping is free. Trip 13 hikers who need a place to stay overnight could hardly find a better site than this. Then our road winds northward to join southbound SNF Road 24S28 (5.1, 62.2), signed "Mountain Meadows Girl Scout Camp," 85 yards south of **Roadhead 10**, where Trip 13 begins. At least 8 cars can be parked off the road in this area.

R11   Continue driving Road 23S16 past the start of Trip 13 (0.0, 62.2) and soon you will reach Portuguese Pass (0.5, 62.7), where paved SNF Road 24S06 comes in from the west and drivers taking the quickest route from Northern California might meet us.

*   *   *   *   *

Shortcut from Northern California to Roadheads 11–14

From Roadhead 20, (0.0, 7.1), take *TC Road MTN 109* southeast. After you've driven about ½ hour, your road veers east-northeast, becoming *Road MTN 1* where paved KC Road 447Z (14.9, 22.0) begins and heads south. Shortly your route changes its code to *"MTN 3"* where paved KC Road 421Z (2.3, 24.3) takes off to the south. Your drive then takes a while to reach first the Posey Post Office and then the next junction with a paved road (3.1, 27.4). There you turn west-northwest onto TC *Road MTN 9*, which winds up a long ridge, and at length narrows near Sugarloaf Lodge to become poorly paved *SNF Road 24S06*. As such, it winds past numerous unpaved spurs and eventually arrives at the Portuguese Pass junction (10.8, 38.2), where you turn north onto *SNF Road 23S16*.

* * * * *

Leading drivers northward from Portuguese Pass (0.0, 62.7), Road 23S16 soon bears away from northeast-forking SNF Road 24S09, the access to Panorama Campground, a shady site that is hardly panoramic but free to use. It's the last source of water and the last place to camp for Trips 15 and 16. We continue to skirt the crest of the Greenhorn Mountains, and presently turn north onto *SNF Road 24S50* where other drivers turn east onto paved SNF Road 23S16 (2.3, 65.0) toward Roadheads 12–14. (They skip to the R12 entry.) Our road instantly loses its pavement, later crosses the Greenhorn Crest twice and eventually leads to an offset 4-way intersection (3.6, 68.6). We take the road leading east, *SNF Road 24S86*, which is signed for "Frog Meadow Campground." A very short drive now takes us past Frog Meadow Guard Station to the campground, **Roadhead 11** (0.4, 69.0), where water gushes from a piped spring. Please park off the road in the ample space just outside of the campground unless you plan to stay the night here.

R12 Paved *Road 23S16* leads us generally east from Road 24S50 (0.0, 65.0) until we reach the first dirt road to the south-southeast, signed SNF Road 24S03 (0.7, 65.7). While drivers bound for Roadhead 14 continue to follow Road 23S16, we who are heading for Roadheads 12 or 13 turn onto *Road 24S03*. Touching no other major junctions, it presently merges with *SNF Road 24S35* (1.5, 67.2), onto which we go straight ahead. This road now winds around 2 minor south-trending ridges and then, by the seasonal creek in the next canyon, finds **Roadhead 12** (1.0, 68.2). Hikers embarking on Trip 15 for Deep Creek can park about 6 cars here.

R13 From the Deep Creek roadhead (0.0, 68.2), our road loops around 2 parallel ridges and then meets signed Bull Run Trail 32E39 of Trip 16 at **Roadhead 13** (1.7, 69.9).

A turnout near the trailhead offers room for 5 vehicles.

R14 Paved *Road 23S16* curves north from its signed junction (0.0, 65.7) with Road 24S03, then meanders and eventually gains signed "Dunlap Saddle" where we turn east onto signed *SNF Road 24S02* (2.8, 68.5). This road winds across Baker Ridge past a lesser spur road, and then ends upon reaching a ridge that extends to Baker Point. Up to 8 cars may be left here at **Roadhead 14** (3.2, 71.7) by hikers taking Trip 17. Overnight camping is possible here, although water is not available.

R15 Paved *Burlando Road* (KC Road 495Z) continues northeast from its junction with State Highway 155 (0.0, 48.3), past gas stations that are open for business only during daylight hours. These stations mark the entrance to the Wofford Heights commercial district, where water faucets, markets, motels, laundromats, phones and a post office can be found. Upon leaving Wofford Heights, our road narrows and its legal speed increases. (More details about it can be found in Trip 20 of *Self-Propelled . . . , Volume One*.) Not long afterward, our road flares to 4 lanes again, enters the Kernville commercial district and arcs eastward, becoming *Kernville Boulevard* (4.1, 52.4) where Burlando Road turns north. Backpacking, camping, hunting and fishing supplies, along with postal, phone and cleaning services, plus food, gas and lodging may be bought here. The two-story log building housing USFS Cannell Meadow District Ranger Station is 0.1 mile north at the corner of Burlando and Whitney Roads. For information about goods and services available here, turn to "Sequoia National Forest" in the "Organizational Resources" section. We next bridge the Kern River and turn north-northwest onto 2-lane paved *KC Road 521Z* (0.5, 52.9) at a **T** intersection. This road, fully described in Trip 21 of this book's companion volume, soon leaves Kernville, where gas stations rarely stay open later than 9 p.m. Soon the road comes to the USFS Upper Kern Canyon Entrance Station, a converted house trailer (2.3, 55.2—see "Organizational Services" section), and shortly thereafter we note in passing the market, phone, water faucet and gas station in the small town of River Kern. Now the road enters Tulare

County, becomes **TC Road MTN 99**, then
passes consecutive junctions with west-
trending paved and signed roads giving access to Headquarters, Camp 3, Hospital Flat
and Gold Ledge campgrounds.(In all of
these campgrounds, sites cost $3 per night,
while numerous nearby "undeveloped
campgrounds" cost nothing.) Our riverside
road continues north from Gold Ledge
Campground and presently reaches signed,
paved SNF Parking Lot 23S39 (12.7, 67.9),
which lies west of the main road just north of
McNalley's Fariview Resort. Here at
Roadhead 15, hikers taking Trip 18 to Flynn
Canyon can leave about 15 cars. Additional
parking room is available in 23S38, the next
paved lot north. Overnight campers are en-
couraged to stay in Fairview Campground,
whose entrance is found between the 2 lots.
Water faucets that operate only in summertime are located there.

Roadheads 16–19: Glennville Area

From Los Angeles, drive generally north,
first on **Interstate 5**, and then on **State Freeway 99** to Bakersfield, the last source of spe-
cialty supplies and late-night gas en route.
Exit the freeway on paved **Airport Drive** and
follow it north through residential Oildale.
Presently you cross railroad tracks and immediately afterward turn east onto paved,
signed **Norris Road**. Drive this road to the
first major cross-street, paved **Chester Avenue**, and turn north onto that signed route.
It soon narrows from 4 to 2 lanes and leaves
Oildale, then turns northwest, forks north
from signed James Road and becomes
known as the "**Bakersfield-Glennville Road.**"
On it, we wind into the foothills and presently reach Woody.

From Fresno, go southeast on **State Freeway 99** to Delano, the last source of late-
night gas. Leave the freeway there and take
State Highway 155 east to Woody.

R16 **Highway 155** winds generally east
from Woody (0.0, 0.0) and presently reaches
a junction with KC Road 421Z, signed "Jack
Ranch Road" (8.6, 8.6). Here drivers bound
for Roadheads 17–19 turn north and skip to
the entry marked R17, while we continue up
Highway 155 to the Glennville Post Office.
Here at **Roadhead 16** (1.1, 9.7), across the

state highway from a market, laundromat
and gas station, we can find room to park
about 8 cars along the street before setting
out on Trip 19. If you're looking for a place
to camp, try driving Highway 155 about 10
miles farther east to find Cedar Creek
Campground.

R17 Signed "**Jack Ranch Road**" leads
north from its junction with State Highway
155 (0.0, 8.6) and quite soon crosses paved
KC Road 447Z at a signed junction,
Roadhead 17 (0.7, 9.3), where 5 to 8 cars can
be parked on the road's wide shoulders.
Water is available to the southeast in
Glennville.

R18 Continuing northeast on the signed
"Jack Ranch Road" beyond Road 447Z (0.0,
9.3), we might see bicyclists on Trip 20,
which describes part of our route. We enter
Tulare County, where our road becomes **TC
Road MTN 3**. Moments later, our route abruptly turns east-northeast upon meeting
TC Road MTN 1 (4.8, 14.1), another paved
2-lane road. We fork right (east) through the
next 2 junctions with paved roads. Then our
route goes through the community of Balance Rock, and eventually we reach a
ridgetop swale and encounter a signed 5-way
junction (5.1, 19.2). Here we start southwest
on twisty **SNF Road 24S07**, whose surface is
narrow and usually rough. After a tedious
drive on it, we find **Roadhead 18** (3.1, 22.3)
in a cluster of campsites by Peel Mill Creek.
At least 8 cars can be left here by runners on
Trip 21.

R19 Making sure our canteens are full before we leave the Peel Mill campsites (0.0,
22.3), we then drive the bumpy road briefly
southwest to meet the Telephone Trail of
Trip 22 in a saddle on Telephone Ridge (0.7,
23.0), **Roadhead 19**. Here 3 or 4 cars can be
parked off the road.

Roadheads 20–42: Western Divide Recreation Area

From Los Angeles, drive north, first on
Interstate 5, then on **State Freeway 99** and
finally on **State Highway 65**. This 2-lane road
for high-speed driving leads almost 30 miles
north, then passes under railroad tracks, and
shortly afterward intersects paved **TC Avenue 56**, signed for "Ducor." Here we turn

east, joining the course that Northern Californians take.

From Fresno, take *Freeway 99* southeast, then leave it at the Earlimart exit (last late-night gas) and drive east on *Avenue 56* until you reach Highway 65.

R20 Avenue 56 leads us east from Highway 65 (0.0, 0.0), soon passing through the town of Ducor and then crossing railroad tracks. Shortly we pass from the San Joaquin Valley plains to the foothills of the Sierra Nevada, presently reaching an "Old West"-style restaurant at Fountain Springs. A few yards farther east, TC Road MTN 109 (7.1, 7.1) intersects our road at Roadhead 20. Cars can be left in the intersection's northwest corner or off the road just west of the restaurant. Overnight camping is only possible with the permission of the restaurant owners.

R21 Drivers intending to take the "Northern California Shortcut" described earlier should turn southeast onto paved Road MTN 109 at its junction with Avenue 56 (0.0, 7.1) and leaf back a few pages to catch the description of that road. Our road, meanwhile, continues east with a slightly changed code: *MTN 56.* (Its first segment is fully described in Trip 23.) Eventually, our road enters Deer Creek valley, passes the entrance of Leavis Flat Campground ($2 a night) and then weaves amid the cluster of cottages named California Hot Springs. There we skirt the old hot springs resort (a shell since it was gutted by fire in 1968) just before leaving town. Just up the road we come to a **T** intersection (20.3, 27.4) where Road MTN 56 turns south and signed, paved TC Road MTN 50 starts north. Drivers heading for Roadheads 24-44 turn north here and skip to the R24 description, but we turn south. Quite soon, we meet signed SNF Road 23S04 (0.2, 27.6), which branches east and leads away drivers bound for Roadheads 22 and 23. They skip to the R22 entry while we drive south into the town of Pine Flat (0.4, 28.0). A restaurant, store, gas station, phone and water fountain attract people in need here. Soon our road passes the last Pine Flat cabin, then loses its pavement and becomes *SNF Road 23S05.* This dusty, sometimes bumpy road winds over Capinero Saddle and eventually reaches the start of White River Trail 31E58 (4.0, 32.0), which is de-

scribed in Trip 24. Although there is no room for parking here, room can be found by driving a few yards farther and then taking *SNF Road 24S05* briefly south to **Roadhead 21** (0.1, 32.1). Off-road parking for at least 10 cars can be found just outside of the White River campgrounds (free), where water is dispensed from pipes.

R22 From its beginning at Road MTN 56 (0.0, 27.6), *Road 23S04* winds east, soon passing through a gate kept unlocked when the road is least muddy and least covered with snow. We now drive up a slight ridge, cross a large clearing and then find signed Thompson Camp Trail 31E54 on which Trip 25 ends at **Roadhead 22** (1.3, 28.9).

R23 Road 23S04 continues east from the cattle guard (0.0, 28.9) and forks in a few minutes with a short, rough road (0.5, 29.4) on which we drive south to **Roadhead 23** on a ridge crest. Deer Creek Ridge Trail 31E55, the initial link in Trip 25, begins at the large campsite here, beside parking for about 10 cars. Water is available just up the road at Deer Creek Mill Campground.

R24 From the **T** intersection (0.0, 27.4) east of California Hot Springs, we take paved *TC Road MTN 50* north and instantly meet eastbound SNF Road 23S01 (0.1, 27.5). This road serves Uhl Ranger Station headquarters of the Hot Springs District of Sequoia National Forest (see "Organizational Services" section). The county road winds beyond, and shortly bridges Tyler Creek where eastbound Lion Ridge Trail 31E52 (1.5, 29.0) begins. (The turnout here is the last place to camp and get water for outdoorsmen about to take Trips 26–30.) A few hundred yards ahead, Parker Meadow Stock Driveway 31E51, a steep shortcut to Cold Springs Saddle for cattle and hikers, crosses the road. Then we proceed to the side of Merry Creek and come to **Roadhead 24** (2.6, 31.6) on the road's first switchback. Trip 26 begins here on signed Rube Creek Trail 31E46.

R25 Beyond the Rube Creek trailhead (0.0, 31.6), our road switchbacks up past Dead Mule Saddle, then skirts Cold Springs Peak and arrives at Cold Springs Saddle (5.2, 36.8), **Roadhead 25.** Further progress is often blocked, and parking space is limited, by snowdrifts here in winter. Trips 27–30 for skiers and snowshoers begin here.

R26   Paved Road MTN 50 winds northeast from Cold Springs Saddle (0.0, 36.8), soon crossing the crest of the Greenhorn Mountains at Parker Pass. From there, our pavement leads east and shortly intersects paved TC Road MTN 107 (3.4, 40.2), onto which drivers with Roadheads 32–42 in mind turn north. While they skip to the R32 entry, we continue reading here. Our road descends east from the junction and presently nears the abandoned, once bustling lumber town of Johnsondale. Near the north edge of town, we turn north to begin driving signed, paved *SNF Road 22S82* (6.2, 46.4), a winding route that soon transports us past a fork with signed SNF Road 22S02 (2.5, 48.9), a shortcut to Road MTN 107. Not far beyond, a small sign indicates that the narrow paved road (0.2, 49.1) straight ahead leads to the Boy Scouts' Camp Whitsett. Drivers with Roadheads 27–31 in mind veer northeast here and skip to the R27 description, but would-be Sentinel Peak climbers take the *Whitsett road* east. Minutes later, they come to a fork in the road and pull off in one of the many parking alcoves found between here, **Roadhead 26** (0.2, 49.3), and the gated Camp Whitsett entrance to the south.

R27   *Road 22S82* beyond the Scout camp road (0.0, 49.1) meanders generally east for a while, and then turns abruptly north, topping a prominent ridge that juts from Sentinel Peak in a saddle. The eastward exit of SNF Road 22S53 here signifies that climbers bound for Elephant Rock should pull off to the south and park at **Roadhead 27** (1.4, 50.5). The local pines and oaks shade space for as many as 10 cars, but fail to screen overnight campers from the road's traffic.

R28   Our pavement weaves generally north from the saddle (0.0, 50.5), and presently forks with a furrowed road (2.1, 52.6) to the Alder Creek Slides. During past holiday weekends, this attraction for slab-seeking sunbathers—and all roadside campsites within 5 miles—was obnoxiously crowded, and the local sheriff was prompted to station officers at this junction. The main road next outflanks Sand Hill Ridge and at length touches the entrance to Lower Pep-

permint Campground, where campers are charged $3 a night. Some drivers prefer merely to hesitate here, filling canteens from the campground's faucets. This campground and campsites close to it mark the usual northern limit of Kern Canyon holiday-weekend congestion. Our road crosses Peppermint Creek a few yards north of the campground entrance and then jogs briefly southeast before resuming a northward course. Just as it resumes that course, 2 roads fork southeast within yards of each other. Now, while other drivers go straight ahead and skip to the R29 entry, we take the second, northernmost, *chuckholed road* (5.8, 58.4) southeast. Minutes later, we top a minor hummocky ridge, and our road ends amid oak-shaded spaces for numerous sleeping bags and at least 6 cars. Kern River-bound backpackers decamp from **Roadhead 28** (0.2, 58.6) here on Trip 33.

R29   *Road 22S82* continues beyond the Durrwood Camp turnoff (0.0, 58.4), shortly crosses Needlerock Creek, and receives detailed description from there on in Trip 34. Our road then traverses a ledge blasted from a precipitous flank of The Needles. There is some danger of rockfall where a midway chute meets the road, so make the traverse cautiously. Once beyond the bare granite flank, we presently reach the crude Freeman Creek Basin Entrance Station (6.7, 65.1), where a Forest Service employee issues permits to backpackers who will be entering Golden Trout Wilderness on Trip 35. Shortly thereafter, Road 22S82 crosses Freeman Creek and then climbs a short distance north to meet the signed, patched pavement of *SNF Road 20S67* (2.2, 67.3). Recreationists intending to take Trips 34 or 36 should stick to the main highway and skip to the R30 entry while we follow Road 20S67 southeast. Quite soon it goes through a creekside zone of large campsites where sleeping bags can be parked overnight with more comfort than at Roadhead 29. Then our road passes over signed "Lloyd Meadows Creek" and later meets signed Kern Flat Trail 33E20 just a few dozen yards before ending. Sparse Jeffrey pines on the dusty volcanic flat here at popular **Roadhead 29** (2.2, 69.5) shade some of the 25+ makeshift spaces for cars. Backpackers about to begin Trip 35 should leave at least 1 car here before going to the next roadhead.

R30 North of its junction with Road 20S67 (0.0, 67.3), *Road 22S82* leads on for about 5 minutes, and then crosses Lloyd Meadows Creek and parallel signed Fish Creek Meadows Trail 32E12 at **Roadhead 30** (1.1, 68.4). More than a dozen cars can be left in the creekside lot here. Places to throw down a sleeping bag are plentiful in the area. Wilderness Permits should be carried by those who embark here on Trip 35 or 36.

R31 Bicycle-toting drivers continue on Road 22S82 past the trailhead (0.0, 68.4) and quickly reach the large, unpaved cul-de-sac (0.4, 68.8), **Roadhead 31**, where Trip 34 begins. Off-road camping is possible here also, but water is scarce.

R32 Paved *TC Road MTN 107* leads north from its start on Road MTN 50 (0.0, 40.2) and on it we pass, during the next 5 minutes, campgrounds with 10 tables (Holey Meadow—$2/night), 15 tables (Redwood Meadow—$3/night) and 5 tables (Long Meadow—free). Our route presently forks north from Road MTN 107, on which drivers intent on reaching Roadheads 34–42 continue northeast. While they skip to the R34 description, we begin taking *SNF Road 22S03S* (4.8, 45.0). That narrow, oft-rutted road switchbacks up the flank of Mule Peak, presently delivering us to a fork (3.9, 48.9) just west of Crane Meadow. Those bound for Roadheads 32 and 33 part company here, as **Roadhead 32** drivers take a very short *spur road* north to their destination, an 8-car-capacity lot (0.1, 49.0). The best nearby spot for overnight camping can be found in the woods beside Crane Meadow, nearly 100 yards east of here, where canteens can be filled at Crane Spring (treat before drinking).

R33 *Road 22S03S* goes northeast of the Crane Meadow fork (0.0, 48.9) and in minutes we pass an eastbound spur to the campsites recommended above. Shortly thereafter, we top a saddle (0.9, 49.8). Groups should leave some cars here because parking space at the next roadhead accommodates only about 3 cars. Now the road begins switchbacking down to Mule Meadow, and at the second switchback, signed Summit Trail 31E14, which we want, begins. Overnight camping here at **Roadhead 33** (0.4, 50.2) would be precarious at best.

R34 Our drive on *Road MTN 107* beyond Road 22S03S (0.0, 45.0) takes us past several lateral roads and then weaves at length past spectacular views and a rockfall zone, cutting through a transverse ridge just before reaching the start of eastbound *SNF Road 21S69* (6.8, 51.8). Again drivers separate, with those going to Roadheads 35–42 continuing on the main road while we take the side road. It leads a few hundred yards along the transverse ridge, passes several large campsites and then, minutes later, ends in a swale by Dome Rock (0.6, 52.4) at **Roadhead 34**. Space for more than 8 cars brackets the road in this waterless site.

R35 Following *Road MTN 107* north from the Dome Rock junction (0.0, 51.8), we soon dip toward Peppermint Creek and then intersect signed SNF Road 21S07, which leads a mile east to reach 19-unit Upper Peppermint Campground (free). Once past Peppermint Creek, we presently meet SNF Road 21S79 (west) and paved TC Road MTN 168 (east) at Ponderosa Lodge (1.9, 53.7). Short-term housing, gas, a store, cafe and a phone await customers here at Roadhead 50 (skip to that description for other services offered). Not far beyond the lodge, we skirt Holey Meadow and then find westbound, signed SNF Road 21S78 at **Roadhead 35** (1.0, 54.7). Bicyclists on Trip 39 can leave their cars on the main road's east shoulder and also just to the west off the spur road (21S79). Backpackers bound for Trip 40 take the spur road further west while drivers bound for Roadheads 37–42 go north and skip to the R37 entry.

R36 *Road 21S78* quickly leads west from Road MTN 107 (0.0, 54.7) over hilly terrain to the crest of the Western Divide, where it flares to make room for at least 6 cars at **Roadhead 36** (0.7, 55.4). Camping is possible but is more comfortable to the northeast at Quaking Aspen Campground, the only dependable source of water. Summit Trail 31E14 comes in from the north here and starts leading Trip 40 backpackers south about 100 yards farther up the road.

R37 Just a few yards northeast of Road 21S78 (0.0, 54.7) on *Road MTN 107*, we turn northeast onto *SNF Road 21S05*, whose sign implies misleadingly that it runs all the way to The Needles Lookout. It really leads only

Larry L. Norris

Ponderosa Lodge in winter

part way there, sporadically passing large campsites, and presently ends in a 20-car lot by overgrown, unreliable Needle Spring (2.8, 57.5), **Roadhead 37**. The Needles Trail 32E22 begins here, and many climbers on Trip 41 will tread it to its destination.

R38   Beyond The Needles junction (0.0, 54.7) *Road MTN 107* cuts through the crest of the Western Divide and then descends briefly to an intersection (0.6, 55.3) with SNF Roads 21S14 (west) and 21S99 (east). (An alternate route to this point via time-consuming Highway 190 is covered in the description for Roadheads 43–50. Once here, drivers will find that the 55 tables and parking slots of Quaking Aspen Campground, where canteens may be filled from taps and camping costs $2 a night, flank paved Road 21S14 beginning just west of the main highway. Wilderness permits are issued at the campground's guard station.) We take *Road 21S99* from the junction and fork northeast a few minutes later where drivers going to Roadheads 39–42 turn northwest (0.6, 55.9). Still on Road 21S99, we drive toward a large cul-de-sac where Freeman Trail 33E20 of Trip 42 begins at **Roadhead 38** (0.2, 56.1). Very little remains of the old pack station that once squatted here. Now there is abundant room for camping and water is available in nearby Freeman Creek, reached along the trail.

R39   From the fork with Road 21S99 (0.0, 55.9), a yards-long *northwest connector* guides us to paved *SNF Road 21S50* and then that road leads us northward. The pavement presently ends at a signed junction (3.6, 59.5) where, after leaving at least one car at Roadhead 40 to the northwest, we turn north onto *SNF Road 20S79*. (Drivers heading for Roadheads 40–42 continue on Road 21S50 past the junction and skip to the R40 entry.) After an initial switchback, Road 20S79 weaves over an unimpressive portion of the Western Divide, and shortly thereafter curves northwest through a signed junction (1.6, 61.1) with *SNF Road 20S53*, on which we head northeast. Minutes later, we arrive at a 12-car lot at **Roadhead 39** (1.1, 62.2), the end of the road. Sites in which to lay sleeping bags can be found nearby, although the lot can get unpleasantly dusty during holiday-weekend nights. Backpackers on Trip 44 and rock climbers on Trip 43 get underway at this usually waterless site.

R40   We persist in tracing *Road 21S50* past Road 20S79 (0.0, 59.5) and presently bear north where SNF Road 20S81 peels off to the west. Moments later, we enter the Clicks Creek watershed thru a swale and shortly find signposted Clicks Creek Trail 32E11 (1.6, 61.1) on a slight hill by Log Cabin Meadow. A few dozen yards beyond the trail, we enter a large clearcut patch and there encounter a dusty 15-car parking lot, **Roadhead 40**. Sleeping bags may be rolled out a few steps away, although sites with less dust and more privacy can be found a few hundred yards north of the road by the Clicks Creek Trail.

R41 Your road runs generally northwest from the lot (0.0, 61.1), shortly crosses a stumpy 5-acre clearing and afterward meets signed and gated SNF Closed Road 20S71 (1.2, 62.3) at **Roadhead 41**. Parking is limited to the few nearby spots where you can pull off to the side and avoid blocking traffic.

R42 Beyond the junction with Road 20S71 (0.0, 62.3), we take Road 21S50 north-northeast, presently crossing North Fork Clicks Creek and soon afterward meeting signed Summit Trail 31E14 in a patchcut at **Roadhead 42** (2.1, 64.4). Up to 10 cars can be left in off-road alcoves nearby. The best spots to lay a sleeping bag are beside the North Fork just over 100 yards southwest of here. The trailhead sign marks the end of Trips 45 and 56, which begin at Roadhead 40; so after leaving at least 1 car here, we head back to that roadhead.

Roadheads 43–55:
Tule River Recreation Area

From Los Angeles, drive *Interstate 5* and then *State Freeway 99* northwest before going north from the northern outskirts of Bakersfield on *State Highway 65*. It leads in about an hour to the ramp signed for eastbound *State Highway 190*, which we take.

From Fresno, go southeast on *Freeway 99*, then take the offramp signed "Poplar" and start east on *Highway 190*. It presently divides, becoming a 4-lane Expressway at a cloverleaf interchange with State Freeway 65 in Porterville.

Porterville is the source of all self-propelled sports supplies and late-night gas that is nearest to this series of roadheads. The gas station is located 2 miles north of the State 65/190 interchange and a few hundred feet east of State Freeway 65 on Henderson Avenue.

R43 From its interchange with State Freeway 65 in Porterville (0.0, 0.0), 4-lane State Highway 190 leads east past a few

"stop" signs and signals, shortly reduces in width from 4 to 2 lanes, and later skirts Lake Success and the shower-equipped lakeshore campground. Soon, after crossing the Tule River for the first time, we pass an alerting "U.S. Ranger Station" sign and find, shortly thereafter, the USFS Tule River District Ranger Station (12.2, 12.2) across a paved lot north of our road. Prospective takers of Trips 44–47 and 52 who happen to be here when the office is open should stop for their requisite Wilderness Permit. (See "Organizational Resources" section for some of the other goods and services it offers.) Fast, easy driving prevails over the few miles from the station to the town of Springville, but there a 30 MPH limit is enforced. Some stores offer limited camping and backpacking supplies, and elsewhere in town you'll find gas, water, phones, a laundromat and also a fire station where you can ask about conditions in Mountain Home State Forest. Bicyclists beginning Trips 49 and 50 should turn southwest next to the station on paved *TC Road MTN 189A* and park along its shoulder, **Roadhead 43** (4.2, 16.4). Overnight camping is never condoned in a residential zone such as this.

R44 Northeast of the fire station (0.0, 16.4), *Highway 190* soon leaves town and forkswith paved, signed TC Road MTN 239 (0.8, 17.2) in front of a large, whitewashed barn. Drivers intent on Roadheads 51–55 take the county road north, skipping to the R51 entry, and those—ourselves included—aimed at Roadheads 44–50 continue on Highway 190. Quite soon our road bridges North Fork Tule River, our canyon narrows, and then the road makes tortuous hairpin turns. Less than ½ hour from Springville, we pass the entrance of Coffee Campground, a 20-unit facility where the overnight charge is $1. (In hot or balmy weekends—especially holiday weekends—a short stretch of the state highway here becomes as congested as roads along the Kern River ever get. Slabs by and pools in the nearby cascading river are thronged then with bathers soaking in the sunlight, and then a pollution hazard arises. Please, if you can, avoid this area during such times.) Our road switchbacks by the campground entrance and later, while winding, is bridged by a flume. The underpass signals an impending signed fork with paved **TC Road MTN 208A** (7.2, 24.4), a narrow, stripeless road. It leads us northeast while drivers determined on getting to Roadheads 46–50 continue along the state highway and skip to the R46 description. Our road soon enters a canyon along the North Fork of the Middle Fork Tule River. Nearly halfway to its advertised destination, Camp Wishon, our road curls in a nook and crosses a seasonal south-trending brook. By a turnout with room for 4 cars here at **Roadhead 44** (1.7, 26.1), Dunn Trail 30E16 starts up a roadside bank and leads away hikers on Trip 51. (If you plan to start hiking the morning after your drive, continue up-canyon and sleep safer in Wishon Campground.)

R45   The segment of curvy road beyond the Dunn Trail (0.0, 26.1) takes less than 5 minutes to drive and leads up-canyon past a USFS guard station to a fork with SNF Road 20S03 (2.0, 28.1). This right-hand road leads northeast among the 28 sites of Wishon Campground, where camping before we hit the trail costs $3 a night. Should your canteens need filling, spring water can be tapped in the campground. When heading for the roadhead, however, we take the left-hand road at the junction, then pass the cabins, cafe, store and phone of the Camp Wishon resort. A locked gate (0.3, 28.4) spans the road near the resort's easternmost structure. Up to 10 cars can be parked on the worn, oak-shaded flat just to the south, **Roadhead 45**, where hikers embark on Trip 52.

R46   At the fork (0.0, 24.4) where TC Road MTN 208A begins, **State Highway 190** starts dropping east toward a one-lane bridge across the North Fork of the Middle Fork Tule River. A roadside phone booth is lodged a few hundred yards beyond the bridge in an electric-power generating complex. Then, after the highway switchbacks twice, it winds tortuously up-canyon toward Camp Nelson upslope from the South Fork of the Middle Fork Tule River. At the Moorehouse Springs Fish Hatchery (4.5, 28.9), midway on our ascent to Camp Nelson, anglers can learn which streams of the Southern Sierra are stocked, how often and with what. One sign that Camp Nelson is close at hand comes later, when we reach the roadside fountain of cold Pierpoint Spring

(2.4, 31.3), an opportune canteen-filler for trips accessible from this road. Just a few minutes beyond the spring, the Pierpoint Spring Resort (0.4, 31.7) stands just south of our road. A store, cafe, laundromat and the Camp Nelson post office are housed in the main resort building, and gas pumps stand in front of it. Cabins accumulate by the state highway beyond the resort and quite soon we reach Camp Nelson's main junction (0.6, 32.3), a 3-pronged fork. Now, while others take aim on Roadhead 47 by taking the middle fork (they skip to the R47 entry) and seekers of Roadheads 48–50 take the upper fork (they skip to the R48 entry), we take the lower fork: signed, paved **TC Road MTN 192A**. It drops southeastward, soon bridging the river, leads through the Slate Mountain Summer Home tract, passes the signed start of Bear Creek Trail 31E31 and almost instantly afterward comes to a 4-car pullout, **Roadhead 46** (1.1, 33.4), just shy of Bear Creek. Here energetic backpackers intent on taking Trip 53 leave one or more shuttle cars before backtracking to the 3-pronged junction and heading to Roadhead 47.

R47   The middle paved road at the 3-pronged fork (0.0, 32.3) signposted "**MTN 193A**," winds generally east from Highway 190 and is soon distinguished from Camp Nelson crossroads by its width. (Trip 54 details the road's distinction further.) Soon after passing a county fire station, we leave Camp Nelson and then arrive at the entrance to signed Belknap Creek Campground. Trip 54 runners and Trip 53 backpackers looking for someplace to sleep before getting their exercise will find this 15-unit campground more comfortable than Roadhead 47 if they don't mind paying $3 a night to stay here. The main road east of the campground, now signed "20S10," soon loses its pavement midway along a short line of riverside cabins. Just beyond the easternmost cabin, drivers of low-slung cars would be wise to park before the road makes a bouldery ford of a snowmelt creek. Beyond the ford, a roadend lot with room for more than a dozen vehicles marks **Roadhead 47** (2.0, 34.3), where Quaking Aspen Trail (signed "Camp Nelson Trail") 31E30 begins.

R48   The upper road at the 3-pronged fork (0.0, 32.3) is center-striped **State Highway 190**, which twists northeastward, avoiding most Camp Nelson cabins. Eventually this road connects with a south-trending spur road signed "20S54/Tulare County Dump," Trip 55 bicyclists start riding at a 4-car turnout a few dozen yards east of this junction, the turnout of **Roadhead 48** (2.2, 34.5). Potable water and private spaces in which to camp are scarce in this vicinity.

R49 Beyond the turnout (0.0, 34.5), Highway 190 winds time-consumingly past the village of Cedar Slope, where a pay phone is stationed, then switchbacks and later turns sharply at Boulder Creek to cross the worst wintertime ice patch between Camp Nelson and the Ponderosa Lodge. (Chains or snow tires may be required at any time from here on in winter and early spring.) Our upgrade shortly eases while we begin a half-mile stretch of eastward creekside travel. The main road starts to curve south at the end of this stretch, becoming TC Road MTN 107, and paved though unplowed SNF Road 21S50 starts northeast from that curve, marking **Roadhead 49** (6.7, 41.2), where state snowplows maintain parking alcoves roomy enough for 20 cars. Trip 56, an alpine ski tour to Jordan Peak, starts here, but camping (unless in your car) is out of the question.

R50 Parking is not allowed along sporadically plowed *Road MTN 107*, which curves south of Road 21S50 (0.0, 41.2), tops the Western Divide in ½ mile and shortly leads to a junction with plowed, northeast-trending *TC Road MTN 168* (1.8, 43.0). The Ponderosa Lodge, whose owners rent cabins and snowmobiles and run a cafe and gas pumps, occupies a private inholding at this junction's northeast corner. About 10 cars can be left in the lodge's parking lot (**Roadhead 50**) by skiers on Trips 57–59, although camping is discouraged.

R51 From State Highway 190 (0.0, 17.2) near Springville, paved *TC Road MTN 239*, signed "Balch Park Drive," leads north near the North Fork Tule River in a segment described in greater detail in Trip 49. At length, we take the first paved road to the east, signed and paved *TC Road MTN 220* (3.4, 20.6). Our narrow road almost instantly bridges the North Fork Tule River, then climbs steadily, presently touching the signed entrance to "SCICON—The Clemme

Gill School of Science and Conservation" and eventually crossing Bear Creek near an apple orchard. (Norman Cook, manager of Mountain Home State Forest, advised me in 1978 that occasional winter storms have in the past left the road piled with snow all the way up from here to the usual snowline at Slick Rock. Afterward, the snowline took a few days or even weeks to retreat to its usual place.) Beyond the Bear Creek bridge, our road switchbacks and winds at length toward Slick Rock. There the road switchbacks for the last time, looping around space in which at least 4 cars can be parked. Only those sleeping inside their cars would want to camp here at usually waterless **Roadhead 51** (9.6, 30.2) before taking Trip 60.

R52 Road MTN 220, still paved, leads northward from the Slick Rock switchback (0.0, 30.2), and after a while it enters Mountain Home State Forest and meets a spur road (3.3, 33.5) starting left (north) to the Forest Headquarters. If you have questions about local history, forestry or trail maintenance, this is the place to seek answers. Beyond the headquarters turnoff, the main road winds over a slight ridge and touches Summit Road (1.1, 34.6) in a signed triangle junction. While drivers on their way to Roadheads 53–55 turn east here and skip to the R53 entry, we stick to the only paved road, going straight ahead. It quickly leads us past the campgrounds ($3 a night) at Balch County Park, and later, when it joins *TC Road MTN 247* (2.1, 36.7)—the first paved road past the park—we make a hairpin turn northeast onto that road. In minutes we pass the entrance to the Frazier Mill Campground, and just a few dozen yards beyond it we find the Bogus Meadow trailhead (0.3, 37.0) at **Roadhead 52**, where Trip 61 begins. Parking spots (not campsites) in the nearby campground are the best places to leave cars before taking this short hike, and drinking water is dispensed from faucets throughout the area.

R53 From the triangle junction (0.0, 34.6) wittRoad MTN 220, dusty *Summit Road* leads past several narrower roads before meeting the signed end of Road MTN 247 (2.6, 37.2). Just a few yards north of that fork, River Road starts leading seekers of Roadheads 54 and 55 away to the east. While they skip to the R54 description, we proceed north, shortly passing the signed entrance to Shake Camp Campground, where tap water is available. Moments later, we drive into a parking lot with room for at least 24 cars, **Roadhead 53** (0.3, 37.5). Hikers begin Trip 62 here.

R54 After beginning at a signed junction (0.0, 37.2) with Summit Road, *River Road* alternately rounds ridges and canyons. On or near the ridges, it touches the start of 3 downslope-trending roads that lead off to the right. While drivers en route to Roadhead 55 go straight ahead, we turn off River Road (2.0, 39.2) onto the third *spur road*, which is signed conspicuously for "Moses Gulch Campground." It winds down into the canyon of the North Fork of the Middle Fork Tule River and presently forks east from a logging road (0.6, 39.8). Shortly thereafter, we switchback northwest on a terrace near the river just before reaching the end of the road in a 30-car parking lot (0.3, 40.1) for the walk-in Moses Gulch Campground. Water is piped to a faucet at the east end of the fallen sequoia that bounds the lot on the north. Appropriately enough, the Moses Gulch Hike, Trip 63, gets underway here.

R55 A few minutes' drive on *River Road* beyond the start of the spur road (0.0, 39.2) to Moses Gulch Campground leads to another fork (0.4, 39.6), where we swerve left. This short spur road serves the 20-car lot in front of the walk-in Hidden Falls Campground, an example of outstanding landscape architecture. Our road skirts the lot and then crosses the river on a concrete slab. Don't attempt this crossing if water more than a foot deep is pouring over the slab, as it sometimes does during snowmelt floods in late spring. Just beyond the crossing, we find a 5-car parking lot on the south, **Roadhead 55** (0.1, 39.7), where hikers embark on Trip 64, climbers on Trip 65. Before leaving the parking lot, look south from its perch toward the river to take in a puzzling scene. You'll see the river disappear into a deep, shadowy slot, but you won't be able to hear the roar of its Hidden Falls. The slot's brink by the campground is well worth a visit, for there you can see the falls themselves; but watch out! The brink is slippery.

Roadheads 56–66: Via Visalia

From Los Angeles, drive *Interstate 5* northwest then *State Freeway 99* north past Bakersfield to the Tulare Avenue (*State Highway 137*) exit. Take 137 briefly east through the outskirts of Tulare, then turn north on *State Highway 63* and trace it north for nearly 15 minutes. Then you turn east onto a *frontage road* for depressed *State Freeway 198* signed "Noble Avenue," and almost instantly veer northeast to get on the freeway.

From Fresno, drive *State Freeway 99* southeast, then get onto eastbound *State Highway 198* and drive it until it becomes a freeway and meets State Highway 63 in Visalia. (Merchants in this town offer a wide range of supplies and services for self-propelled sports. Star Shoe Shop on South Mooney Boulevard (Highway 63) ranks among the state's best boot-repair establishments.)

R56 Beyond Highway 63, (0.0, 0.0) *Freeway 198* leaves Visalia (last late-night gas) and shortly becomes an expressway, which presently narrows to 2 lanes upon entering the Sierra foothills. After a while it starts into the Kaweah River canyon and skirts Lake Kaweah. Here the U.S. Army Corps of Engineers operates several campgrounds that charge $3 a night and offer electrical hookups and hot showers. Quite soon after leaving the lake, we bridge the bouldery South Fork Kaweah River and almost instantly meet southeast-trending *TC Road MTN 347* (28.7, 28.7). While travelers aiming for Roadheads 58–66 speed past on the main highway (they skip to the R58 description), we turn off on this paved, striped county road by an inconspicuous "Old Three Rivers Drive" sign. Our road bends east in a few dozen yards and then joins a loop of abandoned cement pavement, **Roadhead 56**, on which 3 or 4 cars can be parked.

R57 Beyond the loop (0.0, 28.7), we continue east, soon starting up paved *Lane 347* (0.5, 29.2), signed "Blossom Drive," where the main road diverges. We swiftly reach the first crossroad (0.1, 29.3) and turn south there onto paved *TC Road MTN 348*, which Trip 66 describes fully. It winds up the South Fork Kaweah River canyon, crossing the river twice before its pavement gives way

Richard C. Burns, National Park Service

Squirrel Creek potholes by Mineral King road offer refreshing bathing

to washboard dirt. This dirt road, bordered by fences, presently bridges the river again, then switchbacks before entering Sequoia National Park. Then it cuts through the South Fork Campground (piped water) where a trailer sometimes serves as a ranger station. Beyond, the road narrows, touches the South Fork trailhead, continues 50 yards farther and ends at **Roadhead 57** (12.2, 41.5), a parking lot with room for 6–10 cars. Trips 67–71 get underway here.

R58   Driving *Highway 198* beyond Road MTN 347 (0.0, 28.7), we soon pass a general store and, later, a shopping center with a drug store and a laundromat on the outskirts

of Three Rivers. (Most businesses in this town close by 8 or 9 p.m.) Our road then leads through the town's main commercial district, where a post office stands near gas stations, markets, fruit stands, cafes and motels. (Motorists heading to Mineral King should check their gas gauge here before driving up the access grade, which consumes much more gas than they'd expect.) Not long afterward, we slow where the highway bends sharply around a ridge, and then we encounter paved *TC Road MTN 375* (5.3, 34.0) at a junction amply signed for "Mineral King." Although drivers bound for Roadheads 62–66 continue northeast up the state highway from here (and skip to the R62 description), we turn east onto the narrower county road. (Backpackers intending to take Trip 77 should first drive northeast to Roadhead 63, leave a shuttle care there, backtrack to this junction and then take the Mineral King Road to Roadhead 59.) Immediately we come to a sign describing the crowdedness of campgrounds and parking lots at Atwell Mill and Mineral King. National Park Service officials use this sign to notify would-be visitors when the facilities are full, saving them from an intensely frustrating drive. If the roadhead we're aiming for is signed "open," we proceed up the road, almost instantly passing the California Department of Forestry's Hammond Fire Control Station, where emergency services can be obtained around the clock. Our road then switchbacks and winds steeply up the East Fork Kaweah River canyon, and eventually we enter Sequoia National Park (no entrance fee). Shortly thereafter we round the ridge where the Lookout Point Ranger Station (10.2, 44.2) is perched. When the flag flies outside, there's a ranger inside who can provide emergency services. Beyond the station, we quickly rise toward a belt of forest, and at length find the first sequoias en route by a radiator-water trough at Redwood Creek. Here at **Roadhead 58** (4.9, 49.1), a short loop of old road passes behind the sequoias, affording room to park several cars where the main road is usually first blocked by snow in winter. Skiers usually start out from here on Trip 72.

R59   Beyond Redwood Creek (0.0, 49.1), our road continues in summer as a dirt route, and it presently leads into the Atwell Grove of sequoias, where pavement briefly resumes. Here we pass the usually-manned Atwell Mill Ranger Station (2.8, 51.9) and a roadside kiosk. Often this kiosk is the only source of Wilderness Permits anywhere near Mineral King. Then we pass the Atwell Redwood Trailhead and afterward skip the first entrance (the signed one) to the Atwell Mill Campground to find the eastern, or second, entrance (0.3, 52.2). Drivers on their way to Roadheads 60 and 61 continue up the main road from here, but we turn south onto *SEKI Road 5–3*. It instantly leads downslope into a dozen-car parking lot, **Roadhead 59**, where Trips 73–77 for hikers and backpackers begin. Water faucets are located in the campground.

R60   Beyond the campground (0.0, 52.2), *Road MTN 375* shortly reverts to dirt again and enters Cabin Cove, where we slow to pass between 2 pines that closely flank the road. Minutes later, we pass the store at Silver City (1.2, 53.4), which doubles as a cafe and gas station, and offers a public telephone, hot showers, rental cabins and campsites. (It operates only in daylight hours.) From there, the road, fully described in Trip 72, winds up-canyon, becomes paved again, then threads rows of cabins at Faculty Flat and presently meets a southbound *campground road* (2.4, 55.8). It leads south into 28-unit Cold Spring Campground, the only campground in Mineral King. Camping in this ranger-patrolled site costs $2 a night. In the meantime, our road (MTN 375) skirts one more cabin and in a few yards touches **Roadhead 60**, a parking lot on the south with room for 4 to 5 cars. Runners on Trip 78 embark here, just a few dozen paces west of the Mineral King Ranger Station (0.1, 55.9). Runners completing their trip can enjoy long drafts of delicious water, while others can fill canteens. During the Summer of 1978, Wilderness Permits were issued here from sunrise to sunset.

R61   Then the county road leads a bit farther east from the station (0.0, 55.9) and passes a pair (0.3, 56.2) of parking lots, each with room for at least 20 cars. A sign here states that use of the lots is limited to 7 days. The road then proceeds a few hundred yards before cutting through a 40-car parking lot at the start of the Sawtooth Pass Trail (0.5, 56.7). Afterward, our route forks south-southwest from the *pack station road* (0.2, 56.9) and soon after crossing the river for the last time, we park in a 20-car lot at **Roadhead 61** (0.1, 57.0), the end of the road. Camping on private property such as this is never condoned. Backpackers set out on Trips 79 and 80 beside the public telephone here.

R62   From the start of the road to Mineral King (0.0, 34.0), we proceed northeast on *State Highway 198*, bridging the East Fork Kaweah River quite soon and passing a motel, restaurant and phone booth immediately afterward. The Texaco station here offers the last gas of any brand for the next 21 miles. Just beyond this enclave of commerce, we pause at a booth (2.0, 36.0) on the edge of Sequoia National Park and pay the $3 entrance fee. Employees are present to take your cash during daylight hours all year, and also all night from Memorial Day through Labor Day. Check the blackboard here for campground, road and weather conditons.

State Highway 198 becomes SEKI Road 1, the *Generals Highway*, at the entrance station; and while driving it several hundred yards beyond, we come to a series of turnouts where the road is flanked on our left by a picnic area, on our right by Park headquarters (1.0, 37.0). The refrigerated drinking fountain here is a treat in the usual summer heat, and the restrooms rank among the cleanest and best-equipped in the park. Backpackers intending to take Trip 82 can pick up a Wilderness Permit daily from 8 a.m. to 5 p.m. at the reception desk, where the Park's natural-history association sells many useful books and maps.

Upon leaving the headquarters, we drive just over 5 minutes u-canyon, either passing under or bypassing Arch Rock midway. Then, parting company with drivers bound for Roadheads 63–66 (who skip to the R63 description), we turn north into the signed "Potwisha Campground" on paved *SEKI Road 11–1* (2.7, 39.7). Moments later we turn right, directed by signs, and travel part of a one-way loop through this weekend-popular campground. At the northernmost part of the loop we branch north onto a dirt road and immediately pull off to the left at **Roadhead 62** (0.2, 39.9). When the few parking spaces are taken here at the start of the Marble Falls hike, return to the main highway and park in its turnouts. Staying overnight in the campground, where piped water can fill canteens, will not cost you extra.

R63   Continuing awhile up the *Generals Highway* beyond the campground entrance (0.0, 39.7), we encounter the Hospital Rock Picnic Area off to the left just before the highway starts switchbacking up to Giant Forest. The picnic area, with its restrooms and drinking fountains, stands just across the main road from a small "Buckeye Flat" sign marking the start of paved *SEKI Road 12–1* (2.3, 42.0). While drivers aiming for Roadheads 64–66 stick to the Generals Highway, we take the narrow branch road and shortly fork east through a **Y** (0.6, 42.6). Now on the washboard dirt of *SEKI Road 12–2*, we presently reach a cul-de-sac lot (1.3,

43.9) in which as many as 12 cars can be parked. This is **Roadhead 63**, an uncomfortable place to camp perched on a slope a few hundred yards west of Moro Creek. (Drivers on their way to the start of Trip 77 leave shuttle cars here before backtracking to the Mineral King road.) Just east of the lot stands the Moro Creek Corral, which backpackers on Trips 77 and 82 pass through on the Middle Fork Kaweah Trail.

R64   The *Generals Highway* past Hospital Rock (0.0, 42.0) switchbacks gradually up past several springs offering water for radiators, and eventually connects with paved *SEKI Road 13–1* (8.3, 50.3) while making a switchback. Travelers intent on reaching Roadhead 66 (or a gas station) remain on the main highway (they skip to the R66 entry) while we branch northwest here past a "Crystal Cave" sign. Our road winds down a mild grade into the Marble Fork Kaweah River canyon. After a while we cross cascading Little Deer Creek and then pull off into a 6-car turnout, **Roadhead 64** (1.5, 51.8), in the west. The Marble Fork Trail of Trip 83 starts north just across the road, and additional parking space can be found across the road's high bridge to the west. Overnight camping is not allowed here. The safest creek for filling canteens can be found near the overflow parking lot.

R65   Just beyond the last trailhead (0.0, 51.8), our road bridges the river gorge, then meets a down-sloping spur road to the overflow parking lot, in which 2 dozen cars could fit. Our pavement winds west at length, crossing into the Yucca Creek watershed at a saddle. Some time later, we park in the looping lot at road's end, which has room for at least 50 cars. Here at **Roadhead 65** (4.8, 56.6), where camping is prohibited and drinking fountains are present, hundreds of visitors daily start their summertime stroll to Crystal Cave (Trip 84).

R66   Beyond the Crystal Cave turnoff (0.0, 50.3) the *Generals Highway* soon divides to pass between the Four Guardsmen, the first giant sequoias en route. Less than 5 minutes later, we turn southeast onto paved *SEKI Road 14–1* (2.1, 52.4) by the cafeteria and market at Giant Forest Village. (The nearest gas station can be found 4 miles northeast of here via the Generals Highway.) After a short drive on Road 14–1, passing the Auto

Log en route, we fork right twice through a *triangle junction* onto a narrow, paved *one-way road* (1.3, 53.7). It winds to the edge of the Giant Forest plateau and presently flares to the south, making a parking lot (0.4, 54.1) large enough for 15 cars. Although camping is not permitted and water is not available here at **Roadhead 66**, the Moro Rock Trail of Trip 85, which starts here, is so short that the deprivations usually don't matter.

Roadhead 67: Via Dinuba

From Bakersfield, drive *State Freeway 99* northwest, then take the ramp onto eastbound *State Freeway 198* and turn north moments later onto paved *Road 80*, signed "J19." It permits high-speed travel while leading through orchards and fields, and eventually it reaches Dinuba. Here we turn east onto *Avenue 416*, joining drivers headed to the same roadhead from the Fresno area.

From Fresno, we drive *Freeway 99* southeast and then take the *Mountain View Avenue* offramp right after passing the town of Selma. Mountain View Avenue, coded "*Avenue 416*," leads us east from the interchange, bridges the Kings River midway to Dinuba and, upon reaching Dinuba, crosses Road 80. Here we join Southern Californians on their way to the same roadhead.

R67 All together now, we drive east on *Avenue 416* beyond the junction (0.0, 0.0) in Dinuba (where a poorly signed limit of 25 m.p.h. is strictly enforced) and presently cross paved Hills Valley Road (5.0, 5.0), where Southern Californians en route to Roadheads 68–78 turn north. The crossroads doesn't concern us because we continue straight into Orosi (1.0, 6.0), the last source of water, food and daytime gas en route. Just a few minutes later, in the midst of a citrus grove, we park at **Roadhead 67**. It's located near a palm-tree-marked ranch house at the junction with north-south Road 152 (3.0, 9.0). Roadside camping at this waterless site can't be done without the owner's permission. A winsome bicycle tour, Trip 86, starts here.

Roadheads 68–80: Via Highway 180

From Bakersfield, trace the approach to Roadhead 67 as far as *Hills Valley Road*, then take this high-speed road north. It merges with *State Highway 63* by and by, continuing straight ahead, and later we slow on the state highway where it starts winding up into Sierran foothills. Eventually we turn east onto paved *State Highway 180* at the end of Highway 63. Here we join drivers from Fresno and points north.

From Fresno, we drive east on *Highway 180*, picking up speed upon leaving the suburbs and entering agricultural lands. Eventually, this highway too starts ascending Sierran foothills, and early in the ascent it meets abundantly signed Highway 63.

R68 Beyond Highway 63 (0.0, 0.0) everyone takes 180 east past the gas pumps and post office at Squaw Valley to the phone booth, gas stations and geodesic dome that distinguish Clingans Junction (7.1, 7.1). Most everyone can drive through this junction unconcerned, but bicycle-toters heading for Roadhead 68 should check their tires and canteens before leaving the gas stations, and then turn south here onto paved *Dunlap Road*. Winding through pastoral country dotted with ranches and oaks, it presently leads through a triangle junction with Ruth Hill Road (3.4, 10.5), a signal for us to watch the north roadside a few hundred yards beyond for the Dunlap post office. We then leave our cars in the large lot in front of the office at **Roadhead 68** (0.3, 10.8) where bicycle trips 87 and 88 begin. Overnight camping here is out of the question. If you need to camp, take Trip 88 in your car toward Cedarbrook Picnic Area and camp near there.

R69 Speeding beyond Clingans Junction (0.0, 7.1) on **Highway 180**, we make a long ascent, passing Snowline Lodge and its cafe midway, and eventually come to a signed fork (13.5, 20.6) where *State Highway 245* begins. Recreationists bound for Roadheads 71–78 should ignore the fork, except to skip to the R71 description. We, in the meantime, drive on 245 south from the fork. After negotiating many of the state highway's tortuous curves, we touch the start of a paved southbound route signed "Visalia Road" (4.2, 24.8). That's for takers of Trip 90. Our route continues down 245, immediately switchbacking into the outskirts of Pinehurst. Shortly we pass a cafe, phone, store and gas station before pulling off to the west and parking in the paved lot in front of the Pinehurst Ranger Station (see the "Organizational Services" section of Chapter 4). At least a dozen cars can be left here at **Roadhead 69** (0.8, 25.6) by bicyclists getting underway on Trip 89, and although water is obtainable on request at the ranger station, overnight campers can find far quieter places to stay along SNF Road 14S46 east of here (see Map 63).

R70   After *Visalia Road* starts south from State Highway 245 (0.0, 24.8), it presently enters Tulare County, where its designation changes to *Drive 254*. (For points of interest en route, turn to the Trip 89 description.) A little later we turn northeast onto paved *TC Road MTN 465* (4.6, 29.4) and proceed a few hundred yards to a store, gas station, phone, the Badger post office and a picnic area on the right. When parking along the road here at **Roadhead 70** (0.3, 29.7), please leave enough room for the store's patrons. Water is yours for the asking here at the start of Trip 90, but if you need a place to sack out the night before your trip, go 7.2 miles farther to the Eshom Creek Campground.

R71   The next notable point along *Highway 180* beyond its fork with Highway 245 (0.0, 20.6) is the Big Stump Entrance Station (2.8, 23.4) of Kings Canyon National Park. Here a $3 entrance fee is collected from drivers on their way to Roadheads 71, 73 and 80. Others who tell the official here that they're headed for the national forest will get a free passage through the Grant Grove Section of the Park.

Just beyond the station, we curve past a large parking lot beside restrooms and a drinking fountain, and not long afterward our road splits at a triangle junction (1.7, 25.1). The route to Roadheads 71 and 72, which we take, curves north through the junction. (Drivers who only go as far as Roadhead 71 will leave shuttle cars there before backtracking to this junction. Then they'll join drivers en route to Roadheads 73–79 in heading south and skipping to the R73 description.)

To reach Roadheads 71 and 72, we drive north on 180 from the junction, shortly touching both ends of a loop road to the store, cafe, motel and phone at Wilsonia. Moments later, we turn east, off the approach to Roadhead 72, onto paved *SEKI*

Road 24–10 (1.3, 26.4). In a few dozen yards, it passes between the Grant Grove Visitor Center, on our right, and a restaurant, gift shop, bar and gas station on our left. The capacious parking lot here at **Roadhead 71** is usually kept clear of snow, so we leave some shuttle cars before going on to Roadhead 73.

R72   Summertime drivers intent on reaching the start of the Hume Lake Bicycle Tour should stick to Highway 180, continuing north past the visitor center (0.0, 26.4). They shortly leave the Park, then cross Cherry Gap and descend into Indian Basin, where the first paved road (5.8, 32.2) north of the park forks east. This is *SNF Road 13S09*, and we take it eastward around Park Ridge. After a spell, we branch south onto paved *SNF Road 13S43* (3.0, 35.2) which shortly veers southwest through a **Y** intersection (0.2, 35.4). In seconds we turn southeast onto paved *SNF Road 13S24*, really a large, long parking lot fronting the USFS Hume Lake Ranger Station. Here at **Roadhead 72** (0.1, 35.5), we park and start preparing our bikes for Trip 91. Water faucets and other overnight camping facilities can be found in the spacious Hume Lake Campground, for which users pay $3 a night.

R73   South of Grant Grove, the triangle junction (called "The Wye"—0.0, 25.1) through which Highway 180 passes marks the start of the *Generals Highway*. Initially leading us south, it winds along the Kings-Kaweah divide and presently reaches Quail Flat (3.6, 28.7). This is sometimes as far as the road is plowed after intense wintertime storms pass through. Cross-country skiers can park 10–15 cars in the plowed off-road space here at **Roadhead 73** and embark on Trip 92 (and sometimes on Trips 94–95 and 97–98 as well).

R74   *SEKI Road 23–1* starts indistinctly southeast from Generals Highway at Quail Flat (0.0, 28.7), then tops a slight knoll, switchbacks down the other side and becomes unmistakable. Its bumpy, narrow surface presently leads to Redwood Saddle (1.7, 30.4), where we turn south on *SEKI Road 23–2*. It ends in less than 100 yards at a lot large enough for 24 cars, **Roadhead 74** (0.1, 30.5). The Redwood Canyon and Sugarbowl trails of Trip 93 start here. Although camping is prohibited here, and water is not available, Eshom Creek Campground offers the necessary facilities 4.2 miles southwest of here along Road MTN 465.

R75   Beyond Quail Flat (0.0, 28.7) the *Generals Highway* winds southeast, soon passing a spectacular turnout at Kings Canyon Overlook, and later rounding Big Baldy Ridge at the start of the signed, south-trending "Big Baldy Ski Touring Trail" (3.0, 31.7). The 5-car turnout here at **Roadhead 75** serves Trip 94, a year-round trip; and Trip 95, a wintertime ski trek. Because the site is just outside the National Park, summertime visitors can use the medium campsite just a few paces from the road. Unfortunately, water is not available here, except what can be melted from snow in winter. Extra space for parking—at least enough for a dozen vehicles—can be found in a pullout a few hundred feet beyond on the road. The pullout overlooks the buildings and skating pond of the Montecito-Sequoia Lodge, which can provide towing, meals, cabins, and lessons in Nordic skiing for a fee. For further information, call the lodge's Bay Area reservation office at 415-967-8612 or write them at 1485 Redwood Drive, Los Altos, CA 94022.

R76   Moments after leaving the Big Baldy Ridge turnout (0.0, 31.7), summertime drivers aiming to reach Buck Rock leave the Generals Highway and start north on destination-signed *SNF Road 14S11* (0.2, 31.9)—everyone else goes straight ahead and skips to the R77 description. Road 14S11 winds across the mildly hilly Big Meadows plateau past numerous minor spur roads and at length reaches signed *SNF Road 13S04* (2.8, 34.7) 0.9 mile short of the Big Meadows Guard Station. Now taking 13S04 north, we quickly pass Buck Rock Campground and presently ascend to the Big Meadows Creek/Tenmile Creek drainage divide. Minutes after spying Buck Rock Lookout in the north through ridgecrest woods, we meet northbound SNF Closed Road 13S04A (1.9, 36.6) of Trip 96. **Roadhead 76**, just northeast of the junction, offers room for 3–5 vehicles to pull off the road and park. Overnight camping is possible here, but the only water available is what you bring yourself.

R77   From the Big Meadows turnoff (0.0, 31.9), we continue on the *Generals Highway*,

reaching the start of east-trending SNF Road 14S18 (1.1, 33.0) quite soon. Skiers intending to take Trip 97, which starts at this fork (**Roadhead 77**), should pull off the highway at the nearest plowed turnout.

R78   After we pass Road 14S18 (0.0, 33.0), the Generals Highway bends along a canyon and shortly meets southbound SNF Road 14S29 (0.9, 33.9—**Roadhead 78**) where another ski tour, Trip 98, begins. Again one should look for the nearest plowed turnout.

R79   After the snow has melted from *Road 14S29*, climbers can drive it south from the Generals Highway (0.0, 33.9) and shortly bear west with it through a signed junction with SNF Road 14S56. We then wind south awhile, passing a few retired logging spurs, before forking south on a short, well-used *spur road* (2.8, 36.7) that ends in a big cul-de-sac (0.1, 36.8) at **Roadhead 79**. Although roadside camping is possible here, again running water is absent. The jeep road on which climbers begin Trip 99 starts just to the south in the broad saddle here.

R80   Now there is only one user group advancing on the *Generals Highway*—hikers eager to reach the start of Trip 100. Beyond the exit of SNF Road 14S29 (0.0, 33.9), these summertime drivers proceed past a southward turnoff (2.5, 36.4) serving a gas station, restaurant, laundromat and rental shower-room. Then they cross Stoney Creek, where the road is flanked by a large campground and picnic area. Afterward they enter Sequoia National Park, presently cross Dorst Creek at a sharp bend in the road and then watch for a road that starts south, signed for "Dorst Campground." Once they get on this narrow, paved road, *SEKI Road 21–1* (4.9, 41.3), it leads them across the huge campground, then loops through the westermost cluster of sites, signed for "groups only." At its westernmost point, the road flares, offering space enough to park several dozen vehicles. Trip 100 starts west at a "Muir Grove Trail" sign here at **Roadhead 80** (1.0, 42.3).

Chapter 4: Using Trip Terms and the Tripfinder Tables

The Trip

Let's inspect a typical cluster of trip headings to see how each heading was formulated and what it means. (The information placed after each heading was taken from Trip 5.)

Season mid-March through mid-November

Distance 21.0 miles (33.8 km) shuttle trip

Steep Upgrade 1.8 miles (2.9 km)

Elevation Gain and Loss +6100 ft (+1859 m), −6000 ft (−1829 m)

Exertion/Duration easy/4 days, moderate/3 days, strenuous/2 days

Skills/Gears moderate route-finding, Class 1 climbing/ ("Gears" entry limited to bicycle trips)

Registration/Permits ("Registration" entry limited to snow trips)/campfire permit required

Roadheads/Maps R3, R5/M2, M3

Canteens (Entry limited to easy 1-day trips)

Description

The **Season** heading appears first because readers will probably want to know if snow conditions will allow them to take the trip, and if objectionable weekend or holiday crowds might be present.

This is where hikers, backpackers, climbers and bicyclists are told in which months they'll probably find the surface underfoot dry enough for good traction. This is where snowshoers and skiers are told in which months the snow will likely be best for them on designated slopes. (The meaning of "designated slopes" will be explained later in this chapter, under the "Description" heading.)

The phrases "weekdays only" or "nonholiday weekends only" appear next to the months for those trips that would otherwise land you smack in the middle of unpleasant crowds or heavy traffic. Heed these phrases and your chances of finding conflict-free recreation will improve. In short, the "Season" entry tells when the desired experience is usually available to the intended visitor.

Distance headings for most trips indicate totals of between-points measurements provided in the trip description. There, the figure after the slash—for example, (6000/ 2.8)—is always in miles, but here in the heading the distance is given in both miles and kilometers. The "total" distance given for climbing or skiing trips is usually a measurement of the approach route plus the easiest route on the rock or slopes.

After the distance, the kind of trip is specified. A "shuttle trip" is a one-way hike that cannot begin until at least 2 cars are driven to the end of the route. One car is left there, and the other car continues to the start of the route. A "round trip" involves backtracking to your car. A "semiloop trip" combines a loop with a round-trip route used for reaching the loop; and a "loop trip" is just what it says.

Steep Upgrade totals the distance en route up slopes exceeding 12° (grades exceeding 21%). (However, the total doesn't show the complete length of the steep upgrade for trips on which you can choose from any number of routes on the destination rock or slope.) The longer the steep upgrade, the more challenging the ascent; if what you want is an easy, comfortable outing, shun the trips with the longest steep upgrades.

Elevation Gain and Loss occupies the next line. The figures next to this heading are totals for most trips (some climbing and skiing trips are the same kind of exceptions as mentioned above). These totals were derived from counting contours on the map, not from adding or subtracting elevations given at strategic points within each trip description—for example, (6000/2.5), in which the first figure is an elevation. When elevation gain equals loss in a trip, only one figure—the amount of each—appears after the heading.

The process by which **Exertion/Duration** ratings were determined was complicated. The author began by studying travelers' perceptions of their daily exertion, and found that, in general, an "easy day" meant maintaining an easy pace, speed or rate for a total of up to 5 hours, a "moderate day" a moderate rate for up to 7 hours, a "strenuous day" a strenuous rate for up to 9 hours, and an "extraordinary day" an extraordinarily taxing pace for more than 9 hours. Then he determined how much time it would take if one hiked, snowshoed or skied that part of a trip that used smooth, obvious routes at the set of rates presented below in the left-hand column; and then did the same for cycling, using the set in the right-hand column. He recognized that other factors affecting trip durations—inexperience, a necessarily heavy pack or rugged, roadless or pathless terrain—can slow a traveler's pace by *at least* 0.5 mile per hour, and he adjusted his calculations accordingly.

Exertion	Hiking Pace	Bicycling Speed
Easy	1.5 MPH	5 MPH
Moderate	2.0 MPH	10 MPH
Strenuous	2.5 MPH	15 MPH
Extraordinary	3.0 MPH	20 MPH

One hour for every 1000 feet of gain was added to all of the times determined, the hours were converted to days, and the ratings you see in the headings resulted. These ratings reflect the attitude of travelers in 1) good physical condition, 2) good health, 3) good spirits and 4) good weather. If one or more of these four conditions is fair or poor instead, an "easy" pace may seem moderate, a "moderate" one strenuous, a "strenuous" one impossible and an "extraordinary" one unthinkable. These ratings are only estimates, for they do not take the camping situation into account. Only you can choose campsites large enough to accommodate your group from among those shown in this book's maps. You may find that you have to vary your pace and the time spent in transit to reach a suitable campsite each night, bearing in mind that the day at winter solstice is only 10 hours long, while the longest day of summer spans 16 hours. You might discover suitable campsites that the maps fail to show, so keep your plans flexible as you explore the Southern Sierra.

Skills/Gears, the next heading, refers first to route-finding, climbing and skiing *skills;* and then to the desirable range and size of bicycle *gears,* a heading that will appear only above bicycle-trip descriptions. Bicyclists may want to skip the following definitions of skills because they can get all the guidance they need by making frequent comparisons of the maps and text in this book with landmarks and routes in the field.

Route-finding

The degree of route-finding skills needed depends on the difficulty of the route, and a route may be termed "easy," "moderate" or "difficult." Everyone will feel most secure on routes rated "easy." To follow such a route requires observation of various clues in the field. For instance, one should know how to find the right routes even when signs are missing, as they are at many route junctions. (Keep in mind that although the signs mentioned in this book were present when I passed by, they may have disappeared since then.) Numerous obvious clues are found in and along heavily used, often-maintained trails that are free of snow. Trails not so obvious, even when free of snow, along with cross-country routes, are labeled "wild-routes" in this guide. Trees along neglected trails are often scarred with blazes, usually carved in the form of a large, lower-case "i." Such trees are blazed on 2 sides, and each blaze faces a corresponding blaze on a distant tree, so that they show you the route. The Homers Nose Wildroute of Trip 71 and the Newlywed Wildroute of Trip 46 are exemplary blazed, neglected trails. Along the ski-route of Trip 97, however, painted metal tags take the place of blazes.

Low stacks of rocks called "ducks" work just as blazes do but are less reliable clues to

A duck offers guidance

where the route may be found next. "Cairns" are tall rock stacks, sometimes found at junctions and summits. "Streamers" are plastic ribbons which, when tied to protruding objects, also work like blazes. Because ducks, cairns and streamers disappear much faster than blazes, a guidebook cannot name a trip that well illustrates the use of such markers.

Memorable landscape features can be used as guides when both sides are deliberately observed. Ridges that branch from crests followed by the Jacobsen Wildroute of Trip 52 and the Homers Nose Wildroute of Trip 71 exemplify such features.

Moderate route-finding skills, involving alertness to subtle clues, are called for when trails or routes (such as the cross-country ski-route of Trip 70) are so obscure that maps and compasses must be used. Summertime clues include a trail's color and texture, which distinguish it from its surroundings. Grass in a trail through a meadow is often a darker green. Pine needles often collect in trails, giving some faint trails a shaggy appearance. Examples of these phenomena can be found on the Jacobsen and Newlywed wildroutes. The needles collect in "treads," those strips along the trail that were depressed by foot, hoof and wheel traffic. If your neglected path coincides with a retired

logging road, as happens on Windy Gap Trail 31E42, watch for treads on each of the transverse mounds of earth (called "water bars") en route. "Treadless trails," a phrase cropping up in a few descriptions, refers to short lengths of virtual cross-country routes that follow a corridor cleared by man of logs, branches and brush.

Sometimes, the remains of downslope retaining walls (such as those found along the Homers Nose and Summit Lake wildroutes) will be the most prominent clues to a trail's former alignment. Another route-finding clue is contained in the texture of tree and shrub breaks. Stubs that are smooth result from either axing or sawing, which was often done to make way for the trail. (Don't bother to look for this clue in areas that have been logged.) Moderate cross-country routes are usually found in stands of the oldest, most mature timber, for that is where brush is no obstruction.

Following a "difficult route" often requires an altimeter and a compass, plus the ability to choose and then travel the safest, most efficient passage. A guidebook is no substitute for the proper skills and equipment when one must cope with intermediate or difficult route-finding.

Skiing

Skiing skills depend on whether one's style is nordic or alpine. A trip rated "beginner nordic" is meant for people with no previous experience who want to find out whether cross-country skiing is a sport they'd like to pursue. "Novice nordic" trips are designed for skiers who have been introduced to waxing and walking techniques, who can at least make snowplow turns, and who know how to stop themselves without injury. Such trips follow gently sloping cross-country routes and snow-covered roads. "Intermediate nordic" trips involve roads and slopes of moderate gradient on which some esoteric turns must be made. A "difficult" rating means that one should know every trick in the book to cope with steep slopes on the trip's cross-country routes. Some ability to forecast weather and snow conditions is also essential on these trips.

While "nordic" ski touring stresses horizontal movement, "Alpine" touring focuses on downslope runs. Because alpine touring is more hazardous, this guide offers no alpine trips for beginners, who should try the slopes at a commercial, patroled ski area such as Shirley Meadows or Wolverton before venturing into less-visited parts of the Sierra. Trips rated "novice alpine" are present here; they take advantage of moderately steep open slopes with good run-outs near regularly plowed roads. "Intermediate alpine" runs can range farther away from plowed roads and often require turns more difficult than the snowplow. The criteria for "difficult alpine" trips are almost identical to those for "difficult nordic" tours.

Climbing

Climbing skill ratings include familiarity with climbing tools, of which one makes increasing use as the difficulty, risk and corresponding class number increase. The class number pertains only to the most difficult pitches on a route, not the entire route.

Class 1: Ordinary street shoe soles are adequate for traction.

Class 2: Lug-soled boots are needed for traction and foot protection. (For running trips only, close-fitting jogging shoes are recommended instead of boots.)

Class 3: A rope for belays is sometimes called for, as cliffs from which one could fall are present.

Class 4: A belay rope for the climber— and "nuts" or "chocks" for anchoring the belayer—are required for safety.

Class 5: "Nuts," "chocks" and other specialized hardware are secured in the rock by roped climbers, not only at belay points but also en route, to ensure protection.

*   *   *   *   *

The "Gears" heading appears only in bicycle trips. Bicycle dealers call gears "speeds" and market their bikes in 1-, 3-, 5-, 10-, and 15-speed models. Gears themselves come in two kinds, conventional and alpine. One can use conventional gears on any ride not specifically rated "Alpine." Alpine gears enable the cyclist to climb with ease extremely steep grades while toting a heavy load. Bikes

National Park Service

Leaving Hockett Meadow Ranger Station

with such gears are rarely displayed in the store; you have to ask for them. This entry tells which gear options are most appropriate for each proposed ride. (Nevertheless, the bike suited for all rides here is a lightweight 10-speed bike with alpine gears.)

Yet another dual heading is **Registration/Permits.** "Registration" is a service to snowshoers, skiers and winter mountaineers, whose sports are best when the weather is least stable and hence involve unavoidable risks. Before embarking on their trip, they can file an itinerary with the appropriate county sheriff's substation or National Park ranger station (see the "Organizational Resources" section of Chapter 2). A home phone number or a relative's home phone number should be prominent in the itinerary. Then, if the snow travelers do not return when they said they would, searchers sent out will know where to look for them. After their trip, snow travelers should save rescue groups the outrage and expense of needless searches by cancelling the registration promptly. "Registration" is only a supplement to, not a substitute for, the standard procedure of leaving an itinerary and return time with someone who will lose a loved one if you don't return.

There are two kinds of permits, one that allows you to build campfires in parts of National and State Forests outside of designated Wilderness, and one that allows you to camp and build fires in the Wilderness of National Forests and Parks. When obtaining either permit, you agree to abide by the regulations listed on it, so it's wise to read it carefully before signing. Wilderness Permits for the National Parks may be reserved as early as 3 months before your trip, and groups must reserve their permits at least 2 weeks in advance. To be sure of getting entry permits for Golden Trout or Dome Land Wilderness, call or write the headquarters of Sequoia National Forest no later than 10 days before your trip.

The subsequent **Roadhead/Map** heading refers one to the appropriate parking spot described in Chapter 3 and to the numbered maps in the back of this book appropriate to the trip.

Canteen needs are explained in the next heading, but only for easy 1-day trips. Seasoned travelers taking the more difficult trips should gauge the reliability of water sources and the distance between them, and the probable heat and the exposure to sunlight en route, and thereby determine when and where to carry how many canteens of what size. It's helpful to know that many intermittent streams begin flowing again in late August when willows and other water-loving plants become dormant, stop drinking and let the underground water level rise.

Matter under the **Description** heading contains some logs, codes, ratings and land-use information that require explanation. The log is the most apparent unusual feature within these descriptions; here it appears wherever the routes of 2 or more trips coincide. It saves you the effort of flipping back and forth between trip descriptions while you're following obvious or familiar routes in the field. Each trail or road has its own log for a given direction of travel, with its name centered in bold type above 4 columns of words and numbers. In the first (left-hand) column, one is referred to the trip in which further description appears; if, for example, you find a "T4" in this column, you'll find the description from that point on in Trip 4. The second column lists names of

features, places and routes one will encounter along the route logged. Column 3 presents the elevation at each of these points; and in column 4 appears the mileage one has traveled since passing the previous point. Whenever the course of a trip encounters a route which it begins to follow in a new direction, you'll find the encounter recorded in the last line of the log just finished. Beneath this line, a new log, with a title, begins. Because the new log's first line records the same location, its entry in the mileage column is always 0.0.

Route names on signs in the field are rare, and do not always agree with the names in this guide, but codes are both frequently seen and usually consistent wherever they're seen. (Nowhere else but in this book will you see *every* coded route on the map labelled with its code.) Of the 3 types of route codes referred to in this guide, the one most frequently seen is the Forest Service code. A prefix often appears with the code: for roads maintained by Sequoia National Forest, it is SNF; for Mountain Home State Forest, MHSF; and for Sequoia-Kings Canyon National Parks, SEKI. The code itself consists of 2 digits, a letter, and 2 more digits. The letter is "S" for maintained roads and "E" for jeep roads, cyclepaths and foot trails. This code is based on a grid pattern which organizes all land in the western United States according to township and range. Maps issued by Sequoia National Forest explain how it works, but you won't need to know that in order to use this book.

County codes appear every mile, stenciled on paddles, along primary county roads. For Kern County (KC), there are 2 kinds of code, illustrated by KC Road 287X, a road maintained by the county, and KC Road 5176, a road maintained by private interests or not at all. A road first referred to as 287X can become 287Y by the time it is mentioned again; the code's final letter is useful only to the Kern County Road Department. "TC" codes, as in "TC Road MTN 99," identify roads maintained by Tulare County.

Camping facilities noted in the text also need explaining. "Campgrounds" with toilets and readily drinkable water are always convenient to roads. "Campsites" lack all such facilities and are classified either as "large," accommodating 3 or more 2-man tents, "medium," for only 2 such tents, and "small," only for one tent. Inside Sequoia-Kings Canyon National Park, "camping zones" rather than campsites are identified. These zones contain slight slopes on which one can camp almost anywhere and still catch the earliest sunlight. Snow-trip descriptions don't mention camping at all because one can camp on firm snow anywhere that a level site can be found or made.

Skiers and snowshoers can estimate snowpack depths on designated protected slopes by using the conservative readings of local average annual precipitation provided in the appropriate trips. In each past year of average snowfall, the snowpack at its maximum was as much as 5 times deeper than all the water that fell from the clouds that year would have been if it could have remained as water in the rain gauge. Designated areas, such as "Loggy Slopes" offer skiers the thickest, most enduring, most stable snow, and are identified in the text and in the maps. The thick snowpacks found in such areas not only help one pass over obstacles but also hide stock manure and other blights on the landscape.

The Forest Service manages commercial grazing by allowing herds of cattle or horses to occupy separate allotments when forage is most available and snow is least present. Each time a route described here enters a new allotment, the people who own the herd are named, the size of the herd is specified, the grazing season is given and the gates that keep cattle under control are brought to the reader's attention.

During wet years, cattle become evenly distributed throughout each allotment and seldom disturb travelers, but during dry years they congregate in narrow strips of wet meadow, polluting streams and fouling nearby campsites. Then one should always take time to treat or boil water for drinking; wilderness purists might want to avoid such allotments altogether while grazing is still going on.

Before setting out on any trip, one should check with the district ranger to see whether any part of it crosses land in the USFS zone of ongoing logging. Trails there may be temporarily obliterated by current operations, and the noise and debris could be offensive. Call the appropriate district ranger to find whether this will affect your trip.

Those who take the trips as presented, during the season recommended, will enjoy the most freedom to relax and enjoy the Southern Sierra experience, for the design of each trip helps one avoid, among other hazards, conflicts with motorized recreation. Where such recreationists can't be avoided, this book helps you plan for the encounter by describing their use of vehicle routes as "heavy" (more than 300 vehicles per year), "moderate," or "light" (less than 30 vehicles per year). These ratings were derived from the estimates of the most knowledgeable Forest Service officials, but will probably change in future editions as truly scientific ratings emerge.

Ski-touring camp

Dave McCoard

Tripfinder Tables

Statistics for every trip in this book are gathered here for comparison to help you find the right trip fast.

Most entries in the Intersport Tripfinder are taken directly from beside the headings of individual trips, and need no further explanation. But some of these entries are abbreviations, and others appear nowhere else, and readers might need some help before they can put either to use.

Abbreviations, considered alphabetically, include an "A" following a number or numbers (as in "15A") meaning that the bicycle must have alpine gears; the numbers refer to the minumum number of "speeds" (gears) needed in order to finish the ride. A "C" after a number or numbers means that the ride requires no more than conventional gears. Elsewhere, a "D" means "difficult," an "E," "easy;" an "I", "intermediate;" and an "m," "moderate." An "O" preceding a number or numbers (as in "O4–5") means that though climbers can try routes of the specified difficulty (the numbers are Class ratings), such routes are *optional* and easier alternatives are available. An "R" followed by a Class rating means that because no other route to the destination is easier, you must be able to cross surfaces of the specified difficulty. The "R" stands for "required" and usually refers to the only route described.

Entries found nowhere else in the book appear in the two columns headed "Driving Time from Los Angeles" and "Driving Time from Fresno." In the past, these cities have been either the starting points or points en route for the majority of travelers bound for the Southern Sierra; that's why they're used as starting points here. In Los Angeles, this point is the downtown interchange of the Harbor and Hollywood freeways, while in Fresno it's the interchange of State Freeway 99 and State Highway 180.

These times were determined while driving 5 m.p.h. slower than the maximum posted—or the safe—speed in clear, calm, frostless weather and on uncrowded roads. (When fog or airborne dust and sand cuts visibility; when roads are made slippery by rain, snow or ice; or when roads are congested, these travel times are only useful as relative indicators—the drive itself will take longer.) These times reflect the quickest access to each of the roadheads, using the routes described in Chapter 3.

The routes in that chapter were chosen because they took less time to drive, not because they were necessarily shorter than others. For instance, a glance at the map will tell you that it is shorter to drive from Porterville to Dome Rock via State Highway 190, but anyone who knows that twisty 190 makes for excruciatingly slow driving can tell you that the access through California Hot Springs, though longer, is quicker.

In the Intrasport Tripfinder tables, trips are grouped together by sport and listed in order of increasing difficulty. By referring to this table, readers can make quick comparisons; and many, especially beginners, will want to start taking trips in the order listed. That way they can start with the easiest trip and improve their skills and physical fitness a bit at a time, a method that builds both confidence and enjoyment.

Inter-Sport Tripfinder Table

Trip Number	Hike	Backpack	Climb	Cave Tour	Run	Bicycle Tour	Ski Tour	Snowshoe Tour	Jan	Feb	Mar	Apr	May	Jun	Jul	Aug	Sep	Oct	Nov	Dec	Weekdays only	Non-holidays only	Easy	Moderate	Strenuous	Extraordinary	Steep Upgrade (miles)	Route-finding	Rock Climbing (class number)	Nordic Skiing	Alpine Skiing	Gears	Round	Semiloop	Loop	Shuttle	From Los Angeles	From Fresno
1							•		•	•	•												2	1			0.1	E		E			•				3:06	3:06
2							•		•	•	•												3	2	1			E		I			•				3:00	2:55
3	•												•	•	•	•	•	•	•				1				0.2		1				•				3:37	3:26
4	•								•	•	•	•	•	•	•	•	•	•					1				0	E	1				•				3:16	2:55
5		•										•	•	•	•	•	•	•	•				4	3	2		1.8	M	2						•		3:22	3:02
6	•								•	•	•	•	•	•	•	•	•	•	•	•				1			0.1	M	1				•				3:30	3:13
7			•								•	•	•	•	•	•	•	•	•					1			0.5	M	5				•				3:30	3:21
8							•		•	•	•											•	1				0	E		N						•	3:24	3:28
9							•	•	•	•	•												4	3	2		0.1	E		I					•		3:38	3:21
10								•	•	•	•											•	1				0	E		B			•				3:54	3:36
11					•							•	•	•	•	•	•	•							1/12		0	E					•				3:55	3:52
12	•												•	•	•	•	•	•							1		1.3	M	R2 03–5				•				4:01	3:55
13	•												•	•	•	•	•	•					1				0	M	1				•				3:50	3:59
14			•									•	•	•	•	•	•								1/12		0.1	E	2				•				3:13	3:00
15	•												•	•	•	•	•	•					1				0.2	M	2				•				3:13	2:18
16		•												•	•	•	•	•					2				0.2	E	2				•				3:38	2:18
17	•													•	•	•	•	•					1				0.1	E	2				•				3:40	2:35
18	•										•	•	•	•	•	•	•	•							1		0.1	E	2				•				3:03	2:17
19					•				•	•	•	•	•	•	•	•	•	•		•		•			1/12		0	E	2						•		3:37	2:24
20						•						•	•	•	•	•	•	•	•	•	•	•	1				0	E				1C–15A	•				3:35	2:32
21					•							•	•	•	•	•	•	•							1/12		0	E					•				3:43	2:32
22		•												•	•	•	•						2				0.5	E	2				•				3:51	2:32
23						•			•	•	•	•	•	•	•	•	•	•	•		•	•			1		0.1	E				5C–15A			•		5:51	5:31
24	•											•	•	•	•	•	•	•	•				1				0	E	1				•				5:38	2:49
25		•											•	•	•	•	•	•			•	•	3	2			0.4	E	2							•	4:08	2:51
26	•										•	•	•	•	•	•	•	•	•			•			1		0.1	M	2				•				4:10	3:10
27							•						•	•	•	•	•	•					1				0	M		N			•				4:29	3:31
28							•		•	•	•												2	1			0	E		N			•				4:45	
29							•		•	•	•												3	2	1		0.1	M		I	I				•			
30								•	•	•	•												4	2	1		0.6	M		I	I					•		
31			•									•	•	•	•	•	•	•					1				0.6	E	R4 05				•					
32			•									•	•	•	•	•	•	•					1				0.1	M	R2 03–5				•					
33	•												•	•	•	•	•	•					2				0	E	R1 03–5				•					
34						•						•	•	•	•	•	•	•	•				1				0	E				3C–15A	•					

Inter-Sport Tripfinder Table

Trip Number	Trip sport	Season	Easy	Moderate	Strenuous	Extraordinary	Steep Upgrade (miles)	Skills (Route-finding / Rock Climbing / Nordic / Alpine)	Trip type	Gears
35	Hike	Apr May Jun Jul Aug Sep Oct Nov	4	2			0	E 1 / R3	Shuttle	
36	Backpack	May Jun Jul Aug Sep Oct		1			0.1	M 04–5	Round	
37	Hike	May Jun Jul Aug Sep Oct		1			0	E R1 04–5	Round	
38	Backpack	May Jun Jul Aug Sep Oct; Non-holidays only		1			0	E R1 03–5	Round	
39	Run	May Jun Jul Aug Sep Oct	2	1			0	E	Round	5C–15A
40	Backpack	Jun Jul Aug Sep Oct		2			0.1	E R1 03–5	Loop	
41	Backpack	Jun Jul Aug Sep Oct		1			0.1	E R1 5+	Round	
42	Backpack	Jun Jul Aug Sep Oct		2			0	E 1	Round	
43	Backpack	Jun Jul Aug Sep Oct		1			0.4	M R4 05	Round	
44	Backpack	Jun Jul Aug Sep Oct	9	5	4		0.5	E R1 03–5	Loop	
45	Backpack	Jun Jul Aug Sep Oct	4	2			0.1	E 1	Shuttle	
46	Backpack	Jun Jul Aug Sep Oct	6	4	3		0.7	M 2	Loop	
47	Backpack	Jun Jul Aug Sep	6	4	3		0.9	M R2 03–4	Semiloop	
48	Hike	Jun Jul Aug Sep		1			0	E 1	Round	
49	Bicycle Tour	Jan–Dec		2	1		0	E	Round	10A–15A
50	Bicycle Tour	Jan–Dec		2	1		0	E	Loop	10C 15A
51	Hike	Apr May Jun Jul Aug Sep Oct Nov Dec; Non-holidays only		1			0	E 1	Round	
52	Backpack	May Jun Jul Aug Sep Oct	4	3	2		0.2	M 2	Semiloop	
53	Backpack	Jun Jul Aug Sep Oct		2			0.6	M 2	Loop	
54	Cave Tour	Apr May Jun Jul Aug Sep Oct Nov			1/12		0	E 2	Round	
55	Climb	May Jun Jul Aug Sep Oct		1			0	E	Round	5C–15A
56	Ski Tour	Jan Mar Apr	3	2	1		0.1	M / Nordic I / Alpine I	Round	
57	Ski Tour	Jan Feb Mar Apr		2	1		0.4	M / Alpine D	Round	
58	Ski Tour	Jan Feb Mar; Non-holidays only		1			0.1	E / Nordic B	Round	
59	Ski Tour	Jan Feb Mar	3	2			0	E / Alpine I	Round	
60	Ski Tour / Snowshoe Tour	Jan Feb Mar	3	2	1		0	E / Nordic N	Loop	
61	Hike	Apr May Jun Jul Aug Sep		1			0	E 1	Round	
62	Hike	Apr May Jun Jul Aug Sep		1			0.1	E 1	Loop	
63	Hike	May Jun Jul Aug Sep Oct		1			0.2	E 1	Loop	
64	Hike	May Jun Jul Aug Sep Oct		1			0.1	E 1	Loop	
65	Climb	May Jun Jul Aug Sep Oct; Non-holidays only		1			0.7	M R3 04–5	Round	
66	Climb	Jan–Dec		1			0	E	Round	1C–15A
67	Hike	Apr May Jun Jul Aug Sep Oct		1			0	E 1	Round	
68	Backpack	Jun Jul Aug Sep		4			0.3	M 1	Loop	

Driving Time (From Los Angeles / From Fresno), packed values as printed:

4:53 4:45 4:32 4:32 4:34 4:23 4:22 4:03 4:18 4:18 4:14 4:14 4:31 4:31 4:30 4:37 3:49 3:45 3:27 3:59 3:57 4:09 4:09 4:27 4:11 4:16 4:21 4:44 3:54 4:54 4:12 4:11 4:38 4:53

2:03 1:55 2:51 2:53 2:42 2:41 2:22 2:59 2:55 2:59 2:49 2:56 2:08 2:04 1:46 1:46 2:40 2:38 3:00 3:07 2:52 2:52 2:57 3:02 3:25 2:35 2:52 2:53 2:52 2:53 2:53 2:24 3:39

Inter-Sport Tripfinder Table

Trip Number	Trip sport								Season														Exertion/Duration (days)					Skills				Trip type					Driving Time	
	Hike	Backpack	Climb	Cave Tour	Run	Bicycle Tour	Ski Tour	Snowshoe Tour	January	February	March	April	May	June	July	August	September	October	November	December	Weekdays only	Non-holidays only	Easy	Moderate	Strenuous	Extraordinary	Steep Upgrade (miles)	Route-finding	Rock Climbing (class number)	Nordic Skiing	Alpine Skiing	Gears	Round	Semiloop	Loop	Shuttle	From Los Angeles	From Fresno
69	•											•	•	•	•	•	•	•	•	•			1				0	E	1				•					
70							•	•	•	•	•	•												4	2		1.2	D		D	D		•					
71		•												•	•	•	•	•							2		0.4	D	R1 05				•					
72							•			•	•	•	•												2		0	E		N	N		•					
73	•													•	•	•	•						1				0	E	1					•				
74		•													•	•	•	•						4			0.2	M	R2 03–5				•					
75		•													•	•	•								3		0.1	M	2				•					
76	•													•	•	•	•									1	0	E	1				•					
77		•													•	•	•							4			0.3	E	2				•					
78			•												•	•	•				•				1/7		0	E	2				•					
79		•													•	•	•				•				3	2	0.9	E	R2 03–5				•					
80		•													•	•	•						6				0.2	E	1					•				
81	•										•	•	•	•	•	•	•	•	•	•			1				0.1	E	R1 04				•					
82		•									•	•	•	•	•	•	•	•	•						2		0.1	E	R1 03–5				•					
83		•												•	•	•	•	•					1				0	E	1				•					
84					•									•	•	•	•				•		1/4				0.1	E	1						•			
85	•	•										•	•	•	•	•	•	•	•		•		1/12				0	E	R1 05				•					
86							•			•	•	•	•	•	•	•	•	•	•					1			0	E				10C–15A			•			
87							•			•	•	•	•	•	•	•	•	•	•					1			0	E				3C–15A			•			
88							•			•	•	•	•	•	•	•	•	•	•					1			0.1	E				5C–15A			•			
89							•				•	•	•	•	•	•	•	•	•		•			1			0	E				5C–15A			•			
90							•							•	•	•	•	•					2	1			0	E				10C–15A			•			
91							•							•	•	•	•	•					2	1			0.1	E				5C–15A	•					
92							•			•	•	•	•										1				0.3	E		N					•			
93	•													•	•	•	•	•								1	0	E	1				•					
94		•		•						•	•	•	•	•	•	•	•	•	•				variable				0	E	R2 05	N			•					
95							•			•	•	•	•										1				0	M		N			•					
96	•	•												•	•	•	•	•					1/12				0.1	E	R1 05				•					
97							•			•	•	•												1			0	E		N				•				
98							•			•	•	•	•										1				0	E			I				•			
99		•													•	•	•	•	•				1/5				0.4	E	R2 03–5				•					
100	•													•	•	•	•	•			•		1				0	E	1					•				

Driving Time — From Los Angeles: 5:22 5:13 5:07 5:06 5:16 5:04 5:03 4:54 5:19 5:08 4:59 4:31 4:07 5:37 5:39 5:25 5:08 5:10 6:00 6:00 5:57 6:39 5:48 5:48 5:39 4:28 4:53

Driving Time — From Fresno: 1:44 1:35 1:28 1:29 1:38 1:26 1:25 1:17 1:41 1:27 1:19 0:53 0:43 2:47 2:49 2:35 2:18 2:20 3:10 3:07 3:49 2:47 2:03

Intra-Sport Tripfinder Tables

Hikes

short, easy, non-technical (beginners welcome)

↑

long, strenuous, technical (experts only)

CODE	NAME
T96	Buck Rock
T85	Moro Rock
T84	Crystal Cave
T37	Mule Peak
T62	Shake Camp
T61	Bogus Meadow
T17	Baker Point
T15	Deep Creek
T3	Lightner Peak
T13	Sunday Peak
T48	Jordan Peak
T73	Sequoiaside Falls
T83	Sunset Rock
T100	Muir Sequoias
T63	Moses Gulch
T69	Cedar Creek
T51	Dunn Trail
T81	Marble Falls
T4	Mill Creek
T24	Ames Hole
T67	Garfield Grove
T26	Rube Creek
T64	Hidden Falls
T18	Naturalist's Trail
T93	Redwood Canyon
T6	Delonegha Creek
T76	Paradise Peak
T12	Black and Split Mountains

Backpacks

short, etc.

↑

long, etc.

CODE	NAME
T33	Durrwood Camp
T42	Freeman Redwoods
T16	Bull Run
T82	Mehrten Creek
T22	Telephone Ridge
T40	Freezeout Meadow
T25	Southernmost Sequoias
T53	Slate Mountain
T77	Middle Fork's Canyon
T45	Mountaineer Creek
T35	Kern Flat
T52	Alpine Meadow
T74	Ansel Lake
T75	Evelyn Lake
T68	Hockett Lakes
T5	Breckenridge Mountain
T71	Homers Nose
T79	Silver Lake
T80	Mineral King
T46	Silver Knapsack Trail
T47	Coyote Lakes
T44	Two Rivers

Bicycle Tours

short, etc.

↑

long, etc.

CODE	NAME
T20	Linns Valley
T87	Dunlap
T55	Hossack Meadow
T34	The Needles
T66	South Fork
T89	Badger
T88	Miramonte
T90	Eshom Valley
T91	Hume Lake
T86	Drum Valley
T23	Fountain Springs
T39	Western Divide
T49	Blue Ridge
T50	Yokohl Valley

Runs

short, etc.

↑

long, etc.

CODE	NAME
T19	Glennville
T21	Peel Mill
T54	Camp Nelson
T11	Shirley Meadows
T94	Big Baldy
T78	The Sierra's Most Controversial Valley
T14	Tobias Peak

Ski Tours

short etc.

↑

CODE	NAME
T10	"Cook Peak Point"
T58	Dome Rock
T8	Alta Sierra
T94	Big Baldy
T95	Big Meadows
T27	Parker Peak
T92	Park Ridge
T98	Chimney Slopes
T97	Lower Shell Mountain
T28	Redwood Meadow
T1	Squirrel Meadow
T59	Nobe Young Slopes
T60	Balch Park
T29	Speas Meadow
T57	Slate Mountain
T56	Jordan Peak
T72	Mineral King
T2	Breckenridge Mountain
T30	Greenhorn Crest
T9	Tobias Peak
T70	Hockett Meadows

↓

long etc.

Climbs

(described route)
Rock climbers: Please check with governing agency for current climbing policies

short etc.

↑

CODE	NAME
T38	Dome Rock
T85	Moro Rock
T96	Buck Rock
T99	Chimney Rock
T32	Elephant Knob
T41	The Needles
T94	Big Baldy
T36	Castle Rock
T65	Moses Mountain
T43	Hermits Dome
T31	Sentinel Peak
T7	Bat Rock

↓

long etc.

Snowshoe Tours

CODE	NAME
T1	Squirrel Meadow
T60	Balch Park
T70	Hockett Meadows
T30	Greenhorn Crest
T9	Tobias Peak

Chapter 5: 100 Adventures

T1   Squirrel Meadow Snowshoe and Nordic Ski Tour

Besides requiring the shortest drive for Los Angeles area snow travelers, this first trip introduces its takers to the touring styles and settings of later trips in this book. It's difficult to get lost on this trip because steep slopes form the boundaries of its compact touring terrain. The highland bowls en route offer open or wooded slopes to try, and most visitors will find at least one slope that's as gentle or as steep as their tastes and skills demand.

Season   January through March

Distance   12.8 miles (20.6 km) round trip

Steep Upgrade   0.1 mile (0.2 km)

Elevation Gain and Loss   1360 feet (415 m)

Exertion/Duration   easy/2 days

Skills   easy route-finding, novice nordic skiing

Registration/Permits   Kern County Sheriff's Department/USFS Campfire Permit

Roadhead/Maps   R1/M2–M3

Description   Pine Flat (5400/0.0) is a natural place to begin this tour, for here Breckenridge *Road 28S06* first enters coniferous forest on its way up the mountian, and here the winter snowpack usually blocks the rarely-plowed road.

As we get underway on snowshoes or skis, we might be gliding along the tracks of snowmobiles, which are driven here in light numbers, mostly on holiday weekends, by cabin owners and recreationists. It's more likely that we'll find the road's snowpack tamped down by the tracks of snow-cats—tanklike vehicles used by 2 Bakersfield television stations to service their Breckenridge Mountain broadcasting towers. When these vehicles aren't around, we can appreciate the snow's capacity to absorb sound.

We stride at length up the road's gentle grade through snow-draped broadleaf and conifer woods. The road twists around several ravines in this shady north-facing slope, and we can observe that the more trees there are lining the road, and the more the road winds, the more we seem to have the mountains all to ourselves.

Eventually we pass a snow-disguised private driveway, and then we encounter southbound SNF Road 28S22 (5820/2.6), an easily missed turnoff 0.3 mile short of Lucas Creek. Some skiers may want to cut south from here to enjoy swift runs down selectively logged slopes near Breckenridge and Munzer meadows. Most of us, however, will continue on Road 28S06. It crosses shrubbery-hedged Lucas Creek just before the clearing of Breckenridge Meadows. (Now the road is well coated with snow, but snowshoers or skiers with 10-speed, alpine-gear-equipped bicycles at home should note that in spring and fall this spot makes a fine destination for a tough, exciting bicycle ride up from Bakersfield. The pavement ends here at the creek, and deep chuckholes beyond prevent most bicyclists from continuing to the summit of Breckenridge Mountain.)

In the meantime, we cross the clearing beyond Lucas Creek and later touch the start of SNF Road 28S08 (5820/0.5). This northwest-trending road to Golf Meadow begins in the midst of the easternmost of the cabin-occupied inholdings along the main road.

Our course beyond the fork sometimes alternates between crusty, wind-packed snow and tacky snow while rising 440 vertical feet across wooded, west-facing slopes. After considerable huffing and puffing, we enter the Mill Creek watershed through a saddle and then resume crossing north-facing slopes. Southwesterly winds during winter storms pile up snow into drifts on these slopes, but avalanches have been quite rare.

Now we negotiate the twisting road for more than an hour, and afterward cross Mill Creek and switchback upslope toward Squirrel Meadow. Quite soon we fork southeast onto a *spur road* (6650/2.5), still tracking the TV-station snow-cats, and then we enter the isolated, shallow bowl containing the meadow. In minutes we join southeast-trending **SNF Road 28S07** (6610/0.2) and sight Squirrel Meadow's clearing ahead.

U.S. Weather Bureau statistics, reported in 1964, showed that the average winter snowpack on slopes rising from this meadow—the Squirrel Bowl Slopes—had been more than 20″ deep, and it's a safe guess that drifts had been much deeper than that. These slopes have been selectively logged repeatedly during the 20th Century, so skiers and snowshoers can wander across them at will. Snow hides most of the old logging scars, and when snow-draped, the forest here is satisfyingly scenic and fun to explore. The compact Squirrel Bowl Slopes are surrounded by much steeper slopes, and that distinct boundary ensures that if people do get lost here, it won't be for long.

Road 28S07 leads to another part of the Squirrel Bowl Slopes, and while tracing it southward from the meadow, we soon bear southwest where a snow-smothered road (6630/0.1—see Trip 5) starts east. We presently cross Mill Creek, then veer northwest by a bilobed clearing where the summit of Breckenridge Mountain first appears. At the clearing's west edge, we turn southwest onto **SNF Road 28S21** (6620/0.6), which quickly leads to Breckenridge Campground (6630/0.1). Viewpoints surrounding the campground bowl beckon, and a wide range of slopes invite runs, ensuring plenty to do here.

When it's time to leave, we backtrack to our cars.

Snow ghosts

Beverly Steveson

T2   Breckenridge Mountain Nordic Ski Tour

When tule fog quilts the floor of the San Joaquin Valley in white, when glittering snow clothes the trees of Breckenridge Mountain in white, when ice-crusted Breckenridge Mountain Lookout shimmers in strong between-storms daylight: that's when the panorama from there highlights an intensely blue middle-ground Lake Isabella and the vivid green of young plants that flourish in close-at-hand Walker Basin.

Season   January through March

Distance   18.8 miles (30.3 km) round trip

Steep Upgrade   none

Elevation Gain and Loss   2360 feet (719 m)

Exertion/Duration   easy/3 days, moderate/ 2 days, extraordinary/1 day

Skills   easy route-finding, intermediate nordic skiing

Registration/Permits   Kern County Sheriff's Department/USFS campfire permit

Roadhead/Map   R1/M2, M3

Description

Eastbound *SNF Road 28S06* Log

T1	Pine Flat	5400	0.0
	Lucas Creek	5810	2.9
	SNF Road 28S08	5820	0.2
	cutoff road	6650	2.5

Southeast-bound *Cutoff Road* Log

Road 28S06	6650	0.0
SNF Road 28S07	6610	0.2

Southeast-bound *Road 28S07* Log

cutoff road	6610	0.0
SNF Road 28S21	6620	0.6

Initially tracing Road 28S07 southwest from the exit of Breckenridge Campground Road 28S21, we make tracks alongside and in the snowy depressions left by snow-cats of the TV stations ahead. The forest instantly narrows our horizons, which will remain close to us until we crest the main west-trending ridge of Breckenridge Mountain.

Confined in that forest, our road meanders up the mountain, leveling for several hundred yards along the Mill Creek/Lucas Creek divide. Then it steepens while making a few hairpin turns and transfering from draw to draw. Eventually the access road (7480/2.4) to Bakersfield TV station KERO's transmitter branches off to the west, and shortly thereafter we extricate ourselves from the view-denying forest and start traversing south-facing slopes "daylighted" by the 1970 Breckenridge Fire. Getting occasional vistas south toward Mt. Pinos and Bear Mountain on the rim of the San Joaquin Valley, we glide along the mildly rolling, sometimes icy, snow-filled roadbed, early skirting the broadcasting tower of TV station KBAK and later leaving the route of the snow-cat's patrol where a spur road (7460/0.5) branches west to a maintenance building. Our road leads east for a few hundred yards beyond the fork and ends at the foot of the rime-ice-encased lookout tower atop the high point on Breckenridge Mountain (7548/0.1). We take in the spectacular panorama and then backtrack to the cars.

T3 Lightner Peak Hike

A Lightner Peak hike samples habitats where edible miners lettuce and sugar-pine cones may be found. The hike alternates between sunny slopes and dark woods, offers orienting views of Southern Sierran landmarks and finds evidence of enlightenment in the new Forest Service policy for contructing firebreaks.

Season   April through November

Distance   2.8 miles (4.5 km) round trip

Steep Upgrade   0.2 mile (0.3 km)

Elevation Gain and Loss   1140 feet (347 m)

Exertion/Duration   easy/1 day

Skills   easy route-finding, Class 1 climbing

Permits   none

Roadhead/Map   R2/M3

Canteens   1 quart

Description   Our hike begins where a sign indicates that Remington Ridge Trail 32E51 once split north from **SNF Road 28S19** (5950/0.0). The trail has disappeared since the sign was installed, so we descend northeast on the road, which quickly becomes rough and steep—fit for 4WD vehicles only. It winds down among black oaks and shortly breaks into the open, levels and then arcs northwest as another jeep road (5620/0.3) departs to the east. Our road now crosses a willow-lined gulch just above undependable O'Brien Spring. Then it meanders back into the woods and up a slight gulch, continues northwest where faint jeep tracks lead east, and soon climbs along a small ridge, presently reaching a swale where the **Remington Ridge Trail** (5960/0.4) begins. (The road beyond here becomes quite steep.)

Our path initially leads northwest and makes a gentle ascent along the east side of Hobo Ridge, linking northeast-facing slopes where sugar pine and miners lettuce flourish. In *Wild Food Plants of the Sierra*, Steven and Mary Thompson advocate shaking down cones of the sugar pine by bouncing on its branches a long way up from the ground, as the Miwok Indians did. Your reward would be the cone's nuts, which the Thompsons report are tastier, once extricated, than piñon nuts. What they neglect to point out is the short lifespan of the average early California Indian, which most readers would probably not want to imitate. So cone-gathering is out unless you can steal from a squirrel in the act of winter harvesting. The cones are reportedly ripe for such theft in mid-September. Safer to gather is miners lettuce, which the Thompsons say was a source of vitamin C to gold-rush miners. When boiled, buttered and salted, the leaves make a pleasing vegetable.

Your path turns from west to northnorthwest upon crossing a southwesttrending gulch inside the second (northern) sugar-pine grove. This turn is your cue to leave the path (6110/0.6) and start heading southwest on a **cross-country wildroute.** Quite soon you reach a saddle on Hobo Ridge and turn northwest to climb the **firebreak** on the crest. You'll notice that the firebreak's edges are unusually irregular, and that some shrubs were allowed to remain inside the firebreak. Such irregularities are intended to give wildlife more hiding places and escape routes to use when feeding. Most of the clearing here was done amid Brewers oak to spare the adjacent pine forest, which Margaret Bell and other Forest Service biologists, writing in 1973, considered to be more valuable to wildlife of the area.

The firebreak quickly leads past southwestward views of Breckenridge Mountain and gains the northernmost (highest) pile of rocks on forested Lightner Peak (6430/0.1). Views of Lake Isabella in the northeast and Walker Basin in the south can be found by roaming around the summit. Lightner Peak and Lightners Flat commemorate Abia Lightner, a local pioneer of the 19th Century. From the summit we backtrack to our cars.

T4   Mill Creek Hike

Easy year-round access and vividly complementary settings draw hikers to this trip. Among the scenes encountered en route, are intimate, woods-sheltered nooks with murmuring streams that part among rounded, mossy boulders, which complement open slopes where wildflowers sometimes make dazzling displays.

Season   all year

Distance   7.2 miles (11.6 km) round trip

Steep Upgrade   none

Elevation Gain and Loss 1400 feet (427 m)

Exertion/Duration   easy/1 day

Skills   easy route-finding, Class 1 climbing

Permits   none

Roadhead/Maps   R3/M3

Canteen   1 quart

Description   *Mill Creek Trail 31E78* begins in lower Kern Canyon at a turnout on paved KC Road 214H (2390/0.0). The trail initially zigzags, then leads south across slopes above the highway. These slopes always bear a sparse growth of oaks, often nurture grass bitten short by trespassing cattle and sometimes display a prodigious array of lustrous-petaled wildflowers. Quite soon our path rounds a ridgelet and enters the canyon of Mill Creek, then undulates gently upcanyon, crossing a few game trails and cowpaths. We presently reach the first Mill Creek ford, a treacherous boulderhop in spring that is safer when dry in the fall. Poison oak in the creekside colonnade of alders and sycamores makes the prospect of on-the-spot picnicking unappealing.

Next the path rises, crosses a small ridge at a swale, recrosses Mill Creek and then splits off from a barely discernible path (2710/1.4) that leads northeast to a mining prospect. We proceed southeast from the fork, fording the creek twice more and then climbing easy switchbacks to a signed stock-fence gate in a ridgetop swale. Now obscured by grass, the path becomes more discernible 100 yards to the southeast, where it parallels the branch of Mill Creek draining Lightners Flat.

Quite soon you bear southeast at a fork and begin hiking *Farmer Riggs Trail 32E53* (3260/1.2) while backpackers on Trip 5 take the Mill Creek Trail south. Beyond the fork, your path is sometimes disguised by a thick mat of sycamore and alder leaves as it enters a shady, mossy cleft where miners lettuce and gooseberries thrive. Quite soon you hop the creek 4 times, passing a number of picnic sites and perhaps finding one that is right for you. The path goes on to ford the creek twice more, then fades near a box canyon at the sixth ford (3720/1.0). This trail originally extended from here up to Lightners Flat, but disuse and lack of maintenance have let that part disappear. From the current end of the trail, you follow your footprints back to your car.

T5   Breckenridge Mountain Backpack

The 6000–foot ascent involved in this backpack from the Kern Canyon confines up to the Breckenridge Mountain panorama is a grueling test of physical fitness and stamina. No other trip in this book ascends longer steep grades than this one. Hikers prepared for its challenges will probably appreciate its often-cool conifer highland more, having come there up slopes exposed to the sun, and later will honor its rare trees more, having found that they cast the only shade for miles around. This Spartan adventure is best either in the spring, when wildflower-lined freshets spill along its route, or late in the fall, when its forests become flecked with reds.

Season   April through November

Distance   21.0 miles (33.8 km), shuttle trip

Steep Upgrade   1.8 miles (2.9 km)

Elevation Gain and Loss   +6100 feet (1859 m), −6000 feet (1829 m)

Exertion/Duration   easy/4 days, moderate/ 3 days, strenuous/2 days

Skills   moderate route-finding, Class 2 climbing

Permits   USFS Campfire Permit

Roadheads/Maps   R3, R5/M3, M5

Description

Southeast-bound *Mill Cr Tr 31E78 Log*

T4 KC Road 214H	2370	0.0
obscure trail to prospect	2710	1.4
Farmer Riggs Tr 32E53	3260	1.2

At the Farmer Riggs Trail junction, the most challenging part of the Mill Creek Trail looms ahead—3.8 miles of moderate, sometimes steep, grade gaining 3430 feet. Because that waterless path segment is often exposed to the sun, backpackers would be wise to check their canteens before leaving the junction. The Lightners Flat fork of Mill Creek, not far north of the junction, can usually be relied upon to fill any empty canteens.

After leaving the junction, we ascend a mild grade amid live oak and buckeye along a ravine, then cross the ravine and zigzag 6 times amid chaparral before gaining a large ridge that trends south-southeast. At the sixth zigzag, the path turns up the ridge in a swale and shortly steepens, becoming worn down to quartz-diorite bedrock. Eventually we rise into the welcome shade of Kellogg

oaks, and then it's not long before we encounter more and more white firs, sugar pines, and Jeffrey and ponderosa pines amid the oaks.

Then our path veers away from the ridge and slants up across wooded slopes west of it. Our course shortly zigzags, then leads briefly up another ridge and afterward traces a grassy ravine. In minutes we gain a saddle set in a transverse ridge, where a jeep road starts southeast by a large, waterless campsite and a trailhead sign. Here at the saddle we enter the 46,550-acre Breckenridge Allotment, where 200 of Helen Rankin's cows usually graze from early April until mid-October.

Sauntering down the *jeep road,* we quickly reach, then turn west onto, *SNF Road 28S06* (6670/3.9). It bends southeast in a few yards and skirts Squirrel Meadow, a fenced area signed "administrative pasture." Midway along the meadow's west edge, we stroll straight ahead through a signed junction onto *SNF Road 28S07* (6640/0.2). Soon afterward, our course joins a northwest-trending spur of Road 28S06 (6610/0.1), then passes the meadow's southern tip and meets a road (6630/0.1) departing to the east-southeast. This road is mistakenly signed as the access to "Flying Dutchman Trail 32E32" (32E54 is correct).

Much later in this trip, after we backtrack from the Breckenridge Mountain Lookout, we will turn onto this road. Now, however, we walk southwest on Road 28S07, approaching and later crossing Mill Creek and its line of willows. Here the forest parts around a bilobed, grassy meadow, then rises southward to the crest of Breckenridge Mountain.

Beyond the creek, the road bears northwest beside the meadow and presently touches the start of **SNF Road 28S21** (6620/0.5). Noting the junction's "Breckenridge Campground" sign, we turn south-southwest onto 28S21 and pace briefly along the road. Now skirting corn lilies that fringe the meadow, we pass among the campground's 6 tables and then reach road's end (6630/0.1) at a faucet dispensing piped spring water.

Here we start east on a **cross-country route** that will involve gaining 830 vertical feet. A few minutes' stroll by the meadow leads to an intermittent fork of Mill Creek. Its canyon soon bends southward, then leads up a moderate, sometimes steep grade almost directly to Breckenridge Mountain. At length we turn east onto **Road 28S07** (7460/1.2) in a ridgecrest swale. (The spur road to the west leads to broadcasting facilities of Bakersfield television station KBAK, Channel 29.) A short, brisk walk up Road 28S07 from the swale gets us past portals made by the 1970 Breckenridge Fire and subsequent salvage logging. At last the road ends at the foot of the tower topped by Breckenridge Mountain Lookout (7548/0.1).

A car parked at the base usually means that a technician is on duty during the day and can unlock the lookout's trap door for you. Even if you can't get onto the catwalk surrounding the lookout, you'll find in the exhilarating panorama that expands as you climb the ladder some reward for having pushed yourself nearly 6000 feet up from Kern Canyon. While Walker Basin, 4100 feet lower, shows up only a few miles away in the east, a prominent V-shaped pass on the Kern Canyon Fault draws the most attention to the northwest. The pass is lined up with Lake Isabella, some 15 miles away, and also with the isolated hump of 12,123-foot Olancha Peak, 63 miles away. The view is best in the afternoon, when shadows make the landscape's many wrinkles stand out.

Before long the chilly wind common to lookouts will have brought to mind the thought of departure, especially if you hadn't prepared for temperatures usually ranging from 26°F to 39°F colder than those at Bakersfield. After signing the lookout's register, we backtrack down the road to the swale (7460/0.1), then down the **cross-country route** to the campground (6630/1.2). Aware that a long, sometimes hot hike looms ahead, we refill canteens at the campground's

spring, the last reliable water source of the trip.

Now we follow our footprints northward on **Road 28S21,** and then more or less eastward on **Road 28S07** (6620/0.1), before turning east onto the former Flying Dutchman Road (now **SNF Road 28S06**) (6630/0.5 mentioned earlier). Now, for variety, we pass by sides of Squirrel Meadow that we haven't seen before. Our road meets south-trending Flying Dutchman Trail 32E54 (6630/0.1) quite soon, and then turns north on the forested rim of the Squirrel Meadow bowl. We pass several large campsites, then pass a dirt road segment of 28S06 (6750/0.4), leave the Breckenridge Allotment and then saunter down the rolling divide between the Mill Creek and Havilah Creek canyons.

Oaks dominate scattered, large, waterless campsites at grassy Lightners Flat, which we presently reach. The "Farmer Riggs [misspelled 'Ridge'] Trail 32E53" sign posted here marks the end of a nearly untraceable wildroute (5840/2.4—see Trip 4). We stroll a few minutes beyond the sign and then turn north onto **SNF Road 28S19** (5837/0.1), incorrectly signed "28S06A."

This rolling road along Hobo Ridge soon leads into clearings with downslope views to the east of historic Havilah and other points covered in this book's companion volume. While enjoying the view, we veer across part of the ridge's east flank and soon regain the shade of oaks and Jeffrey pines. Our course presently rounds an east-trending ridge and meets a jeep road (5950/1.5) departing southeast. Then we dip briefly northward into a swale, where a muddled sign advises that "Remington Ridge Trail 32E30" (should be 32E51) starts here (it doesn't), and reaches "State Highway 178" (now Road 214H) in "5" (really 5.8) miles.

Northeast-bound
SNF Jeep Road 28S19 Log

T3	auto road at swale	5950	0.0
	O'Brien Spring road	5620	0.3
	Remington Ridge Trail 32E51	5960	0.4

Northwest-trending
Remington Ridge Tr Log

Jeep Road 28S19	5960	0.0
Lightner Peak Wildroute	6110	0.6

Beyond the departing wildroute, our north-trending path descends a gentle, occasionally moderate grade, along hummocky

Hobo Ridge. We presently drop into open chaparral, getting a heady northward view that includes the seemingly touchable Kern River valley and the aloof High Sierra.

At length our path outflanks hill 5582, then bends northeast along the ridge and enters the Bureau of Land Management's Bakersfield District lands through a stock gate (please close). The Remington Ridge Trail then leads into a grove of the rare, short tree called Piute Cypress, which resembles its relative, the juniper. We first stroll through part of the grove that was burned in a 1966 wildfire, and observe the return of cypresses there. Our course then touches a jeep road (5020/1.9) leading southeast toward ugly mining scars, and reaches unscathed cypress hedges that shade the only good resting place for miles around. Botanist Ernest C. Twisselmann wrote in 1967 that this grove, one of the 6 known to exist (all local), remains from a vast prehistoric woodland that gradually broke up 2–5 million years ago.

Just before leaving the grove, we meet a faint path (4973/0.1) to the southeast and, in chaparral 175 yards later, our path bends abruptly northwest. The path's surface just ahead is jarringly hard where we pound down the trip's steepest grade, losing 1860 vertical feet in 1.4 miles. Midway down the grade, we re-enter National Forest at a stock gate, and soon afterward we are treated to a whiff of the laurel bunched close to a seep spring.

The grade ends in a cove, and then our trail rises slightly alongside and then past a fence, skirting pits probably bulldozed by uranium prospectors during the early 1950's (See Trip 6). We shortly skirt one of the pits while rounding the Hobo Ridge crest; then the trail flares into a *jeep road* while crossing slopes of Kern Canyon. Quite soon a jeep track (3100/1.8) from the south joins our own, and as one they wind past the signed "Buckeye Claim," then switchback down to the trip's end, a signed junction (2480/0.7) with KC Road 214H on a knoll above the hidden but heard Kern River.

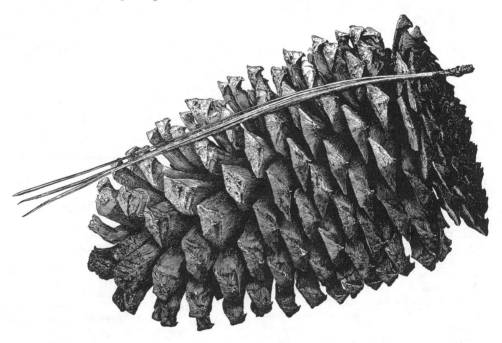

Jeffrey pine

T6   Delonegha Creek Hike

*Among the interlocking ridges sloping into Kern Canyon, seasonally
prominent wildflowers lie nestled by glades, talus caves, pebble-strewn
brooks and sycamore colonnades. But in 1983 the mine's gate at the start of
this trip was locked and posted "No Trespassing." Therefore, try this trip
in reverse by hiking up the jeep road west of Delongha Creek, then hike east
on the described route, stopping before the mine area.*

Season   all year

Distance   10.4 miles (16.7 km) round trip

Steep Upgrade   0.1 mile (0.2 km)

Elevation Gain and Loss   1370 feet (418 m)

Exertion/Duration   strenuous/1 day

Skills   moderate route-finding, Class 1
climbing

Permits   none

Roadhead/Maps   R4/M4B-M5

Description   This trip begins on a flat
along the west side of State Highway 178
(2400/0.0) 5.9 miles southwest of Lake
Isabella (the town). Near the southern edge
of the flat, the **Kergon Mine road** begins, and
while you saunter west on it, make a mental
note to cautiously watch for rattlesnakes and
to maintain protection against ticks by spray-
ing repellent on skin and clothes after intervals of several hours. If you have mistimed
your hike and have missed the cool morning
of a hot day, you might be already thinking
of switching to a high-country trip. But if
you have come at an opportune time, you
stride ahead buoyantly, soon topping a swale
among piñon pines and live oaks on the rim
of Lilly Canyon, and finding there one end
of a north-trending segment of Kern River
East Trail 32E49 (2430/0.1). (Anyone with a
yen for a workout can track this segment,
and the disused jeep and auto roads it connects with, all the way northeast to historic
Keyesville, the first Caucasian settlement
hereabouts. See Trip 20 of this book's companion volume for details of Keyesville history.)

Our road now leads southwest, soon dips
across a gulch whose stream seldom appears,
and then joins a spur road coming northwest
from a private cabin. The main road guides
us up a narrow ridge between buildings of a
ranch, and then peels off from an old mining road (2450/0.3), coursing southeast for
200 yards past several tunnels and ram-
shackle structures of the Kergon Mine.
Radioactive autunite, a lemon-yellow mineral formed where local granodiorite was
wrenched and ground under great stress,
was extracted here millions of years after
formation, as geologist E.M. MacKevett, Jr.
reported in 1960. Both this mine and a mine
to the south on the opposite side of Kern
Canyon were busiest during the local
"uranium rush" (1954–56) when the raw ma-
terials for atomic bombs and reactors were in
demand. That "uranium rush" left slopes in
30 square miles of lower Kern Canyon
scarred with prospect pits, most of which
proved unprofitable.

Nearly 200 yards from the ranch buildings, our road switchbacks west on a small
ridge parallel to the Kern River, where
another mining spur forks east. The main
road next guides us through 280 yards of
ascent past pockets of shady piñon pines before curving south at a junction with yet
another spur road, this one trending north.
The final segment of main road makes 3 ascending hairpin turns before giving way to
another part of the **Kern River East Trail**
(2750/0.7). This path switchbacks, weaves
and then twines with an abandoned road,
and after hiking on it briefly we leave the
mined watershed through a swale.

Now with our attention free of roads we
can gaze at the seasonal filaree, baby blue-
eyes, poppies and other striking wildflowers
bunched amid a vast trailside velveteen of
grass. The path contours at length, crosses
intermittent Little Creek, and then takes on
a slight upgrade, on which we presently step
across Greenhorn Creek and later skirt talus
caves. Soon afterward, that part of the Kern
River East Trail (other parts exist farther
down-canyon) yields to the **Greenhorn Creek
jeep road** (3200/2.9), which comes in from

the east. This road ascends gently west from the junction through rich pasture and scraggly woods, and shortly joins **SNF Jeep Road 27S35** (3220/0.1) atop a long, slightly rolling ridge.

That road in time leads us down into the watershed of intermittent Delonegha Creek, passing alcoves with buckeye displayed. Then we fork north-northwest onto another jeep road (2830/0.6), which soon skirts an abandoned shack. The road shortly shrinks to become **Tenant Wildroute 31E76,** whose tread is just barely visible through intruding grass. Within a few minutes, our path fords boulder-studded Delonegha Creek (2950/0.4) and then goes beyond while we tarry

alongside the creek, admiring adjacent sycamores and recalling what made restless men of all races poke and prod in the pebbly water during the early 1860's. Richard C. Bailey of the Kern County Museum traced the creek's name in 1959 to origins among the Cherokee Indians, to whom the word "delonegha" signified "where there is gold."

Because the pathfinding east from here along Tenant Wildroute toward Bakersfield would test the judgment and equipment of the most practiced modern pioneers, we leave it to them, preferring the comparatively obvious route on which we came for backtracking to our cars.

T7   Bat Rock Climb

This and most other climbs in this book take advantage of rocks that mainly have southern exposures, for they offer climbers a long season and warmth from the sun in winter. This climb of Bat Rock, however, deserves special attention because its driving approach from Los Angeles is the easiest and quickest of all. William Craig and John Newman climbed it in 1975 and report that its granite is sound, its route possibilities many and its view outstanding. Bat Rock juts skyward and dominates rumpled terrain in sight of Lake Isabella, the Piute Mountains behind the lake and the V-shaped pass on the Kern Canyon Fault between the Piutes and Breckenridge Mountain.

Season   March through November

Distance   1.4 miles (2.3 km) round trip

Steep Upgrade   0.5 mile (0.8 km)

Elevation Gain and Loss   1660 feet (506 m)

Exertion/Duration   strenuous/1 day

Skills   moderate route-finding, Class 5 climbing

Permits   none

Roadhead/Maps   R6/M6B

Description   Your route leaves State Highway 155 (4340/0.0), heading north on a narrow dirt **powerline service road.** That road bends west almost immediately, but your **cross-country route** continues north,

winding through passages in the pathless chaparral and soon passing under the powerline. Soon you gain a little ridge and then work your way up across the west slope of a canyon parallel to the ridge. The route presently reaches an intermittent fork of Shirley Creek, follows it momentarily and afterward takes the first ravine departing to the northeast. The ravine inclines steeply up and shortly ends at the base of Bat Rock, where a variety of Class 5 routes to the top (6000/0.7) begin. Craig reports that a 150-foot rope should prove adequate for rappeling off the shortest face (the north one) when you descend to the base. From there you backtrack to the cars.

T8 Alta Sierra Nordic-Alpine Ski Tour

This easy loop among trees caped in dazzling white, past sculptures in ice, gives access to optional ski runs and offbeat spur roads of interest to alpine skiers and explorers. Those taking this tour should at least know how to slow and stop themselves on the moderately steep descent midway on the loop. They might want to avoid this tour during holiday weekends to save themselves from having to cope with snowmobiles on the unplowed roads and automobiles on the plowed ones.

Season   January through March

Distance   4.4 miles (7.1 km) loop trip

Steep Upgrade   None

Elevation Gain and Loss   590 feet (180 m)

Exertion/Duration   easy/1 day

Skills   easy route-finding, novice nordic skiing

Registration/Permits   Kern County Sheriff's Department/none

Roadhead/Map   R7/M6B, M11

Description   We leave Greenhorn Summit and State Highway 155 (6010/0.0) heading north on drifts overlying **SNF Road 23S16,** a road that initially traverses steep, forested, west-facing slopes of peak 6606. This road is a favorite of a small band of snowmobile enthusiasts whom you are most likely to meet during holiday weekends. Although the snowmobilers' ranks thin as you get farther away from Greenhorn Summit, they have been rumored to range as far north as Tobias Meadow. Our trip, however, is not so ambitious. We shortly return to the crest of the Greenhorn Mountains at a right-handed junction (6020/0.9) with **SNF Road 25S16.** Now taking this road east-southeast, we ski up its gentle grade, catching fugitive northward views of the Calf Creek watershed.

Then you arrive at Black Mountain Saddle, where a face-tingling descent begins soon after you turn south onto **SNF Road 25S20** (6230/1.1). Oaks are more in evidence now and views are more easily caught: Shirley Peak and Breckenridge Mountain are sometimes visible in the south. Your narrow road, with its moderate grade, soon intercepts the cleared right-of-way of a powerline. This long, cleared strip parallels State Highway 155 and would make an exciting descent for intermediate alpine skiers. (They should not try to follow it all the way east to Highway 155, however: the last 100 feet down to the busy highway are steep and treacherous.)

Our road, meanwhile, soon joins the **state highway** (5720/1.2), which snowplows sometimes make into a walled passage. Then it is safest to remove skis and descend gingerly, perhaps helped by a short length of rope. While most visitors will prefer to walk the usually snowfree state highway northwest of here, some may wish to explore on skis the unplowed roads of Alta Sierra. They will cross the highway, descend slightly, pick up the first of those roads and find their way back to Greenhorn Summit using the maps in this book. Meanwhile, we take the simpler state highway northwest, returning to Greenhorn Summit (6010/1.2) before them.

T9   Tobias Peak Nordic-Alpine Ski and Snowshoe Trek

Uniqueness, variety, advantage and opportunity commingle in this adventuresome exploration along the crest of the Greenhorn Mountains. This crest and adjacent slopes collect more rain and snow, preserve it longer, and catch the morning sun better than most other slopes closer to the winter recreationists of Los Angeles. Of all the slopes in the Greenhorn Mountains, those visited on this trek are the largest that offer a low risk of avalanche. Of all the wintertime treks in this book, this one is among the longest and most comprehensive. It offers explorers ample opportunity to leave and rejoin the described route, letting them discover attractions along additional loop excursions on their own. To snowshoers and novice nordic skiers, this trek offers miles of gently inclined snowy roads; to experienced nordic skiers, a melange of old packed and new powder snows; and to alpine skiers and vista collectors, slopes that have been strategically stripped of some or all trees, which increased their potential for outstanding runs and views. Just as these chainsaw-created clearings are never more beautiful than when snow conceals evidence of their artificiality, so is the lookout en route enhanced when wind-driven water freezes to it in horizontal wedges. The Tobias Peak Lookout panorama takes in Mount Whitney while extending to distant horizons in all directions. All these advantages more than make up for the scarcity of running water, the occasional nuisance of zero-visibility fog and the weekend incursions of a few snowmobiles into this otherwise isolated area.

Season   January through March

Distance   26.9 miles (42.3 km) semiloop trip

Steep Upgrade   0.1 mile (0.2 km)

Elevation Gain and Loss   3080 feet (939 km)

Exertion/Duration   easy/4 days, moderate/ 3 days, strenuous/2 days

Skills   easy route-finding, intermediate nordic and alpine skiing

Registration/Permits   Tulare County Sheriff's Department/USFS campfire permit

Roadhead/Maps   R7/M11, M17–M18

Description

Northbound *SNF Road 23S16* Log

T8	Greenhorn Summit	6010	0.0
	SNF Road 25S16	6020	0.9

After parting company with skiers of modest ambitions at the junction with Road 25S16, we continue generally north on winding *Road 23S16.* Local USFS Ranger Bruce Waldron noted in 1976 that although, in the recent past, a few weekend snowmobilers had tracked this road, they were sometimes impeded where snowdrifts had filled some road cuts, restoring the terrain's original slope. Self-propelled travelers, undaunted by drifts, advance up the road through pine-and-fir forest past junctions with eastbound SNF Road 25S18 (6020/0.1) and north-northeast-trending SNF Road 25S11 (6030/0.2). Now the main road leaves the crest to climb a gentle grade past peak 6852, joining Road 25S12 (6210/0.7) midway. While rounding this peak, one can glimpse the High Sierra on the northern horizon. Its profile will become more picturesque and familiar as our trip progresses.

In the meantime, our road touches the crest again briefly, then leaves it to pass drift-hidden SNF Road 25S06 (6590/1.9), which leads northeast, serving Tiger Flat Campground in drier times. Now we skirt Sunday and Portuguese peaks and enter Tulare County, presently noting where SNF Road 24S28 (7280/2.2) departs south-southwest toward the Mountain Meadows Girl Scout Camp. A few hundred yards beyond the fork, we come to the multiple junctions of Portuguese Pass. First a route (7350/0.4) the intrepid have skied to Portuguese and Sunday peaks departs trending south, then SNF Road 24S10 departs northeast toward Portuguese Meadow, and finally, just beyond, signed Road 24S06 (7360/0.1) drops away to the west.

Down at Portuguese Meadow, a gauge maintained by the U.S. National Weather Service averaged more than 60″ of rain and melted snow each year from 1957, when it was installed, until 1964, when Kern County statistics were last reported. The closest that skiers dependent on machine-driven lifts had come to this great accumulation of snow was at Sugarloaf Ski Lodge, 5 miles northwest of Portuguese Pass along Road 24S06. There, 2 ropes repeatedly towed skiers up a cleared slope from 1947 until 1968, when lack of patronage forced the lodge owners to get out of the skiing business.

Now our road again leaves the crest and crosses its east-facing slopes, with the Sierra Crest and the Kern Plateau sporadically in view. In between view-framing portals in the forest, we might amuse ourselves by identifying animal tracks in the snow, which could make the trek past Road 24S09 (7350/0.8), the Panorama Campground road, to Road 24S50 (7350/1.5) seem to take less time than it does. We will later return here from the east-northeast on Road 23S16, but now we continue north on **Road 24S50**, skirting Bull Run Peak to reach Bull Run Pass (7580/0.8). Here, in summer, cattlemen of Linns Valley cross the road while driving their herds to pastures along Bull Run Stock Driveway 32E38.

Now your road switches to the west side of the crest, meandering north past picturesque snags across open slopes of Tobias Peak before returning to forest and reaching the swale of Tobias Pass (7550/1.5). Here one encounters for the last time the south-bound tracks of cross-country skiers and snowshoers taking Trip 30. Turn northeast here onto **Road 24S24.** Soon you can spy the clearing of Tobias Meadow through the artificially thinned forest. By now you may be wondering who was Tobias and what did he have to do with these places. Hisorian Francis P. Farquhar wrote in 1924 that Tobias Minter homesteaded a meadow at the base of Tobias Peak. After his death in 1884, his sons named the peak for him and, much later, geographers extended the name to a creek, 2 meadows and a pass because they happened to be near the peak.

In minutes we emerge in a ridgetop clearcut and turn south on **SNF Road 24S08** (7680/0.7). Its gradual grade leads up semiforested, east-facing slopes for more than ½ mile and then it winds onto the ridgecrest, where it steepens and becomes first a jeep road and then, near Tobias Peak Lookout, a trail. That drifts usually disguise the trail does not keep us from working our way, with or without skis, up from the timberline roadend to the lookout-capped summit (8284/0.9).

Later we backtrack from Tobias Peak to the point where we left **Road 24S24** (7680/0.9) to resume skiing east on it. It soon curls across the east face of Tobias Peak, affording a swift descent toward a snow bowl shorn of all trees.

Watch for the fork where the road bends northeast, leaving the bowl. Here you turn south onto **SNF Road 24S25** (7000/1.4), which quickly curves west, returning you to the bowl. From there your road inclines gently up to cross a fork of Bull Run Creek, quickly trading completely cut for selectively logged forest.

Now our road follows a contour southward, soon crossing unnoticeable Bull Run Stock Driveway 32E38 (7220/1.8) and presently reaching a **T** intersection with **Road 23S16** (7220/0.5) in a swale atop a transverse ridge. (Alpine skiers may wish to detour 1 mile east on this road to enjoy descending north-facing slopes cleared of trees above Tyler Meadow.) We turn southwest at the **T** intersection and soon return to Road 24S50 (7350/0.2), where we begin backtracking south toward our cars at Greenhorn Summit (6010/8.8).

T10

"Cook Peak Point" Nordic Ski Tour

A gentle descent through forests and meadows transformed by snow, along which you have oblique, downward views of Lake Isabella, is the modest reward of this trip designed for people who want to find out if nordic skiing is right for them. Would-be skiers from Los Angeles will find it in this trip's favor that it is not only the easiest nordic ski tour in the book but also among the easiest to reach by car.

Season   January through March

Distance   4.0 miles (6.4 km) round trip

Steep Upgrade   none

Elevation Gain and Loss   600 feet (183 m)

Exertion/Duration   easy/1 day

Skills   easy route-finding, beginning nordic skiing

Registration/Permits   Kern County Sheriff's Department/none

Roadhead/Maps   R8/M6B

Description   Our trip begins on plowed, paved *KC Road 465Z* at its junction with snow-coated SNF Road 25S17S (6790/0.0), the north-northwest-oriented entrance of Shirley Meadows Campground. The Swiss-style buildings of the Shirley Meadows Ski Resort stand just across the road. We stroll northwest from the campground down KC Road 465Z past where SNF Road 25S17N (6750/0.1) departs northwest and SNF Road 25S22 (6710/0.1) southeast. Quite soon we round a small ridge, meeting a small road from the Shirley Meadows Summer Home Tract, and soon afterward turn south-southeast onto *SNF Road 25S21* (6480/0.5). This road is both unpaved and unplowed, and leads down a quite gentle grade. In years when snowfall is average (20″) or better, this road serves admirably the needs of those new to nordic skiing.

Winding southward, our road shortly crosses an old road (6450/0.1) connecting the summer-home tracts of Shirley Meadows and Alta Sierra. Shortly thereafter we cross a few headwaters branches of Shirley Creek and pass through a clearing. Much later, as our road traverses east-facing slopes of Cook Peak, black oaks become liberally mixed with the conifers that have shaded us since the beginning. Views toward Lake Isabella and the Kern Plateau occur more often as we approach a watershed divide. While "dry-season" runners on Trip 11 continue along the road as it curves around this divide at "Cooks Peak Point" (6190/1.2), we turn around and begin to backtrack through winter snow to the cars.

T11

Shirley Meadows Run

Campers staying near Alta Sierra may want to use this loop of roads to "stretch their legs" and acquaint themselves with the multidirectional vistas offered by forest portals and meadows arrayed on all sides of the Shirley and Cooks peaks massif. That these roads are seldom driven increases this run's appeal.

Season   May through October

Distance   6.2 miles (10 km) loop trip

Steep Upgrade   none

Elevation Gain and Loss   850 feet (259 m)

Exertion/Duration   strenuous/1 hour

Skills   easy route-finding

Permits   none

Roadhead/Map   R8/M6B

Description

North-northeast-bound *KC Road 465Z* **Log**

T10	SNF Road 25S17S	6790	0.0
	SNF Road 25S17N	6750	0.1
	SNF Road 25S21	6480	0.6

Southeast-bound *SNF Road 25S21* Log

KC Road 465Z	6710	0.0
tract road	6450	0.1
Cook Peak Point	6190	1.2

(Of course, no sensible person would run the route of Trip 10 when it is still coated with snow, and so when referring to that trip's description, readers should imagine the setting snow-free and more colorful, with plants that are identifiable.)

Pacing ourselves on Road 25S21, which gently undulates west beyond "Cooks Peak Point," we cross the south-facing slopes of Cooks Peak and occasionally glimpse Breckenridge Mountain in the south. The road soon begins a gentle upgrade and presently curves southward, now in the shade of a dense coniferous forest. After a few minutes more of panting we reach a junction (6420/2.8) with SNF Road 26S07, which departs straight ahead to the west, and *KC Road 465Z*, which we begin to follow northward. We crossed the crest of the Greenhorn Mountains just before reaching the junction; the road we're running on now crosses the crest several more times during our climb toward Shirley Meadows. We presently pass portals in the forest that open on Cedar Creek canyon and the Linns and San Joaquin valleys in the west. While passing those portals, our road levels out, skirts Shirley Peak and splits with SNF Road 25S49 (6810/1.2), which gives access to a summit microwave tower. In just a few minutes more we return to our cars near Shirley Meadows Campground (6790/0.2). Sequoias shade part of the campground, but having been planted they do not qualify as the Sierra's southernmost grove.

T12
Hiking to Black and Split Mountains

Although the split in Split Mountain arouses the curiosity of travelers who spy it from Breckenridge Mountain, the Piute Mountains, the Kern River valley, Point Lovely Rogers, Harley Mountain and Baker Point, the grueling bushwhack out to Split Mountain guarantees that the register book there names only the hardiest mountaineers. For those who don't reach Split Mountain, the panorama from easily climbed Black Mountain is compensation. For those who do manage the climb to both summits, that panorama adds to their substantial satisfaction.

Season May through November

Distance 8.0 miles (12.9 km) round trip

Steep Upgrade 1.3 miles (2.1 km)

Elevation Gain and Loss 4090 feet (1247 m)

Exertion/Duration extraordinary/1 day

Skills moderate route-finding, Class 2 climbing (Class 3–5 pitches optional)

Permits none

Roadhead/Maps R9/M11–M12

Description (Climbers Paul Lipsohn and John Backus provided some details for this description in 1975.) *Cane Spring Trail*

32E46, a retired logging road, begins on SNF Road 25S20 (6234/0.0) in Black Mountain Saddle. Our roadbed climbs east up a grade at first steep, then gentle, in the shade of white fir, Jeffrey pine and Kellogg oak. The way presently steepens again, and afterward ends its climb in a swale (6880/0.6). Here at a large, waterless campsite the *Black Mountain Wildroute* forks southsoutheast and we take it. The initial steep slopes soon give way to a gently rolling summit plateau where Inyo gilia, hound's tongue and the rare Cuyamaca campion can be found nestled among granite outcrops.

Sauntering south across the plateau, we top two hills before reaching the highest pile of rocks, Black Mountain (7438/0.5). After admiring the vista, an expansion of that given to Trip 7 climbers, we backtrack to the swale (6880/0.5) and resume hiking the **Cane Spring Trail**. Still recognizable as a logging road, this dim, eastbound path descends a steep ridge. Shortly we reach a broad saddle (6170/.07) 50 yards south of intermittent Cane Spring. Sierra lilies, made rare by the depredations of grazing cattle and garden-plant collectors, may still be gracing the spring when you arrive.

East of the saddle, the faint road soon narrows to trail-width and presently it vanishes

altogether. Now we bushwhack generally east on a **cross-country wildroute** through dense but passable brush, remaining just south of the crest to avoid the impassable chaparral on north-facing slopes of this ridge. Eventually we descend to a pass just west of Split Mountain, then note occasional ducks while making a taxing ascent to the summit (6800/2.2). The cleavage for which the mountain was named opens dizzyingly to the east, tempting climbers of Class 5 rock to exercise their skills. After taking in stunning views of Lake Isabella and the upper Kern Canyon, we backtrack without climbing Black Mountain again and, exhausted, return to our cars.

T13   Sunday Peak Hike

Atop Sunday Peak, from the foundations of a lookout burned in 1954, you can get views of the Southern Sierra unsurpassed by those from any other peak this far south in the Greenhorn Mountains. Adventuresome children with parents in tow will find this hike a special treat.

Season   June through October

Distance   3.0 miles (4.8 km) round trip

Steep Upgrade   none

Elevation Gain and Loss   1000 feet (305 m)

Exertion/Duration   strenuous/1.5 hours

Skills   moderate route-finding, Class 1 climbing

Permits   none

Roadhead/Maps   R10/M10–M11

Canteens   1 quart

Description   **Sunday Peak Trail 31E51** begins at the junction of the main road and the Girl Scout camp road (7300/0.0). It leads you west, in general, up the retired logging roads, becoming trail width.

Now your path climbs a moderate grade across slopes where strips of exposed chinquapin and manzanita alternate with strips of sheltering pine and fir. The path soon merges with a faint track (7680/0.7) that climbs to here from a Girl Scout camp. Just west of the junction you touch the Greenhorn crest in a saddle between Sunday

and Portuguese peaks. If you need water, you can begin a cross-country detour 600 yards west to Water Gap Spring. But if you have enough water with you, trace the path south from the saddle, past where it switchbacks, turns a corner and then climbs across west-facing slopes. Soon our path joins the route (7830/0.3) of Trip 22 and enters a vale forested with what botanist Ernest Twisselmann identified in 1967 as the southernmost Shasta red fir in North America. Continuing south toward the rim of the vale, the Sunday Peak Trail soon joins an unmaintained path from the northeast and then turns abruptly southeast at a signed junction with Telephone Trail 31E67 (7920/0.2).

Now our path leads a few yards up a gentle slope, meets a faint, north-trending lateral, and continues beyond up the slope to a swale on Telephone Ridge. Here the path turns north and then exits from the forest. Then we begin forging through hip-deep, prickly snow bush and chinquapin, parting the brush ahead with our hands to follow the overgrown trail. It leads 200 yards north of the swale, switchbacks southeast, and then quickly climbs the granite talus of Sunday

Peak (8295/0.3). Vivid red blossoms of a penstemon called "pride of the mountains" snuggle against blue-violet Brewers lupine in crannies amid the talus.

A lookout was built here in the early years of this century so watchers could scan distant landscapes for fires. Leonard Barkley, who worked for the Forest Service when the lookout was in use, said in 1974 that the watcher here kept in touch with Fulton Ranger Station near Glennville using a phone line that descended Telephone Ridge. But Tobias Peak blocked the view to the north, Barkley said, so a new lookout was built there in 1937 and the structure here was abandoned. Later, in 1954, the Forest Service set this old lookout on fire but neglected to finish cleaning the site. The shake roof of the lookout's outhouse can still be seen in the brush to the south. From the site we backtrack to the cars.

The unneeded Sunday Peak Lookout was destroyed by the Forest Service

Courtesy Mike Mortenssen, U.S. Forest Service

T14   Tobias Peak Run

Not many runs combine visits to a silvery-spouting, delicious spring, vistas of stunning meadows, laps along deep-forest lanes, and a breathtaking panorama suddenly revealed, as this run does. Few other runs offer even the fastest runner more opportunity, challenge or inspiration to better their pace and technique.

Season June through October

Distance 6.8 miles (10.9 km) round trip

Steep Upgrade 0.1 mile (0.2 km)

Elevation Gain and Loss 1140 feet (347 m)

Exertion/Duration Strenuous/1:12 hours

Skills easy route-finding, Class 2 climbing

Permits none

Roadhead/Map R11/M17

Description   Our run gets underway on **SNF Road 24S86** near the gushing spring hydrant at Frog Meadow Campground (7460/0.0) and initially leads through the elongated meadow itself, affording views of corn lilies in fringes around the meadow, augmented by a ruined, silvery log cabin at the meadow's far edge. Our steadily ascending course soon skirts the Frog Meadow Guard Station (7630/0.3—manned in summer), then enters red-fir forest and bends abruptly southeast onto signed **SNF Road 24S50** (7670/0.1).

Almost instantly we pass the exit of northwest-bound SNF Road 24S82, then lope along the mildly undulant road through the usually cool woods. The private pasture of brilliant green Tobias Meadow is soon glimpsed to the east, and later, at Tobias Pass, Panorama Cyclepath 31E57 (7550/1.3) strikes our road from the southwest.

Here we turn northeast onto signed **SNF Road 24S24,** which leads past the meadow through patches of cut forest invaded by snow bush. Soon we exert outselves in a steady ascent, which swiftly gets us atop an oblique ridge and continues as we take **SNF Road 24S08** (7680/0.7) south from there. At length, this dusty auto road ends in a swale by a lot (8140/0.8) with room for 15 cars, and then a steep jeep road guides us 265 yards closer to Tobias Peak. Now we bound up a granite talus trail above timberline, brushing past thickets of bitter cherry and chinquapin for 60 yards and then veering southwest up an indistinct path at a junction where the obvious path forks south. In minutes we pause at the picnic table outside the summit lookout (8184/0.2), which is open to visitors from 8 a.m. to 5 p.m. from May through October or as long as fires pose a threat. Although the lookout is short on water, it's long on inspiring panoramas, in which The Needles, Olancha Peak and Salmon Creek Falls figure prominently. Now we double back to our cars, enjoying some brisk descents en route.

T15   Deep Creek Hike

Aged, redwoodlike incense-cedars shelter a creekside campsite at the end of this short hike, which balances virgin woods with stump-filled clearings, low-angle lanes with precipitous paths and unmistakeable trails with tricky cross-country routes.

Season   June through October

Distance   3.2 miles (5.1 km) round trip

Steep Upgrade   0.2 mile (0.3 km)

Elevation Gain and Loss   450 feet (137 m)

Exertion/Duration   easy/1 day

Skills   moderate route-finding, Class 2 climbing

Permits   none

Roadhead/Map   R12/M11

Canteens   1 quart

Description   *Deep Creek Wildroute* begins at the inside edge of a sharp curve on SNF Road 24S35 (6300/0.0) in the form of an old logging road, abandoned but not retired. A high berm on Road 24S35 prevents drivers from seeing, much less using, the roadbed on which we now stroll southeast. We stay left as the road forks in 0.2 mile, and from here on our route deteriorates among new growth, calling upon us to use our best pathfinding skills. After less than a mile of walking, we near the crest of the Deep Creek/Bull Run Creek divide and then veer southwest where the road forks, just inside several acres denuded within the last few decades by lumbermen. Seedlings of ponderosa pine planted after the logging compete with encroaching brush here.

Our road soon nears the crest again and then turns west, beginning to round a crest-straddling hill. We leave the road (5990/1.1) just as it starts to veer southeast, and work our way southwest, downslope, through the pathless plantation to its west edge, where a piece of the Deep Creek Trail begins amid an ankle-high layer of kit-kit-dizze (*Chamaebatia foliolosa*). In their book, *Sierra Nevada Natural History* (Berkeley: University of California Press, 1970), Storer and Usinger ascribe the common name of this fernlike, sticky, spicy plant to the Miwok Indians, who made a medicinal tea from its leaves. A recreational tea with a taste like hot lemonade can be made *(Wild Food Plants of the Sierra* tells how) from the manzanita berries that ripen in nearby trailside bushes toward the end of summer.

Now our path, the Deep Creek Trail, plummets down a little ridge, then parallels alder-screened Deep Creek for a few yards downstream and afterward turns northwest to ford the stone-strewn stream. (Beware of stinging nettles among the horsetails lining the banks.) We follow the trail a few paces farther west and then leave it upon spying a campsite (5480/0.5) to the south. The trail we have just left climbs ¼ mile west before vanishing near the Portuguese Meadow fork of Deep Creek. Our campsite, guarded by white fir and incense-cedar, overlooks the confluence of that cascading tributary with the unhurried main-stem creek. From here we backtrack to the cars.

Incense-cedar and seeds

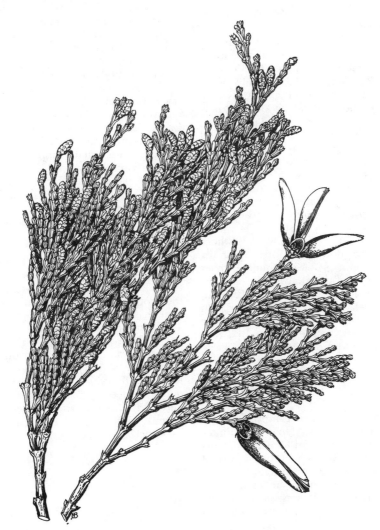

T16   Bull Run Backpack

The chuting cascades, emerald pools, brick-red bedrock, usually temp-
erate climate and juxtaposition of moisture-loving and drought-tolerant
plants in and near Bull Run Basin outweigh the presence of rattlesnakes
there in the minds of its sensibly cautious devotees.

Season   June through October

Distance   8.6 miles (13.8 km) round trip

Steep Upgrade   0.2 mile (0.3 km)

Elevation Gain and Loss   1840 feet (561 m)

Exertion/Duration   easy/2 days

Skills   easy route-finding, Class 2 climbing

Permits   USFS campfire permit

Roadhead/Map   R13/M11

Description   A "Bull Run Trail" sign may still be posted 200 feet south of the actual start of the trail on SNF Road 24S35 (6170/0.0). *Bull Run Trail 32E39* initially leads southeast down more than a mile of steep grade. A ground cover of kit-kit-dizze borders the trail, and ponderosa and sugar pine, white fir and incense-cedar shelter it until it descends amid manzanita, deer brush, Brewers oak, digger pine and black oak in the lower part of its grade. The drought-tolerant plants to which we have descended show that we have entered an area shielded from most rain-bearing clouds by the Greenhorn crest to the west.

The steep downgrade finally ends where the path weaves down to a ford of Schultz Creek. Here, in a glen with thimbleberries and fountain grass shaded by alders, metamorphic stones lead across the braided, cascading creek. Beyond the ford, our path rises briefly, tops a slight west-trending ridge and then descends to the floor of Bull Run Basin. Here we find one of the many large campsites scattered across this basin. Jeffrey pines, white firs, incense-cedars and Kellogg oaks shade the basin floor, while alder is the predominant tree along Bull Run Creek.

Our path skirts the first campsite and instantly fords the creek. Now we saunter across the basin floor and shortly boulder-hop Bull Run Creek again. Having returned to the creek's west bank, we follow it some distance, cross it again at the basin's end and quickly return to the west side. Now the creek beside our path runs into a deepening canyon while we progress into Kern County. The creek soon cascades over outcrops of resistant metamorphic rock, entering shimmering pools while our path crosses slopes above.

We presently climb a brief, steep grade and then cross a ridge into the Deep Creek watershed. When the local flannelbush blooms, your attention may be captured here by its pungent fragrance. Our path descends a few yards from the divide and then meets a trail (4750/3.3), established by use, leading east along Bull Run Creek.

We contour west from the junction for a few minutes and then our path begins winding southwest. Soon we approach Deep Creek and find a cluster of campsites under the widespread boughs of a streamside live oak. Then we boulder-hop the creek where it issues from a large pool, and later hike past a lateral to a medium campsite where Deep and Cow creeks converge. Apropos of Cow Creek, we now enter the Split Mountain Allotment, where the Snow family let 60 head of cattle graze from early May through August of 1977.

The trail beyond the confluence climbs gently along Cow Creek, soon crossing it twice. Presently we step across a tributary at the mouth of its canyon, and then we encounter a medium campsite near a fork with a southeast-trending lateral (4900/0.7). Then our trail fords Cow Creek 5 times in quick succession and ends just beyond the last ford. Narrow and seldom-maintained SNF Road 25S18, which may be barred to the public because it crosses private land, ends here by frail railway tracks leaving the Silver Strand Mine (4970/0.3). From here we backtrack to our cars.

T17   Baker Point Hike

Partisans of the most popular section of Kern Canyon can enjoy com-
prehensive and exciting views of it from Baker Point Lookout, which is
easily reached by the only trail in the Greenhorn Mountains that is closed
to off-road vehicles.

Season   June through October

Distance   2.4 miles (3.9 km), round trip

Steep Upgrade   0.1 mile (0.1 km)

Elevation Gain and Loss   680 feet (207 m)

Exertion/Duration   easy/1 day

Skills   easy route-finding, Class 2 climbing

Permits   none

Roadhead/Map   R14/M18

Canteens   1 quart

Description *Baker Point Trail 32E37* begins at the end of SNF Road 24S02 (7430/0.0) and then leads east. In its first few hundred yards, the wide, level trail crosses a forested, north-facing slope parallel to an older path visible just down the slope. Leonard Barkley, a former Baker Point smoke-spotter, said in 1974 that the new path was built during the 1960's so tractors could ferry supplies out to the lookout. He said that its construction was halted where it now ends because funds ran out, and predicted that the new path would not be completed as long as the lookout is supplied by helicopter.

We soon reach a linkage with the old path and use it instead of continuing on the new trail, knowing that the new trail ends in cliffy terrain impassable to anyone unskilled in Class 3 and 4 climbing. The view-framing forest of white fir and Jeffrey, ponderosa and sugar pines shades us as we advance east beyond the linkage on the old trail. Now we descend a gentle grade across talus to avoid the cliff face where, high above, the new trail ends. Then our path climbs a short, steep grade and afterward undulates east, zigzags, rounds a north-trending ridge and eventually ends above timberline at the foot of Baker Point Lookout (7753/1.2).

Pioneer enthusiasts take note of Carol Moore's report, made when she was employed here in 1977, that cattlemen once drove herds up the precipitous slopes from Kern River banks to here. She maintained that modern pioneers could find remnants of a historic cattleman's blacksmith shop within ⅛ mile of the lookout. From the lookout steps, we backtrack to the cars.

T18   Hiking a Naturalist's Trail

Cliffs of crystallized limestone show strikingly in the midst of
springtime cascades, flashy flowers and sheltering trees in the Flynn and
Tobias Creek canyons. The visual-aural feast in these canyons is at its
best in the spring and fall, when precaution-taking hikers find that the
presence of poison oak, rattlesnakes and ticks can be more challenging
than threatening.

Season   March through November

Distance   8.8 miles (14.2 km) round trip

Steep Upgrade   0.1 mile (0.2 km)

Elevation Gain and Loss   2280 feet (695 m)

Exertion/Duration   strenuous/1 day

Skills   easy route-finding, Class 2 climbing

Permits   none

Roadhead/Maps   R15/M18, M21

Description   Our jaunt begins on a northwest-trending dirt road just south of paved SNF Parking lot 23S39 (3745/0.0) and east of paved TC Road MTN 99. Our dirt route at first skirts McNalley's Fairview Resort and Restaurant, then forks southwest from the road through a small house-trailer colony. We then take **Whiskey Flat Trail 32E35** (3725/0.1), which starts northwest at the colony's edge, where a sign directs us onto a suspension bridge spanning the Kern River. At the peak of snowmelt runoff, this swirling torrent commands attention, just as it did in 1845 when explorer John C. Fremont named it for the artist and cartographer of his expedition, Edward M. Kern.

Once at the west bridge abutment, we turn southwest through a signed junction with the private Fairview Mine Trail (3725/0.1) and saunter across a fenced, private inholding. Although motorbikers had made racecourses throughout this privately owned flat by the mid-1970's, the owners had yet to put up "No Trespassing" signs. If such signs appear in the future, this trip is automatically nullified.

Our path threads the racecourses briefly, then leaves the inholding through a stock gate (please close) and enters the 48,504 acre Kern Canyon Allotment. In 1977, a drought year, 210 cattle with the Sprague Ranches' brand were released to roam the allotment in mid-January, and then were rounded up in mid-March. Since the allotment was opened to grazing in 1964, the herd-size allowance has sometimes been increased somewhat, and the grazing season expanded from October through May, depending on how much forage has grown each year. The chance that cows may be sullying water sources ahead makes toting purification tablets a must.

Midway up the ensuing cross-slope ascent, we leap a dry, chaparral-choked ditch that once diverted water from Tobias Creek in the south to riverside ranches north of here. Shortly we top a slight riverside ridge and then leave the Whiskey Flat Trail (Trip 24 in this book's companion volume), turning abruptly northwest onto **Lila Lofberg Trail 32E33** (3725/0.6). Lofberg, a gifted naturalist and writer, captured the Florence Lake environment in her little-known classic of 11 years' year-round survival in the High Sierra, *Sierra Outpost*. After she and her husband left the post of Florence Lake Dam caretaker, they lived out the rest of their days (Bob Powers told how, charmingly, in *North Fork Country*) across the river from here.

The Lofberg Trail initially leads a few dozen paces northeast before **Tobias Creek Trail 32E34** (3740/0.1) peels off to the southwest, presenting us with an optional excursion along trout-frequented Tobias Creek.

*   *   *   *   *

The Tobias Creek Trail beyond the signed junction briefly rolls through a thick cloak of buckbrush, flannel-bush and yerba santa, then fords the often slack water of Flynn Canyon creek where boulders permit dry-footed crossings. Then one passes among canyon live oaks and piñon pines dispersed along Tobias Creek and presently ascends a moderate gradient across a rust-streaked schist-and-quartzite blend.

Canyon tia, a strain of the plant Mormon tea, thrives on these red rock slopes. As botanist Ernest Twisselmann pointed out in 1967, this Mormon tea makes a hot beverage that is not only tasty but also was thought (by Spanish Californians) to relieve arthritis and (by Mexican *vaqueros*) to cure venereal disease. In the midst of these canyon tia clumps, high above the creek, our path briefly levels, and then our canyon bends east while we make a short, gentle descent to the creek. Here in the shelter of Jeffrey pines and Kellogg oaks, the path skirts a few small, leaf-strewn campsites and ends at an old ford (4190/1.8) just short of a "trail not maintained beyond this point" sign.

At one time the path zigzagged up a long ridge beyond this ford on its way across the Greenhorn Mountains. A huge blaze roared up the flanks of Kern Canyon in 1960, consuming the brush and trees on this ridge and initiating a regeneration of chaparral which obliterated much of the trail. A road was extended south from Johnsondale at Forest Service behest, superseding the rest of the ridge trail amid intense salvage logging. Faced with these obstacles, most travelers will double back at the trail's present end.

*   *   *   *   *

Beyond the Tobias Creek Trail, the **Lila Lofberg Trail** undulates mildly west, outflanking a ridge interlarded with sandstone and crystallized limestone. Now we thread seasonal displays of the lemon-yellow flowers of flannelbush, the creamy, cuplike blooms of mariposa lily, the magenta bristles of Indian paintbrush, and the pale, lacy spikes of buckbrush. Live oak and piñon pine interspersed in the chaparral offer occasional shade, and soon, while entering Flynn Canyon, we're acquainted with some of the floral riches its metamorphic soils support: California coneflower, pennyroyal, larkspur, brodiaea, wild rose, gooseberry, silk tassel, Brewers oak and wild cucumber.

Shortly we step across Flynn Canyon creek—the first ford in a series of 10—and start up a gradual grade in the shade of Kellogg oaks. Keep an eye peeled for poison-oak clumps, which occasionally encroach on the trail ahead. We then ricochet from bank to bank while crossing the creek at progressively shorter intervals, presently skirting a line of alders and viewing an upslope cliff of crystalline limestone in the north.

By the time most hikers attain the eighth ford of Flynn Canyon creek, 850 feet higher than the first ford, they may have wondered whether Flynn was a stockman, like most of the others whose names survived on maps of the Southern Sierra. Bob Powers' research, published in 1974, confirms their suspicion—Matt Flynn herded sheep here nearly 100 years ago.

The eighth ford lets us onto a small flat by an adjoining west-trending canyon, a flat with a flourish of miners lettuce in the deep shade of incense-cedars. A bedframe and mattress take up a small part of the flat, and a large campsite takes up the rest. (Most people will prefer to leave backpacks here and to hike the rest of this trail with a day pack.)

Soon after leaving the flat, we jump the creek yet again, then ascend a short, stiff grade to bypass cliffs that signal our passing onto a mass of erosion-resistant quartzite and schist. Then we briefly contour toward one final ford of Flynn Canyon creek in a streaky, scooped spillway. Moments after we leave the ford, our path cuts into a northwest-trending side canyon, and there starts zigzagging north up a ridge. Zigzags give way to a steep ascent halfway up the ridge, but presently the gradient eases while our path ascends cross-slope beyond the ridge.

That ridge was only a dinky spur of Speas Ridge, which we soon top in a swale (5960/3.6). The trace switchbacking downslope through kit-kit-dizze from this ponderosa-pine-forested swale is part of old Speas Trail 31E31, which is rumored to be sporadically cleared of brush by local cattlemen. Because it ends on private property near the lumber-mill town of Johnsondale (see Trip 40 for its history) this path is not recommended for use. Therefore, while relentless explorers reconnoiter along Speas Ridge, most of us at the swale double back toward our cars.

California sycamore

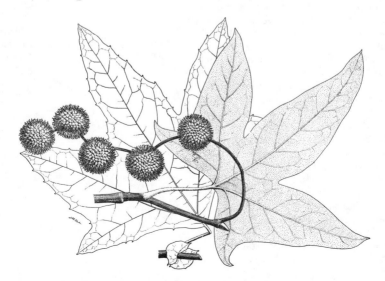

T19   Glennville Run

Roads level or gently rolling with no blind curves, with only avoidable spurts of traffic, and with the beguiling presence of pastoral small-town life rooted in American history make this run one workout for the body that doesn't neglect the mind.

Season   all year (avoid holiday weekends)

Distance   3.5 miles (5.6 km) loop trip

Steep Upgrade   none

Elevation Gain and Loss   220 feet (67 m)

Exertion/Duration   strenuous/1 hour

Skills   easy route-finding, Class 2 climbing

Permits   none

Roadhead/Map   R16/M6A

Description   Our outing begins at the Glennville Post Office (3180/0.0) at the north corner of paved State Highway 155 (west) and KC Roads 110G (northeast) and 447Z (northwest). We first jog up the gentle grade of **Road 447Z,** soon passing the Linns Valley Elementary School. Shortly the live oaks and blue oaks that were dotting distant foothills become our companions, and then we cross a rolling ridge that links our route with the Greenhorn Mountains to the east. We stride down the short ensuing grade, viewing a pastoral scene in which distant Blue Mountain in the west acts as a foil for a close-at-hand Linns Valley ranch.

Ranch buildings stand by 2 corners of our crossroads at the end of the grade with paved **KC Road 421Z** (3060/1.1)—the spot where the Trip 20 bicycle tour begins. Starting to run on that road southwest, we pace ourselves along the edge of the open Linns Valley pasture. Here, in spring, a riot of wildflower color will delight and delay the runner, who later dashes across Highway 155 (3030/0.8) at a signed junction while keeping its two-way traffic in mind.

Then, after striding a few yards more, we pivot east and begin running on paved **KC Road 118G** (3020/0.1), labeled on signposts "Pascoe Road." This road soon leads across intermittent Angel Creek and then parallels that creek while leaving Linns Valley. Quickly striding past foothills lined up south of the road at the valley's edge, we soon pass a north-opening exit to the Glennville Rodeo Grounds. Water-loving plants such as willows soon close in on our road, and

shortly we recross Angel Creek, climb slightly and hit the pavement of **Highway 155** (3180/1.3) where Pascoe Road ends.

*   *   *   *   *

Now we can choose to include or omit a detour of 0.1 mile round trip to the Glennville Adobe State Historical Landmark. Historian Bob Powers wrote in 1970 that Tommy Fitzgerald probably came to California with pioneer trapper Jedediah Smith in 1826 and definitely was the one who built and settled in this hut then.

Gradually others homesteaded nearby land, for the site of Glennville was at the junction of popular gold-rush mining roads. Among the settlers, as Russ Leadabrand recorded in 1968, were James Madison Glenn, a native of Tennessee for whom the town was named, and William Lynn, whose name, misspelled "Linns", came to denote the valley to the west. After examining the historical marker, we backtrack smartly to the junction with Road 118G (3180/0.1).

*   *   *   *   *

Now we make a short final sprint west past the Glennworth shopping complex and then return to our cars at the Glennville Post Office (3150/0.2).

T20   Linns Valley Bicycle Tour

A mountain range draining south once stood here, nearly worn flat between its near-parallel streams. A massive chunk of the earth's crust on which the range stood then began rising and tilting west and, while most streams deserted their old channels to flow west as the slopes of this new Sierra Nevada directed, 2 entrenched streams still flowed south. Many millions of years then preceded the pioneers who named the greater eastern stream "Kern River," the lesser western one "Poso Creek" and a Poso Creek basin with a vast pool of underground water "Linns Valley." Then as now, in average or extra-wet winters, this pool fills up to the valley floor, keeping trees out of the valley's long meadow, germinating a vast array of terrestrial and aquatic plants and renewing some waterfowl-patronized ponds. Every year now, wild roses, poppies, blue dix, tarweed, sunflowers, brodiaea, Oregon golden asters, mariposa lilies, wallflowers, downingia, lupine, mule ears, groundsel, clarkia, violets, clematis, five-spots, farewell-to-spring and other terrestrial annuals blossom into a riot of springtime colors here. Then, when the "riot" wanes and the underground pool and ground-level ponds start to shrink, tiny plants bloom in succeeding concentric circles around each pond, one circle of uniform color at a time, lending distinction to a piece of prehistoric landscape and enticing modern bicyclists to ride the roads that give views of it there in Linns Valley.

Season   March through December

Distance   11.2 miles (18.0 km) loop trip

Steep Upgrade   none

Elevation Gain and Loss   550 feet (168 m)

Exertion/Duration   easy/1 day

Gears   1-speed conventional to 15-speed alpine

Permit   none

Roadhead/Maps   R17/M6A, M8–M9

Canteens   1 quart

Description   We start bicycling on **KC Road 447Z,** signed "White River Road," at its crossing of paved KC Road 421Z (3060/0.0). Our road narrows quite soon and grows knobby while it leads west-northwest from the crossroads. Then this road bridges transitory Poso Creek just north of a landing strip and afterward meanders northwest through Linns Valley, now among blue oaks, now in the midst of clearings, now within sight of windmills, now skirting springtime ponds. In a few minutes, a gated private road branches west toward visible Blue Mountain Lookout, manned by the California Department of Forestry.

Not long thereafter, our road's gentle grade leads beyond the valley meadows into rolling, oak-wooded terrain. Then we cross into the drainage of incipient Arrastre Creek, part of the White River watershed. Almost instantly our route enters Tulare County and turns east on signed, paved **TC Road MTN 1** (3220/4.2), a wider road striped down the middle.

This rolling road skirts Joe Bowen Canyon and later cuts across the north edge of Linns Valley while bypassing Vincent Ranch. The Vincents, a pioneer homesteading family, traditionally drove cattle from here to the Greenhorn Mountains every year until recently.

A **T** intersection in the valley's northeast corner marks the point where we turn south onto signed, paved **TC Road MTN 3** (3250/2.4). It soon bridges Poso Creek, crosses Sand Flat and then enters Kern County, where its code changes to **421Z.** We continue to pedal southward, traversing fingers of the Linns Valley meadow and collections of white, blue and Kellogg oak between them. Shortly we ride past Carver and Bowen Ranch, headquarters of a pioneer cattle-raising family that still divides their years between cow punching in the Greenhorn Mountains and letting their herd graze near home. Wheeling farther along Linns Valley, we skirt Oak Grove Cemetery, a dapper plot where local pioneers were entombed which is carefully tended by valley old-timers. Then we return to the crossroads (3060/4.6) where our cars await.

T21   Peel Mill Run

A sawmill established in 1886 lends its name to this shady-lane run through cedars and pines alternating with oaks. The bumpy dirt lane oscillates between ridges and nooks, linking fern-bordered, cascading streams with forest portals that frame views of the Linns and San Joaquin valleys.

Season   April through November

Distance   6.0 miles (9.7 km) round trip

Steep Upgrade   none

Elevation Gain and Loss   680 feet (207 m)

Exertion/Duration   strenuous/1 hour

Skills   easy route-finding

Permits   none

Roadhead/Map   R18/M10

Description   Our run begins at the cluster of campsites where Peel Mill Creek (5350/0.0) crosses **SNF Road 24S07,** popularly known as "Sandy Creek Fire Road." Some distance from this ford the sawmill that gave the creek its name was in service from 1886 until the depression that followed the Spanish-American War. Emmett R. Berry wrote in his *History of Jack Ranch* (Riverside: Desert Litho Service, 1975) that the mill was uneconomical and was abandoned because it was too far from the market and also because the road from mill to market was in places too steep for horse-drawn wagons.

After we leave Peel Mill Creek, the initial easy loping we do before starting to pant takes us southwest up the road's gentle grade. Now we run in the often-cold shade of dense incense-cedars and pines characteristic of north-facing slopes on this trip. Most runners or joggers have to pant by the time they top a saddle on Telephone Ridge and meet Telephone Trail 31E67 (5630/0.7). From here the road continues to climb on a south-facing slope, although on a gentler grade; and incense-cedars still appear, although mostly crowded out by Brewers and black oaks. Quite soon we cross a transitory tributary of Sandy Creek, presently round a ridge and then descend to the creek itself (5480/1.3). Beyond the creek and its modest stream violets, we make a short, final advance to reach the next ridge, where eastbound Sandy Creek Trail 31E68 (5570/1.0) begins. From here we retrace our steps on the usually quiet road to Peel Mill Creek.

T22   Telephone Ridge Backpack

Backpackers looking for trips that will get them in shape may not want to look farther than this, for Telephone Ridge is often steep, the trail through its dense forest is shady, the campsite near its summit lies near a tasty, dependable spring and its summit is Sunday Peak, the highest and among the most viewful of peaks in the Greenhorn Mountains.

Season   June through October

Distance   7.4 miles (11.9 km) round trip

Steep Upgrade   0.5 mile (0.8 km)

Elevation Gain and Loss   3130 feet (954 m)

Exertion/Duration   easy/2 days

Skills   easy route-finding, Class 2 climbing

Permits   USFS Campfire Permit

Roadhead/Maps   R19/M10–M11

Description Where SNF Road 24S07 rounds Telephone Ridge in a saddle (5630/ 0.0), you begin hiking east up jeep tracks, which narrow in a few hundred yards to form *Telephone Trail 31E67*, which is open to motorbikes. Although your trip follows the border between 4 grazing allotments, it's unlikely that you will see more than a few cattle en route because forage is rare. Beyond the jeep tracks, your path leads briefly straight up the ridge crest, initially with black oak, incense-cedar and ponderosa pine shading a trailside undergrowth of silk tassel and miners lettuce. Tiny-flowered blue lips. brodiaea and lupine thrive on this ridge where sunbeams warm the soil, as they do in a clearing you shortly reach atop the first hill of the trip.

Next your path re-enters the woods and at the same time leaves the crest. Now it inclines steeply up across north-facing slopes, where white fir and sugar pine first appear in the dense forest. The trail presently crosses the crest in a swale and then zigzags east up south-facing slopes a stone's throw from the crest. Presently you return to the crest, go briefly straight up it once more, and then contour southwest to avoid a crestline jumble of boulders. Quite soon the path meets a ravine and then climbs southeast. In a few hundred yards, it reaches a southwest-trending ridge and then winds over hill 7473 to meet the faint path of Bohna Peak Wildroute 31E66 (7390/2.0) beside a sawn-through log in a broad saddle. A bitter spring among hundreds of half-buried cans and bottles can be found 0.2 mile down a gulch that leads southeast from this junction. Campsites of all sizes are scattered between the spring and the junction, but the spring itself is best avoided until the trash has been taken away.

Beyond the junction saddle on Telephone Ridge, the Telephone Trail climbs southeast and soon rounds a slight, south-trending ridge at the remains of a cairn. Then it angles steeply up across an open slope clad in manzanita and chinquapin, passing views showing the Greenhorn Mountains diminishing to the south. You presently regain the ridgecrest and then stroll along it up easier grades amid pinemat manzanita. Soon your path crosses a north-facing slope in dark forest and ends at a signed junction (7920/0.9) with *Sunday Peak Trail 31E51*.

* * * * *

Now we have the option of climbing that peak before or after we make camp. The Sunday Peak Trail, described in Trip 13, takes a short but roundabout route from the junction to the peak (8295/0.3). Once you decide to leave the top, backtrack to the junction.

* * * * *

To reach the campsites, walk the Sunday Peak Trail north from the junction into a shady alpine vale where snow drifts sometimes linger through June. The vale and adjacent ridges can accommodate at least 30 campers. Water Gap Spring is located near thickets of bitter cherry, gooseberry and monkshood where the vale turns from north to west and becomes a ravine. A short *cross-country route* leading north to the spring leaves the path (7820/0.3) where it starts northeast out of the vale. From the spring (7580/0.2), you backtrack to the cars.

T23   Fountain Springs Bicycle Tour

*The exhilaration of those who struck White River gold in 1853 is
almost matched when adrenalin spurts into the blood of cyclists descending the long final grade of this foothill tour of ranches and White River
gold fields.*

Season   all year (avoid holiday weekends)

Distance   27.8 miles (44.7 km) loop trip

Steep Upgrade   0.1 mile (0.2 km)

Elevation Gain and Loss   2780 feet (847 m)

Exertion/Duration   moderate/1 day

Gears   5-speed conventional to 15-speed
alpine

Permits   none

Roadhead/Maps   R20/M7–M8, M13–M15

Description   Our ride begins at a shadeless
picnic table and state historical landmark just
south of paved TC Road MTN 56 and a few
yards west of the rough-hewn, unfinished
wood exterior of the Fountain Springs Saloon (790/0.0). The plaque of the landmark
here calls the attention of passersby to the
origin and movement of the Fountain
Springs settlement. Originally located beside
the springs themselves, more than a mile
northwest of here, Fountain Springs was first
a station on the Butterfield Stage (1858–61)
where the main road to the Kern River
mines split from the Los Angeles-to-
Stockton stage road. Today travelers can ask
to fill canteens inside the relocated saloon, or
use the outside faucet at the California Department of Forestry (CDF) fire station just
southeast of here.

After mounting our bikes, we pedal east
past the saloon and almost instantly turn
southeast onto the 2-lane blacktop of *TC
Road MTN 109.* The eastward view of a
windmill against sensuous curves of Sierra
foothills is marred by high-tension powerlines, which soon cross our road heading
south to Los Angeles. After a few minutes'
ride beyond the lines, we can pause on a
large, wooded lawn by a fire station (810/0.2)
and snack at the shady picnic table there with
the tacit approval of CDF. Eucalyptus,
Modesto ash, pepperwood, apavitas cedar,
maple and elm shelter the site, and to
travelers here on a sunny day the treeless
pastures across the road seem to jiggle because of the heat rising off the road. When

fires don't pose a threat, usually from
November to May, the station is locked and
vacant on weekends.

Heading southeast on the road again, we
make the first in a series of fords of Fountain
Springs Gulch, conduit of an intermittent
creek. Later we skirt a row of black walnuts
near a barn before crossing the gulch 4 more
times, now in environs studded with blue
oaks. Scattered windmills and lichen-
dappled boulders add pleasing focal points
to foothills now flanking the road. Shortly we
leave Fountain Springs Gulch, pass the
signed entrance to "John Guthrie Ranch,"
skirt assorted barns and stockyards, and undulate gradually to a crossing of intermittent
Coho Creek. After topping a nearby divide,
our course makes some sharp curves while

Fast fix for a flat tire

Ron Van Cleave

winding beyond, down into the White River canyon. At an intersection (1150/7.4) near the bottom of the short grade, we choose between taking a brief excursion farther down the same road to the White River ghost town, and pedaling off without delay on signed, paved TC Road MTN 15.

* * * * *

The White River excursion leads in minutes to a narrow bridge over sycamore-shaded White River, and then leads beyond past sites of long-gone saloons to a signposted junction with paved TC Road MTN 12 (1080/0.4), where we pause to imagine what occured here more than a century ago. After DeWitt Biggs and A.J. Maltley first struck gold in the vicinity, a mining town was erected here and called Tailholt. The name was characteristic of the gold-rush miner's rambunctiousness, for its source was a piece of cow tail with which a miner pulled open his front door. But respectability soon overcame whimsy here, and after the local post office opened in 1860 the town bore the name "White River." The mines that had kept the town alive petered out in 1909, and nothing more than a few ruins and cabins remain of the town today. Now, from the historical monument next to the junction, we backtrack to Road MTN 15 (1150/0.4).

* * * * *

Locally known as the "Grapevine Grade," **Road MTN 15** begins by leading east-northeast on the level, its narrow, unstriped pavement being chuckholed, in some places dusty, and everywhere patched. Its roughness makes it good for ascending, but not descending. Ahead, it traverses part of the John Guthrie Ranch, and the cattlemen there reportedly drive their herds up it each year en route to their summertime pasture atop the Western Divide.

Beyond the junction with Road MTN 107, our road soon swerves close to the band of sycamores that indicate the winter-wet course of the White River. Shortly the road starts rolling across increasingly large riverside hills on which wildflowers flourish in spring. Early amid these undulations, we cross transitory, willow-marked Chalaney

Creek and pass another road signed "John Guthrie Ranch." At the end of the undulations we leave the White River for the last time and climb north near a tributary. Quite soon we wheel gingerly through the tributary's sand at a ford, then labor up a steady grade and later turn west onto signed, paved **Road MTN 56** (2520/7.6) in a swale beside Bald Knob. The dark Greenhorn Mountains loom east of the junction.

Now that this 2-lane, shoulderless road has become a trans-Sierra artery, one should ride by the edge of it and be wary of speeding vehicles while one advances northwest from the junction. Soon our yellow-striped road dips briefly toward a tangle of wild grapevines visible in the canyon below, and if we pause somewhere along this descent and look due south we can see Blue Mountain Lookout, the CDF facility seen from the Linns Valley Bicycle Tour (Trip 20). Then we ascend along a gulch packed with wild grapevines and willows, shortly skirting water tanks and presently topping a saddle, the highest point on the trip.

You might want to check your brakes now because from here to Fountain Springs you can coast almost all the way. The first descent takes you rapidly into the watershed of Chalaney Creek past several pools where cattle drink. Then you speed easily past the signed "HB," "Crunon Bluegrass" and "Condor" ranches into the Coho Creek watershed, soon crossing the creek itself to meet signposted TC Road MTN 52 (1670/5.0), locally known as the "Old Hot Springs Road." Then your road undulates slightly past the Hunsaker Ranch, where horses are raised, and the John Guthrie Ranch, where cattle are kept.

Now propelled at a brisk rate, we shoot across Fountain Springs Gulch between two windmills, up a short, slight grade and then down a thrilling incline, soon passing under high-tension lines and crossing Road MTN 109 (790/7.2) at Fountain Springs. Here we return to our cars.

T24   Ames Hole Hike

Among the things that make a trip to Ames Hole a memorable occasion is the place itself. Ames Hole has a grassy glen with a glassy brook coursing over a bed of white sand. Here White River plunges in a 30-foot fall before becoming the glassy brook. Sycamore, live oak, buckeye and alder lend shade to the setting and appear to frame the falls.

Season   March through November (avoid summer weekends and holidays)

Distance   4.6 miles (7.4 km) round trip

Steep Upgrade   none

Elevation Gain and Loss   940 feet (287 m)

Exertion/Duration   easy/1 day

Skills   easy route-finding, Class 1 climbing

Permits   none

Roadhead/Maps   R21/M16–M17

Canteen   1 quart

Description   Your hike starts on **White River Cyclepath 31E58,** which begins at a sign beside SNF Road 23S05 (4070/0.0) and descends west on a gentle grade. Gary Linden and Rich Platt, Forest Service technicians both, told me in 1977 that this path has been heavily used by motorbikers during holiday weekends and weekends in summer. If you hike the path's initial stretch when the bikers are gone, you will seldom be out of earshot of wind-chimes disguised as riffles in brook-width White River. With Kellogg oak, Jeffrey pine and incense-cedar unfurling their awnings overhead, and a pungent catalog of years of fallen leaves underfoot, you'll tread jauntily past the upper and lower White River campgrounds.

Your path runs entirely inside the White River Allotment and is not without cattle spoor. Gordon Heebner, range specialist of Sequoia National Forest, wrote that Oscar Klein again managed 150 grazing cattle here from mid-April to mid-August of 1977, just as he had been doing each year since 1967.

While you progress farther west, canyon slopes close in on the "river" like a vise and your path nears the melodious water. Then the "river" slides away from your trail through a sequence of cascades. The path continues descending, but now across slopes high in the White River canyon. Presently you enter a zone of live oak, chinquapin and deer brush where the trail is no longer sheltered. Then your gentle descent is interrupted by a steep dip down into a southwest-trending ravine in which you skirt a pile of boards. The gentle downgrade then resumes for ¼ mile before the path zigzags down into the glen named Ames Hole (3130/2.3). (A summer-home tract and the popular campgrounds upstream make it unwise to drink from the White River.) From here you backtrack to the cars.

T25   Backpacking Among the Southernmost Sequoias

The small band of Sequoiadendron gigantea *that you'll pass along this trip belong to the Deer Creek Mill Grove, which constitutes the southernmost naturally distributed redwoods in North America. Scarcely less memorable is Frog Meadow, a large, sloping patch of subalpine grass abutting conifers, campground conveniences and a gushing piped spring. These attractions make this trip especially useful to youth groups brimming with energy.*

Season   June through November, non-holiday weekdays only

Distance   14.1 miles (22.7 km) shuttle/loop

Steep Upgrade   0.4 mile (0.6 km)

Elevation Gain and Loss 3800 feet (1158 m)

Exertion/Duration   easy/3 days, moderate/ 2 days

Skills   easy route-finding, Class 2 climbing

Permit   USFS campfire permit

Roadheads/Map   R22, R23/M17

Description   Rich Platt and Gary Linden of the Forest Service said in 1977 that *Deer Creek Ridge Cyclepath 31E55* has been heavily used by motorbikers, and that the small part of this heavy use that didn't occur during holidays and weekends in hunting season happened on other weekends when the paths were not snowbound. The cyclepath leads us southeast from a spur of SNF Road 23S04 (4560/0.0) and shortly enters a stockfence gate and a section of the Lion Allotment. Here, in 1977, drovers of the John Guthrie Estate herded more than 365 head of cattle in small groups from section to section for short periods in each. Forest official Gordon Heebner reported that cattle were present somewhere in the allotment from May through August that year. It's quite possible that you'll see cattle here if you visit in one of those months.

Soon the logging road SNF 23S04 cuts into our trail twice. At the first cut we slant up the road, round the curve, and hike up and along the trail briefly. Next we stroll east along the road for 200 yards, looking to our left for *Frog Meadow Cyclepath 31E56* (5920/1.9) onto which we turn northeast, returning to the woods. Motorbikers used this path just as often, or more so, as they did the path we just left, according to Platt and Linden, who provided estimates of such use for all paths in the northern Greenhorns. This path runs a few hundred feet before joining signed westbound Sequoia Grove Trail 31E55 (5930/0.1), a steep, disappointing track through scars where, John L. Harper indicated in 1974, loggers removed pine and fir amid local sequoias in the 1920's. Of the 131 sequoias scattered across about 180 acres in the Deer Creek Mill Grove, this trail visits only one.

Our path leaves the Deer Creek/Capinero Creek divide just beyond the junction,

threads a cluster of sequoias and then switchbacks up a south-facing slope amid white fir and sugar and ponderosa pines. We then loop around a lustrous glade and later round an adjacent ridge to reach Dead Horse Meadow.

The object of all those halved license plates you've seen supplementing blazes along this trail was to guide snow surveyors up to the signed "D.H.M. Snow Survey Course," located in the forest between the meadow and SNF Road 24S82 to the east. Although helicopters have taken the place of snowshoes as the surveyor's means of getting here, the measurements that he records continue to reveal patterns in the snow's moisture content.

Our path runs between the snow-survey course and the head of the meadow and then swings east, skirting a few patches of corn lilies before ending at a signed junction with *Road 24S82* (7690/2.3). Follow the road south a few yards to a junction with *SNF Road 24S50* just over the Greenhorn crest. We take a few steps north on this road and then turn east onto *SNF Road 24S86* (7670/ 0.1). This inferior road descends along lengthy Frog Meadow past a guard station manned in summer and ends at a commonly uncrowded 10-unit campground (7460/0.4) near a piped spring spouting the best water for miles around. (Hikers eager for extra exercise can take the old Tobias Trail 0.9 mile down along cascading Tobias Creek from the end of Road 24S86 to Road 23S53, and then regain 700 feet of elevation by tracing it back to Frog Meadow.)

We next return to the ridge-crest junction (7670/0.4) and turn north onto *Road 24S50*. Mounds diverting water from the initial section of this road often bend the fenders of cars being driven along it too fast. The mounds offer no resistance to us as we cross a large swath of stumps on a slope overlooking Frog Meadow.

The rolling road soon re-enters selectively logged forest and presently ends at Sand Flat (7750/0.9). Packsaddle Trail 31E49, which has at times been heavily used by motorcyclists, begins here in the form of a retired logging road. Leading us north, it inclines up and across a slope of stumps and logging debris and quite soon reduces to a trail upon reaching virgin fir forest. Manzanita crowds up to the trail in a few clearings we shortly pass through. The trail then leaves the Greenhorn crest for a long west-slope traverse on a gentle downgrade. Clearings en route offer westward views of the San Joaquin Valley that are especially comprehensive during windy days.

A mile beyond where we left the crest, our path passes a medium campsite, bends around a squared-off spur rudge, and runs past several sloping meadows to which willows and corn lilies cling. Then the tread leads straight ahead at a signed junction with abandoned Speas Dirty Trail 31E31 (7560/ 1.8). Our path continues to twist along the headwall of the Deer Creek watershed, passing ground-level flowering pussypaws and blue lips that speckle the slopes which are sunny and free of brush.

You presently reach Lion Ridge and a signed junction (7280/0.9) where the Packsaddle Trail bends sharply northeast. Leave it here to descend a usually gentle but sometimes moderate grade southwest on **Lion Ridge Trail 31E52,** another path open to motorbikes. Several game trails similar to your path split off at intervals, so be wary. The maintained trail descends along the crest for more than a mile to a broad saddle, then switchbacks up to mount a hill and there resumes its descent.

The ridge soon narrows, and views of the bald ridges around California Hot Springs are sporadically revealed through the forest. Then sets of zigzags periodically ease our descent into the realm of oaks, tall grass and cattle. Eventually we reach a signed junction with **Thompson Camp Trail 31E54** (4920/4.1), onto which we turn east-southeast.

After 100 yards, this sometimes grassy path turns south-southeast and then plummets into and later alongside a gully. Now a minor ridge leads down an increasingly gentle grade past myriad seasonal flowers of five-spot, baby-blue-eyes, buttercup and miners lettuce. Shortly we cross the gully we left above, and some time later we step across an intermittent tributary of Deer Creek twice in close succession. Directly south of the second ford, the tributary joins Deer Creek, which we boulder-hop just west of the confluence. Boughs of live oak, black oak and ponderosa pine hover over the braided, boulder-smoothing waters here. A parcel of private land spanning the creek's gulch downstream discourages explorers from forging a creekside route directly west to Uhl Ranger Station (Pronounce the station's first name "you'll" as contemporaries of the namesake homesteader, a vegetable truck farmer, did.)

Upon emerging from the creek, the path inclines steeply up a creekside slope. Midway up the slope, we pass above a water-side medium campsite. Then our path zigzags up to end at a signed junction with **Road 23S04** (4190/1.2), Roadhead 22, where the road crosses a cow-catcher. (Those who did not leave a car here can now enjoy a quick, easy, and—best of all—final ascent on the shaded road east to Roadhead 23.)

T26   Rube Creek Hike

The water that's never far from this route has cut deep box canyons with boldly contrasting settings. This moving water slides, cascades, spreads, pools, narrows; sculptures bedrock, polishes boulders, scours slabs, cuts terraces; and varies in its sound from a fizz to a roar. Two streams flowing all year, plus numerous seasonal tributaries, distribute water to most parts of the Rube Creek Trail. Underground water in snowmelt season fosters variety and showiness in wildflowers en route, and arranges settings so that the flowers and the lush, green, streamside growth contrast with adjacent dry, drab brush. Water beckons the hiker here, but only when the trailbike whine present on holiday weekends doesn't compete for his attention.

Season   March through December (avoid holiday weekends)

Distance   7.6 miles (12.2 km) round trip

Steep Upgrade   0.1 mile (0.2 km)

Elevation Gain and Loss   1740 feet (530 m)

Exertion/Duration   moderate/1 day

Skills   moderate route-finding, Class 2 climbing

Permits   none

Roadhead/Maps   R24/M16, M19

Description   This trip takes hikers through the principal grazing areas of the Rube Allotment, which Gordon Heebner of the Forest Service approved for use by some 320 head of cattle bearing John Hershey's brand from mid-April through August of 1977. Since it is almost a tradition that varying numbers of cattle are allowed to graze here during those months, chances are good that you'll find them here if you visit then.

The chances are also good that if you come here on holiday weekends or weekends in hunting season, you'll meet a different though also legitimate land-user on the trail: the motorcyclist. Forest Service technicians Rich Platt and Gary Linden, familiar with patterns of use on this trail when interviewed in 1977, observed that motorcyclists had made moderate use of it up until then.

Rube Creek Trail 31E46 begins at a sign beside paved TC Road MTN 50 (4260/0.0), leads northeast amid live and black oaks, fords intermittent Merry Creek via steppingstones, turns west-northwest to run at first parallel to the creek and then joins an abandoned jeep road. Immediately the road dips into a northeast-trending gully, fords the gully's transitory stream and then crosses an adjacent slope in the sparse shade of buckeyes and digger pines. Soon the jeep tracks turn to climb the slope, while we continue west-northwest, picking up the trail again. The slopes we cross next, en route to the visible saddle ahead, grow flecked in spring with the kaleidoscopic colors of blossoms of buttercup, brodiaea, fiddleneck, lupine and baby blue-eyes.

Presently we cross the saddle 100 feet northeast of a red-painted metal post labeled "CH6," and afterward drop north to a flat beside Cold Springs Creek. Here we start hiking west on an abandoned jeep road, another part of the Rube Creek Trail. Quite soon it leads us across the steppingstone-studded creek, and then it undulates northwest across rolling, oak-dotted pastures. After a time, we leave Sequoia National Forest at a large metal gate and close it after us, bearing in mind that any abuse of the private land ahead could cause the owners to bar everyone from the privilege of visiting Rube Creek. (If "no trespassing" signs are posted here when you arrive, please heed them and turn back.)

Soon our road runs past the conspicuous start of a northbound cowpath and then quickly narrows to trail width upon reaching a steep, south-facing slope. After crossing this chaparral-covered slope in a moderate-to-steep descent, we soon reach a saddle on the Rube Creek/Cold Springs Creek divide. Now our path makes a knee-shocking descent amid flannelbush, redbud, laurel, gooseberry, deer brush and buck brush, and shortly we step from boulder to boulder in crossing Rube Creek where the trail fords it.

Upon reaching the west bank of the creek, we instantly turn northeast because the wide trail (3520/2.0) curving southwest from here is a stock driveway that leads farther into private land. The section of Rube Creek Trail that begins here is sometimes obscured by washouts and annual grass, and then it requires intense pathfinding. At first we saunter upstream by the creek for 290 yards; then we cross to follow the creek's east bank for the next 100 yards. Then our path reappears on the west bank near a cascade-fed pool. Later it crosses a north-trending tributary gully, crosses live-oak-shaded creekside flats knee-deep in miners lettuce and finally re-enters Sequoia National Forest at a stock-fence gate. Please help keep cattle from overgrazing the land: close the gate behind you.

Our path continues to climb up-canyon, keeping the creek in earshot and meeting popular cowpaths that head off to the west.

Quickly we come to another ford of Rube Creek, from which our path zigzags up the steep east bank and then resumes a gentle upgrade upon reaching a terrace. Now the course gradually returns to the banks of Rube Creek, crossing en route a thin, fizzing snowmelt brook that tumbles down mossy stones from the east. Then, 0.4 mile north of the last Rube Creek ford, we cross again to its west bank.

Now we ascend a moderate grade, screened by alders from the creek's pools and cascades. The path presently zigzags up to an oak blazed with an "X" and then contours northeast to another ford of Rube Creek. Boulders in the wide creek at this ford allow hikers to cross with dry feet. Here the creek emerges from a long pool that it chutes into just up-canyon. Continuing northeast from the ford, we soon step across Rube Creek and then stop at a cluster of campsites (4320/1.7) perched on a flat overlooking the creek. From here we backtrack to our cars.

T27   Alpine Skiing on Parker Peak

At the union of the Greenhorn Mountains with the Western Divide lies a mildly rolling landscape uncommonly receptive to the diversity of intents with which different wintertime visitors enter the Southern Sierra. Some come here as alpine skiers to swoop down the many cleared multiple-gradient slopes—and are pleased with the quick, easy access from their cars to the slopes. Some come as nordic skiers to explore the adjacent, enticing but undescribed slopes—and enlarge their appreciation of the varying snow conditions. Some come here as naturalists to investigate brutal survival stories implicit in animal tracks in the snow—and are sidetracked by sculptures in ice along musical Parker Meadow Creek. Some come here to initiate much more demanding treks—and are assured of the power snow has to beautify remnants where forests ahead were decimated or leveled by chainsaw. Some come for other reasons and discover further enticements, but most come to appreciate the peculiar diversity and versatility of the Range Union Slopes.

Season   January through March

Distance   6.4 miles (10.3 km) round trip

Steep Upgrade   none

Elevation Gain and Loss   800 feet (244m)

Exertion/Duration   easy/1 day

Skills   moderate route-finding, novice alpine skiing

Registration/Permits   Tulare County Sheriff's Department/USFS Campfire Permit

Roadhead/Map   R25/M19

Description (Early in 1978, forester John Bridgewater outlined for the author what might happen to TC Road MTN 50, the main access road for this trip, after it was to be completed later that year. It could, he said, continue to be closed each winter by the Uhl District Ranger Station. It could be left open as far as snowbanks let visitors drive. Or it could be kept open by snowplows across the range to Johnsondale. Bridgewater said that one of these options would be agreed on and implemented in time for the Winter of 1979. The author believes that precedence, jurisdictional differences and economy will dictate that the road will be left open to snowline because most other county roads are, will not be closed by the county because its gate belongs to the Forest Service, and will not be plowed because no winter resorts, few winter recreationists and scant numbers of all-year businesses would benefit from the great expense. Therefore, it's reasonable to assume that you will be able to take this trip as described.)

Elsewhere in the Sierra, especially along the east side, avalanches leave drifts and debris that block roads at low elevations until long after the main snowpack has retreated to higher slopes, making skiers carry their skis, sometimes for considerable distances. That the need for such carrying has rarely occurred here is among the advantages offered by the Western Divide. So, wherever the snowpack blocks further progress up paved *TC Road MTN 50* by car—usually at Cold Springs Saddle (5800/0.0)—we slip on skis and ascend the slightly slanted, continuous sash of snow overlying the road beyond. In so doing, we benefit from another advantage of the Western Divide—a thick snowpack made predictable by the local past annual average precipitation of 25". This average increases to 33" near Parker Peak for those who take this trip; to 40" near Speas Meadow for those who take Trip 29; and to 60" near Portuguese Meadow for those who take Trip 30.

Minutes after leaving the cars, we stride easily past the consecutive north exits of SNF Road 23S66 (5800/0.1) and Parker Meadow Stock Driveway 31E47 (5810/0.1) and then saunter a bit across slopes of the Starvation Creek watershed. Early on this slope traverse, we might see tracks of homeward-bound Trip 29 skiers on incoming SNF Road

23S64 (5930/0.4). Beyond, our curvilinear corridor through needle- and broad-leafed forest continues to lead northeast, and at length starts to take advantage of the fine snow on the Range Union Slopes. A few minutes later, we reach Parker Pass (6420/1.4), where easy skiing begins.

Here we turn northwest, parting with other winter travelers taking Trips 28–30, and take *SNF Road 22S04* through a barely rolling landscape striped by the shadows of bunchy pines and firs, whose forms are recognizable although adorned with snow. In so doing, we cross usually unnoticeable Parker Meadow Stock Driveway 31E47 without delay. Then the road crosses a few of the locally scattered masses of stumps that the snow conceals. The snow may conceal this road segment as well, so if you lose the way, head north into Parker Meadow and, listening for tunneling Parker Meadow Creek, follow its banks a mile upstream into Upper Parker Meadow.

Meanwhile, those who did not lose the road can use a short part of its indistinct corridor to outflank Parker Meadow, and use a succeeding shorter piece to reach a junction (6470/0.7) near the south tip of Upper Parker Meadow. Here, while some independent nordic skiers take Road 22S04 on into apt and often dazzling country, we turn west onto *SNF Road 22S81,* which turns north in an instant and twines among trees bordering Upper Parker Meadow. Our route soon impinges on steep, east-facing slopes that, having been clear-cut, are secretly stumpy and available for repeated cautious but swift descents. (Beware of letting your ski tips be caught by subsurface brush or debris.) The road ends near the north edge (6580/0.5) of the cut forest, and from there we eventually backtrack to our cars.

T28 Redwood Meadow Nordic Ski Trek

Nothing makes the warm orangish-brown of giant sequoia bark stand out more than a cloak of snow on its foliage, and this trip offers in its vistas a potpourri of such impressive colors.

Season   January through March

Distance   11.2 miles (18 km) round trip

Steep Upgrade   none

Elevation Gain and Loss   1240 feet (378 m)

Exertion/Duration   easy/2 days, moderate/1 day

Skills   easy route-finding, novice nordic skiing

Registration/Permits   Tulare County Sheriff's Department/USFS Campfire Permit

Roadhead/Maps   R25/M19–M20

Description

Northeast-bound *TC Road MTN 50* Log

T27	Cold Springs Saddle	5800	0.0
	SNF Road 23S66	5800	0.1
	Parker Meadow Stock Driveway	5810	0.1
	SNF Road 23S64	5930	0.4
	Parker Pass, SNF Road 22S04	6420	1.4

Parker Pass separates the Western Divide to the west from the Greenhorn Mountains to the east, so paved Road MTN 50 heads for the Greenhorn Mountains directly from the pass. In several minutes of striding, we pass through a large, stump-packed clearing and then turn southeast to advance up a slightly inclined segment of road. Soon after passing southwestward views of Sierran foothills, we cross a Greenhorn crest swale, and then we descend at a clip past a signed "Penny Pines Plantation." Forester Hank Abraham said in 1974 that the young ponderosa pines among the stumps and brush here were planted too close together to allow the healthy growth of any. This plantation screens other logged slopes to the north around Holey Meadow from the view of summertime tourists.

Just beyond where the plantation sign protrudes from the winter snowpack, the headwaters bowl of Double Bunk Creek is reached and the Powderhorn Ski-route

(6420/0.9) branches southeast. While takers of Trips 29 and 30 leave the road here, we trace it briefly northwest to a signed junction with paved *TC Road MTN 107* (6380/0.2), known as the "Western Divide Highway." Skiers preferring improvisatory touring will find the surroundings of Double Bunk Meadow, east of the junction on Road MTN 50, much to their liking. Even in an extremely dry winter such as 1976–1977, you may find, as Ted and Sue Beauchamp did, that the snow line remains at the 6000-foot level, still allowing considerable exploration on skis.

But, having made it halfway to the goal of our trip, Redwood Meadow, we track Road MTN 107 north from the junction and almost instantly exit the Double Bunk bowl through a cleft in its rim. Then we shoot down past swiftly glimpsed Holey Meadow, to which snow has restored continuity. The thrill run ends as we cross both the creek draining Holey Meadow and creekside SNF Road 23S06 (6250/0.5). There the Western Divide Highway begins a mild ascent out of the Parker Meadow Creek watershed. Early in this ascent, our highway divides the alders lining that creek, then leaves the Range Union Slopes and crosses northwest-trending SNF Road 23S18 (6230/0.3). That ascent ends when we top the rim of the Long Meadow Creek basin.

Here we encounter the Far-Flung Slopes, a zone in the shape of a grotesque claw that usually collects powdery, stable and long-lasting snow. The downward-angled road now directs us in a brief, bracing slide across these slopes until we cross a cascading stream and then reach *SNF Road 22S09* (6100/1.7). This short, paved, southbound, campground-serving lateral lets us reach Redwood Meadow, an attraction of sustained popularity because of the striking arrangement of tall sequoias surrounding it. These are but a few of the 150 sequoias distributed in groups across the 268-acre Long Meadow Grove.

Given the urge and enough time, explorers could link Trip 30 with this trip and Trip 59 for a grand traverse of the Greenhorn Mountains and the Western Divide by skiing northeast on Road MTN 107 from Redwood Meadow to Nobe Young Creek and beyond. But because the limited ambitions of this trip have been realized, most of us will now backtrack to the cars.

Butch Castro

Crossing a snow bridge on skis

T29   Speas Meadow Nordic-Alpine Ski Trek

David Beck, an expert on nordic skiing in California, remarked in 1974 that the best cross-country skiing terrain in the Sierra could usually be found just east of sequoia groves, because more snow fell there than anywhere else around. If he was correct, the Speas and Tobias Slopes— the goals of this modest trek—hold great promise for skiers. When snow forms a shield over debris, brush and stumps in the large, cleared swaths near Speas Meadow, alpine skiers can find on the slopes with good run-out a spectrum of runs from easy to tough. Nordic skiers can enjoy the ideal terrain going to and from there, and all kinds of skiers can enjoy outstanding views once they are there.

Season   January through March

Distance   15.4 miles (24.8 km) semiloop trip

Steep Upgrade   0.1 mile (0.2 km)

Elevation Gain and Loss   1930 feet (588 m)

Exertion/Duration   easy/3 days, moderate/2 days, strenuous/1 day

Skills   moderate route-finding, intermediate nordic and alpine skiing

Registration/Permits   Tulare County Sheriff's Department/USFS Campfire Permit

Roadhead/Maps   R25/M17, M19–M20

Description

Northeast-bound *TC Road MTN 50* Log

T27	Cold Springs Saddle	5800	0.0
	SNF Road 23S66	5800	0.1
	Parker Meadow Stock Driveway	5810	0.1
	SNF Road 23S64	5930	0.4
	Parker Pass/SNF Road 22S04	6420	1.4
T28	Powderhorn Ski-route	6420	0.9

From the white ribbon of TC Road MTN 50, the cross-country *Powderhorn Ski-route* leads us southeast across the forested headwaters bowl of Double Bunk Creek. Near the southeast end of the bowl, we penetrate a large, open patch of snow-buried stumps and then climb over a low gap into the Bear Creek watershed. Another zone where all trees were cut now offers views of the few recognizably rounded crowns of Powderhorn Grove sequoias among the woods on the first north-facing slope to the south. Redwood researcher P.W. Rundel disclosed in 1969 that none of some 50 sequoias here were reproducing themselves, and predicted that the grove would gradually disappear.

Our logged zone leads southeast, downslope, from the viewpoint to SNF Road 23S17 (6290/0.9), which we cross before skiing through a fringe of forest into the clearing of Powder Horn Meadow. Mounds in the woods to the west appear where a rustic log cabin and an adjoining corral stand buried in snow. Now the ski-route leaves the meadow's southeastern lobe and leads east, diagonally, up gentle, semilogged slopes—the northernmost of the Southern Sequoia Slopes—to the base of a rise on the Windy Creek/Bear Creek divide. Here we turn southeast, then

ski 100 yards down a moderate slope and intercept the ledge of *SNF Road 23S02* (6310/0.6).

We start tracing this winding road south, soon crossing Windy Creek and presently passing a few of the 379 sequoias known to be in the 240-acre Packsaddle Grove. Amid the redwoods runs Packsaddle Creek, which our road crosses and then parallels to the clearing of Packsaddle Meadow. Here a clear-cut from the meadow's edge crosses our road and encompasses a west-facing slope.

At the cut's north edge, *SNF Jeep Road 23S02A* (6630/1.3)—sometimes so thoroughly hidden by snow that a map and compass must be used often to stay on it—leaves Road 23S02 and leads us diagonally upslope into the forest, where it turns east. Soon our road leads through a notch randomly filled with snow across north-facing slopes along the crest of the Greenhorn Mountains. (The snowshoers among us will prefer to follow the crest itself, avoiding this stretch of road.) Midway across the slope we enter a huge patchcut where alpine skiers can race down moderate slopes again and again.

The road forks near the east edge of the cut, and we veer northeast, beginning the *Tomowas Ski-route* (6870/0.8), named with the Tubatulabal Indian word for winter, while Trip 30 skiers go southeast on the Bankalachi Ski-route, named for the band of Tubatulabal Indians that inhabited the Greenhorn Mountains. In a few minutes we leave the Southern Sequoia Slopes and enter an artifically thinned forest where our road has been retired, which means that much of the land's original slope has been restored where the levelled roadbed used to run. A corridor, sometimes diffuse at the edges, directs us on a short, gentle ascent across these forested slopes until *SNF Road 24S73* takes over our guidance at a transverse branch of Packsaddle Creek (7000/0.8).

Having just started traversing the Speas and Tobias Slopes, we advance 100 or so strides along this road and get onto a gently rolling portion of incipient Speas Ridge, here stripped of trees. It soon becomes apparent that this clearing extends south, opening slopes delightful to alpine skiers in the bowl containing Speas Meadow. Our road briefly contours along the bowl's edge, then merges with a *spur road* (6970/0.6), which, while taking us southwest to a flat (6940/0.1) near fir-fringed Speas Meadow, gives us a few minutes of sliding.

A haystack-shaped snowdrift in the vicinity is the cabin called Speas Dirty Camp, established, presumably during the 19th Century, by a reputedly sloppy shepherd. Today, skiers can decorate the clean, snowy slopes above with tracks in voluptuous curves or bold slashes—and mar them inevitably with accidental sitzmarks. All sorts of on-slope descents and off-slope excursions are available here, including a run for experienced alpine skiers from the promontory where Speas, Burnt and Lion ridges unite in sight of the High Sierra. Eastward views of Salmon Creek Falls embellish this and other potential excursions for Speas Meadow campers.

Eventually everyone on this trip backtracks to Packsaddle Meadow and **Road 23S02** (6630/2.3), which one again takes to the south. Quite soon after leaving the meadow and crossing the crest of the Greenhorn Mountains, we ski straight ahead through a **T** intersection and onto **SNF Road 23S64** (6650/0.2). Now as our road descends gentle grades and gradually curves northwest, parallel · to the Greenhorn crest, our

forest-defined corridor opens occasionally on Deer Creek watershed vistas. Now that we've left the Southern Sequoia Slopes for the last time, the under-ski snow is crusty in places, soft and deep in others, and may be sporadically slushy or even bare in spots.

This route takes us through numerous curves before our road cuts through a small, west-trending ridge and, upon touching the ridge's far slope, meets Powderhorn Wildroute 31E50 (6120/1.9)—a steep, long-neglected path. The upslope half of this offset junction lies several dozen yards north, where an old, northbound logging road, now part of the Powderhorn Wildroute, was stranded when our roadbed was cut deeper into the slope.

Beyond that point of departure for dry-season scramblers, our road arcs periodically, then crosses Starvation Creek in a cove and starts curving southwest. At length we return to the uniform pad of snow overlying paved **Road MTN 50** (5930/2.4), where we begin tracing tracks we made earlier, now heading southwest. Its gentle downgrade takes us by Parker Meadow Stock Driveway 31E47 (5810/0.4) and Road 23S66 (5800/0.1) with a minimum of delay before our trip ends at Cold Springs Saddle (5800/0.1).

T30   Greenhorn Crest Snowshoe and Nordic-Alpine Ski Trek

A smorgasbord packed with Southern Sierran sights and impressions—all you could want to consume at once—is figuratively set before skiers and snowshoers who contemplate taking this trip. There is the boldness in the notion of trekking the length of the greater part of the Greenhorn Mountains that will appeal to the ambitious. There is snow accreted to everything—here as fluffy as powdered sugar, here grainy like little peas, here concealing logging debris, here cascading in bridal veils from fir boughs onto natural meadows. Snow in varying forms and depths, embellishing groves of giant sequoias and spread across a mammoth collection of slopes allows uncrowded, inexpensive, reassuring-to-hair-raising alpine skiing in settings that have never recorded an avalanche. Intimate forests are interspersed across these slopes with astonishing views, including one that aligns Sentinel Peak with The Needles and the highest peak in the contiguous United States, Mount Whit-

ney. Salmon Creek Falls, visible too, brings to mind the chimes of creeks and the howling of wind that sometimes enrich the Trip 30 experience. But fog or sun is as likely as wind, and protective forests amid the widely distributed clearings keep exposure to weather from becoming monotonous or dangerously lengthy for the capable explorer. Other treats on the trip are the numerous optional "do-it-yourself" detours that add risk and discovery to the adventures that can be had on this trek. Only the most jaded will leave this snow trek without vivid, prominent memories.

Season January through March

Distance 23.2 miles (37.3 km) shuttle trip

Steep Upgrade 0.6 mile (1.0 km)

Elevation Gain and Loss +3000 feet (+914 m) and −2800 feet (−853 m)

Exertion/Duration easy/4 days, moderate/2 days

Skills moderate route-finding, intermediate nordic and alpine skiing

Registration/Permits Tulare County Sheriff's Department/USFS Campfire Permit

Roadheads/Maps R7, R25/M11, 17, 19, 20

Description

Northeast-bound *TC Road MTN 50* Log

T27	Cold Springs Saddle	5800	0.0
	SNF Road 23S66	5800	0.1
	Parker Meadow	5810	0.1
	Stock Driveway		
	SNF Road 23S64	5930	0.4
	SNF Road 22S04	6420	1.4
	at Parker Pass		
T28	Powderhorn Ski-route	6420	0.9
T29	SNF Road 23S17	6290	0.9
	SNF Road 23S02	6310	0.6
	SNF Road 23S02A	6630	1.3
	Tomowas Ski-route	6870	0.8

Upon forking southeast from the Tomowas Ski-route, the initial segment of the cross-country ***Bankalachi Ski-route,*** (our route)—a jeep road barely traceable through overlying deep drifts—briefly ascends to the Greenhorn crest and there gives way to a longer cross-country segment. The Packsaddle Trail veers southwest from here in summer, but in winter and early spring it loses allure because it gets packed with hard snow just as steep as the slopes it crosses, and because its passage through often-dense forest is narrow and easily lost. Snowshoers and nordic skiers will find that the Greenhorn crest offers easier going and emphatically better views.

Our crestline route beyond the jeep road enters untouched forest and initially climbs east, but after a few hundred yards, both crest and route swerve southeast. Now on the edge of Speas and Tobias Slopes, the route sometimes undulates briefly but steeply, and elsewhere climbs a moderate grade, finally leading above timberline to a stunning panorama. A promontory here at the union of Speas, Burnt and Lion ridges makes visible a High Sierran horizon extending from Mineral King past Mount Whitney. Tall, domelike Olancha Peak and apronlike Salmon Creek Falls dominate views of the Kern Plateau and the rounded Sierra crest in the east.

Now our course on the Greenhorn crest rolls south, reaching in ½ mile a lobe of Speas and Tobias Slopes that extends, partly above timberline, down to a bowl in the east—a slope that will challenge the most sophisticated of intermediate alpine skiers.

Condensation fog frequently forms on this crest and sometimes spills down the east slope, eliminating visibility. This condition calls for extreme care in crestal route-finding and abandonment of any plans to ski down adjacent slopes, where it is easy to get lost. And keep to the west when walking the crest—cornices that can collapse underfoot may conceal the verge of steep, east-facing slopes.

Taking these hazards into account, we undulate on beyond the lobe and presently drop below timberline. Quite soon our route merges with ***Packsaddle Trail 31E49*** and we take note of its blazed trees while gliding south on billowy drifts among snow-encrusted pines and firs. In less than a mile, at Sand Flat (7750/3.4), southbound ***SNF Road 24S50*** begins to guide us. Animal tracks become more prevalent in the short time it takes us to leave Speas and Tobias Slopes, bypass Frog Meadow and cross an offset junction (7670/0.9) with SNF Roads

24S86 (east) and 24S82 (west). Our road's corridor soon winds over a low transverse ridge, then becomes riddled with holes framing views of the glaring snow that coats Tobias Meadow. Eventually, after striding easily past the meadow, we arrive at Tobias Pass (7550/1.3) and take note of departing SNF Road 24S24. From here we take the first half of Trip 9 in reverse to our shuttle cars at Greenhorn Summit.

Southbound *Road 24S50* Log

T9	Road 24S24	7550	0.0
	SNF Road 23S16	7350	2.3

Southbound *Road 23S16* Log

SNF Road 24S50	7350	0.0
SNF Road 24S09	7350	1.5
SNF Road 24S06	7360	0.8
SNF Road 24S10	7350	0.1
SNF Road 24S28	7280	0.4
SNF Road 25S06	6590	2.2
SNF Road 25S12	6210	1.9
SNF Road 25S11	6030	0.7
SNF Road 25S18	6020	0.2
SNF Road 25S16	6020	0.1
State Hwy 155 at Greenhorn Summit	6010	0.9

T31   Sentinel Peak Climb

Truly the panorama-commanding sentinel of the middle Kern River watershed, this climb's destination, Sentinel Peak, stands in the midst of a boldly rimmed basin where vivid vegetation offers contrast to expanses of polished, bare light-gray granodiorite. Sentinel Peak guards the way to elephant-profiled Elephant Rock, hemispheric Dome Rock and a low-elevation imitation of the famed Whitney Crest, The Needles. Within one's view from Sentinel Rock, rich forests delineate north-facing slopes, drought-tolerant plants indicate south-facing slopes, and foliage stung by fall frosts into flaming hues defines intervening drainage courses. Newcomers to middle Kern climbing should find tackling this sentinel an appropriate initiation.

Season April through November

Distance 2.4 miles (3.9 km) round trip

Steep Upgrade 0.6 mile (1.0 km)

Elevation Gain and Loss 1480 feet (451 m)

Exertion/Duration easy/1 day

Skills easy route-finding, Class 4 climbing (Class 5 pitches optional)

Permits none

Roadhead/Map R26/M21

Description The *Bankalachi Trail,* named for the band of Shoshonean Tubatulabal Indians who inhabited the eastern slopes of the Greenhorn Mountains and the Western Divide, was forged to the summit block of Sentinel Peak in the 1960's by Dave Jaqua when he was a 16-year old Eagle Scout. Subsequent generations of scouts staying at Camp Whitsett have kept this crude, steep but fairly direct trail passably marked and free of brush.

It starts east from a black oak by the Camp Whitsett road (4720/0.0) amid thick manzanita and mountain mahogany interspersed with digger pines. Quite soon the path bridges a gulch in the midst of deer brush and holly-leafed redberry clumps. Then it leads some 140 yards beyond to cross paved SNF Road 22S82 (4780/0.1) near the road's bend around the south ridge of Sentinel Peak.

Beyond the road, the path trends northnortheast and, in 70 yards, starts ascending along the ridge crest. Flannelbush dispersed among the chaparral adorns the ridge in May and June with showy yellow petals. We presently clamber over Class 2 chunks of rough granodiorite, keeping just east of the crest.

Shortly thereafter we meet a path departing southwest to nowhere and then, guided by red-tipped yellow stakes, we climb a series of steep, sandy pitches in a northeast advance away from the ridge. Live oak and Jeffrey pine offer intermittent shade while we pant up these loose slopes, where encompassing views of terrain drained by Nobe Young and Dry Meadow creeks can be had.

Nearly 190 yards after leaving the ridge, our path turns northwest, reverts to stabler footing and briefly offers an easier grade. Then we work up steep west-facing slopes on an indistinct trail segment past specimens of incense-cedar, and soon gain a southeast-trending divide, which becomes our route.

In minutes we clamber up slabs and subsequent talus along the divide, and then reach the smooth west wall (6120/1.1) of Sentinel Peak's summit fortress. Although the Boy Scouts have left an anchored rope dangling to the foot of this 30-foot wall (the shortest pitch on Sentinel Peak), the rope is weakened by weathering and shouldn't be climbed. Numerous 5th and some 4th Class routes are available to those determined to reap the giddily sweeping summit panorama. Rewarding portions of this view can be found by scramblers poking around the base of the summit fortress.

Exfoliating granodiorite bulges are visible near the level of Sentinel Peak and both southeast of it and a few miles southwest of it. Called "Nobe Young Bluffs" by Pete Kirchner, who climbed them in 1976, these bulges, although inferior to Dome Rock and The Needles, offer sound holds on eastern exposures and require ropes no longer than 150 feet. Kirchner rated the easiest route here Class 5, and observed that the rock's proximity to SNF Road 22S82 made it advantageous for practice climbs.

Eventually everyone doubles back from Sentinel Peak via the trail to the cars.

Beverly Steveson

T32   Elephant Knob Climb

The profile of an elephant's head appears in the knob's south face when it is viewed from within private property to the west. Like most other sheer south faces in the Southern Sierra, not only is this one a product of the mammoth chiseling force exerted when water freezes and thaws in cracks but also it is a haven of warmth during the day for climbers when High Sierra faces are glazed with ice.

Season   March through December

Distance   1.2 miles (1.9 km) round trip

Steep Upgrade   0.1 mile (0.2 km)

Elevation Gain and Loss   450 feet (137 m)

Exertion/Duration   easy/1 day

Skills   moderate route-finding, Class 2 climbing (Class 3–5 pitches optional)

Permits   none

Roadhead/Map   R27/M21

Description   Beginning at the saddle-top junction (4760/1.2) where SNF Road 22S53 splits off paved SNF Road 22S82, the *Elephant Knob Wildroute* leads southeast in a firebreak up the crest of a ridge. Quite soon it becomes apparent in over-the-shoulder views that this ridge extends from domineering Sentinel Peak to connect with Elephant Knob. Stiff, thick mountain mahogany pinches off the firebreak before we get 300 yards from the cars, and we then weave through corridors in the brush, favoring slopes just east of the crest, which soon dips east to a saddle. From there on we follow the crest through tangles of live oak and other brush through which some black oaks and digger pines protrude. In so doing, we quickly top a second hill and then a third, which proves to be Elephant Knob (5090/0.6). Here we overlook pools and cascades set in the pine-bordered spillway of Nobe Young Creek, which arcs around the bare, steep, exfoliating Class 3–5 granite on the south face of our viewpoint. Eventually the views and climbs here lose their hold on us and we backtrack to the cars.

T33   Durrwood Camp Backpack

Smoothly scooped, slick chutes through which Peppermint Creek plummets entice travelers toward ample midway pine flats and oak-sheltered destination campsites secreted in back of boulder bars lining the boisterous Kern River.

Season   April through November

Distance   4.2 miles (6.8 km) round trip

Steep Upgrade   none

Elevation Gain and Loss   1020 feet (311 m)

Exertion/Duration   easy/2 days

Skills   easy route-finding, Class 1 climbing (Class 3–5 pitches optional)

Permits   USFS Campfire Permit

Roadhead/Map   R28/M25

Description   (This is tick country, so spray yourself and your clothes liberally with insect repellent. Since rattlesnakes have been seen here also, carry a long stick and probe any obscured spot into which you might have to reach or step.) A log felled across a spur (5280/0.0) of SNF Road 22S82 on the crest of a minor ridge marks the start of eastbound *Peppermint Falls Wildroute 32E42,* on which we start hiking east. Initially a retired logging road, our route soon evolves into intertwining cowpaths while descending along a low divide to a saddle (5160/0.1). Here we turn south onto unmistakable *Bean Camp Cyclepath 32E29,* often stippled by cow tracks. In droughty 1977 the cattle belonged to Dennis Carver, who managed them here from mid-May through mid-August. (Usually the cattle remain until mid-September.) Carver owns the 320-acre inholding in which our trip begins, but much of his land has remained unfenced, and "No trespassing" signs are unknown here. Nevertheless, if anyone abuses his land while passing through, Carver can close it to the public, effectively nullifying this trip.

While descending the cyclepath's moderate grade from the saddle through sagebrush, we're soon treated to beguiling glimpses of Peppermint Creek plunging more than 100 feet from a sheaf of exfoliating granodiorite. Our path presently levels, skirting numerous large creekside campsites while crossing part of a Jeffrey-pine-sheltered flat. Eventually we branch east on a narrower path, **Durrwood Camp Trail 32E44** (4910/0.7), and finish crossing the flat. (The Bean Camp Cyclepath veers south here and fords Peppermint Creek in ¼ mile, where any hikers who missed the turnoff usually realize their mistake.)

Our path, meanwhile, veers southeast a few yards from the fork, then rolls amid chaparral-cloaked knolls and shortly thereafter slants down a mild gradient while Peppermint Creek, some 250 feet downslope, swirls over polished granodiorite, pooling and cascading. Presently we switchback down onto iron-rich (and hence rust-stained) interlayered sandstone, mudstone and tuff.

Then our course meets a use trail of breakneck steepness which leads southeast down a divide to visible flats at the confluence of Peppermint Creek and the Kern River.

Our path beyond the use trail rounds the divide and enters the shade of live oak, Kellogg oak and silk tassel. After ¼ mile of gentle northward descent, the trail drops in a steep ravine, making 9 tight zigzags, each firmly buttressed with mortarless masonry. The path then fades away upon reaching the Kern River floodplain (4260/1.3) several dozen yards from the river. A loamy, oak-sheltered channel runs north and south from this point, offering an assortment of campsites.

The ruins of Durrwood Camp, a resort built by Bill Calkins during the 1920's, stand ⅓ mile upstream by the river's east bank. According to historian Bob Powers, Calkins built the Bean Camp Cyclepath and Durrwood Camp Trail, plus a bridge spanning the river, in the same year he erected the camp. When the river flooded in 1966, ripping out the bridge and a resort cabin, these events plus already declining tourism forced the camp's owners to abandon it. A solitary prospector occupied a camp cabin in the early 1980's. A cable car spanning the Kern was built at his behest. It is similar to the one pictured on page 100, which is now a part of river memorabilia.

Eventually we retrace our steps to our own cars.

T34   The Needles Bicycle Tour

Beyond linking increasingly more impressive displays of erosion, and in addition to demonstrating how not to build a road, this trip exposes in curious juxtaposition the easternmost grove of Sierra sequoias, a precipitous gorge, and some towering, Whitney-like pinnacles.

Season   May through November

Distance   15.4 miles (24.8 km) round trip

Steep Upgrade   none

Elevation Gain and Loss   680 feet (207 m)

Exertion/Duration   easy/1 day

Gears   3-speed conventional to 15-speed alpine

Permits   none

Roadhead/Maps   R31/M25, M32

Canteens   1 quart

Description   Our jaunt begins in a rutted, ridge-mounted cul-de-sac at the unpaved end of **SNF Road 22S82** (5890/0.0) in the midst of ponderosa and Jeffrey pine, incense-cedar and black oak. A thick mat of pungent kit-kit-dizze borders the route where we coast an initial hundred yards, gaining pavement early. Hermits Dome, tapering skyward like a banana, appears profiled on the western horizon, flanked to the south by a closer, forested dome with exposed overhanging arches like those at Yosemite. The arches provide an outstanding display of exfoliation in action. Like most rock formations we'll see on this trip, the rock of this dome was crystallized nearly 90 million years ago from a huge mass of molten "recycled" rocks. Its crystals formed while it was still 5 miles deep under older rocks, and so the crystals were accustomed to a pressure nearly 2200 times that of the atmosphere. As erosion stripped away the overlying rock, the pressure on the granodiorite crystals decreased and they expanded. When this rock was finally exposed at the surface, layers like the layers of an onion developed and sloughed off by themselves. The repeated freezing and thawing of water seeping between the layers accelerated the sloughing until domes like the one before us were streamlined into likenesses of Hermits Dome.

Eager to reach the startling views of Hermits Dome ahead, we complete our first-stage stint by crossing signed Fish Creek Meadows Trail 32E12 (5840/.04) and Lloyd Meadows Creek in tandem. The trail's name is deceptive—Fish Creek Meadows was washed out more than 35 years ago. The current badlands where the meadows were illustrate more than the erosion accountable for so much of our trip's fascination, for—as field botanist James R. Shevock pointed out in 1977—these badlands reveal layers of peat, the remnants of at least 10 previous meadows buried in the gravels of earlier floods. These badlands impress one most with the instability of granitic soils, the naturally brief life of the beauty it nurtures, and the swiftness with which the Southern Sierra can change its appearance.

Nearly 100 yards beyond the creek crossing, one can catch the first unobstructed vista of Castle Rock in the northeast. This fissured granitic tower is one of few granitic outcrops near Lloyd Meadows to have been shaped solely through ice wedging. Then we bear down on our pedals briefly to cross a low ridge parallel to the creek, and are rewarded with a glimpse of The Needles Lookout shining in the south next to some tantilizing tips of The Needles themselves. The frontal view of that spectacular formation will be the ultimate reward for our journey today.

Now freewheeling down from the ridge, we quickly scoot past the signed terminus of Lloyd Creek Trail 32E19 (5850/0.4), then zip through the signed exit of southeast-trending dirt SNF Road 20S67 (5700/0.6). It leads toward Lloyd Meadows and an adjacent outlier of the Little Kern Basalt Flow. (See Trip 35 for the flow's origin and subsequent history.)

Road 22S82 displays the better pavement and rolls southward from the junction, soon linking SNF Roads 22S82A, B and C, logging spurs all. A, the only spur starting southeast, gives access to Ten Minute Meadow—the haunt of nature-study groups from nearby R.M. Pyles Boys Camp (see Trip 35 for details). Just beyond that spur, we trundle across signed "Freeman Creek Trail" 33E20 (5620/0.8) and the adjacent hummocky, willow-packed flood plain of Freeman Creek.

The easternmost sequoias in the Sierra are situated not far to the south in the 1700-acre Freeman Creek Grove, in the opinion of local naturalist Larry Norris the most impressive grove of big trees on the Western Divide. He attributes this unique grove to the funneling of Pacific storms through the gap between Slate Mountain and Jordan Peak. The masses of snow deposited here soak north-facing slopes of the tall, jutting ridge crowned by The Needles (hidden from here), in prolonged doses, attacking the underlying granodiorite to deepen the already rich soil (Trip 88 tells how). Sequoias, said Norris, thrive under these conditions. Close-up views of the Freeman Grove sequoias are easily reached by hiking cross-country south from the junction of SNF Road 20S66 (ahead), by strolling 1.3 miles west on the Freeman Creek Trail, or by taking Trip 42 from near Quaking Aspen.

Next, our road skirts a cluster of large, creekside campsites, leads along a rustic-fenced outpost of the Robertsons' "P.A.C." (pack) Station, headquartered high to the west by the headwaters of this drainage. Shortly we cross a branch of Freeman Creek, then catch a glimpse of the Flat Fire scar to the east before cutting through a granite bulge and getting a close-up look at subsurface exfoliation. Breathtaking views of Hermits Dome, in the northwest, are available here in an orienting panorama that displays Castle Rock on the ridge between Hermits and Dual domes. On the far side of this bulge, we pedal past north-trending Road 20S66 (5680/0.9), the signed entrance to R.M. Pyles Boys Camp—not a public campground.

A brief jaunt beyond brings us across another Freeman Creek branch to a stained-plywood USFS Entrance Station (5700/0.6), where permits may be obtained for entering Golden Trout Wilderness to the north. The panorama (which here includes the Great Western Divide) dwindles while we work quickly up some easy grades beyond the station, then becomes suddenly striking again where our road cuts through a divide overlooking the Kern River gorge. Customary plant associations and life zones are telescoped here. Drought-tolerant piñon and digger pine and mountain mahogany thrive on the rim of this gorge—little over a mile from sequoia and red fir, which need a heavy snowpack each year to survive. A signed segment of the Kern Flat Trail ends here at the divide (5740/0.8).

Now our road crosses extremely steep slopes while approaching, then rounding Voodoo Dome at the eastern extremity of The Needles. According to local wrangler Bruce Cates, the ledge for this segment of road was blasted, then bulldozed from sheer granodiorite during the Summer of 1969. Historian Ardis Walker said that the road was extended north through this segment from Johnsondale to give loggers there access to Lloyd Meadows basin timber sales before the advent of Environmental Impact Reports and public scrutiny of USFS engineering proposals. This road segment gives ample evidence of the need for such public review, for it demonstrates not only how not to build a road but also how man has increased erosion, careless of the consequences.

Among the reasons why roads can increase erosion disclosed by USFS hydrologist Walter F. Megahan in 1977, those exhibited here include stripping away the plants that held the soil in place, creating slopes too steep and too loose to allow future plants a

foothold, failing to bridge an avalanche chute, and funneling sheets of storm and snowmelt runoff into destructive freshets along the road. Since Megahan was generalizing and not writing of this road in particular, he failed to mention that surface rocks of The Needles ridge were already being shed through exfoliation (explained earlier) and ice wedging (explained later). Loosened more by the road's construction, these masses of rock crash onto the road each winter, justifying the inference that this road is among the most expensive to maintain in Sequoia National Forest. Erosion here also sends silt and debris down the Kern River to Lake Isabella, making it smaller until the muck is dredged out again at great taxpayer expense.

Bearing in mind that this road segment could be closed soon by landslides or taxpayer revolts, we savor its spectacular setting while dodging its pits and rocks. Soon after we leave the end of the Kern Flat Trail, cascades in Freeman Creek's cream-colored spillway, chunky postpiles and massive bluffs in the dissected, mauve Little Kern Basalt Flow, and a blue-green sash marking the rumbling Kern River appear in the east. Midway along this trail segment we cross the avalanche chute—where snow sometimes lingers until early May—and eventually reach the segment's end where the road curves west out of the Kern River gorge. Outlying layers of Little Kern basalt displaying stages in the flow's history are visible in the south, along with the long, rolling defile marking the Kern Canyon Fault.

Now our course contours into the recess of Needlerock Creek, crossing en route a cattle guard by a large southern viewpoint turnout. Oaks predominate here on the southern flank of The Needles ridge, and occasionally shade us while we approach a rock-climbers path (5550/2.9) starting northwest through kit-kit-dizze. Our road proceeds to pierce a pocket of incense-cedar, white fir and alder, quickly leads past a large, downslope creekside campsite and then crosses usually signed "Needlerock Creek."

At a turnout (5530/0.3) just beyond the creek we start to double back, but pause when struck by the just-revealed northern horizon. There stand The Needles, a row of sheer, towering spires and massive domes; and a tribute to the power of ice wedging, explained by geologist Jeffrey P. Schaffer in 1974. When The Needles' granodiorite cooled, it contracted along widespread vertical cracks that geologists call "master joints." By the time erosion had stripped overlying rock and debris from this granodiorite, soil acids borne by percolating water had attacked the rock along each joint, cleaving it deeply into a number of domes that would exfoliate independently. The water that seeped behind flakes and through cracks of the south-facing slopes froze nightly, expanding with the force of 1000 pounds per square inch, and then thawed the next day, peeling The Needles to smooth spires. Each thaw and each storm flushed more shattered rock

from the sheer facade, revealing the formation that moved Fred Beckey, an internationally eminent climber, to write in 1974: "here is startling, exciting rock-climbing terrain on a scale suited to individual rather than institutional ventures, an opportunity to gain self-knowledge in solitude." (Beckey's leads are impossible for all but the most practiced climbers to follow, and those who would emulate him should develop their skills step-by-step on easier rocks than The Needles.) Now fortified with some knowledge of the process, problems and products of erosion, we backtrack to our cars at the end of Road 22S82.

T35   Kern Flat Backpack

Spectacular gorges worn in granitic masses, flanked by palisades and postpiles of volcanic basalt, contain frenzied rivers and lush riverside meadows along this near-loop of paths. Despite the devastation wrought en route by the 1975 Flat Fire, the surviving scenery is such that this trip is still among the most popular circuits in the Golden Trout Wilderness. Try it during spring or fall to catch the scenery at its best and the weather at its balmiest.

Season   April through November

Distance   20.4 miles (32.8 km) shuttle trip

Steep Upgrade   none

Elevation Gain and Loss   +3320 feet (+1012 m) and −3380 feet (−1030 m)

Exertion/Duration   easy/4 days, moderate/ 2 days

Skills   easy route-finding, Class 1 climbing

Permits   Wilderness Permit

Roadheads/Maps   R30, R29/M32, M33

Description   A posted register box (please sign in) and a *"Fish Creek Meadows Trail 32E12"* sign by the north side of SNF Road 22S82 (5840/0.0) mark the beginning of our trail. At first we ascend the low-angle crest of

a small ridge along Lloyd Meadows Creek, a ridge that soon joins the steeper massif of the Little Kern/Freeman basin divide. We ascend the massif while the trailside ground-hugging web of kit-kit-dizze sporadically yields to Brewers oak and manzanita. Also during this climb, the trail is either deeply entrenched, shallow but broad, or split into multiple, independently weaving paths, all because it was once legally and heavily used by motorbikers. Such use was no longer permitted after 1978, when Congress drew the Golden Trout Wilderness boundary on the crest of the ridge we're ascending.

Our path's angle of ascent presently lessens and, a few minutes later, it levels upon reaching the ridgecrest in ponderosa-pine shade. Here we enter the Wilderness. The trail descends slightly for a few paces north from the crest, and then forks (6890/1.3) just shy of Jerkey Meadows. (The Fish Creek Meadows Trail leads straight ahead from the fork, almost instantly cutting through skimpy Jerkey Meadows, and then leads to Grey Meadow via an exhaustingly steep grade and the badlands of Fish Creek Meadows—see Trip 34.)

From the junction we take a northeast-trending *cutoff*, bypass the meadow, start dropping into a ravine and soon find our cutoff merging with **Lewis Camp Trail 33E01** (6840/0.2). This path leads briefly northeast, then forks where a sign (6700/0.5) directs now-outlawed cyclists north and hikers and horsemen northeast. Here the ravine we just descended flares and almost levels.

While climbers bound for Castle Rock start east on a trail-less wildroute (see Trip 36), we descend either the Lewis Camp Trail or Bypass #1. Both skirt manzanita patches and penetrate semidense woods, but the short northern path offers the more gradual descent before the paths reunite (6300/0.4) just short of languid Jug Spring. This signed seep issues from the base of a boulder that flanks our trail's northern edge, and supplies sometimes tepid water to patrons of a close-at-hand camping zone.

A few minutes' stroll beyond the spring brings us to the signed beginning of initially north-trending Grey Meadow Trail 32E15 (6160/0.4). The first few hundred yards of this path were once part of another Lewis Camp Trail motorbike bypass (Bypass #2), which now affords the hiker an alternate route to the Little Kern River bridge ahead. Our path leads northeast from the fork onto a mauve outlier of the Little Kern Basalt Flow. Arising from the earth's inner crust via vents near present-day Burnt Corral Meadows, this melted portion of crust filled ancestral Kern River watershed canyons for more than 18 miles—sometimes to depths nearing 800 feet. Solidification throughout this basalt flow was very fast, and it formed some vertical, 6-sided columns like those far to the north at Devils Postpile. The Little Kern postpiles are especially evident along the ascent from Forks of the Kern to Lloyd Meadows basin, toward the end of this trip. Their basalt was tested by geologist G. B. Dalrymple in 1963, and found to be nearly 3.5 million years old.

Minutes after leaving the Grey Meadow Trail, we on the Lewis Camp Trail pass a small campsite atop a basalt knob and then descend diagonally into the incipient Little Kern gorge. Soon we move to soils derived from granodiorite which, like the basalt, was once molten rock. Unlike the basalt, however, the molten granodiorite failed to surface, and instead cooled deep within the earth, close to 85 million years before the basalt solidified.

Presently we join the alternate trail and switchback down to a suspension bridge spanning the Little Kern River. Ken Fox, who was the local District Ranger in 1955, recalled in 1978 that the original suspension bridge (100 yards downstream from the replacement span we use today) was cut and mangled late that year when a warm tropical storm melted the snowpack, swelling the Little Kern to 100 times its average volume.

An assortment of campsites are situated by the shores visible from the bridge, which sways underfoot. Once we leave the span's northern abutment, our path quickly leads into a tributary canyon, then leaves it via a moderate upgrade. Soon we start treading dusty volcanic soils through sparse Jeffrey pines and then round a declivitous ridge, spying parts of the downstream chasm through which the Little Kern River flows.

Willow Meadows Cutoff 33E14 (5990/1.5) then branches north by a treed sign, affording Trip 44 backpackers who are unwilling to climb to Hockett Meadows a shortcut that could save several miles and many feet of gain. Lewis Camp Trail leads southeast from the junction, ascending gradually now, and on it we shortly swing into, then cross, a gulch containing a large campsite and a transitory stream. From there our mildly rolling course leads a mile southeast, allowing views of the cross-sectioning slice that the Trout Meadows stream made in the basalt-capped granodiorite. Trout Meadows itself soon appears in the southern foreground and our path arcs along it. Then, where the Lewis Camp Trail starts north toward a guard station 0.6 mile away, we branch south onto **Deadman Wildroute 33E11** (6100/1.8), incorrectly signed "33E10."

Initially a path, this route spans the meadow's soggy southern extremity via a rickety corduroy bridge, then turns southeast, joining a lateral from a private cabin. A painterly scene appears in the north which includes the terminal peak of the Great Western Divide, Angora Mountain.

Beyond the meadow, we ramble no more than 20 minutes through conifers, then leave the track of the Deadman Wildroute (6330/0.6) where it bends abruptly southeast. Our course uses a northeast-trending **connector,** which quickly desposits us on a switchback of *Doe Meadow Trail 33E10* (6350/0.1). Here we part company with takers of Trip 44 and follow this meandering trail eastward. We shortly traverse a field of mountain dandelions ringed by Jeffrey and ponderosa pines, and then step across a seasonal stream that drains a flank of Hockett Peak.

A mass of dark gray gabbro underlies much of that peak in addition to some of the Trout Meadows defile and the next 1.5 miles of the Doe Meadow Trail. The course then undulates mildly in the shade of Jeffrey pines interspersed with manzanita, and in time joins signed but indistinct Cold Spring Cutoff 33E12 (6560/1.2) near the head of a short-grass meadow. Delicious pipe-delivered water fills a trough at Cold Spring, a few yards east of the junction—our last source of water (when snowmelt is gone) for the next 3.7 miles. Although campsites abound near the spring, the one most favored is situated south of the trail a few dozen yards east of the spring.

Now our path inclines briefly up to cross a divide through a swale (6760/0.4) that was scorched in the Flat Fire of 1975. A forest of mixed conifers once welcomed travelers here, but now that forest is decimated and naturally lagging behind brush in making its recovery. Switchbacks and some long side-slope traverses now ease our protracted descent in the drainage of a transitory stream toward Kern Flat, and multiple crossings of that stream give ample opportunity to slake any early-summer thirst. We eventually reach a long-legged triangle junction with *Kern Flat Trail 33E20* (5120/3.2) and pause to choose from the options available.

*   *   *   *   *

The northeast leg can be quickly descended to join the main trail (5000/0.1) near the north end of the Kern Flat meadow. The northbound path leads past an assortment of riverside campsites, then fords intermittent Hockett Peak Creek and meets a trans-Kern River lateral (5050/1.0) to Sacratone Flat Trail 33E50. The bridge here affords the only safe crossing of the river in Golden Trout Wilderness.

North of the lateral, the Kern Flat Trail soon exits the Flat Fire scar, reaching more campsites on ponderosa-pine-shaded terraces alongside the river. It presently ends (5180/1.5) near where trailblazer John Jordan drowned, attempting to ford the river in 1862 (see Trip 50.)

The lateral itself leads east from the Kern Flat Trail, then bridges the river and quickly joins the Sacratone Trail (5050/0.2). Backpackers can head northeast on this undulating trail and, quickly leaving the Flat Fire swath, ramble through black oak, white fir and incense-cedar, cross Manzanita Canyon creek in time and eventually latch onto Jordan Hot Springs Trail 34E19 (5440/2.3), the route of Trip 83 in this book's companion volume.

The alternative at the bridge-linkage junction is to start southwest on the Sacratone Trail, making a long riverside journey relieved by midway views of grassy Kern Flat. That journey ends not far beyond an Osa Creek ford at a junction with Lion Trail 33E21 (5020/2.6), also described in *Self-Propelled in the Southern Sierra, Volume One,* but this time as Trip 75.

*   *   *   *   *

Travelers who lack time to explore the terrain surrounding Kern Flat usually descend the southeast leg of the triangle junction and then turn south onto the **Kern Flat Trail** (5000/0.1). Here we touch the edge of Kern Flat's grassy expanse, but leave it quite soon while stepping across the stream we often forded on the last segment of the Doe Meadow Trail. Some 15 minutes beyond that ford, the nearby river swings around a rib of resistant quartz diorite and the canyon narrows. Our path climbs slightly to cross the rib and then parallels riverbank wattles of willow interwoven with wild rose. (Riverside campsites will appear at the rate of at least one every ½ mile until we reach Forks of the Kern.)

Nearly a mile past the rib, the canyon flares somewhat to admit Osa and Soda creeks, which tumble in from the east. Our path rises slightly in passing the Osa Creek confluence and overlooks the site of a riverside shelter used by the R.M. Pyles Boys Camp until 1977, when the camp staff dismantled it. The shelter was the first structure built after Pyles and fellow oilmen established this camp in 1949 for boys in need of guidance, said camp packer Bruce Cates, interviewed in 1978.

A moment's jaunt beyond the site brings us to a "soda spring" sign that points to the Soda Creek-Kern River confluence, and then we saunter along the river past trailside niches emblazoned now and then with California coneflowers and other wildflowers. At length our course fords a murky but transitory dribble of water issuing from Deadman Canyon—a dribble signed "Lower Deadman Spring." Shortly thereafter, a trace of Deadman Wildroute 33E11 (4950/3.0) departs west, giving orienteering specialists equipped with maps and compasses access to the Flatiron.

Backpackers contour away from the river beyond the junction in the midst of a Kellogg-oak grove, soon bearing west. Then they gain a southward view of Rattlesnake Creek spilling from an impressive granodiorite gorge to join the river. The California Highway Commission envisioned proposed trans-Sierra State Highway 190 bridging the river here, and adopted this route in 1966. Subsequent austere construction budgets and looming energy shortages caused California Department of Transportation spokesmen to express doubt in 1974 that the highway would ever be built.

Now our path switchbacks down toward the river before cutting briefly across dynamited granodiorite slabs. Then we return to soils derived from the darker quartz diorite and brush past riverside willows, presently passing a loop trail to dismantled Lower Pyles Camp.

Here the canyon leads into a zone of much lighter rock—granite mixed with quartz monzonite—but more than a mile downcanyon we reach an inclusion of reddish-brown schist and quartzite. A gauging station, slightly hidden from the trail, held one end of a cable arcing across the Kern River. By pulling hand-over-hand, one could in

1974 work across the river while riding a cable car, but now it exists only in Kern River annals.

Shortly after entering metamorphic rocks, our canyon joins the Little Kern River canyon at Forks of the Kern, where we pass a travertine spring and then a sandy, boulder-strewn floodplain. Our path then fords the swift Little Kern River, but most hikers will traipse upstream, seeking a wider, shallower channel to ford. In late spring, when snowmelt surges down this channel, most backpackers should be roped and belayed across it. Campsites abound amid piñon pines, Kellogg oaks and willows beyond the narrow Flat Fire scar at Forks of the Kern and are heavily used by fishermen. Here in September 1975 a campfire fanned by gusty winds roared out of control, spreading devastation as far as Kern Flat within

**Aerial self-propulsion
in the Southern Sierra—now gone**

hours and lingering for days afterward, becoming known as the Flat Fire.

Once we've crossed the river, passed most of the riverside campsites and regained the Kern Flat Trail, we meet North Rincon Trail 33E23 (4710/3.1) on a sand bar. It leads a few dozen paces south to a Kern River ford where a couple drowned on Memorial Day in 1974. Except when the river ebbs, usually in late summer, this ford should not be attempted.

Our path zigzags west from the Rincon Trail junction up through aprons of sedges watered by springs that issue along the Kern Canyon Fault. Quite soon we traverse ⅓ mile north past a few steep downslope laterals departing toward scattered riverside campsites. Spicy-scented kit-kit-dizze and violet-flowered brodaiea border our trail along this traverse before it switchbacks south into exposed chaparral. The landscape-determining influence of the Kern Canyon Fault is abundantly illustrated in views south from this ascent. Presently we round a declivitous ridge and leave Golden Trout Wilderness. The trail soon skirts seat-sized chunks of many-sided basaltic columns that rolled here from an impressive upslope postpile. Budding geologists will want to pause to examine the evidence for the basalt-flow processes explained earlier, while most everyone else will ogle the cleft into which the Kern River pours southward. Soon afterward, the path switchbacks toward the postpiles, then crosses basaltic soils just downslope from them and, after a time, gains the shelter of incense-cedars and Jeffrey pines. Shortly we enter the Freeman Creek watershed, passing through a swale, and then utilize a short length of retired logging road to reach dirt SNF Road 20S67 (5780/2.4), where we left our shuttle cars.

T36   Castle Rock Climb

Climbers drawn to the central Southern Sierra by the well-publicized awesomeness of The Needles but then repelled by the great popularity of The Needles will find that nearby Castle Rock, though it looks dowdy, actually has secluded, spectacular faces, a wealth of challenging routes for climbers of all capabilities and a fine summit panorama. That view is better than the one from The Needles because it extends across huge basins to the flamboyantly ragged horizons that embrace them.

Season   May through October

Distance   7.6 miles (12.2 km) round trip

Steep Upgrade   0.1 mile (0.2 km)

Elevation Gain and Loss   2280 feet (695 m)

Exertion/Duration   moderate/1 day

Skills   moderate route-finding, Class 3 climbing (Class 4–5 pitches optional)

Permit   none

Roadhead/Map   R30/M32

Description

Northwest-bound *Fish Creek Mdws Tr 32E12* Log

T35 SNF Road 22S82	5840	0.0
Jerkey Cutoff	6890	1.3

Northeast-bound *Jerkey Cutoff* Log

Trail 32E12	6890	0.0
Lewis Camp Trail 33E01	6840	0.2

Northeast-bound *Trail 33E01* Log

Jerkey Cutoff	6840	0.0
bypass trail	6700	0.5

We take the sign at the bypass trail junction as a cue to strike east, off-trail, beginning a segment of protracted gradual ascent on the **Castle Rock Wildroute**. Early in this segment we leave the flared ravine, and then we cut across slopes of duff and rotten granite in conifer forest, dodging patches of chinquapin and manzanita to which the forest sometimes gives way. Less then ⅓ of the way along this segment we cross a tiny, undependable brook. Later the segment is nearly ⅔ completed where it touches the broad arc of a saddle on the divide that we crossed earlier. The segment is completed after the route leads across northeast-facing slopes, skirting crest-straddling hill 7576, and regains the crest in a saddle.

Castle Rock is now apparent in the south-east, and it justifies its name. A short, steep length of crest now leads to a gap between a gendarme and one of Castle Rock's spectacular faces. A sheer chute that plummets southward from here along the rock's base makes our first view of that face a giddily breathtaking one. Class 5 climbers might want to start unloading equipment here, but those intent on the easiest route to the summit will skirt the north face and climb the blocky east face, where ramps are linked by pitches of Class 3–4 rock. Of the dual turrets of Castle Rock (7740/1.8) the northern one gets the more comprehensive panorama of the Little Kern basin, where the "Southern" and "High" Sierras meet, and the southern turret (the higher) seems the airier, perched as it is in confinement atop dizzying palisades. From here we backtrack to our cars.

Approaching Castle Rock on the rim of the Little Kern Basin

T37 Mule Peak Hike

An opportunity—with little prolonged effort—to attain an inspiring panorama and to observe a nerve center of fire-fighting operations make this lookout-topped peak a favorite of children of all ages. Serious climbers will also be attracted here by the exclusive cliffs and pinnacles on the southwest face of the peak.

Season   June through October

Distance   1.2 miles (1.9 km) round trip

Steep Upgrade   none

Elevation Gain and Loss   460 feet (140 m)

Exertion/Duration   easy/1 day

Skills   easy route-finding, Class 1 climbing (Class 4 and 5 pitches optional)

Permits   none

Roadhead/Maps   R32/M19, M20

Canteen   1 quart

Description   Our excursion begins in a lot (7680/0.0) where a spur of SNF Road 22S03S ends. *Mule Peak Trail 31E43* leads west from the lot up a moderate-to-steep grade across a large patch of stumps. Panting as we climb it, we soon cross a ravine, turn southwest, and enter an untouched stand of red fir and lodgepole pine. After a few minutes our path attains the crest of the Western Divide, then zigzags up it, and finally meanders north across the flat top of buttelike Mule Peak to the summit lookout (8142/0.6). The lookout is unusually squat, but the panorama from there is breathtaking. While rock climbers can find some Class 4–5 rock to interest them about 250 yards southwest of the lookout, almost everyone else will backtrack directly to the cars.

T38

Dome Rock Climb

Easy access, an orienting panorama and a broad, firm footing make Dome Rock a satisfying destination for newcomers to hiking and climbing in the south-central Sierra Nevada. Although Dome Rock's optional technical slabs are too steep for beginning climbers, people who have climbed some low class 5 routes will find these slabs a romp.

Season May through October (avoid holiday weekends)

Distance 0.2 mile (0.3 km) round trip

Steep Upgrade none

Elevation Gain and Loss 60 feet (24 m)

Exertion/Duration easy/1 day

Skills easy route-finding, Class 1 climbing (Class 3–5 pitches optional)

Permits none

Roadhead/Map R34/M24

Description Although our *path,* a retired section of road, starts east from the end of SNF Road 21S69 (7160/0.0) amid red firs, serious rock climbers will start northeast or southwest instead. While they descend, curving around the dome to its base, we ascend the path's short, moderate grade and arc south into the clearing atop Dome Rock (7221/0.1). This great bulge of granodiorite overlooks a broad basin slashed by multiple canyons, and offers dramatic views of The Needles and the eastern scarp of the Kern Plateau. Although the slope around Dome Rock's summit is gradual, it quickly bends down out of sight toward cracks and ledges where roped climbers have forged routes, partly with their hardware and rock-gripping boots but mostly with strength and nerve. Please don't roll rocks or trash off the dome—let the climbers live!

When our time runs out, we backtrack to our cars.

The Needles add interest to the Dome Rock panorama

T39   Western Divide Bicycle Tour

This Western Divide sampler for the aspiring naturalist-bicyclist leads from the divide's middle crest to its southern terminus. It starts on a high plateau amid sleek meadows, symmetrical red firs and autumn-crimsoning, quaking aspens. Beyond the plateau, this trip intercepts a panorama establishing the scenic supremacy of Dome Rock and The Needles while crossing steep, cascade-dissected quartzite and schist inlaid in granodiorite. Bicyclists here in autumn are next treated to vivid green forests flecked with the scarlet of oaks and barred with the orangish-barked shanks of sequoias.

This prodigious visual diversity complements the lengthy alternating mild ascents and breezy coasts that make up for the occasional risk posed by speeding motor vehicles during holidays and some weekends. The pavement is wide, its blind curves are few, and Forest Service landscaping makes its cuts and fills, the abundance of campsites and campgrounds along it, and the ongoing logging near it seem to blend in with nature. Greater convenience for bicyclists is conferred by the local profusion of water sources (carry purification tablets); by the store and cafe near the trip's start; and by the ride's moderate access drive (less than 4 hours from Los Angeles).

Season   June through October

Distance   30.6 miles (49.2 km) round trip

Steep Upgrade   none

Elevation Gain and Loss   2440 feet (744 m)

Exertion/Duration   moderate/1 day, easy/2 days

Gears   5-speed conventional through 15-speed alpine

Permits   USFS Campfire Permit for overnight riders only

Roadhead/Maps   R35/M19–M20, M24

Description   Our ride begins on the centerline-dashed pavement of *TC Road MTN 107* where it cuts through the Western Divide (7220/0.0), 0.7 mile south of Quaking Aspen Campground. Our southward course initially sweeps across the furrowed plateau drained by Peppermint Creek, encountering quaking aspen, red fir, white fir, and lodgepole and ponderosa pine. Very early in this traverse we zip through offset junctions with SNF Road 21S05, the main access route to The Needles, and SNF Road 21S78, which connects with the Summit Trail en route to a religious camp. Before the traverse is ⅓ complete, we meet a northeast-trending, paved subdivision backroad, TC Road MTN 180B (7190/0.4), then note a rough southeast-trending road (7180/0.2) to visible picnic tables, and soon afterward skirt Holby Meadow, crossing the creek that drains it. Our road then cuts through a slight rise and at once intersects SNF Road 21S79 (7190/0.4)—aimed southwest and signed for a Methodist camp—and TC Road MTN 168—the northeast-trending pavement that instantly flares to provide a lot for the Ponderosa resort. Here, a year-round store with gas pumps, a cafe, bar and rentable cabins blocks our view of the subdivision beyond. Aspens are absent along the second third of our plateau traverse, which quickly leads past a "snow not removed beyond this point" sign, presently touches east-trending SNF Road 21S06 (7120/0.5) and finally meets westbound SNF Road 21S09 (7130/0.4) just short of a Peppermint Creek crossing. Our last segment across the plateau ascends from the crossing, soon meets eastbound SNF Road 21S07 (7090/0.3)—which leads to Peppermint Campground—and later meets westbound pavement of SNF Road 21S21 (7200/0.7), which leads to an USFS heliport and fire-crew barracks.

You'll notice many young incense-cedars, ponderosa pines and sugar pines planted in cuts and fills by the road. Besides beautifying and stabilizing the immediate earthwork, the trees screen fresh scars of ongoing logging in the foreground from motorized passersby.

Our road crosses one such planted embankment in getting across a ravine from the heliport junction to the exit of eastbound SNF Road 21S69 (7200/0.1). Some cyclists with clincher tires may want to ride this route—others will prefer to walk their bikes along it—to catch a breathtaking panorama from atop Dome Rock (Trip 38). Hidden climbers may be inching up the face of this rock when you arrive, so for their sake please don't throw anything.

Beyond the Dome Rock junction, we pass through a cut and start a long but swift coast toward Redwood Meadow. Our speed and need to watch the road for cars and fallen rocks limit our recognition of the roadside ground cover to manzanita and bitterbrush on exposed slopes and kit-kit-dizze in the shade. Moments after starting to coast, we freewheel around a "Dome Creek" signed canyon, and then, less than five minutes later, we round a bend into Horse Canyon, where the contact between iron-stained quartzite and once-molten invading granodiorite is prominently displayed. The falling-rock hazard is most acute in a huge roadcut just beyond the canyon's cascading brook.

Much of Kern Canyon, the Kern Plateau rim and the Greenhorn Mountains are evident as we continue coasting southward. Kellogg oaks that turn scarlet during the first fall frosts shortly appear amid the prevalent bright green of ponderosa pine and straggly incense-cedar and Jeffrey pine in the immediate roadside scenery. Dome Rock, with The Needles behind it, soon figures in northeastward views that compel most cyclists to pause. Presently, patches of mountain alder at crossings of signed, sometimes-dry Ice and Middle creeks herald our crossing of Alder Creek, which disappears only during severe droughts.

Minutes beyond the creek, we touch the start of a southeast-trending logging road, which provides entry to a large assortment of campsites plus an alternate approach for independent climbers bound for Sentinel Peak. Then in a brief hiatus from

downgrades, our road nearly levels, meets westbound SNF Road 22S03N (6320/4.7) in a dense stand of Jeffrey pines and then crosses the pine-obscured groove of Nobe Young Creek. Shortly thereafter, we pass through a gap, enter the Bone Creek watershed and coast a few minutes to a signed junction with eastbound SNF Road 22S02 (5980/1.3), part of a shortcut to Johnsondale.

A gradual upgrade begins at the junction, and pedalling up it we shortly observe the northward departure of SNF Road 22S03S (6020/0.8). Cyclists subsequently cross the willow-and-alder-packed canyon of Bone Creek and finally pass among banks of snow bush to crest another drainage divide at a broad saddle. The ensuing pleasant descent lasts less than 10 minutes and passes an eastbound exit to Long Meadow Campground, SNF Road 22S08 (6100/1.5), in half the time. Our road's descent ends quite close to Redwood Meadow Campground, reached via southbound SNF Road 22S09 (6100/0.6). Not far along the straightaway past the campground, the first roadside giant sequoias appear. Mixed with white fir and incense-cedar, these redwoods are the only ones of which our route offers close-up views.

Now we bump across a cattleguard in the road, transfer to the next watershed via mild undulations, meet northwest-bound SNF Road 23S18 (6230/1.7) and almost instantly scoot across signed "Parker Meadow Creek" on a high embankment. Then a few old logging roads leave our road's east shoulder for nearby campsite clusters and, directly afterward, SNF Road 23S06 (6250/0.3) leaves the west shoulder bound—as advertised—for Holey Meadow Campground. A short, stiff ascent from the foot of Holey Meadow gets us through a breached ridge to a signed intersection with paved **TC Road MTN 50** (6380/0.5). The 100 yards of county road extending south from this junction indicate that (as Russ Leadabrand reported in his out-of-print 1968 guidebook) county and forest engineers had planned to extend high-speed Road MTN 107 south on the crest of the Greenhorn Mountains to Bakersfield. Current economic inflation and energy shortages have presumably caused this plan to be shelved, and now the stub of road serves as a repository of asphalt and gravel.

The last forward stage of our tour guides us westward from the junction along the pavement of MTN 50. After a brief initial ascent, we pass through a swale beside an old clearcut now packed with ponderosa pines. A nearby sign informs us that these pines were planted in 1963 under the auspices of the Forest Service's Penny Pines Program. Holey Meadow can be glimpsed in the northern foreground from here.

Soon our nearly-level road pierces the crest of the Greenhorn Mountains, passes a campsite-access road, overlooks foothills near California Hot Springs and finally meets northeast-bound SNF Road 22S04 (6420/1.0) atop Parker Pass. This gap links the Greenhorn Mountains, just to the east, with the Western Divide, just to the west, and offers a fitting double-back point for our Western Divide reconnaissance.

T40   Freezeout Meadow Backpack

This journey's contrasts of logged and natural forests and mountains intensify hikers' appreciation of environments in which man is a visitor, not a meddler. Meddlers have created this trip's starting and ending close-up views of stump-packed tracts, and in-between middle-ground scenes strewn with patchcuts that manifest much of the logging history of the Western Divide. These sights contrast starkly with Slate Mountain's unspoiled red-fir forest, its dells, its cliffs, its meadows, its Southern-Sierra-encompassing views, its outlook on supremely distinctive Mount Whitney and Farewell Gap, allowing Slate Mountain's insulation from most of the man-made chaos at large to work its spell on backpackers.

Season   June through October

Distance   11.5 miles (18.5 km) shuttle trip

Steep Upgrade   0.1 mile (0.2 km)

Elevation Gain and Loss   2240 feet (683 m)

Exertion/Duration   easy/2 days

Skills   easy route-finding, Class 1 climbing (Class 3–5 pitches optional)

Permits   USFS Campfire Permit

Roadheads/Maps   R33, R36/M20, M23B, M24

Description   Leaving our cars at the northernmost turnout along *SNF Road 21S78* (7160/0.0), we saunter more than 100 yards southwest along the road to get this trip underway. Then we fork south by a sign onto *Summit Trail 31E14* (7160/0.1), which initially rises along a ravine in selectively logged red-fir forest, then briefly levels upon gaining the crest of the Western Divide by a slender meadow. Beyond the meadow, our path cuts across strips of chainsaw-cleared land, intersects grooves dug by trees being dragged to mill-bound trucks, and also

meets several roads on which the loaded trucks left for the mill.

We presently leave the inconspicuous divide and angle upslope, and most of us exit the logging zone less than 45 minutes into our trip. Now our path switchbacks up past a spring bordered with fern and thimbleberry, gaining 680 feet to a swale with a large, waterless campsite. A granitic knob stands just east of the swale, offering short, puzzling pitches to climbers testing techniques and tools.

Soon acquiring borders of pinemat manzanita, the path rises on a moderate gradient through a ponderosa-pine grove and after a while touches a cairned saddle on the Western Divide. Here we have the option of leaving the trail and tracing the undulant ridgecrest nearly ½ mile northwest. Yokut Spire, a spectacular tooth of volcanic schist with an engaging panorama of a Tule River fork's canyon is the lure for this excursion. Climbers forcing their way up the tooth's technical face will find little need for rappelling because the tooth has a back side that almost anyone can walk up.

Back at the saddle, we resume our ascent of the trail, taking our first steps on soils derived from the quartzite and schist which make up the bulk of Slate Mountain. While we ascend west along the ridge, soon tackling a steep grade, western white pine replaces ponderosa pine amid the predominant red fir. By and by, our path contours for nearly ½ mile, veering southwest from the divide across slopes where snowdrifts usually remain well into July.

Next we meet northwest-trending Bear Creek Wildroute 31E31 (9050/4.0—see Trip 53) atop a ridge separating the South Fork and Middle Fork Tule River watersheds. The junction offers yet another optional side excursion, this one an 0.3-mile clamber east up blocky, disheveled slate to the panorama-commanding apex of Slate Mountain (9302′).

The Summit Trail south of the junction slants briefly down across headwaters slopes in the South Fork Tule River watershed, then starts a lengthy stretch of tracing the crest of the Western Divide. We presently rise somewhat to mount hill 9054 and enter the sprawling Summit Allotment, whose boundary we've been following since meeting the Bear Creek Wildroute. For quite some time now, cowhands of the John Guthrie Estate have transfered more than 400 head of cattle early each July north to this spread from the Lion Allotment, and have rounded them up by mid-September each year.

Hill 9054's steep south flank soon leads us onto a mildly undulant segment of crest. Early in our stroll along this segment, we branch northeast onto a *trace* (8640/1.5) that leads in a few minutes' descent to Freezeout Meadow (8500/0.1). In his 1924 inquiry into the origin of Sierra place names, Francis P. Farquhar speculated that "freezeout," a gold-rush miners' card game in which a player drops out when bankrupt, might have lent its name to this meadow. The meadow-side campsite's appeal diminishes in late summer when the brook alongside it dries up.

After backtracking to the *Summit Trail* (8640/0.1), we saunter south at length along the rest of its mildly undulating segment and then fork southeast on a dim **path** (8520/0.9), continuing on the ridgecrest. Tracing this path, we soon meet an abandoned east-trending spur (8540/0.1) that fades out in downslope logging plots. Meanwhile, our path soon veers southwest, then ends a few hundred paces from a colorfully rocky point (8704/0.4) labelled "VABM Wes" on the topo.

A series of large patchcuts extends from this point's intermediate slopes south to a bowl where plumes of smoke marked the now deserted lumber-mill town of Johnsondale. Why were loggers allowed to cut so much here? Why does the logged slope to the west-southwest, seen through Windy Gap, look devastated even from 2 miles away? For some of the answers we turn to an article in the May 27, 1940, *Bakersfield Californian,* in which then-Forest Supervisor Joe Elliott told of the exchange that was mostly responsible for what we see here. In 1886, said Elliott, John P. Fleitz, a Michigan lumberman, acquired a scattering of parcels—including many sequoia groves—extending from Double Bunk Meadow (southwest of our viewpoint) to Camp Nelson and Lloyd Meadows (hidden north of here). Elliot, presumably spurred by the devastation wreaked by loggers on sequoias to the northwest (details in Trip 91), secured the Fleitz sequoias' protection in 1935 by adding Fleitz land to Sequoia National Forest in exchange for the right to cut local commercial timber intensely. A forerunner of American Forest Products, now part of the conglomerate Bendix Corporation, was engaged to cut the exchanged timber, and has since fed its Johnsondale mill with logs from the southwestern Kern Plateau, the Piute and Greenhorn Mountains and the Western Divide, as sheaves of USFS contracts attest. While mulling over this information, we backtrack to the **Summit Trail** (8520/0.5).

Beyond the junction this trail switchbacks west down the flank of Slate Mountain, alternately in the midst of manzanita and of mixed conifers. After losing 900 feet of elevation, we skirt a woods-sheltered medium campsite, then stroll some 100 yards farther and ford a bouncing snowmelt brook. The gully in which the brook cascades offers the last exposure of metamorphic rocks on this trip.

Shortly beyond the gully we contour into Windy Gap just upslope from the mauled earth of some clearcuts to the west. Here our path disappears under a Gap crossing logging road (7570/1.8). We can find our offset path by hiking 150 yards up the road's hairpin curve to where our trail, indicated by a tree blaze, continues. During this romp we pass the now obscure junction of Windy Gap Trail 31E42, trending southeast.

The Summit Trail continues southwest through the junction, starting a moderate ascent across southeast-facing slopes where scattered sugar pine, manzanita, chinquapin, snow bush, fern, blue lips, dwarf monkey flower and forget-me-not mingle engagingly. Then we regain the Western Divide and trace it several hundred yards southwest through mixed conifers. Our path then skirts part of emerald-green Onion Meadow,

afterward fades in the meadow's downslope flank and quite soon fords the ephemeral brook draining the meadow.

The trail regains its obviousness on the brook's southern bank, then drops briefly beside the brook to a willowy pocket glade. An ensuing rise takes us over a minor west-trending ridge where gooseberry, currant and pussypaws parade in the trailside patchwork of underbrush. A subsequent short stint of contouring leads to a final, sometimes steep descent. After fording an intermittent streamlet midway along the descent, we approach the end of our trip by dropping into a stumpy clearcut. There we meet SNF Road 22S03S (7680/2.0) close to our shuttle cars.

T41   Climbing The Needles

Despite its precarious appearance, The Needles Lookout has withstood pummeling winds, lightning strikes, and rock-splitting freeze and thaw for over 40 years. For visitors who can overlook the spindly appearance of its underpinnings, the clatter of its airy catwalks and the sheerness of the granodiorite that plummets from its heights, the lookout stands ready to compensate them with views of a rock-climber's paradise, a thumpingly good feeling of accomplishment and the thrill of facing beauty and danger simultaneously.

Season   June through October

Distance   3.8 miles (6.1 km) round trip

Steep Upgrade   0.1 mile (0.2 km)

Elevation Gain and Loss   800 feet (244m)

Exeration/Duration   easy/1 day

Skills   easy route-finding, Class 1 climbing (Class 5+ pitches optional)

Permits   none

Roadhead/Map   R37/M25

Canteen   1 quart

Description   Our brief hike begins by a trailhead sign at the end of SNF Road 21S05 (7730/0.0), just southeast of unreliable, sometimes signed "Needle Spring." (The sign indicating our path, **Needles Lookout Trail 33E22,** is now and then changed to read "*Needless* Lookout.") The path itself starts as a retired logging road, then narrows after a few hundred yards and ascends a

gentle grade around a pair of hills. Although red firs and some ponderosa pines shade most of this traverse, they sometimes thin out, permitting chinquapin to thrive in patches and offering vignettes of Hermits Dome in the north.

We presently start the last ¼ mile of rounding the hills by catching a view of the lookout ahead. Afterward our path switchbacks briefly down past kit-kit-dizze and scarlet penstemon to a saddle. Beyond the large, waterless campsite here, the popular path zigzags up sparsely treed, manzanita-clad slopes. The trail soon ends in a small, rocky cove that picnickers frequent on holiday weekends. (Rock climbers sometimes leave our route here and traverse north-facing slopes toward the eastern needles.)

A ladder leads up from the cove to a pinnacle, and from there a catwalk several hundred yards long bears us over a knife-edge ridge. One final ladder then completes our ascent of the highest rock in The Needles, and gets us to the lookout (8245/1.9).

While taking in the spectacular view, look southwest to see if Wizard Needle doesn't look like a huge gorilla, and Warlock Needle a bunch of bananas. The lookout's employees can point out these features for you, but please don't ask them for water—they have enough only for themselves. After signing the register at their home, we backtrack to our cars.

Sheer cliffs plummet on each side of this approach to The Needles Lookout

T42   Freeman Redwoods Backpack

This jaunt to the easternmost Sierra sequoias is ideal for families with young children. It proceeds parallel to a fascinating creek; it follows lines of least resistance when food is weighing down children's packs, and doesn't ask them to ascend until their packs are lighter, relieved of food, and they are homeward-bound. The campsites offer some privacy, and bears that raid backpacks for food at night have never been reported here. The trail that leads to the campsites is distinct; it mostly slants down gentle grades; and people who ought to know have described it as one of the best-maintained paths in Sequoia National Forest.

Season   June through October

Distance   4.4 miles (7.1 km) round trip

Steep Upgrade   none

Elevation Gain and Loss   1350 feet (411 m)

Exertion/Duration   easy/2 days

Skills   easy route-finding, Class 1 climbing

Permits   USFS Campfire Permit

Roadhead/Map   R38/M31

Description   This weekend adventure gets underway beside buildings and corrals of the Robertson's "P.A.C. [pack] Station," where SNF Road 21S99 (7190/0.0) ends in a parking lot. From the lot we stroll northeast on *Freeman Creek Trail 33E20,* descending a mild slope past shanks of Shasta red fir. The path leads quite soon to an elongated meadow along Freeman Creek, and then follows a wooded strip between the meadow and occasionally stumpy slopes. The rounded crowns of giant sequoias appear in the trees hedging the meadow—they're part of the 849-acre Freeman Creek Grove. (On the grove's far side stand the Sierra's easternmost sequoias.)

After somewhat more than ½ mile of walking, we reach a headwaters fork of Freeman Creek signed "Trail Crew Creek." Dogwood, hazelnut and fern, in descending order of height, deck the creek banks at this ford. Not far beyond the crossing, we saunter past semilogged stands of white fir and ponderosa pine and then cross a ridge while veering away from the creek.

Our path subsequently switchbacks down a ravine parallel to Freeman Creek, bordered here and there by kit-kit-dizze, manzanita and snow bush. Most of the switchbacks lead through shade where Kellogg oak

and sugar pine join the forest. Our downgrade soon shifts from moderate to slight, then nears the creek in the midst of impressive sequoias and skirts some large campsites. Later, the trail slants down another moderate grade past a few more memorable campsites (5840/2.2). (Other fine sites can be found to the south, away from the trail.) Mileage and elevation gain for the trail east of here are not included in the trip-heading totals.

      *   *   *   *   *

The trail beyond makes a pleasant spare-time excursion, and plants along it illustrate that most rain in the Freeman Creek basin falls on its south and east flanks. As we advance from the campsites, sequoias and ponderosa pines soon drop out of the forest, and Jeffrey pine becomes dominant. Then we cross a glassy, sand-floored brook from the west, and our course starts undulating slightly across the broad, warped floor of the basin. Just east of the ford, along Freeman Creek, hazelnut and dogwood give way to wild rose and willows—another sign of decreasing elevation and increasing dryness. Because the ensuing route makes for a dull, dusty ramble, most people turn back before reaching northeast-trending Lloyd Creek Trail 32E19 (5630/1.1) or, beyond it, paved SNF Road 22S82 (5610/0.2). Some energetic hikers have followed the trail beyond the road to a creek-isle soda spring east of Pyles Camp (see Trip 34). Eventually, from wherever they stopped, everyone backtracks to the cars.

T43   Hermits Dome Climb

The sheer 700-foot south face of Hermits Dome has shed onionlike layers, leaving the face inscribed with a rainbow outline that beckons the climber who's climbed everywhere. Fred Beckey is that kind of climber. He made the first recorded ascent of Hermits Dome in 1969 and afterward described the rock as "reminiscent of Yosemite's domes" and "one of the many surprises the Sierra still yields."

Season   July through October

Distance   1.8 miles (2.9 km) round trip

Steep Upgrade   0.4 mile (0.6 km)

Elevation Gain and Loss   840 feet (256 m)

Exertion/Duration   easy/1 day

Skills   moderate route-finding, Class 4 climbing (class 5 pitch optional)

Permits   none

Roadhead/Map   R39/M31

Description   Our *cross-country route* to the back side of Hermits Dome begins at the end of SNF Road 20S53 (7630/0.0) on a slight north-south ridge. It slants up a moderate, sometimes steep grade south from the parking lot through sparsely cut Shasta red fir and shortly veers southeast to trace a near-level section of ridge. The underbrush along this ½-mile section, and the subsequent moderate ascent, is easily avoided; and western white pine joins the conifer overstory where we turn southwest onto the crest of Fish Creek Ridge. Climbers bound for the challenging Class 5+ routes on the face of Hermits Dome should leave the main route here and gradually arc southwest, descending across southeast-facing slopes. To intercept the dome, they shouldn't lose more than 500 feet on this descent.

In the meantime, our route skirts brush and outcrops along the crest, and presently climbs to the granite slabs (some shattered, some intact) on the back side of the dome. Climber Jim Shevock reported in 1978 that the easiest route to the summit (8465/0.9) involved a short Class 4 pitch. (Beckey's route up the other side, the longer south face, involves Class 5 and Aid climbing.) The ascent's reward is the series of bolt-upright rocks in the summit panorama, from Yokut Spire in the southwest to The Needles in the southeast, Castle Rock in the east and the Great Western Divide in the north. There's plenty of inspiration for future climbs here.

Eventually we backtrack, making a short rappel en route to the cars.

Approaching an overhang

Pete Kirchner

T44   Two Rivers Backpack

The southernmost part of the Great Western Divide presents paradoxical sides. Its western flank appears rounded and horizontally striped, and the stripes distinguish the bright, rolling shoulders and crest from the darkly forested flanks and greater plain of a basin drained by the crooked Little Kern River. The divide's eastern side looks deeply dissected, patched with woods, and cut short by a deep, amazingly straight trench occupied by the Kern River, Kern Lake and Little Kern Lake. This exploration of the divide leads past an abundance of campsites and water sources that make the going easier. Nevertheless, those who take this trip must have extraordinary endurance and physical fitness, plus substantial river-fording and route-finding savvy.

Season   July through October

Distance   50.5 miles (81.3 km) shuttle trip

Steep Upgrade   0.5 mile (0.8 km)

Elevation Gain and Loss   10,270 feet (3130 m)

Exertion/Duration   easy/9 days, moderate/5 days, strenuous/4 days

Skills   easy route-finding, Class 1 climbing (Class 3–5 pitches optional)

Permits   Wilderness Permit

Roadheads/Maps   R39, R40/M31–M33, M47–M49, M41–M42

Description   *Lewis Camp Trail 33E01* starts west from SNF Road 20S53 (7630/0.0), then curves east to switchback down a gulch a while under mixed-conifer canopies. We then move onto the Fish Creek/Freeman Creek drainage divide, which slants down a short, steep pitch before rolling gently east. A scattering of thick manzanita and buckbrush patches abut the trail along this divide. After 0.2 mile of rolling going, we meet an extremely steep Fish Creek-bound stock driveway (7050/0.9). Jack Shannon's 200 cattle diverge from the Lewis Camp Trail here in mid-June, when they are usually herded into the 53,000-acre Little Kern Allotment. (We entered it at the roadhead.) The allotment's vast acreage would make one expect to see very few cows on this trip, but according to the USFS Little Kern Environmental Statement of 1977, only 2693 acres of brush, meadows and open timber (about 5% of the allotment) provide cattle with forage. Because quite a large part of this trip traverses such forage, we can expect to see quite a few cows until they are rounded up in mid-August.

Our undulating crestline traverse continues some minutes beyond the junction and then leaves the main ridge, crossing signed Fish Creek Meadows Trail 32E12 (6900/1.7) just north of Jerkey Meadows. Quite soon our path drops along the ravine draining the meadows, and shortly connects with the Jerkey Meadows Cutoff (6840/0.2), which comes in from the southwest.

Northeast-bound *Lewis Camp Trail 33E01* Log

T35	Jerkey Meadows Cutoff	6840	0.0
	bypass #1 (entrance)	6700	0.5
	bypass #1 (exit)	6300	0.4
	Grey Mdw Tr and		
	bypass #2 (entrance)	6160	0.4
	bypass #2 (exit)	5810	0.8
	suspension bridge	5780	0.1
	Willow Meadow		
	Cutoff 33E14	5990	0.6
	Deadman Trail 33E11	6100	1.8

Southeast-bound *Trail 33E11* Log

Lewis Camp Trail 33E01	6100	0.0
lateral and Deadman		
Wildroute 33E11	6330	0.6

Northeast-bound *lateral* Log

Deadman		
Wildroute 33E11	6330	0.0
Doe Meadow		
Trail 33E10	6350	0.1

Splitting from the ranks of Trip 35 takers, we pound the **Doe Meadow Trail** north from the junction, contouring under Jeffrey-pine cover. In minutes we turn east onto dim *Hockett Mountain Wildroute 33E06* (6320/0.1), which weaves through chest-high manzanita in the scar of an old burn. (Unless you are an excellent pathfinder, skip this wildroute loop and continue north to rejoin Lewis Camp Trail.)

Then we encounter a seasonal brook where the path disappears amid a profusion of monkey flowers, buttercups, lupine and clover. Turning north-northwest here, we skirt the brook and presently regain the trail where it wanders through sagebrush 30 yards west of the brook. After a while, our path leaves the burn scar, then leads across an ephemeral creeklet, passes a medium campsite in a Kellogg-oak grove and starts up a sometimes steep, north-trending ridge, leaving the Shannon range. The chess-piece parapet of Castle Rock can be glimpsed in over-the-shoulder views of the southwest horizon while we labor up the exposed, often hot ridge. The path presently turns north-northwest and descends slightly into a gully with sheltering Jeffrey pines, white firs and incense-cedars. The ensuing steep grade leads northwest, soon gaining a ridge that the path then ascends ½ mile on a north-northeast bearing.

Easy going resumes where we leave the ridge. The path initially drops slightly, then contours ⅓ mile across slopes of weathered rock (gabbro) to cross a semicircular ridge that culminates in Hockett Peak. A subsequent short descent through thick red firs (many blowdowns) leads to the isolated emerald expanse of Hockett Meadows. Our path skirts the meadow to an identifying sign at its north end, where a short lateral (7520/3.2) forks east to cross a sluggish, sometimes dry stream draining the meadow and reach a large campsite in the midst of mixed conifers.

Aiming northwest beyond the meadows, our trail undulates slightly for quite a while, passing northeast-oriented vignettes of the deep Kern River canyon. Then our course crosses a rounded ridge and zigzags steeply west, downslope, passing live oak and mountain juniper on its way into the Trout Meadows defile. The trail's surface deteriorates during this descent, becoming loose and gravelly in its final ¼ mile.

Then we turn north onto the **Lewis Camp Trail** (6480/1.7) and start a gradual ascent through the defile, tracing the Kern Canyon Fault (see Trip 35). In less than 25 minutes we saunter past a "Radio Spot"-inscribed post marking the start of a northeast-

Good reception spot

trending abandoned part of Hole-in-the-Ground Trail 33E05 (6650/0.6). According to Willie Craig of the Forest Service, those posts, scattered across the Little Kern basin, show backcountry rangers where the reception is best for their shortwave radios. Our path briefly levels beyond the trail fork, then starts descending, at first gradually, near an intermittent stream. Shortly we switchback through ponderosa pines singed years ago in the Betty Fire. We presently cross a permanent part of the creek we hiked near earlier, and soon afterward meet a maintained, southeast-trending segment of Hole-in-the-Ground Trail 33E05 (6080/1.9), which is described as Trip 100 of *Self-Propelled in the Southern Sierra, Volume 1: The Sierra Crest and The Kern Plateau.*

Declining northeast, the Lewis Camp Trail soon runs through the cold, tasty waters of Angora Creek, then becomes briefly rocky and dusty. Then it curves north and levels upon reaching the boulder-heaped Kern River flood plain. Jeffrey pine, incense-cedar, alder, Kellogg oak, scrub oak, and willow endure by the trailside ahead. After a brief hike on the level, we pass through a stock gate next to a "Grasshopper Flat" sign. Quite soon we boulder-hop Leggett Creek, and afterward pass numerous large, oak-shaded campsites.

At the head of the flat we pass through a clearing, then begin climbing zigzags. Two thirds of the way up the zigzags, our course nears a cold, tangy brook where wild rose, penstemon and Bigelow sneezeweed flourish. But don't drink the brook water here. Wait till after we find it beyond the next zigzag upslope, for there the brook enters, then briefly descends, the tread of this horse-frequented trail.

Presently the zigzags abate while we approach a narrow pass. Geologist A. C. Lawson observed in the course of his pioneering 1904 reconnaissance that the pass was eroded along the Kern Canyon Fault, effectively isolating the buttress east of the pass from the canyon slope proper.

Here at the pass (6600/2.3) the path begins a moderate northward decline. Soon its grade diminishes as it bridges Little Kern Lake Creek. The creek's braided waters hiss among granite boulders, and a sheltering stand of alders invites the hiker to linger. A masonry ditch intercepts the creek by the bridge, diverting fresh water a few hundred yards north to a cluster of large campsites.

The trail ahead soon bears north where a lateral (6290/1.0) to the campsites splits off to the east. Then we skirt photogenic Little Kern Lake, pass a signed north-lakeshore lateral, and then climb south-facing slopes toward another pass. This grade is mercifully much less steep than that to the previous pass. From this one (6575/0.4) we gaze beyond muddy Kern Lake to Tower Rock, which stands near an entrance to Sequoia National Park.

The California Legislature set aside the lake and the segment of river from the Park boundary downstream to the lake for the rearing of Kern River rainbow trout in 1932, and will prohibit fishing in them until 1984, according to the 1977 USFS *Little Kern Environmental Statement.* That report went on to say that the 10-acre lake, filling with silt, has dwindled from the 100-acre pool that was backed up by a massive landslide in 1876.

After a brief, moderate decline, the path

levels and then runs along a marshy extension of Kern Lake. Then it fords an inlet stream near a medium campsite (6235/0.6). The river flows into an adjoining embayment, away to the east. Above Kern Lake, it flows stealthily through several channels sometimes obstructed by beaver dams among horsetails and alders. Phil Pister, a California Department of Fish and Game (DFG) biologist, lamented in a 1976 *Los Angeles Times* article that the beaver, introduced in the Southern Sierra during the 1940's to help increase forage for cattle, has caused the gravels in which trout lay their eggs to be buried in mud. Hence Pister's agency has permitted some beaver hunting here (contact the DFG for details).

Our path, meanwhile, leads north from the ford. Past moist slopes of columbine and clover, it runs by a marsh luxuriant with leopard lilies and then passes a reedy pond. Then the path briefly inclines up a moderate grade, crossing a steep riverbank. Now we bear north where a lateral (6360/1.7) to the Golden Trout Trail peels off down a steep slope. We can see from the junction that it initially leads to a group of large riverside campsites. Nearby rapids magnify the river's sounds raucously.

Now our path curves gradually west, crossing a southwest-trending ridge on the boundary of Sequoia National Park. Wilderness Permit statistics for 1973-78 (which only register intentions) show that the heavy use this entrance was intended to get peaked in July and August, despite this spot's remoteness from roads. Much of that use came from horsemen with pack stock, and a 1976 survey directed by David J. Parsons of the Park Service showed that most of the horsemen (backpackers too) planning to stay in the Kern River trench reached it via this entrance. (It was also implicit in Parsons' figures that most of the people we're likely to see ahead on the slightly used Farewell Coyote Trail will be traveling in the opposite direction.)

From the Park boundary we contour through a dark stand of Jeffrey pine to a signed junction (6456/0.1) with the westbound *Farewell Coyote Trail.* Taking this path, we bypass the Kern Canyon Ranger Station and pass through a "camping zone" (see Chapter 4 for the meaning of this term). Then we ramble farther amid natural

Claus Engelhardt

Little Kern Lake and Kern River

forest litter by Coyote Creek before switch-backing steeply up out of the Kern trench. After gaining nearly 800 feet, our path clings to precipitous slopes past views of cas-cading Coyote Creek and (across the Kern trench) Volcano Falls. The trail slants up these slopes and at length leads to gentler slopes and a ford of Coyote Creek. In times of high water, a search of the creek bank often reveals a creek-spanning log.

The north bank offers a small camping zone before our upslope grind resumes. The nearly continuous shade of mixed conifers, an early ford of a burbling tributary and a trailside string of enticing bathing holes in Coyote Creek make this 1300-foot ascent a pleasure. By the time our grade eases, lodgepole pine comes to dominate the woods and partly screens us from a glade just to the north, signed "danger/poison forage."

Quite soon we enter a large camping zone, then ford Coyote Creek where its banks are accented by monkey flower and columbine. Soon afterward we step across a transitory tributary, then cross a meadow where tasty scarlet strawberries ripen in August. Our path shortly joins a faint, east-trending seg-ment of the Top-of-the-World Trail (9360/4.9). It offers access to the Coyote Lakes at the cost of moderate route-finding and steep scrambling up a slope scarred by multiple trails.

Beyond the signed junction, the Farewell Coyote Trail leaves the headwaters-bowl camping zone and winds up a moderate grade past increasingly straggly pines and firs. Presently passing from duff underfoot-ing onto decayed granite, we gain northward vistas of rarely visited crags and cirques while ambling the last few hundred yards to the signed Park boundary at Coyote Pass (10,160/1.0). Parsons' survey revealed that most of the people passing this moderately used entrance in 1976 were backpackers in-tending to make week-long loops out of Mineral King. Although more than half of them planned to return via Franklin Pass (while some ranged as far as Mount Whit-ney), their contribution to the wear and tear of Park campsites and trails was negligible.

Now we meander slightly downslope (northwest) for several minutes, passing a few small, exposed campsites, and then skirt a medium campsite ringed with red heather and labrador tea beside intermittent

Tamarack Creek. "Tamarack" was the word that John Muir and his contemporaries used for what we now call lodgepole pines—which, aptly enough, shelter the campsite here.

After fording the creek, our course leads up a short, gentle grade to a broad 10,335-foot-high saddle, and from there we stride down switchbacks that get progressively longer and less steep. The switchbacks' final, long, southward traverse guides us into the cooling shade of firs and pines. Beyond the last switchback, the route makes a cross-slope descent northwest, crosses an avalanche swath and then alternates between strips of woods and exposed, afternoon-hot man-zanita. In time we ford a Rifle Creek fork, then ascend ½ mile of moderate grade, gain-ing 300 feet to cross a saddle in a ridge athwart our route. Beyond the large, water-less campsite here, our path undulates for nearly a mile on ball-bearing-like granite grit and afterward passes upslope from a small, slope-perched campsite and fords shrub-bordered Pistol Creek.

Jeffrey pine makes its Little Kern basin encore where we scramble a few minutes upslope to reach an admirably engineered stretch of trail that was realigned during the 1960's. The pattern for the next few miles is established here: red fir on west-facing slopes, exposed brush on slopes facing south and east. At length we approach shattered granite that conceals gurgling Shotgun Creek. Here our route turns off the Farewell Coyote Trail (8980/5.5) several dozen yards short of the Shotgun Pass Trail (Trip 79) and leads down a steep *use trail* beside the apron of rocks.

In less than 100 yards we pass a pair of small campsites and then, after scrambling a bit farther downslope onto quartzite and schist, we step onto **Lion Meadows Trail** **32E02** (8780/0.1) and start south on it. The vegetation pattern established at Pistol Creek on the Farewell Coyote Trail holds true for the next 1.1 miles of the Lion Meadows Trail. After this sequence ends at our second and final Pistol Creek ford, our path's gentle downgrade continues a mile farther. Then we pass through a slight saddle and begin a moderate descent of a gully. Shortly we stroll briefly down alongside frolicsome, bubbly Rifle Creek, then ford it and almost instantly meet a southwest-trending creekside part of abandoned Little Kern Trail 31E12 (7430/2.7).

Our path rolls mostly southeast from the junction with Trail 31E12 through thick Jeffrey pines, and on it we soon arrive in the midst of a cluster of medium campsites graced by the trunk-mounted skull of a cow mouthing an empty whiskey bottle. A placid spring issues a few steps east of the trail in a glade that the campsites flank. An outhouse located just upslope from the spring elicits raised eyebrows from would-be drinkers.

Our path now descends gradually west along the meadow's south edge, turning south to round J.C. Jenkins Knob. (Named for the author of this book who, as a wilderness ranger, was stationed at this camp.) Presently we hike above corn lilies that conceal a from a nook where corn lilies conceal a spring. While metamorphic gravel clinks underfoot, we soon hear the roar of the Little Kern River and sight, on the opposite canyonside, furrowed quartzite streaked with magenta and orange and stained chartreuse with blotchy lichens.

Then we re-enter the Little Kern Allotment through a barbed-wire stock gate. (Please close it to keep Shannon's cattle out of the upper Little Kern meadows.) After a spell, our path swerves away from the river, and then its prolonged descent on quartzite gives way to a moderate upgrade on granite just short of a leap-across brook. Less than 20 minutes later, we top a slight gap with exposed brush patches, then undulate a mile down through lodgepole-pine shade to a ford of Tamarack Creek. One small campsite can be found just downslope from the trail on the north bank, while past the ford, several others are situated just upslope from the path. While skirting the campsites beyond the ford, we pass a pocket meadow ringed by corn lilies and a barbed-wire fence.

Our course starts rising gently several hundred yards from the creek, passes a north-trending lateral to a large campsite beside Tamarack Creek, rambles up a ravine and shortly touches more exposed patches of brush while topping a broad saddle. The subsequent Jeffrey-pine-shaded jaunt takes us some distance along a ravine before we encounter Coyote Lakes Trail 32E04 (6870/4.3) and mingle with hikers on Trip 47. A small, shady campsite lies just southwest of the junction, near the north bank of Willow Creek.

The Lion Meadows Trail continues southeast from the junction, almost instantly dipping to a leap-across ford of Willow Creek. Then our course rolls slightly for ½ mile, fords a Willow Creek branch lined with grass, drops briefly through manzanita, snow bush and blue lips to ford narrow Lion Creek, contours and presently meets a north-trending segment of Top-of-the-World Trail 32E05 (6680/1.2).

Now we start south across an inholding of 120 acres acquired by R.M. Pyles Boys Camp in 1977, and our path leads along a fence enclosing a tin-roofed cabin we can glimpse through the woods. A very brief stroll gets us to the terminus of a cross-country segment of Nelson Cabin Trail 32E08 (6670/0.1), which comes in from the west-southwest. Then we pass a large creekside campsite where toads sometimes promenade at night, and almost immediately afterward jump a fork of Lion Creek.

Lion Meadows lies next to the creek here, severed in two by a short length of our trail. A stock gate (please close) near the meadow's south edge marks an entrance to more public land. The path now rolls over a low ridge, presently fording depressed Table Meadow Creek, then traces the corn-lily-lined edge of baizelike Table Meadow.

Easy strolling continues while the path leads across a rounded creekside ridge, soon fords a grass-bordered brook and undulates slightly. At length we meet and turn southwest onto signed **Clicks Creek Trail 32E11** (6240/2.4).

It leads gradually downslope at first, touching Sagebrush Gulch in some 15 minutes and shortly thereafter turning northwest to ford the Little Kern River. The river can run chest-deep, and quite powerfully so, when snowmelt torrents peak. When that occurs, inexperienced forders will find the only negotiable crossing nearly two miles downstream. There the river flares and allows a long, thigh-deep wade to those using Burnt Corral Trail 32E13. Even there, waders should cross diagonally, using a walking stick or an ice axe as a downstream brace.

The Clicks Creek Trail river ford leads to a spit between the river and Mountaineer Creek. Here we meet an obscure, north-trending segment of Nelson Cabin Trail

32E08 (6060/0.6) before turning south and fording Mountaineer Creek. (The only obvious path at this point is the misleading track of fishermen heading 200 yards up the creek.) Our path, initially faint, continues south from the stream bank across floodplain gravels and an adjacent dusky flat where Jeffrey pines shelter an assortment of campsites.

Then the course rolls over several slight ridges, midway diverging southwest from a lateral to Grey Meadow (6210/0.5). Later we cross signed Fish Creek Meadows Trail 32E12 (6150/0.3) after completing most of the undulations. Patchy manzanita now and then fringes our route southwest of the junction, but it soon becomes scraggly, just as the Jeffrey pines do, beyond the last undulation. Now we work up a gradual rise into Clicks Creek canyon, crossing a band where incense-cedar predominates and is wreathed at the base by kit-kit-dizze.

Shortly we meet signed, east-trending Grey Meadow Cutoff 32E16 (6460/1.0) and next enter the Jordan Allotment, where 225 head of Hanggi family cattle roam from July through mid-September, just as their cattle have done since 1900. Some time later we ford boulder-studded Clicks Creek while crossing a strip of quartzite and related metamorphic rocks. At least 3 small campsites can be found near the Richardson's geraniums that poke from beneath bankside rocks at the ford. We then traipse a few hundred yards up-canyon, passing the confluence of Clicks Creek and

its north fork before transferring to granite soils and later zigzagging upslope within earshot of the tumultuous creek. A subsequent length of gentler grade amid red firs takes us onto an open slope luxuriant with tiger lily, groundsel and numerous other wildflowers. A tumbling snowmelt brook amid the flowers gives hikers a chance to refill canteens for the impending final ascent of the trip.

Advancing a few yards from the clearing, we note a short spur departing west toward 3 medium meadowside campsites. Then our path slants up moderately to gain 600 feet, alternately zigzagging up, and crossing, slopes that hide thimbleberry-graced nooks. The grade terminates near our next-to-last ford of Clicks Creek, and beyond the ford we skirt the creek southward. The creek soon splits a long, slender meadow emblazoned with cinquefoil, corn lily, bleeding heart and shooting star. We parallel the meadow's edge for nearly ⅔ of the meadow's length, then note a sign indicating that a trail once led west from here to Jordan Peak and Camp Wishon.

The junction precedes a small meadowside campsite, succeeded in turn by the meadow's south end and our last ford of Clicks Creek. Thereafter we pace a few minutes near the creek, then leap across an intermittent tributary and start a final ¼ mile of sauntering through red firs and lodgepole pines. Upon reaching the trailhead on *SNF Road 21S50* (7850/4.2), we start hiking northwest on the road toward our shuttle cars, a few hundred feet away.

Little Kern River above Mountaineer Creek

Thomas Winnett

T45   Mountaineer Creek Backpack

The charms of this trip along 2 brooks and part of the Western Divide are mostly found in the foregrounds along the way. There, tangy water spills in silvery curls, pools in rockbound hollows and splashes nearby wildflowers. Banked against brooks. sprinkled throughout meadows and hanging from crannied cliffs, the rainbow-colored wildflowers perfume the air hikers breathe.

The panorama that climaxes our trip contrasts the vast flats of the Little Kern Basin and the San Joaquin Valley with the abrupt, jagged slopes of the Tule River's canyon and the Great Western Divide. The stump fields in which this trip begins and ends show what might have happened to the foregrounds that frame such panoramas had they not been spared from logging by the establishment of Golden Trout Wilderness in 1978.

Season   July through October

Distance   16.4 miles (26.4 km) shuttle trip

Steep Upgrade   0.1 mile (0.2 km)

Elevation Gain and Loss   +4000 feet (+1219 m) and −3740 feet (−1140 m)

Exertion/Duration   easy/4 days, moderate/2 days

Skills   easy route-finding, Class 1 climbing

Permits   Wilderness Permit

Roadheads/Maps   R40, R42/M30–M31, M39–M41

Description   At a parking lot beside **SNF Road 21S50** nearly 6 miles north of State Highway 190, our journey gets underway when we stroll a few hundred feet southeast along the road. This jaunt puts us amid thick lodgepole pines, where we turn northeast onto signed **Clicks Creek Trail 32E11** (7850/0.0). The trail presently fords a seasonal fork of Clicks Creek, then crosses the stride-wide creek itself, skirts a long creek-bank meadow and meets an abandoned west-trending path by a medium campsite midway along the meadow. Our course then runs past the rest of the meadow's sprinkling of cinquefoil, corn lily, bleeding heart and shooting star while descending slightly along the creek. Shortly we leap to the creek's east bank, and proceed to lose 600 feet in elevation by alternating between zigzagging and slope-traversing past thimbleberry-graced alcoves. Then the path's gradient eases, and we touch a short westbound spur trail to 3 meadow-side medium campsites.

Beyond the campsite turnoff, we cross a clearing packed with wildflowers, hopping an intermittent brook midway. Almost ½ mile later, our trail zigzags downslope. Soon we skirt 3 small campsites, then boulder-hop Clicks Creek again where sprigs of Richardson's geranium poke from beneath bankside rocks. We then traipse away from the creek, presently passing through a stock gate that marks the boundary between 2 grazing allotments. On the west side is the Jordan Allotment where, since 1900, the Hanggi family has been permitted to let their 225 head of cattle roam. On the east side is the Little Kern Allotment, where Ruben Shannon has pastured his 200 head of cattle in a tradition dating back to 1917. Both ranges are grazed only during summer months, after most of the Western Divide's winter snowpack has melted.

We then cross a few forested slopes where incense-cedar is wreathed at the base with kit-kit-dizze, later meet east-trending Grey Meadow Cutoff 32E16 (6460/4.2) and afterward continue northeast, into stands of Jeffrey pine. At length, we encounter a signed junction (6150/1.0) and turn northwest onto **Fish Creek Meadows Trail 32E12.**

Treading on a layer of sand and dust, we ramble at length beyond the junction across the wrinkled, well-drained floor of the Little Kern basin. Past clumps of manzanita we dip to a boulder-heaped flood plain of Mountaineer Creek just west of a shady, large campsite. Then our course crests an elongated hump into which the creek has cut a bluff not far to the north. Just upstream from the cliffy passage, the creek spills through a succession of granite-bound pools, while our path forks west from a yards-long northwest spur. The spur gives access to a collection of large campsites in the protected midst of an assembly of Jeffrey pines, white firs and incense-cedars.

Continuing up the main trail, backpackers next pad across decomposing granite slabs and later skirt alder-covered gravel bars along the creek, shortly fording the creek where it debouches from a canyon. The ensuing ascent of a southeast-facing slope involves zigzagging through kit-kit-dizze, then outflanking a huge blowdown and, at a nearby junction (6460/1.7), meeting signed *Mountaineer Trail 32E10.*

Now we hike the westbound Mountaineer Trail, the first segment of which rolls steeply, then mildly. The trail segment shortly leads into the Jordan Allotment and then ends at a sometimes-stagnant tributary. That path segment's sequel is at least 3 times as long and undulates more steeply, but it now and then offers compensatory downslope vistas of Mountaineer Creek combing through a series of granite-locked pools. The final steep undulation passes a pool 30 feet in diameter which fills a deep gouge by a slope of gabbro bedrock that our path has been blasted across. What makes some backpackers stop here is not so much the floral accompaniment of mariposa lily, forget-me-not and Richardson's geranium as the long, slick slide down which Mountaineer Creek whisks into the pool.

A short interval of contouring past the pool brings us to a creekside "Cow Trail" sign misplaced beside the confluence of Mountaineer and South Mountaineer creeks. The sign was meant for a path that starts south several dozen yards up-canyon, beyond a bouldery ford of Mountaineer Creek. This spur path (6880/2.1) is a short remnant of the South Mountaineer Trail, which now leads only as far as some medium campsites where Jacobson Creek arrives from the west.

Meanwhile, the first 15 yards of the Mountaineer Trail beyond the junction, which hug the bank of Mountaineer Creek, are overrun with monkey flowers, gooseberries and cinquefoil. The path then resumes and our course fords the creek twice more in

quick succession. The next ford, reached in a moment, is not immediately apparent—it's just upstream from a slab cantilevered over the creek like a diving board.

Now on the north bank, we briefly ascend a steep section, and then for a long while hike easily past flowers of larkspur and pennyroyal. Afterward, at another creek ford, the path disappears in the south-bank sod. It can be regained by striking south-southwest toward a visible tributary ravine, which quickly proves to contain a brook. Here the path resumes.

The path and its parallel brook, now deep into the crag-companionate red fir's domain, shortly arc west-northwest through a scattering of glades. In the highest glade the brook issues from a small, round pool by the path. Beyond, and after a brief jaunt through a swale, the path dips, fords Mountaineer Creek again, and again disappears, now in a sloping meadow.

Our cross-country route through this sometimes sodden meadow stays at least 30 yards from the creek, and shortly regains the path in a corridor where the woods close in. We then polish off a moderate ascent, by and by leaving the woods at an old posted "Mountaineer Creek" sign. It precedes yet another ford where soggy sod hides the route. We persevere west-northwest from the ford and shortly resume the path where it skirts the south fringe of Mowery Meadow. Although only one large campsite is found here, the meadowside environs—which receive early morning light—can accommodate many more campers. Shortly beyond this emerald oval, we turn southeast through a signed junction in a pass onto *Summit Trail 31E14* (8100/2.4).

This path at first intertwines with the Western Divide, then crosses a transitory brook, and then skirts a meadowy strip. Beyond the strip, the path again crosses the divide, now beside slopes sprinkled with dwarf lupine, cinquefoil and pussypaws. We next proceed past a grassy strip named Jacobsen Meadow and the corn lilies, mountain bluebells, buttercups and shooting stars that it showcases.

Shortly after outflanking the meadow, we stroll through a red-fir corridor and spot a "31E19" sign where the long-vanished Yellow Jacket Trail once started down along Jacobson Creek. Then the Summit Trail touches a southwest-trending segment of Jacobsen Wildroute 31E21 (8360/1.3) and afterward rises 250 feet in a zigzag ascent of the divide. We top a ridge athwart the divide, dip somewhat into a shallow saddle, and afterward saunter along an open crest, intercepting the most comprehensive views of this trip.

The path next re-enters red firs where silver pines put in a skimpy appearance, shortly bypasses knob 8738, then switchbacks down an adjoining northeast-trending ridge. After consuming lots of yardage, we touch the Western Divide again in a saddle. At this point we turn east, hike some distance downslope along a ravine, then arc south on an eroded, root-riddled path to ford South Mountaineer Creek just upslope from a perched medium campsite. The creek's 2 cascading headwaters forks convene at the ford, bounding a 50-foot wall of hanging gardens. Water surfaces at the wall's brink, then drizzles over a profusion of ferns, corn lilies, mountain bluebells, shooting stars, buttercups, Sierra corydalis and other wet-meadow wildflowers.

The ensuing, nontaxing ascent takes nearly a mile to mount the Mountaineer Creek/Clicks Creek divide, where we leave the signed "Golden Trout Wilderness" on the brink of a swath of brush, stumps and logging debris. The path now bears south, merging in 15 yards with an abandoned logging road. This road leads south, down and across the mauled slope, presently meeting an irrelevant road to the west-southwest. Continuing south for 90 yards past the junction, we then resume the Summit Trail, which forks south from the road and descends a moderate grade. It ends some 200 yards later by signposts adjoining **SNF Road 21S50** (8090/3.7). A final walk of 200 yards northeast on the road brings us to our shuttle cars in the trailhead parking lot.

T46

Backpacking the Silver Knapsack Trail

Despite its stiff ascents and demanding route-finding, this trip has long been a favorite of the Boy Scouts (who've dubbed its circuit the "Silver Knapsack Trail") because it leads among the Western Divide's showiest waters. In one place, the water fizzes in travertine-rimmed soda springs; in others, it fills granite-cupped lakes. Whether spilling comblike from pool to pool, dashing downslope and spattering flourishes of wildflowers, or gathered into a beach-lined, deep and powerful river, the water along this trip appears in many of its most scrumptious forms.

Season   July through October

Distance   31.5 miles (50.7 km), shuttle trip

Steep Upgrade   0.7 mile (1.1 km)

Elevation Gain and Loss   +6410 feet (+1954 m), −6150 feet (−1875 m)

Exertion/Duration   easy/6 days, moderate/4 days, strenuous/3 days

Skills   moderate route-finding, Class 2 climbing

Permits   Wilderness Permit

Roadheads/Maps   R40, R42/M30–M31, M39–M41, M46–M47

Description

Northeast-bound *Clicks Creek Trail 32E11*

T45	SNF Road 21S50	7850	0.0
	Grey Meadow Cutoff 32E16	6460	4.2
	Fish Creek Meadows Trail 32E12	6150	1.0
T46	lateral to Trail 32E12	6210	0.3
	Nelson Cabin Trail 32E08	6060	0.5

Our path, the **Nelson Cabin Trail,** starts north from the Clicks Creek Trail on a gravelly spit between converging Mountaineer Creek and Little Kern River. First we climb north up a bank, entering Jeffrey-pine woods, then we undulate northwest. After slogging across well-drained granitic grit for less than ½ hour, hikers may note a sign indicating a "soda spring" to the southwest. A diligent search can reveal the spring some 150 yards from the trail, bubbling through Mountaineer Creek where it pools and slides near its confluence with Alpine Creek.

The main trail continues rolling monotonously past the sign on a course that roughly parallels Alpine Creek. At length we ramble across some sandy barrens and then veer north through a triangle junction with Mountaineer Trail 32E10 (6300/1.7), which we do not take. The first segment of this trail, though often faint and obstructed by blowdowns, leads near the site of Parole Cabin, demolished by fire some years ago. Harry O'Farrell, whose alias, "Parole," commemorates his release from prison, headquartered his hunter-for-hire service here in the mid-1800's. In 1964, historian Tom Porter credited O'Farrell with the discovery of Mineral King, and reported that he often hunted deer there to supply trail crews with venison. Today, large campsites sprawl across the creekside flat where the Parole Cabin once stood.

Now we take the Nelson Cabin Trail, which rolls north from the junction, almost instantly crossing a sand flat with subtly colored pussypaws. Afterward we thread manzanita patches, and shortly our trail forks north-northeast from the abandoned Alpine Creek Trail. That route to the crest of the Western Divide is so thoroughly blocked by blowdowns, brush and landslides that only the keenest observer accustomed to scrambling on cliffy, unstable slopes could trace it.

Our path next leads over the low Alpine Creek/Soda Spring Creek divide before rolling over another slight ridge and eventually reaching the GT Campsites, so called by the Boy Scouts, who have given them a beaten look. Some of these large campsites lining Soda Spring Creek are inside our trail's triangle junction (6420/1.6) with *Newlywed Wildroute 31E13,* while others are scattered near downstream banks. We bear northwest through 2 of the triangle's corners, taking the wildroute's first-segment trail.

Not far to the northwest we come to a "Nelson Cabin" sign posted in a midsummer-sere, sloping glade. When questioned in 1974, the local district ranger, Bob Werner, said that the cabin, located near the head of this glade, was never completed. It was never built higher than the present few tiers of logs.

Now our path slants up across an expanse of steep, predominantly east-facing slopes through a mixed conifer forest. A reddish ridge in the middle distance can help us gauge our progress, while the Great Western Divide looms in the far distance, inspiring us to persist in our efforts. Foreground diversions, especially welcome where our grade steepens, include sprays of Richardson's geraniums and brittle outcrops of hornfels and slate. The path presently dips into a gully, then rises to overlook a broad saddle and afterward disappears in crossing a squishy hanging meadow. Corn lily, monkey flower, cinquefoil and sunflower relatives

Sugar pine cone

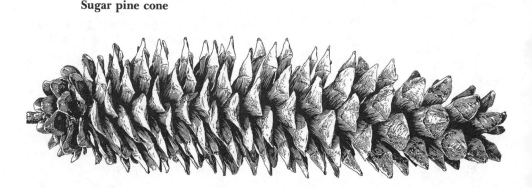

jam the meadow, having obliterated the trail long ago. We gingerly pick our way across, heading north and ignoring an old sign near the meadow's upslope fringe.

Soon leaving the meadow, we instantly regain the trail where it fords a meadow-side seasonal brook and afterward curls around drafty Walker Cabin. Ranger Werner observed that since the cabin was built by sheepherders in 1886, it has been sporadically used as an outhouse, making it undesirable as housing and increasing the attractiveness of a large, close-at-hand campsite.

We leave the cabin heading west on a deteriorating trail segment, at first zigzagging, then briefly weaving and finally straining straight up an utterly taxing slope. This luckily forest-sheltered segment gains 500 feet before dovetailing into a segment no better than a game trail. Now we ascend more gradually while rounding a squared-off ridge and recognizing Indian paintbrush, forget-me-not, pinemat manzanita, and currant in clearings along the way. Many blowdowns lie athwart this segment, and together with numerous pendulous boughs they make it impassable to pack stock.

Eventually our makeshift trail passes a small, sloping campsite just before rounding a canyon through shoulder-deep, dank clumps of willow, wild rose, tiger lily, aster, yarrow and goldenrod—all fed by 2 seasonal brooks. Near the north edge of this fragrant foliage, an abandoned segment of Hanging Meadow Trail 31E16 (8070/2.9) starts southwest by a sign-tacked lodgepole pine. That path once ascended quite steeply en route to Maggie Lakes, but most of it has either been overgrown, obstructed by blowdowns or sloughed off the slope.

Our still-nebulous path begins a gently rolling segment at the sign and shortly reaches aspen-bordered Newlywed Camp, a large campsite named for the wedding night that Springville packer Frank Negus and his bride spent in it. Then we proceed beyond a wet meadow, some snowmelt brooks and a few gently rounded, red-fir-clad ridges to finish the lengthy segment on the Hidden Lake Slopes, where snowdrifts sometimes last until early July. The ensuing steep descent along a ravine involves more blowdown hurdling and a 600-foot elevation loss.

The trail forks near the foot of this grade, and a short lateral (7820/1.9) leads east from the fork to the signed "Soda Butte Campsites"—9 small sites clustered near an orange-travertine-rimmed soda spring. Certain flavor additives can make the somewhat sulfurous water delicious. Try mixing orange drink with it for a flavor like breakfast eggs washed down with orange juice. The terraced campsites near this raised spring have the wan, worn look diagnostic of exceedingly heavy use and should be bypassed in favor of the enticing meadow-side sites to be found not far ahead near Quinn Cabin. The spring drains over glistening tufa ledges into adjacent Soda Spring Creek, where fishing is prohibited.

The Newlywed Wildroute fords this creek where blowdowns assist flood-time travelers to get across dry-shod. Moments later, we cross a tagged boundary and enter Sequoia National Park, where the trail displays vastly better maintenance. It ascends a gentle grade by an ingratiating bit of the creek bordered with columbine, pennyroyal and scarlet gilia, and sporting its own grove of quaking aspens.

Soon after veering north from the creek, we saunter up through a large camping zone (a new concept defined in Chapter 4) to Quinn Patrol Cabin. Originally, this was the summertime haunt of Harry Quinn, a turn-of-the-century sheepman. Nowadays the cabin, although a signed snow-survey shelter, is more often used in summer by the Hockett ranger on patrol.

Incipient **Atwell Hockett Trail 90,** marked by diagonally halved license plates tacked high up on wayside trees, leads us away from a cabin-side junction (8330/0.9) and early fords the occasional brook draining the meadow. Shooting star, monkey flower, forget-me-not, lupine and corn lily verge on this brook, exuding a heady aroma. We soon begin a moderate, sometimes steep ascent through predominant red firs past scattered conglomerations of gooseberry, Indian paintbrush, owl's clover and mountain bluebells. Rare strains of bleeding heart and trillium found where the forest thins are in danger of extinction because of the flower pickers who have misused this trail. Please leave the blooms intact so these plants can reproduce and be enjoyed by future hikers.

With grit and duff underfoot, we shortly advance to exposed slopes checkered with various subalpine brush varieties, then pass near an avalanche swath. Eventually we round a corner of Windy Ridge, where a rewarding panorama of the Little Kern Sierra can be had by turning to face southeast. Then we turn southwest on a short **lateral to Summit Lake Trail 102** (9510/1.7) a few hundred yards south of Windy Gap.

The lateral begins an ascent soon made easy by lodgepole-pine-shaded zigzags, and then we turn southwest onto the **Summit Lake Trail** (9570/0.1). In minutes we top Windy Ridge, a crest on the Western Divide, and enter not only a slender camping zone but also a clearing that includes distant Kern Peak in its Little Kern basin panorama. We stroll across the clearing's grit, oscillating along the crest while observing a scattering of wildflowers. Our course presently contours southwest, leaving the crestline camping zone, and soon traverses a corner of the widespread Cyclone Slopes, where snowdrifts sometimes add to the hiker's exertion and route-finding difficulty.

Eventually our route turns southeast at one tip of a signed triangle junction with **Summit Trail 31E14** (9620/1.9) 0.6 mile short of the intensely used campsites ringing Summit Lake. Averaged USNPS Wilderness Permit statistics for 1973–78 indicate that although the lake's visiting season has been a long one (March through November), most of its moderate packstock and heavy backpacker use has occurred in July.

Meanwhile, we briefly ascend southeast before touching a lateral to the Summit Lake Trail (9750/0.1) at the southernmost point on the triangle. Then we work south up a short, rocky grade to leave the Park at the "Pecks Canyon Entrance" sign, which stands in a broad saddle beside Sheep Mountain on the Western Divide. Here we enter Golden Trout Wilderness and Sequoia National Forest at the highest point on this trip. (We also resume identifying individual campsites according to size.)

The Summit Trail next zigzags down a metamorphic-rock outcrop flecked with the annual blossoms of Douglas phlox and wallflower. Dwarf lupine and chinquapin patches dispel monotony while we skirt a meadow seen in slices between lodgepole pines. Then we veer south to catch the start of Maggie Kincaid Trail 31E17 (9520/0.7). (Those who do not intend to use this trail should bear southeast through the fork,

going ahead on the Summit Trail and skipping to its description.)

*   *   *   *   *

The **Maggie Kincaid Trail** starts southwest down a mild grade amid dense lodgepole and silver pine. Shortly we cross a south-trending gully, pass an isolated small campsite, and afterward touch a few of the heavily used campsites—8 medium and one small—ringing Twin Lakes (9140/0.6). The lake water sometimes stagnates before midsummer, requiring treatment.

A crease that drains snowmelt freshets from the lakes is crossed in the midst of these campsites. Beyond the crossing, our trail descends a glacial moraine along the crease, which quickly deepens, exposing to view a cross-section of the moraine. We then ford a bouldery seasonal brook, whose playful tumbling sprays the adjacent ground cover of labrador tea.

The faint, ducked path meanders a few hundred paces from the ford down a slope of shattered granite, remaining within earshot of the lilting creek. Then the course turns south again, effects a quick though rocky ascent and presently crosses a log-jammed stream between the 2 Frog Lakes (9000/0.8). The larger lake, west of us now, is flanked on its northeast shore by a large campsite and southeast by a medium one.

Jumbled, hummocky chunks of granite mantle a rise not far south of the Frog Lake ford, and our course meanders over this rise. Then we drop through a blocky passage and sight the lowest of the Maggie Lakes, snug in a glacier-scooped bowl and backed by an eye-catching fin often mistaken for Maggie Mountain. Frank Knowles, who guided Sierra surveyor Clarence King in his unsuccessful bid to be first (he was second) up Mount Whitney during the 1870's, named Maggie Mountain for Maggie Kincaid, a San Joaquin Valley teacher. We reach the lowest lake's shore at a trail junction (9020/0.7).

*   *   *   *   *

A lateral departs here for the largest and uppermost of the Maggie Lakes. It starts southwest by the lowest lake, fords a stone-strewn inlet stream bordered with heather, and shortly slants diagonally up a low, spot-

Upper Maggie Lake

tily forested ridge. Quickly cresting the ridge, we make a slight descent south to meet a path (9180/0.3) parallel to the upper lake's shore. A large campsite situated north of this fork near the lake's outlet can be reached by the northern shore trail, while the southern track first skirts a pair of small campsites and then a pair of medium ones before ending on a wooded flat suitable for large groups.

*   *   *   *   *

In her 1977 survey of Western Divide campsites for the Forest Service, Kris Jackson estimated the capacity of the bruised, campsite-ridden north shore of the lowest lake at 50 sleeping bags a night. Camping is not recommended at this often noisy, firewood-poor site, despite the presence of an outhouse. Campsites in Pecks Canyon, not more than 90 minutes east of here, offer ample firewood, more seclusion, less fishing competition, better protection from wind and lightning, and plants that can take accidental mutilation and still thrive.

The Maggie Kincaid Trail leaves the lower lake's junction (9020/0.0) and leads east by the shore across the campsites. Then we ford the outlet—Pecks Canyon creek—and weave east over a rise, veering southeast quite soon where a traceable segment of Hanging Meadow Trail 31E16 (8960/0.2) starts northeast.

Beyond the fork, our trail swiftly deteriorates while initially rounding a wet meadow, and then makes a slight cross-slope descent to a north-south ravine. A rotting log aligned with the ravine and blocking our path is our cue for clambering up the ravine, gaining 50 feet before the bouldery path resumes, contouring eastward. Soon the trailside slopes diminish as our trail becomes outlined in rocks, while a red-fir canopy keeps us cool. Then we pass a medium campsite and subsequently turn south onto *Summit Trail 31E14* (8910/0.8) a few dozen yards west of a transitory brook. (Now we skip the following description, which is meant for those backpackers who don't want to use the Maggie Lakes Trail, preferring to take the Summit Trail all the way.)

*   *   *   *   *

After touching the north end of the Maggie Kincaid Trail (9520/0.0), we on the **Summit Trail** roam south-southeast, still descending a moderate grade in shady woods and crossing numerous ruffles and grooves in the slopes along the way. Shortly we pass a medium campsite, then enter a 160-acre inholding thoroughly posted with "private property" signs. It's probable that the Forest Service will buy this land for Golden Trout Wilderness before the current owners get irritated enough with hikers to post "no trespassing" signs. But if you do see such signs, leave the Summit Trail immediately and contour west to catch the Maggie Lakes Trail near Twin Lakes, outflanking the inholding.

The Summit Trail quickly encounters a group of shacks, one of them with a tin roof and a refrigerator outside. A nearby tree tacked with destination signs pointing off in many directions marks our intersection with Hanging Meadow Trail 31E16 (8880/1.1). The *western* segment of this trail is fairly easy to follow and leads to Maggie Lakes. (To find that segment, go 30 yards south from the tree across a sloping bog.) The *eastern* segment is now little more than a straightforward cross-country route to the Newlywed Trail.

Our path, meanwhile, meanders farther downslope to meet an 0.7-mile-long lateral (8620/0.6), which starts south-east toward a series of large Pecks Canyon campsites. We then leap a fork of Pecks Canyon creek to find a lateral forking west toward a large campsite 30 yards from the Summit Trail. A moment's jaunt takes us south from the junction to wide, boulder-studded Pecks Canyon creek. Past a large campsite just south of the ford, we trudge up a moderate grade through the woods, skirting chinquapin clumps and a small glade. Usually no more than 40 minutes pass before we rejoin the Maggie Kincaid Trail (8910/0.8).

*   *   *   *   *

Working up a moderate grade on the Summit Trail beyond the Maggie Kincaid Trail we initially pace 40 yards, then step across a willow-hedged, transitory brook and switchback up onto a shoulder of Maggie Mountain. Now we rove south amid red firs, often encountering snowbanks before midsummer. Our path shortly levels, then contours past a small campsite by an often-wet meadow and, minutes later, connects with the signed terminus of southwest-trending Griswold Trail 31E18 (8890/1.8).

Next we mount a low, broad saddle on the Western Divide, where a departing westbound trace wrongly signed "31E18" runs 100 yards, then ramifies into confusing game trails. The saddle marks our entrance to the Jordan Allotment, since 1900 the summertime range of the Hanggi family's 225 cattle. Our course zigzags down along the divide from the saddle, shortly skirting a sloping meadow, then swerves next to a small campsite and later passes a lateral (8500/0.9) that starts southwest and is signed for "Neva Point." This 0.2-mile-long lateral gains 150 feet in reaching the point, where the westward panorama (especially vivid at sunset) contrasts a deep Tule River canyon in the middle distance with the vast, smooth San Joaquin Valley in the background.

Beyond the Neva Point turnoff, the Summit Trail leads nearly 300 paces east to a cluster of campsites altogether roomy enough to hold 28 sleeping bags a night. Intensely green Alpine Meadow lies just across Alpine Creek from most of the campsites. (Two large campsites can be found on the meadow side of the creek).

Now we turn south through a swale, then quickly descend a moderate, sometimes steep grade via zigzags into a pass on the divide. Mountaineer Trail 32E10 comes in from Mowery Meadow to a signed junction with our route in the pass (8100/0.6).

Southeast-bound *Summit Trail 31E14* Log

T45	Mountaineer Trail		
	32E10	8100	0.0
	Jacobsen Wildroute		
	31E21	8360	1.3
	SNF Road 21S50	8090	3.7

T47   Coyote Lakes Backpack

A "top-of-the-world" panorama and a popular pair of cirque-nestled lakes draw hikers despite the vastness of the intervening Little Kern basin and the occasional rattlesnakes and snowmelt torrents en route. Add these obstacles to the destination's remoteness and you'll only begin to grasp the physical, mental and spiritual challenge of this trip to the Great Western Divide.

Season   July through October

Distance   33.2 miles (53.4 km) semiloop trip

Steep Upgrade   0.9 mile (1.4 km)

Elevation Gain and Loss   8450 feet (2576 m)

Exertion/Duration   easy/6 days, moderate/4 days, strenuous/3 days

Skills   Mod. route-finding, Class 2 climbing (Class 3–4 pitches optional)

Permits   Wilderness Permit

Roadhead/Maps   R10/M31, M41, M42

Description

Northeast-bound *Clicks Creek Tr 32E11* **Log**

T45 SNF Road 21S50	7850	0.0
Grey Meadow Cutoff 32E16	6460	4.2

The incipient **Grey Meadow Cutoff** leads down a moderate slope, shortly nearing willows along Clicks Creek, then fording the creek itself. Next we roll briefly not far from the creek through Jeffrey pines that now and then thin to admit manzanita clumps. Then our course leads over a low, rounded divide, presently turning southeast onto **Fish Creek Meadows Trail 32E12** (6170/1.0), and then meeting Burnt Corral Trail 32E13 (6160/0.1), where we first glimpse Grey Meadow through the trees. Large campsites intermittently flank the meadow, which— historian Harold G. Schutt wrote in 1973— was named for the Grey brothers, Harvey P. and R.P., who presumably camped here while driving sheep hereabouts in 1877. Their herd came in the midst of a summertime influx of San Joaquin Valley sheep that began in the drought of 1864 and ended some 30 years later with federal banishment of sheep after Sierran meadows had been nibbled nearly bare. Although most meadows have recovered, Fish Creek Meadows to the south did not, and they continue to look devastated.

The Grey Meadow Guard Station stands near Trail 32E12 just a few dozen yards southeast of here, offering emergency services and Wilderness Permits from June through early October when the ranger is not out on patrol. A spring issues not far behind the guard station.

(Hikers arriving here in spring or early summer who lack the experience or equipment to wade across a powerful river should take the Grey Meadow Trail 2.5 miles east, a lateral 0.2 mile northeast and then a Lewis Camp Trail bypass 0.3 mile northeast. Afterward, they should trudge the Lewis Camp trail, which bridges the river 0.6 mile northeast from the junction, then ascend the Willow Meadow Cutoff 1.3 miles and finally ramble 1.6 miles west on the Lion Meadow Trail to rejoin our route at the lower end of the Deep Creek Trail. This detour adds 3.2 miles and 1000 feet gain to the trip totals for those who take it.)

Now we take the **Burnt Corral Trail** northeast, presently crossing several often soggy lanes extending west from Grey Meadow. Beyond the grass we roam 0.4 mile across dry, gritty slopes where lupine and pussypaws lie along with other manifestation of the 10–15 inches of rain that the Little Kern basin floor has averaged in past years. Then we encounter a breach in the basin floor and hear the slithering of a river that drains heights receiving 3 or more times the rainfall that our standpoint gets. Here our course briefly weaves down a steep bank to a strand where stately pines shelter a couple of campsites.

Immediately we wade across the Little Kern River's widest, shallowest ford. Nevertheless, the river here is swift and waist-deep when the winter snowpack hereabouts is melting most heavily. The recommended course therefore slants diagonally across the current and beaches downstream from where it began.

Once on a narrow, Jeffrey-pine-canopied flat beside the north shore, we locate the trail starting northeast through an assortment of campsites. Barbara Rose, who inventoried most of the Little Kern basin campsites for the Forest Service in 1977, estimated their capacity at 18 one-person tents.

Just past the campsites, the trail enters, then briefly leads up alongside, a moderately steep ravine, shortly attaining a broad terrace. There we fork northeast from a spur path that cuts north into Burnt Corral Meadows. Our path skirts this large, sandy pasture for several hundred yards near some of the highest remnants of the Little Kern Basalt Flow (discussed in Trip 35). Geologists speculate that this flow originated somewhere close to this clearing. Near the clearings' northeast corner, we turn east onto signed **Lion Meadows Trail 32E02** (6160/1.3).

Near-level trudging through Jeffrey-pine forest consumes our time monotonously until our path cuts downslope across a sloping, oft-mushy meadow nearly a mile from the junction. We then step across a sporadically present rivulet and afterward briefly ascend granite slabs. Moments after surmounting the slabs, we arc around Round Meadow, passing a large campsite midway, and then meet southeast-bound Round Meadow Wildroute 32E14 (6230/1.2). This wildroute, a seldom-maintained trail, reportedly has been used only rarely, and it has faded away in its central section, which includes a treacherous ford of the Little Kern River.

Continuing east on Trail 32E02, we start up a mild grade, alternating between patches of manzanita and woods where the scurry of lizards across pine-bark chips is often heard. After less than 40 minutes of attentive sauntering, we spot a signed junction and there turn north onto **Deep Creek Trail 32E06** (6420/0.8), joining those hikers who took the bridge bypass.

The dense Jeffrey pines at this junction mingle with sparse incense-cedar, which shortly drops out of the pathside sequence while our course leads over a low, rounded divide. We presently leap across Deep Creek at a willow-lined ford by a large campsite. A long, gentle grade leads up along Deep Creek from the ford. Our ascent eventually steepens where the creek entrenches itself downslope from the trail. Here we encounter a short lateral to a small creekside campsite, then zigzag briefly upslope and resume the creek-paralleling ascent.

Our path shortly fords a Deep Creek tributary, then rounds a slight ridge, crosses another trickle of snowmelt runoff, passes just upslope from a corn-lily-ringed spring and finally becomes overgrown in a grassy lupine field. A large campsite can be found at the west edge of this clearing, a few paces east of the creek and just north of a large blowdown. The path then grows distinct again upon re-entering forest where red fir vies with pines for predominance. On it, we quickly gain several hundred feet and ford a narrow, transitory headwaters segment of Deep Creek. Now the grade eases and soon it levels in manzanita corridors separated from stubby White Mountain by a broad saddle.

Maintaining a cautious watch for rattlesnakes, we shortly swerve north through a junction onto **Top-of-the-World Trail 32E05** (8290/3.7). A medium campsite lies by this junction several hundred yards south of the nearest water, which can be reached via westbound Trail 32E05. Our course, in the meantime, progressively zigzags farther east and upslope, presently skirting a spring with a complement of wallflowers and larkspur. Past the small, levelled campsite here, the path leads around a slight ridge and across an ensuing south-facing slope where exposed snow bush makes for prickly going. More and dustier zigzags subsequently lead up along a sporadically meadowed draw, soon abating near a blank board tacked to a trailside tree. Schulers (large) Campsite, a 19th Century sheepherder's retreat, is perched several hundred yards southeast of here across an intervening meadow.

Now our course rolls steeply over a redfir-clad transverse ridge and then weaves briefly upslope, mounting the Great Western Divide at a saddle (9740/3.0) not far from its southernmost peak, Angora Mountain. This easily reached peak was named (according to Farquhar) by a shepherd some 100 years ago for a prized shaggy-fleeced Angora goat in his flock.

After leaving the saddle, the path weaves steeply downslope in the manner of old-fashioned sheep driveways. Letting it guide us, we course past numerous chinquapin patches, intercepting vistas of a gaunt rib of metamorphic rock athwart the canyon

Easternmost Coyote Lake

ahead, and shortly we bisect 2 consecutive sloping meadows. Campsites overlooking the second meadow offer enough room to spread out 20 sleeping bags. This campsite group (9200/0.6)—labelled "Kramer Horse Camp" on the USFS map—is perched just south of the trail along an intermittent headwaters fork of Grasshopper Creek.

Our easing, red-fir-shaded descent past the campsites is soon succeeded by some 2 miles of steeply ascending trail. It directs us past several obstructing blowdowns back to the heights where foxtail pines are predominant. Then we approach the Great Western Divide again, where a row of granite tines makes an appearance. We presently rise above timberline and top the divide near a gritty and often wind-buffeted point, hill 10885—the ultimate height for the trip. Encircled by far-flung horizons, and impressed by the nearness, sheerness, depth and straightness of the Kern trench, we absorb a panorama with contrasts that emphasize the region's spaciousness. When we loosen ourselves from the spell of the place, we scuff north on the grit, presently nearing the great

scoop in which the Coyote Lakes are nestled. Then we romp down a short foxtail-pine-timbered slope onto a crest-straddling saddle.

Here we turn east through a signed intersection (10,500/2.2), and start down zigzagging *Coyote Lakes Trail 32E04*. Its moderate grade prescribes a quick descent to the westernmost, largest and most popular of the 10 campsites next to this lake's north shore, where as many as 36 people at the same time have bedded.

Shores of the eastern lake, where the trail ends (10,070/0.5), have suffered from crowding less, exhibiting 4 sites that altogether have held as many as 20 campers. Potential explorations from base camps at these lakes include Class 2–4 climbs of the Coyote Peaks to the north, along with forays east (for experienced mountaineers only) down a virtually vanished sheep driveway that once connected the Coyote Lakes with Little Kern Lake in the Kern Trench.

When the time comes to leave the lakes, we backtrack to the saddle-top junction with the Top-of-the-World Trail (10,500/0.5). From there we continue west on the Coyote Lakes Trail, now a ducked **wildroute**, and weave down a long, steep slope from mixed subalpine forest to chinquapin-embellished stands of red fir. Then we negotiate several fords of Willow Creek. It cascades in silvery peals near the final ford, where a small campsite is perched.

Here the creek jogs southeast to trace the contact between granite and layers of quartzite with schist. Rocks and tree roots jutting into our unmaintained path make an obstacle course of its ⅓ mile descent on the west bank of this offset segment of creek. Then we turn west and so does the creek, now cutting through the metamorphic rock. Ducking past branches of young white firs, we soon contour away from the creek, return to soils weathered from granite and then start down a low ridge dappled with manzanita into Jeffrey-pine woods. During this final descent parallel to Willow Creek, we outflank several more blowdowns before reaching a signed junction with Lion

Meadows Trail 32E02 (6870/3.8). (A "Hunters Trail" sign posted here really points up the Coyote Lakes Trail.)

Southeast-bound *Lion Meadows Trail* Log

T44	Coyote Lakes Trail		
	32E04	6870	0.0
	Top-of-the-World Trail 32E05	6680	1.2
	Nelson Cabin Trail 32E08	6670	0.1
	Clicks Creek Trail 32E11	6240	2.4

Southwest-bound *Clicks Creek Trail* Log

Lion Meadows Trail		
32E02	6240	0.0
Nelson Cabin Trail 32E08	6060	0.6
Grey Meadow lateral	6210	0.5
Fish Creek Meadows Tr 32E12	6150	0.3
Grey Meadow Cutoff 32E16	6460	1.0
SNF Road 21S50	7850	4.2

T48   Jordan Peak Hike

Crested with spiky rock and crowned with a lookout, Jordan Peak offers a panorama that contrasts the depth and stubbiness of the middleground Middle Fork Tule River canyons with the breadth of their backgrounds—the San Joaquin Valley and the Southern Sierra.

Season   July through October

Distance   3.4 miles (5.5 km) round trip

Steep Upgrade   none

Elevation Gain and Loss   875 feet (267 m)

Exertion/Duration   easy/1 day

Skills   easy route-finding, Class 1 climbing

Permits   none

Roadhead/Maps   R41/M30

Canteens   1 quart

Description   *SNF Closed Road 20S71* starts west from a gate in a red-fir corridor at a signed junction with SNF Road 21S50 (8240/0.0) and rises gradually through several large patches of stump-riddled brush, presently crossing McIntyre Creek (8580/

1.1). This glinting seasonal stream flows just north of a bog, while our path, *Spring Trail 31E25*, starts across the road in the mauled forest. We climb immediately, ascending a moderate grade via 10 zigzags. They presently lead among clumps of currant and pinemat manzanita, then reach shattered, chunky metamorphic rocks when the lookout appears in the southwest. A short stroll suffices to get us there (9115/0.5), where the panorama is as sweeping from outside the lookout as in. The lookout is staffed from June through October, or till the annual fire hazard abates, and it maintains a register for visitors. They eventually backtrack to their cars.

T49   Blue Ridge Bicycle Tour

The approach to Blue Ridge Lookout demonstrates that, for extraordinarily varied adventures, self-propelled recreationists need not look beyond the foothills of the Sierra Nevada.

Season   all year

Distance   39.4 miles (63.4 km) round trip

Steep Upgrade   none

Elevation Gain and Loss   4700 feet (1433 m)

Exertion/Duration   moderate/2 days, strenuous/1 day

Gears   10- and 15-speed alpine

Permits   USFS Campfire Permit for overnight riders only

Roadhead/Maps   R43/M27, M36–M37

Description   A bubbly spring (now privately owned) by the Tule River not far from Roadhead 43 gave rise to the name "Springville" when a town rose around the spring in 1889. Historian Russ Leadabrand related in 1968 that the stimulus for that early development was the sawmill and box factory that Avon M. Coburn installed here. Coburn's crews reportedly logged giant sequoias, pines and firs in what is now Mountain Home State Forest, high in the mountains northeast of town, and then transported them to the mill here. Today, tourism is both the mainstay of the town and the main use of the State Forest.

From the junction of TC Road MTN 189A and **State Highway 190** (1030/0.0) by the Springville fire station, we propel our bikes northeast on 190, soon observing an imposing retirement home signed "Sierra Dawn" off to the north, set amid the oaks and chaparral that dapple Sierra foothills hereabouts. When asked in 1978 about the history of this facility, Larry Norris, a local geographer, said that it had been vastly renovated after being occupied as a state tuberculosis hospital. A few minutes' ride beyond takes us past the neat, green-trimmed white buildings of a Forest Service work center. Our route then branches north where a huge, white, barnlike structure (1060/0.8) stands amid bucolic views at the outskirts of Springville.

Now tracing paved, center-dashed **TC Road MTN 239,** the signed main access to Mountain Home State Forest, we initially find ourselves flanked on the west by a ditch packed with cattails and on the east by a white board fence with a large private reservoir behind it. Just east of the reservoir, a band of sycamores, alders, cottonwoods and willows signifies the sometimes-slack presence of North Fork Tule River, which flows near our route for more than half of this journey. Shortly we cross the hidden Mount Whitney (irrigation) Ditch and then pass a landing strip that is almost concealed by the burner and debris of a derelict mill yard. Buckeyes scattered among local blue oaks herald our crossing of Buckeye Gulch, namesake of a knurled tree that sheds its leaves earlier annually than any other in the Sierra.

A sprinkling of roadside cattle-ranch houses and old-timer's homes varies the scenery as we progress through a North Fork canyon, and in time we arrive in a great basin that is blotchy with clearings. Horses and sheep are occasionally seen separately in a few of the fenced pastures ahead. Soon after reaching the basin, we catch the signed incipient pavement of TC Road MTN 220 (1380/3.4), locally known as the "Bear Creek Road." It offers the self-sufficient bicyclist access to undescribed territory; the budding ecologist, the Clemmie Gill School of Science and Conservation; and the sequoia-seeker, Mountain Home State Forest.

Observing the seasonally showy wildflowers along the next section of MTN 239 helps pass the time until we pass ranch-serving, paved TC Road MTN 231 (1630/1.6) and subsequently arc north onto paved **TC Road MTN 296** (1800/1.1), where Trip 50 riders branch northwest.

Our easy ascent continues while we pedal across a bridged, nameless creek just beyond the junction, and then the route curves past the Paradise Ranch entrance. Moments later, we cross an old bridge spanning the bleached-boulder floodplain of North Fork Tule River. Sycamores, white oaks, mountain alders, interior live oaks, redbuds, willows and blackberry vines are assembled here in a likeness of thickets ahead. Orchards fill gaps in the thicket at random; the first soon abuts our road to the west. Other openings in the thicket enclose more ranch houses and, in fall, feature bright-colored foliage on exotic trees in the front yards.

Our course shortly touches a high riverbank and then veers away among dinky reservoirs. Reeds and cattails fringe the pools that aren't left to dry in postrain heat waves. Blue oaks again provide most of our shade while we cycle past the reservoirs toward the exciting southwest face of Dennison Peak.

Conical domesticated sequoias presently signal a fork with paved, northbound TC Road MTN 256 (2420/3.0), which leads toward Battle Mountain. There, historian Annie R. Mitchell wrote in 1966, the Yokuts Indians waged a last fight to retain their ancestral homes. Nearly a century ago, mistreated Indians armed with bows and arrows held off besieging Caucasian settlers until, distracted by howitzer fire in front, they were caught by outflanking riflemen. Their descendants inhabit the South Fork Tule River drainage in a reservation to the south.

Beyond the Battle Mountain turnoff, black walnut, elderberry, wild grape and wild fig mingle in a brambly strip between our road and a parallel stream. Apples are grown in the interspersed orchards, and in the fall some growers sell them at roadside stands. Windmills add a visual delight as we make our way closer to Dennison Peak, and shortly we pass south of chicken houses before turning north onto paved **TC Road MTN 276** (2920/1.5). Signs at the junction mark the eastward extension of Road MTN 296 to Mountain Home State Forest as "J37." Confirmed pedal-pushers will find its ascent to Mountain Home a challenging bonus exploration, but the warning of J. D. Miller of the Forest Service that reckless drivers cut the blind curves of this road on weekends causes many cyclists to stick to the route of our trip.

Predominant chaparral indicates the paradoxical dryness of the elevation we've attained, but in spring the dense blooms of chamise, flannelbush, deer brush, buck brush and yerba santa hereabouts seem to invalidate the paradox. Our road assumes a moderate grade, offers northwestward views of our Blue Ridge Lookout destination and

presently bridges North Fork Tule River in sight of the eastern-horizon crags and ribs of Moses Mountain.

The stalwart bicyclist quickly ascends from the bridge to an easy-to-miss junction with northeast-trending SNF Road 19S09 (3200/0.8). Parts of this road follow a course blazed in the mid-1800's by Nathan Dillon to haul cut sequoias out from his mill in the Dillonwood Grove, northeast of here. He traced the course of the Dennison Trail, which his predecessor, Dennison, had forged across the Western Divide before dying, caught (wrote historian Floyd Otter in 1966) in his own bear trap. Logging sequoias rarely brought profits, as Dillon's descendant, Mildred Egenes, conceded in 1970, so in 1877 Dillon and friends extended their road to a gap on the horizon by the crags of Moses Mountain. Then he attempted—without success—to popularize Dillonwood as a wilderness-threshold resort. Dillonwood has remained to this day a private enclave in public lands, despite a flood in December 1966 that washed out much of the road system there and set back its current owner's plan to operate it as a tree farm.

Our pavement beyond the Dillonwood junction is quickly ridden to a Backbone Creek crossing and then patiently negotiated past the clustered cabins of a religious retreat. The black oaks that shelter the cabins also shade much of our road's next few miles and make our ongoing ascent pleasant. Before long, we enter Sequoia National Forest by bumping over a cattleguard near a stockloading pen. The subsequent jaunt through laurel-filled alcoves, past bouldery washes and between large campsites presently leads to dense woods along Kramer Creek, where incense-cedar predominates. Devils Canyon Trail 29E16 (4030/2.8), a jeep road, starts north just inside the creekside woods and links up several slanted, large campsites in its first 100 yards.

Our road, meanwhile, bridges the creek (sometimes dry), then narrows and offers a stiff ascent amid cliffs made more hairraising by over-the-shoulder close-ups of Dennison Peak's awesome facade. (Bicyclists who value their lives usually prefer to walk this road segment on their way back from the lookout to Springville.) Eventually our ascent encounters another cattleguard and turns level. This level road segment soon touches the Blue Ridge crest at a gap covered with lofty boughs of ponderosa pine and lowly wreaths of kit-kit-dizze. Here an abundantly locked gate keeps us off northbound SNF Road 19S36 (4790/2.1) and out of Upper Grouse Valley, a private inholding just to the north.

Leaving the gap, we again ascend slopes south of the crest and skirt nooks inhabited by hazelnut, thimbleberry and chaparral coffeeberry. Our road presently switchbacks out of a cove amid incense-cedar and shortly afterward regains the crest of Blue Ridge. Instantly leaving the National Forest, we pedal almost effortlessly by scattered ridgetop cabins and then—still on pavement—surmount a granite-slab prominence, skirt the microwave relay tower there and finally scoot 100 yards west. Most riders dismount upon reaching the cabin-side base (5733/2.6) of the tall, spindly tower on which the Blue Ridge Lookout is perched. In years of average fire potential, an official of the California Department of Forestry watches for smoke while taking in a comprehensive, breathtaking panorama, and from 9 a.m. to 5 p.m. he is usually glad to share the view with visitors. But even if the lookout's trapdoor entrance is locked, the view from the stairs high in the tower just beneath the door more than adequately rewards this ascent of Blue Ridge. At length, we backtrack cautiously to Kramer Creek and then swiftly to Springville and our cars.

T50   Yokohl Valley Bicycle Tour

If you want to examine the most compact collection of evidence for the cataclysmic events in earth history described in Chapter One, this is the tour to take. Most congenial in winter, spring or fall, this loop of mildly rolling roads offers bonuses for landscape photographers, wildflower enthusiasts, agricultural savants and lakeview connoisseurs in the fascinatingly diverse environs that it links.

Season   all year

Distance   62.0 miles (99.8 km), loop trip

Steep Upgrade   none

Elevation Gain and Loss   3000 feet (914 m)

Exertion/Duration   moderate/2 days, strenuous/1 day

Gears   10-speed conventional to 15-speed alpine

Permits   none

Roadhead/Maps   R43/M22A–M22C, M26A–M27, M34–M37

Description

Northeast-bound *State Highway 190* Log

T49	CDF Springville fire sta	1030	0.0
	TC Road MTN 239	1060	0.8

Northbound *Road MTN 239* Log

Highway 190	1060	0.0
TC Road MTN 220	1380	3.4
TC Road MTN 231	1630	1.6
TC Road MTN 296	1800	1.1

Taking leave of Trip 49 riders at the end of Road MTN 239, we trundle northwest on the pavement of **Road MTN 296,** signed at the fork for "Visalia." The road ahead through Yokohl Valley originated in the trail that John Jordan tried to cut across the Sierra in 1861. His object was to shorten the journey for silver-lode seekers to the rich mines near Owens Lake, and to profit by charging them for the use of the trail. In this he competed with John B. Hockett, who blazed his trail a bit farther north. The competition stopped when Jordan, having reached the midway Kern River, drowned while trying to raft across its snowmelt-swollen torrent.

The gradual ascent which makes up most of our climb to Blue Ridge passes randomly bunched blue oaks interspersed with ranch houses and large private pastures. Early in this ascent we pass the start of northbound paved TC Road MTN 240 (1960/0.7), signed "Stuart Drive," which serves backwoods ranches. Then we pass north of 2 diverting sights: a private, occasionally dry reservoir covering several acres and, 0.2 mile beyond it (and far from any railroad tracks), an inhabited caboose. Eventually our route touches steep slopes, assumes a moderate grade and switchbacks up, with the sheer granite of Dennison Peak and Moses Mountain in view to the east. Before we can work up much of a sweat, we surmount Blue Ridge (2680/2.5) and once there relax, knowing that most of this trip's elevation gain is behind us.

Grit sloughed from granite rotting in roadcuts now and then streaks our road where it switchbacks from the ridgecrest down into Yokohl Creek valley. Dense blue oak and some buckeye blot out most distant views until we round the third and final switchback. From here, the hodgepodge of foothills around Yokohl Valley stretches toward the dark cross-hatching of San Joaquin Valley farmland, backdropped by the profile of the remote Coast Ranges. These stark foothills mark the area where the prehistoric North American continent overrode an expanding ocean floor (see Chapter 1).

Then we swing rapidly around the valley's headwall to a weeping willow in a nook, opposite which a CDF fire-control station (1960/2.2) is perched on an overlook. Canteens can be filled here on request anytime from June through the end of fire season (usually November).

Our moderate descent is prolonged a bit farther, and then it yields to easy pedalling where we pass a stock ranch with an orchard and cross an adjacent, sometimes-dry creek. Beyond the ranch, our road closely parallels Yokohl Creek, where occasionally surfacing water nurtures a line of sycamores, cottonwoods and valley white oaks. Sticker weeds now and then border our route from here on, making spare tubes, a puncture-repair kit or extra tires essential to have along.

Several miles later, we cross the Chickencoop Canyon wash. A subsequent mild ascent to a gap allows our attention to wander southwest toward the defile through which Yokohl Creek veers away from our road. Being steep-sided and narrow, the defile is characteristic of the slate-dominated rocks that roadcuts several miles ahead will expose to our scrutiny. In 1977, geologist Jason B. Saleeby and a University of California research team investigated these Sierran rocks and speculated that they were deposited on an offshore continental shelf that once extended at least 300 miles north across the present Mother Lode country. The shelf deposits had been washed in, not only from the ancestral continent in the east but also from a chain of volcanic islands in the west (see Chapter 1).

Resuming our coasting at the gap, we quickly drop into hilly Yokohl Valley, where ranches are all but absent and trees are scarce. We soon enjoy easy pedalling through cattle-raising country while skirting one of the valley's many stock-truck loading pens and crossing nearby Franklin Canyon wash. Afterward we pass among rocky conical hills of hornblende gabbro.

Quite soon after leaving the gabbro, we pass under high-tension powerlines that extend across Southern Sierra foothills en route from hydroelectric generators on the San Joaquin River south to Los Angeles. Built in 1911 under the auspices of millionaire Henry E. Huntington, these transmission lines represent the first long-distance electrical conduits to appear in America.

A short breezy coast beyond the lines takes us toward Yokohl Creek and Valley, where we arc west, passing north of a roofless rock cabin whose origin historian Harold G. Schutt generalized about in 1965. One of several hundred 19th Century homesteads that once dotted Yokohl Valley, this cabin, Schutt wrote, was one of the few structures spared when the Gill family bought and then cleared the Yokohl and Frazier valleys to make way for grazing cattle, beginning in 1874. Occasional exotic palm trees off to the south show where some of the other homesteads stood.

Road MTN 296 now leads 1.4 miles west toward the valley's narrow middle, and then slices through part of hill 685, exposing provocative rocks for inspection. Some inquisitive bicyclists will know the dominant kind of slate in this roadcut by its clayey odor, microscopic grains and the shiny planes along which it breaks. Saleeby has identified—here and in surrounding ridges—the results of an undersea scrambling of washed-in rocks, slices of ocean-floor lava beds, lodes of sea-dwelling creatures' skeletons, and fragments of an oceanic crust and its underlying mantle. Chapter 1 tells not only where these rocks come from but also how they came to be so transformed that only advanced geologists directed by Saleeby's 1977 "Fieldtrip Guide to the Kings-Kaweah Suture" (see Bibliography) can appreciate them. Bicyclists impatient to get on with the trip, however, will probably be satisfied with the knowledge that outcrops of these rocks, the soils these rocks produce, plus the region's dry climate, low elevation and historic cattle-raising monopoly (now a duopoly) are the agents responsible for the strange starkness of Yokohl Valley.

After the absence of shade by hill 685 prompts bicyclists to leave, they pedal just over ½ mile toward a house·and barns at the headquarters of the Gill Ranch. A big roadside valley white oak offers shade in front of the headquarters, encouraging sunbeaten cyclists to pause and consider some recent history. Talc for talcum powder was mined from the nearby former sea-floor and mantle fragments when the ranch was in Gill family hands. The Gills soon washed their hands of the operation, however, when the talc proved too abrasive to use.

After leaving the shade, we skirt several ranch houses and ride into a wider part of Yokohl Valley, where the stubbly granodiorite island of Rocky Hill stands straight ahead of us. Still cycling past the oak and sycamore that spot the wide Yokohl Creek bed, we soon turn south onto *Road 228* (520/14.6), which bridges that creekbed immediately.

We then wheel a few hundred yards south toward a conspicuous cottonwood and eucalyptus group beside the headquarters of an alfalfa ranch. The trees mark where our road turns, becoming westbound *Avenue 272* (530/0.3). We soon reach the base of Rocky Hill, and there our road turns into southwest-trending *Drive 211* (550/0.7). In minutes it leads past a palm-guarded ranch and nearby orchards before switchbacking up a rounded ridge.

Shortly we enter the San Joaquin Valley through a gap in the ridge and then brace ourselves through a hairpin turn in the subsequent short descent. Then we turn south through a triangle junction onto *Road 216* (520/1.4) and speed across bridges that span the Lindsay Strathmore Irrigation Ditch and the Friant Kern Canal. At long last we leave grazing lands and cycle into agricultural country, a patchwork of citrus groves, farmhouse yards and fallow land. Soon after meeting westbound Avenue 264 (400/0.5), we come close to the canal and parallel ditch where they bend around a hill, and later our course turns east onto *Road 256* (360/1.0). (Tonyville lies ¼ mile south of the junction and is worth detouring to if your canteen is low on water, bikebag low on food or tires low on air.)

Our road presently spans the canal near a station where Lindsay ditch water is pumped to a higher segment of ditch. Moments later, we turn southeast onto paved *Drive 227* (450/0.8) and then roll along the foot of the capped ridge which culminates in Lindsay Peak. This varied course puts us in about 10 minutes onto west-trending, paved *Avenue 248* (450/1.1), which quickly takes us across the canal and then lets us off on *Road 224*

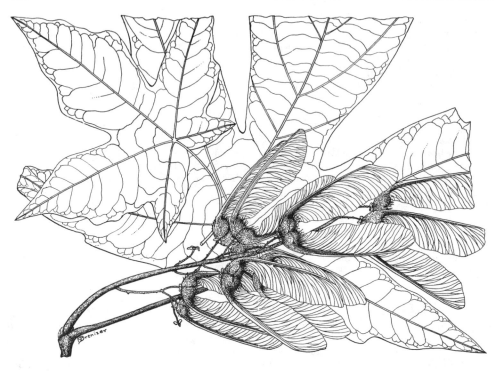

Bigleaf maple

(400/0.3). This paved road leads us south.

In ½ mile of cycling we rise slightly to an overlook by the canal of the farmlands surrounding Lindsay. Now we spin south down from the overlook, almost instantly crossing inlaid tracks of the elsewhere-vanished Visalia Electric Railroad. This company, competing with Southern Pacific and Santa Fe for the business of fruit-packing houses, probably laid these tracks sometime during the period 1915–20 to serve rural packers, wrote Harold G. Schutt in 1978.

Next, our route jogs briefly east on paved "Fir Street"—signed *Avenue 238,* (380/1.2) momentarily passing a colorfully treed housing tract, then bends south onto the asphalt of *Road 228* (400/0.5), here signed "Orange Avenue." Groves of olives and fields of cotton vary the land-use pattern in the short time it takes to reach paved *Drive 236* (410/1.3), on which we turn east. Quite soon we pass over the Friant Kern Canal for the last time, and then our road winds along transitory Lewis Creek at the base of the foothills.

The drive eventually straightens, intersects several paved farm-access roads and finally meets "Peach Avenue"—signed *Road 242* (440/1.9) before deteriorating. Taking this paved road south, we soon jog east on paved *Avenue 224* (442/0.25) past a lake-occupied gravel pit and then wheel south on *Road 244* (459/0.25). This blacktop leads on the level for several hundred yards and then bridges Lewis Creek by a patch of willows and cottonwoods. Quite soon we branch east onto *Avenue 220* (460/0.5), elsewhere confusingly signed "Second Avenue."

Soon our course recrosses Lewis Creek and then runs for nearly a mile sandwiched between the crooked creek on its south edge and the steep Rocky Hills on its north. Like the Rocky Hill we passed in leaving Yokohl Valley, these hills were carved from a mass of light gray granodiorite that had intruded into the plate junction.

The hills shortly recede to the north, and we take the second (easternmost) of 2 roads starting south. Now on paved *Road 254* (520/1.3), signed "Adams Avenue," we skirt an orchard-screened reservoir and an adjacent gravel pit before our route doglegs east on *Avenue 216* (530/0.5) toward more rounded hills. Our pavement soon bends abruptly south, signaling less complicated route-finding ahead. Now signed *"Road 256"* (530/0.5), our guideway intersects 3 pavedroadeleading west before cornering east onto the wide, striped pavement of *Avenue 196* (475/2.5).

Signposts displaying this road's code are confusingly augmentd elsewhere by "Frazier Highway" and "J28" signs. Less than 10 minutes after leaving the junction, we leave the checkered pattern of San Joaquin Valley orchards, fields and farmhouse yards behind at the entrance to Frazier Valley. Stock grazing is the dominant use of the seasonally grassy land hereabouts. Now, if the day is exceptionally clear, the profiles of Moses Mountain, 23 miles away, and next to it Maggie Mountain, 25 miles away, loom on the northeast horizon above the intervening Blue Ridge.

At length we pass south of a derelict barn made conspicuous by an adjacent tall palm tree. Leaving eastbound Avenue 196 soon afterward, we lean into a curve designed to be taken at 50 MPH that initiates us to southbound *Road 276* (600/2.3). This road quickly takes us past a ranch marked with windmills and assorted trees. Afterward, the wide, striped pavement signed "J28" curves east, becoming *Avenue 176* (640/2.3), then leads toward prominent powerlines while passing north of the Frazier Dike, which conceals Lake Success. The squat meshwork of a power substation stands by the road where we pass under the high-tension lines (the same ones we saw in Yokohl Valley).

We shortly roll into view of a shallow Lake Success inlet that is usually bereft of water, and then touch the end of Road 292 (720/2.0) where it comes in from the south. Gabbro is the black rock exposed in the roadcut we pass through just east of the junction, and subsequent roadcuts reveal cross sections of gray quartz diorite and, later, brownish slate.

Now we coast down to the slightly rolling terrace of sand, gravel and cobbles that underlies Pleasant Valley. Quite soon our road joins with paved TC Road MTN 171A (800/2.1) from the west, and then we proceed in a straight line for a bit more than a mile. Early along this straightaway we pass a small olive orchard, note a citrus grove forming a collar around a hill by a palm tree to the north and then pass an apparently unused sawmill. Once at the straightaway's end we

cross a transitory stream just upslope from a small, sometimes dry reservoir. Then, while Avenue 176 forks east and diminishes, the main highway, still signed "J28," starts curving south as *TC Road MTN 176* (740/1.4).

Quite soon we turn east onto paved *State Highway 190* (770/0.4) where traffic is fast and often heavy. Fortunately for us, a slight margin of pavement that we can ride on laps over the shoulders. Immediately to the south sprawls a golf course and residential tract, and soon we find just to the north the main office (800/0.3) of the Tule River District, Sequoia National Forest. (See the "Organizational Services" section for the services offered here and the hours they are rendered.)

Then we meet southbound paved *TC Road MTN 172A* (840/1.0), signed "Globe Drive," just short of signed "Pleasant Valley Ranch" where home-grown fruit is occasionally heaped in a stall to tempt and be bought by passersby. Some cyclists usually detour east on 190 to the ranch, then backtrack to this junction. Others who are especially eager to get back to their cars can take 190 past the ranch directly to Springville. But we may be craving a contrast to the ordered farms and austere ranches we've seen so far, and so turn south onto Globe Drive and aim toward a lake-dappled, pastoral landscape.

First we swoop down this striped but narrow 2-lane road toward its bridge spanning the Tule River, crossing an overgrown historic railroad bed in the dense riverside alders and sycamores. Soon after bridging the river, our course leads across paved TC Roads MTN 161 (west—800/0.5) and MTN 167 (east) near a spacious ranch subdivision.

Bunches of blue and live oaks then shade our road as it gradually ascends past lupines. Quite soon we level off on a terrace and cross the Moore-Witt Ditch, the lower of 2 ditches delivering water to the terrace's many ponds and reservoirs. Then the road turns abruptly east and guides us past scattered reedy marshes, small ranches and rolling pastures, soon taking in Road MTN 167 (870/0.9) from the northwest.

Beyond the junction, our road arcs through a great foothill amphitheatre and presently parallels the Graham-Osborn Ditch, where wild plum and fig trees and oaks are festooned with wild cucumbers, and where monkey flowers are displayed. Our course soon makes a gap in woods along murmuring Graham Creek. A few minutes' ride beyond the creek crossing takes us past patches of wild rose, elderberry, blackberry and grapevine to a view of a serene pool several acres large. Adjacent sycamores and Kellogg oaks increase the landscape's appeal.

By and by we drop to the riverside on a road segment closely flanked by fences and "No Parking" signs, and after making a short tour of Tule River woodland, our course bridges the river, quickly returning us to the state highway (890/3.2). The final minutes of our trip cover our easy ascent north from the junction on **Highway 190's** paved shoulder. We shortly progress past the extended outskirts of Springville, and eventually reach the town's commercial district. After passing the district's park and the familiar CDF firecontrol station beside it, we end our journey upon finding **Road MTN 189A** (1030/1.9) and our cars.

T51   Dunn Trail Hike

Variety and vitality embodied in a slapdash gathering of plants by cascading brooks in glens—all at their best in the winter—make up one of the riches conferred by this compact trip.

Season   April through December

Distance   5.0 miles (8.0 km) round trip

Steep Upgrade   none

Elevation Gain and Loss   2090 feet (637 m)

Exertion/Duration   moderate/1 day

Skills   easy route-finding, Class 1 climbing

Permits   none

Roadhead/Map   R44/M29

Description   This trip begins by leaving paved TC Road MTN 208A (3220/0.0) by an often-stolen trailhead sign and ascending a stiff grade on **Dunn Trail 30E16** across a slope of chamise and buckbrush. A transitory brook that cascades down many mossy boulders marks the slope's base, and is itself marked by hedges of laurel, gooseberry and canyon live oak. In the meantime, we too weave among boulders, and presently ford the creek on slick rock fringed with woodwardia ferns.

A tributary trickle approaches the brook a few hundred yards upstream, and we step across it just north of the confluence. Then we proceed into a cleft glutted with bracken fern, wild ginger, blackberry, kit-kit-dizze, canyon live oak, Kellogg oak, sycamore, sugar pine and white fir. After a while, we recross the brook, then leap a fork of it masked by ferns and, shortly thereafter, make our last step-across ford of the brook.

Our course next leads briefly up a divergent ravine, then switchbacks away, traversing a slope of exposed brush in which manzanita and Brewers oak indicate our advanced elevation. Shortly we gain, then turn northwest on, a briefly flat ridge from which can be seen Black Mountain in the south and Jordan Peak lookout in the east. The ensuing gently rising segment of trail crosses slopes south of the ridge and zigzags briefly between 2 midway ravines. That segment ends, by and by, upon touching a slight, northwest-trending ridge where oak-dotted grass borders chaparral.

Although grass obscures the path here, the route turns up the ridge and skirts several blazed oaks. After a few hundred yards the trail resumes. Immediately we leave the ridge, then work generally west across slopes and at length meet paved TC Road MTN 220 (5300/2.5) where it adjoins a jeep track from the north. A "Dunn Trail" sign marks the spot in this broad, shade-dappled saddle. After taking in the soothing vistas here, we backtrack to the cars.

T52   Alpine Meadow Backpack

Looking for challenging route-finding? A stiff workout? Redwoods?
Pools? Waterfalls? Meadows? Colorful cliffs? Lofty peaks? Comprehen-
sive panoramas? This is the trip for you.

Season   May through October

Distance   18.9 miles (30.4 km) semiloop
trip

Steep Upgrade   0.2 mile (0.3 km)

Elevation Gain and Loss   6000 feet (1829 m)

Exertion/Duration   easy/4 days, moder-
ate/3 days, strenuous/2 days

Skills   moderate route-finding, Class 2
climbing

Permits   Wilderness Permit

Roadhead/Maps   R45/M29–M30, M39–
M40

Description   Our adventure begins at a
usually locked gate across **TC Road MTN
208A** (3930/0.0) where it enters Doyle
Springs Association land in Camp Wishon.
The **private road** beyond the gate at first
leads east-northeast along the bouldery
North Fork of Middle Fork Tule River and
parallel to a boxy concrete aqueduct. When
the fledgling Pacific Gas and Electric Company built the aqueduct as part of a power-
generating complex in the Tule River drainage, early in this century, the resort near
which we parked our cars was named for A.
E. Wishon, the company's general manager.
The resort, snug as it is, was built beyond
reach of the local hot springs, which Tulare
County pioneer J. J. Doyle had pre-empted
several decades earlier. Later, after the formation of the Doyle Springs Association expanded the springs' patronage, the springs
remained the nucleus of a private retreat despite the inflow of tourists on the power
company's roads.

Shortly our road forks north where a spur
road (3980/0.3) bridges the river. We then
skirt an aqueduct-intake dam, take several
dozen strides farther up-canyon and start
north on **Wishon Trail 30E14** (4030/0.1).
Signs here plead with hikers to use the trail
instead of trespassing on the road northeast
of here through a summer-home tract.

Our path zigzags twice quite early, then
traces a sinuous course up a gentle grade

alternately bracketed by ground-shrouding
kit-kit-dizze, exceedingly thick manzanita,
and nook-embellishing bracken fern. Intermittently glimpsing downslope cabins, we
presently stroll down a low ridge and then
quickly fork north from a cabin-bound lateral (4160/0.4). Next, the main trail curls
across a ravine and later continues to rise
gently north past a spur path signifying the
end of Jacobsen Wildroute 31E21 (4330/0.6).
(That's the route on which we'll return toward the end of this trip.)

Moments later, Doyle Trail 30E15 splits
northwest from our course amid signposts
aplenty, and then our grade becomes
moderate. Some 20 minutes of mild exertion
get us to a brief, gentle downgrade, which
signals a brook ford ahead. Sycamore pre-
sides over the ford, where the brook spills
half-hidden by California hazelnut and
thimbleberry bushes.

The path beyond the ford slants down
steeply but briefly, connecting with north-
trending 4H Trail 30E14A (4550/1.3) on a
terrace beside the roaring river. In 1974 the
only signpost present was propped against
the roots of a river-spanning blowdown. (It
identified the river but not the junction.) Besides this batch of large campsites, several
more can be discovered by strolling the cobbly and exquisitely scenic 4H Trail north
from here.

Our route, the Wishon Trail, inconspicu-
ously turns southeast at the junction, then
dips down a short, steep embankment and
fords the boulder-studded river. (When
snowmelt surges submerge the boulders, the
downed tree extending east from the junction serves as a bridge for mountaineers sure
of their balance.) Resuming the trail on the
east bank, we forge through a screen of
riverside alders, then continue southeast
through a floodplain jumble of boulders.
Soon we re-enter mixed broadleaf-conifer
forest, meeting a southbound course signed
"Fisherman Trail" (4550/0.1). It traces the

floodplain fringe ½ mile south before ending in a large, sequoia-shaded campsite.

Beyond the Fisherman Trail, the Wishon Trail curves southeast, then switchbacks north just short of a mucky, orange-stained mineral spring. The ensuing moderate ascent soon leads past a sandstone outcrop on which rain sometimes etches delicate laceworks. This sandstone, together with dominant shales and residual clays (most of them rich in the calcium carbonate from which concrete is made) make up a widespread deposit called flysch. These rocks are easier to wear away than the granite that surrounds them, and that, combined with snowfalls greater than most Sierran locales received, speeded the Tule River's entrenchment.

The path continues ascending beyond the outcrop, presently tops a crosswise ridge in a swale and then dips toward a large, terrace-perched campsite by Burro Creek. Just short of the campsite, we veer east into the Burro Creek ravine and ford the creek near dry-crossing logs a few moments later. Another bunch of large campsites can be found by strolling west parallel to the north bank on a short, pathless route to a wooded terrace beside the river.

Beyond the ford our path angles upslope beside the creek, continuing east momentarily to the brink of an angel-hair waterfall.

The path subsequently switchbacks north, then undulates into sequoia and dogwood environs. It presently passes a few partly caved-in mineshafts that are dangerous even to come near, then guides us up a taxingly steep ridge. In the meantime, the entrenched river remains tantalizingly visible but out of reach in the western foreground. Shortly the grade dwindles to nothing and then we meet an abandoned portion of SNF Jeep Road 19S29 (5090/1.5). We catch the road where it zigs from southeast to north above a junked copper mine and follow it briefly upslope through a zag southeast to its end. The Wishon Trail resumes heading north here, but quickly narrows, being undermined by a roadcut. Once again we undulate, though steeply now, and presently cross a ravine just short of a swale worn in a transverse ridge. There, while takers of Trip 64 turn north on the Wishon Trail, we

swerve northeast onto **Griswold Trail 31E18** (5290/0.5).

This path was among the first to span the Sierra Nevada, historian Floyd Otter observed. Originally a game trail, it was first improved by Indians, and then by pioneering Caucasians when it was known as the Dennison Trail. Its current name commemorates Art Griswold, who engineered its realignment in 1930, adding some 50 zigzags to ease the grade and better serve his Shake Camp pack station. Although this moderate, sometimes steep ridge ascent enjoys nearly continuous forest shade, water has always been scarce en route, so backpackers lacking 2 quarts of water should take a short detour north on the Wishon Trail to tank up at Silver Creek.

Starting up the Griswold Trail's first few dozen zigzags, we inhale the spicy aroma of bordering kit-kit-dizze while panting up along a slight ridge. We presently cut through an unmarked boundary, entering Mountain Home State Forest, and later meet the signed Eastside Trail (6490/1.1), which leads takers of Trip 65 in from the north.

The ensuing zigzaggery shortly gives place to a brief southeast traverse that gets us atop a greater ridge just northeast of a broad saddle. We then wind a few hundred yards upward along this northeast-trending ridge, and later traverse its south-facing slopes for a mile, re-entering Sequoia National Forest midway. The traverse terminates moments after our course jogs north onto a wedge-shaped flat. Subsequently, 12 zigzags mark our progess north past vistas of the Western Divide's sheer, convoluted western facade. Then we touch the northeast-trending ridge next to a large, waterless campsite ensconced in a swale. After entering Golden Trout Wilderness here, we work up 11 more zigs and zags toward another large, ridgecrest campsite, equally waterless but with a better outlook.

The ensuing final set of zigzags leads up just north of the ridge, which presently merges with a gentler, southwest-facing slope. Our zigzags abate when we reach this slope, where lupine obscuring the trail poses a route-finding problem. The problem is most critical for backpackers taking this trip in reverse, who must find the head of the zigzags. Our course, meanwhile, rises 550 yards east through sparse red fir up a mild grade, then tops the Western Divide. Independent explorers seeking ragged timberline plants plus overviews of lake-occupied bowls will find a detour north along the divide to Maggie Mountain more than rewarding. Its bonus treat is a heady panorama of far-flung California features.

Sooner or later, everyone traces the dim Griswold Trail briefly down the divide, and then veers east off the divide, quickly meeting signed **Summit Trail 31E14** (8890/3.3), onto which they turn south.

Southbound *Summit Trail* Log

T46	Griswold Trail 31E18	8890	0.0
	Neva Point trail	8500	0.9
	Mountaineer Trail 32E10	8100	0.6
T45	Jacobsen Wildroute 31E21	8360	1.3

Where the **Jacobsen Wildroute** starts southwest as a faint path from a signed junction with the Summit Trail, we must choose between two alternatives.

*   *   *   *   *

One, which involves moderate skill in route-finding, is to trace the bushy, blowdown-ridden first segment of the wildroute's trail. Leaving the junction (8360/0.0), it quickly vanishes under a hodgepodge of wind-felled red firs, then swerves south from a saddle on the Western Divide. The route shortly descends moderately across a west-facing slope, and resolves into a path, although sometimes it passes through overlapping snow bush and chinquapin. The west-trending ridge we're aiming for is discernible as we approach it, and even more so when, at length, we cross it (8200/0.6). Here we join backpackers who took a brush-bypassing ridgecrest course that offers easier route-finding.

*   *   *   *   *

That course, the second alternative, a favorite of panorama collectors, follows the Summit Trail south from the Jacobsen Wildroute (8360/0.0) in a short, moderate ascent through red-fir forest. The trail presently zigzags, and at its third hairpin turn some hikers leave the trail (8580/0.4) immediately. (Others may want to detour south briefly to

take in the panorama described in Trip 45.) Eventually everyone leaves the path at the same switchback, and then contours southwest, cross-country, pacing off nearly 200 yards. That brings us to a west-trending ridge, which we descend some distance before rejoining the Jacobsen Wildroute (8200/0.3).

*   *   *   *   *

Our difficulties are far from over because, after crossing the ridge, the path veers west over its south-facing slopes and vanishes in a man-tall tangle of prickly snow bush and manzanita. The easiest way out of this mess follows the open ridgecrest several hundred yards west and finally rejoins the trail where it emerges from the brush and returns to the crest.

The pathfinding is easy now as we stroll down along the ridge, soon noticing sugar pine in the midst of the dominant red fir, which has spread to unusually low elevations along slopes just north of the ridge. A subsequent set of zigzags lets us down onto metamorphic rock, which will add to our route's scenic attractions until nearly the end of the trip.

The trail then guides our progressive shuttling across the crest from north- to south-facing slopes and back again for a mile, and afterward starts zigzagging down where the ridge divides into 2 steeper spurs. While ponderosa pine gains predominance and kit-kit-dizze starts hemming the path, we coast down the northern of the 2 spurs for a while, until the trail starts zigzagging down this spur's southwest-facing slope. The 7 zigzags precede a brief interval of diagonal downslope traversing, which gets us to a shady ravine just upslope from a spring nestled in it.

Our course downslope from the spring is crisscrossed by confusing game traces. We make a lengthy descent across a southwest-trending spur of the main Jacobsen ridge, tracing the crest for a few hundred yards midway along the descent. Encountering Kellogg oak and nutmeg along the descent's final stage—a traverse of the spur's south flank—we presently touch an east-trending lateral signed "to Ellister's cabin" (4870/3.6), a private hideaway. Then our course drops from a terrace upslope from hidden North

Alder Creek and shortly connects with a signed lateral (4690/0.2) that starts southeast toward "Healy Cabin," another private summer home.

The descent is nearly complete by the time we sight cascading North Alder Creek and then gingerly tread a sometimes slippery plank causeway across a bog bristling with horsetails. Then the path is lost under a large tufa deposit colored a glistening sorrel where streams issuing from an upslope spring wash over it. Now we bear west-northwest, gingerly picking our way across the thin-crusted slime, being guided by blazed trees.

After emerging from the tufa deposit, the trail leads north a moment, then turns southwest in a ravine and slants down across a North Alder Creek canyonside on a moderate grade overarched by oaks, incense-cedars and—indicative of our low elevation—sycamores. Presently our path curves north around the southwest-trending spur near its base, then arcs south while a northbound path (4400/0.4) peels off midway through the arc. The "Fishermans Trail" sign for this path stands misplaced to the south by our route's ford of Alder Creek, but the trail itself leads to some popular whitewater-fed pools in the North Fork of the Middle Fork Tule River.

A few minutes' stroll south from the junction on a much-trampled path takes us to our descent's terminus, a ford, with boulders for hopping, of signed "Alder Creek." Sunlight periodically filters through alders into the glen where this ford is set, playing on broken-cliff crannies with grass and columbines. Sometimes the sun spotlights leopard lilies and scintillates off the creek beneath.

Now our course rolls over a low ridge that deflects the alder-screened river west. The path then slants down a riverside terrace past many turnoffs of river-bound paths and soon skirts a large, oak-shaded campsite. Shortly we ford the boulder-strewn river, then amble south over a sandy strand and afterward touch the end of the Doyle Springs Association Summer Home Tract road (4170/0.5).

A cluster of signs accompanies the juncture, one of which asks hikers to respect the residents' need for privacy, and to use the tract-bypassing trail instead of this road. The last trail segment of the Jacobsen Wild-route, which constitutes the first part of this bypass, zigzags up a puckered slope, veering southwest minutes later to join the **Wishon Trail** (4330/0.2). Tracking footprints we made earlier, we trace this trail and a subsequent link of **private road** back to our cars (3930/1.4).

T53   Slate Mountain Backpack

When is a trip extraordinary? Could it be when the highest point in the United States outside of Alaska—Mount Whitney—crops up in the trip's panoramas? Could it be when its panoramas include not only the Southern Sierra, the San Joaquin Valley and the Coast Ranges but also the Pacific Ocean? Or when it helps hikers to discover a landscape packed with attractions? What else could describe a trip that leads past volcanic spires, granite-bound gorges, whitewater streams, orangy-shanked sequoias, quaking aspens and rainbow-flowered glades? What else could describe a trip that leads through a giant sequoia, and that leads near a store, cafe and campground midway; a trip that calls for sharp pathfinding skills, and that appeals to geologists, wild-river enthusiasts, botanists, photographers, rock climbers, self-reliant explorers and seekers of off-trail solitude. Those who take this trip usually agree that it is extraordinary.

Season   July through October

Distance   15.1 miles (24.3 km) shuttle trip

Steep Upgrade   0.6 mile (1.0 km)

Elevation Gain and Loss   4890 feet (1490 m)

Exertion/Duration   moderate/2 days

Skills   moderate route-finding, Class 2 climbing

Permits   USFS Campfire Permit

Roadheads/Maps   R46–R47/M24, M30–M31

Description   This Slate Mountain back-pack begins at a signed cul-de-sac (5120/0.0) where SNF Road 20S10 ends and *Quaking Aspen Trail 31E30,* which we take, starts east. Quite soon we sight a large campsite amid the wayside kit-kit-dizze and then boulder-hop across McIntyre Creek. Francis P. Far-quhar's 1924 place-name research revealed that this creek was named for a Tulare County pioneer and 1880's sheepman, Thomas McIntyre.

A trickle spiny with horsetails parallels McIntyre Creek just over 100 yards to the east and, soon after fording it, we amble along the South Fork of the Middle Fork Tule River. Now our course weaves among knots of gooseberries and ferns interspersed on springy humus overshadowed by Kellogg oaks, ponderosa and sugar pines, and McIntyre Grove sequoias. Several minutes into this amble, we skirt a medium campsite and then ford to the south bank of the river. Backpackers wishing to cross with dry feet when the river is swollen with snowmelt can often find a toppled tree spanning the river nearby.

Now we advance along the south bank past another medium campsite, presently zigzag-ging onto a terrace. There our course skirts a large campsite in an exclusive Kellogg-oak grove, afterward crosses a stump-riddled clearing and eventually meets a retired ex-tension of SNF Road 20S46 (5410/1.1). We turn northeast onto the road at an often signless post, take some 70 paces northeast and then turn southeast, resuming the path by another post. Although motorbikers have been allowed to use the path to this point, they seldom do; but if they progress beyond this point, they can be cited for trespass.

Our path now slants up a moderate grade, soon passing through a sequoia trunk where it forks in an inverted **V.** California hazelnut,

yellow violets and horsetails grace this fringe of the Wheel Meadow sequoia grove, which we proceed to traverse. Early in this traverse, still parallel to the hidden river, our trail zig-zags up onto another sloping terrace. Later it rolls across several ravines past chinquapin and labrador tea and eventually leaves the grove. Then we ford the river's headstream and 2 of its nearby converging forks, and afterward switchback northeast, rising 600 feet. Finally the route turns east from a "Camp Nelson Trail"–signed trailhead onto paved *State Highway 190* (6780/2.3).

A short stint of strolling its shoulder takes us out of the river's canyon and onto rolling, red-fir-clad terrain, where we stroll in sight of a fork of the river. Then our route turns southeast from the highway onto a retired road that now serves as a segment of *Summit Trail 31E14* (6880/0.4). It almost instantly crosses the river fork, then cuts across an often-wet meadow, skirts Quaking Aspen Meadow and eventually meets SNF Road 21S78 (7160/0.7).

Southwest-bound *SNF Road 21S78* Log

T40	Summit Trail (north)	7160	0.0
	Summit Trail (south)	7160	0.1

Southbound *Summit Trail 31E14* Log

SNF Road 21S78	7160	0.0
Bear Creek		
Wildroute 31E31	9050	4.0

The first trail segment of the *wildroute* starts northwest from a signed ridgeline fork with the Summit Trail. It leads us down the ridge's moderate incline amid sugar pines to a broad saddle. From there, the wildroute curves east into a bowl and shortly turns north, approaching a spring-fed pond near the base of the bowl. The path—always dim and at times overgrown by dwarf lupine—shortly skirts the pond, then extends a few hundred feet beyond and passes 3 tiers of logs outlining what was once a cabin.

Now we cut through a few large campsites near a dribbling spring (the last water source on the trip). After we tramp briefly beside the dense greenery lining the spring's runoff, we ford it and rise diagonally upslope through pinemat manzanita. To-ward the end of this mild ½-mile ascent, the forest parts in the east to reveal Kern Peak's massiveness, which contrasts in the middle distance with The Needles' slenderness. In the background, a serrate Sierra crest extends from Mount Corcoran south to Olancha Peak.

Then our route crosses the rounded Bear Creek/Tule River divide and begins a drawn-out descent with a brief traverse of a west-facing slope and a subsequent short drop along the divide. We leave the divide just south of a chinquapin-mantled boss, stride several dozen yards down a steep, northeast-facing slope, then turn north beside a landmark outcrop where pink-stained granite is broken as if plowed. A short, gentle cross-slope descent then returns us to the divide at a cairn, and from there we weave down more northeast-facing slopes while dodging or jumping numerous blowdowns.

Shortly the slopes resolve into a steep, broad trough, which we presently leave on a faint path that gradually improves. After gently descending north, the trail contours northeast on the east shoulder of a nearly flat subsidiary ridge. A few hundred yards of contouring past chinquapin clumps bring us to a cairned swale from which our course zigzags briefly west into a ravine. Then we weave briefly down the ravine while the red fir that shades us yields to white fir and sugar and ponderosa pine.

At the 7220-foot level, the trail starts cutting diagonally down a north-facing slope swathed in kit-kit-dizze. We presently edge across the slippery trough of a landslide, and later cut through a sloping meadow flanked by the outmost sequoias of the Belknap Camp Grove. It's but a brief stroll beyond

the grass to an erect, capped pipe stuck in the ground, the cap inscribed "General Land Office/1923". Now the path executes several blowdown-obscured zigzags down a gully, then becomes conspicuous while rounding an incipient, north-trending ridge onto metamorphic rock. Shortly thereafter the trail returns to the Bear Creek/Tule River divide, which we start tromping down.

Osa Trail 31E23 (6200/4.2), an unmaintained lateral to the Belknap Creek Campground, soon branches north while we continue west. Then the divide's gradient eases awhile where knots of gooseberry and shooting star appear among the kit-kit-dizze. Shortly before the divide steepens, we switchback south down its flank, then traverse under the arcing boughs of canyon live oaks and Kellogg oaks which host parasitic mistletoe. This traverse takes us across a few open slopes enlivened with holly, ceanothus, Indian paintbrush and brodiaea. Eventually, we round the divide to its north flank, then switchback southwest near an outlook on the community of Camp Nelson. Shortly afterward our course skirts a water tank serving the downslope Slate Mountain Summer Home Tract.

Just south of the water tank, we meet a wide path (4760/1.7) serving the tract; and then our trail, being much fainter, bears southeast toward a final few switchbacks and a large mud slide near Bear Creek. The trail segment presently ends by a "Bear Creek Trail 31E31" sign, at a junction with paved TC Road MTN 192A (4550/0.5) a few dozen steps from our shuttle car and the creek itself.

T54   Camp Nelson Run

Warm, reddish-brown forest palings encoiled in vivid greenery augment the rusticity of Camp Nelson's historic architecture in a splendid setting for running. Few other trips in this book visit as many convenience and comfort servicers or touch a spring quite so quenching and generous.

Season	March through November	**Exertion/Duration**	strenuous/1 hour
Distance	6.0 miles (9.7 km) round trip	**Skills**	easy route-finding, Class 2 climbing
Steep Upgrade	none	**Permits**	none
Elevation Gain and Loss	700 feet (213 m)	**Roadhead/Map**	R47/M30

Description We start running west on *SNF Road 20S10* from its cul-de-sac (5120/0.0) and almost immediately step gingerly to cross a cobbly, sometimes-dry creek fork. Soon rushing by cabins that line the South Fork of the Middle Fork Tule River, we start running on asphalt midway along the line of cabins. Dense incense-cedar, sugar pine, white fir and an occasional black oak interlace branches overhead as we dart past the cabins and cabin-side slopes of kit-kit-dizze.

Runners then skirt the signed start of Belknap Campground Road 20S05 (4960/0.5) across from the signed beginning of Osa Trail 31E23, and afterward cross Belknap Creek, then stride a short but winding road segment to the outskirts of Camp Nelson. Emigrant John Nelson homesteaded here in 1886, according to an account Russ Leadabrand passed on in 1968. Nelson soon catered to one pressing need of San Joaquin Valley residents—escape from summertime heat. He built a hotel and a clientele. He then provided easier access, starting with pack-train service over the trail from Springville. Nelson's son-in-law and successor, Charles Smith, was there when a road replaced the trail; his subdivision eventually contained some 400 cabins, including the ones we now run past.

Our road changes designations, becoming *MTN 193A,* where we pass a "snow not removed beyond this point" sign on the outskirts of town. (Numerous narrower paved roads branch off our route ahead, but the correct route is usually either obvious or signed.) Quite soon we charge past a county fire station and then find near our bridge over Nelson Creek, in the center of town, a trailer park just south of our road, then a meadow, riding stable and store to the north, followed by a modern successor of Nelson's hotel (where hot showers are sold to runners) to the south. The main Camp Nelson road joins *State Highway 190* (4770/1.5) at a signed triple-pronged fork shortly afterward, and there we take the striped, paved state road southwest.

More oaks appear in the conifer forest as we sprint down a gradual grade through the extension of Camp Nelson called Pierpoint Springs, passing just north of a knoll-top combination store, restaurant, motel, gas station and post office (4540/0.6) in less than 10 minutes. Then we lope briefly while the highway contours, and enjoy an occasional view of the Tule River canyon, before reaching the spouts where Pierpoint Spring (4500/0.4) issues from crystalline limestone and splashes over a mortared stone wall. The spring is always cold and always flows at the same voluminous rate, even during severely dry years. Now we backtrack to our cars.

T55   Hossack Meadow Bicycle Tour

Crag-dominated watershed views plus a brook-threaded subalpine meadow highlight this two-way traverse of a road with mild grades, light residential traffic and a thick, colorful flanking forest.

Season May through October

Distance 12.0 miles (19.3 km) round trip

Steep Upgrade none

Elevation Gain and Loss 1400 feet (427m)

Exertion/Duration easy/1 day

Gears 5-speed conventional to 15-speed alpine

Permits none

Roadhead/Map R48/M30

Description From the 5-car pullout beside State Highway 190 (5430/0.0) our route coincides with that highway while leading a few dozen yards north, then branches west onto paved *TC Road MTN 216,* signed "Redwood Drive." Early in its ascent, this road crosses strips of manzanita, live oak and black oak alternating with ponderosa pine, kit-kit-dizze, elderberry and thimbleberry while winding across corrugated slopes. These trees and shrubs occasionally part to frame southward views of crags near Slate Mountain across a canyon drained by a fork of the Tule River. Although many curves on this road are blind ones, the road's width allows cyclists who ride close to the right shoulder some confidence about their safety. Presently we cross fizzing Nelson Creek, later round a promontory ridge, and then cut across a corner of the same metamorphic rocks that are responsible for the reliableness of Pierpoint Spring, which issues forth a mile southwest—downslope—from here. The addition of white fir to the forest makes it denser from now on, and roadside silk tassel starts to thrive while manzanita grows more scarce. A few dirt roads branch off from our own as we quickly approach and then execute a switchback, and much later the A-frame cafe-store, gas pumps and phone booth of signed "Alpine Village" appear by the inside edge of our road's most viewful hairpin curve. The paved exit of east-trending TC Road MTN 208A (6310/3.0), signed "Alpine Drive," is situated midway on this curve. Our road straightens just beyond and to the west, downslope from a perched motel.

Quite soon we return to dense forest, observing burgeoning snow bush and *Lotus cressifolia* in roadcuts. Our twisty, ascending road continues to yield inspiring views, presently forks with a northbound jeep track that leads to hidden stump fields and before long meets signed SNF Road 19S06 (6240/1.6), which heads toward the low end of Hossack Meadow. Shortly thereafter, our road connects with Hossack Wildroute 31E24 (6330/0.7), here a retired logging road that, in 1977, was officially declared off limits to motorcycles.

Hazelnut's sudden appearance in the shadier roadside nooks is indicative of moist soils and a sign of the elevation we've attained. The junction marks the onset of a gradual, coasting descent for us, which ends soon after we arc across bouncy Hossack Creek with white-fir-fringed Hossack Meadow in view. Chinquapin and lupine complicate the texture of nearby ground cover while we make a short ascent beyond the meadow. Then our road enters a subdivision on part of a 640-acre private inholding, and there its pavement narrows upon crossing signed Hossack and Redwood drives (6290/0.7). A nearby sign labels the neighborhood "Sequoia Crest" and offers cabins for rent. Undaunted by steep grades ahead, inquisitive cyclists may want to take

the main road farther north to see how the Alder Creek Grove of giant sequoias survived the subdividers. We, meanwhile, double back to our cars, enjoying a refreshing descent on the way.

Utter frustration

T56 Skiing on Jordan Peak

Great potential, sometimes realized, characterizes this trek to Jordan Peak. It's here in the peak's fetching panorama: short rows of distant, jagged, snow-capped peaks on the northern horizon beckoningly indicate that there's more to the High Sierra than meets the eye. Part of these peaks' suggestiveness stems from their lean jaggedness contrasting with the Southern Sierra's dominant horizontality. Potential beauty closer at hand is realized not only when the Jordan Peak lookout acquires a jagged fringe of ice, but also when the debris and harsh lines in clearings created by nearby logging are masked by snow, subordinating their artificiality to the clearings' views and usefulness as ski courses.

Some breathtaking alpine runs can be found along and near this trek, including logged slopes overlooking Golden Trout Wilderness that have long been held in reserve as a potential commercial skiing development. Because the potential of this trek's surroundings for beauty and use is only the first of its opportunities, skiers can have the pleasure of learning the place's secrets for themselves.

Season   January through March

Distance   17.2 miles (27.7 km) round trip

Steep Upgrade   0.1 mile (0.2 km)

Elevation Gain and Loss   2200 feet (671 m)

Exertion/Duration   easy/3 days, moderate/2 days, strenuous/1 day

Skills   moderate route-finding, intermediate alpine skiing

Roadhead/Maps   R49/M30–M31

Description   Our journey begins on the snow-burdened pavement of *SNF Road 21S50,* which starts northeast where State Highway 190 (6950/0.0) ends and TC Road MTN 107 begins. Our road initially leads amid snow-cloaked conifers along a headwaters branch of the Tule River. Usually not more than 10 minutes elapse before we pass through a gap in the Western Divide where the wind during Pacific storms can be fierce. Here in a logging-expanded clearing we meet a spur of SNF Road 21S99 (7190/0.5) that is sometimes obscured by snowdrifts. Then our road winds across the uppermost part of the Freeman Creek drainage (where downslope sequoias stay hidden) and presently we can sight the corridor-narrow clearing of Coffee Mill Meadow.

Now our gradually ascending road enters the Boulder Creek watershed through a swale, then splits north from SNF Road 20S75 (7400/1.3) and traverses a couple of patchcuts in the forest. At length we pass the northward exit of SNF Road 20S79 (7680/2.2), which allows for improvisory detours to the generous expanse of ideal nordic touring terrain known as the Loggy Slopes. This road also gives access to breezy alpine ski runs on the back side of peak 8556, which offers a captivating eastward view of Hermits Dome (Trip 43).

Our trek, meanwhile, continues along Road 21S50—which, beneath all the snow, narrowed and lost its pavement at the junction. Offering occasional views down the Tule River canyon, it presently meets southwest-starting SNF Road 20S81 (7900/1.1) and almost instantly afterward recrosses the wandering Western Divide through a saddle. Here we start crossing extra-thick leeward drifts of the Log Cabin Slopes, outflanking Log Cabin Meadow early. Then we observe a "Clicks Creek Trail 32E11" sign (7850/0.5) protruding from drifts for a summertime trail just north of the whitened meadow. A subsequent roadside patchcut precedes by a few dozen yards a signed crossing of Clicks Creek. Then a brief stint of incline-slogging gets us up to the foot of a long 5-acre slope that was cleared of all trees more than 10 years ago. Skier Loren Ross, who had traversed this slope often during the mid-1970's, evaluated its skiing potential in 1978. His downslope slides here were rarely fast ones, hence his recommendation that novice nordic and alpine skiers use these slopes for practicing turns. Although the isohyetal map John Harper drew in 1974 indicates that the average precipitation here reaches 30–35 inches a year, which should ensure that the snowpack would be at least 12 feet deep, Ross said that the southern exposure (we are just off the Log Cabin Slopes) kept the pack less than 6 feet deep. Some of the slope's stumps protruded there, and Ross warned future skiers to check out their runs before descending.

Now the road loops around to pass just above the upper end of the patchcut slope (downslope runs begin here), and shortly thereafter meets **SNF Closed Road 20S71** (8240/1.3). Some skiers may choose to explore view-packed patchcuts proposed for commercial ski development in the upper North Fork Clicks Creek drainage by continuing north on Road 21S50, but we turn west onto 20S71.

A locked green metal gate spans our road near the junction, and getting past it entails some tricky side-stepping. Then our course crosses a few steep patchcuts having poor run-out for schuss-booming but offering invigoratingly fresh sidelong vistas of Slate Mountain and the southernmost Western Divide. Our protracted jaunt along the closed road ends in a southeast-trending ravine, the conduit of a transitory brook (8580/1.1). Though the road continues beyond, we leave it here.

Now we stick wax or skins on our skis and then do the herringbone shuffle (or your own favorite climbing step), gaining some 300 vertical feet west up a steep, red-fir-forested slope. (This **cross-country route** is obscured by the word "Peak" on the map.) Topping the slope some 100 yards southwest of a ridgecrest saddle, we then work southwest up the crest past vistas of a Tule River branch's 4000-foot-deep canyon.

Eventually we emerge from forest, advance a few dozen yards farther and then reap the nearly comprehensive panorama outside of Jordan Peak Lookout (9115/0.6). The structure itself has never been manned or opened for visitors during the months when skiing is best. At length we schuss, slant or sidestep down from the peak, and then our return to the cars is accomplished by backtracking.

T57   Alpine Skiing on Slate Mountain

Slate Mountain's wintertime climbing and schussing potential represents an advancement for many skiers toward alpine ski mountaineering. The southernmost part of the Western Divide to rise above the 9000-foot elevation, Slate Mountain commands panoramas less known but more given over to sheer alpine rock than those of any other Sierra ski tour so close to Los Angeles. Advanced opportunities go hand-in-hand with advanced requirements here. Those who attempt to ski Slate Mountain without knowing how to recognize and deal with avalanche hazards, without having had extensive practice in climbing techniques and schuss control and without having built up stamina are jeopardizing not only their lives but also the lives of would-be rescuers—and the panoramic solitude that makes Slate Mountain, when snowbound, unique.

Season   January through April

Distance   9.4 miles (15.1 km) round trip

Steep Upgrade   0.4 mile (0.6 km)

Elevation Gain and Loss   2230 feet (680 m)

Exertion/Duration   easy/2 days, moderate/1 day

Skills   moderate route-finding, difficult alpine skiing

Registration/Permits   Tulare County Sheriff's Department/USFS Campfire Permit

Roadhead/Map   R50/M24

Description (Parts of the climb ahead are steep and may be icy, ruling out all but the most experienced nordic skiers.) Our journey begins at a stubby, plowed extension of paved *TC Road MTN 107* (7190/0.0) just south of Ponderosa Lodge. The resort offers 15 snowmobiles for rent, and so during holiday weekends, when the numbers of renters are bolstered by San Joaquin Valley snowmobile owners, the road's snowpack is combed with tracks. But few snowmobilers venture off roads, so skiers can usually count on escaping from mechanization ahead, high on the flank of Slate Mountain.

Our snowy roadway leads directly south from the stub, rolling slightly, soon connecting with eastbound SNF Road 21S06 (7140/0.6) and then, minutes later, reaching the start of *SNF Road 21S09* (7130/0.4) before entering a cut some 15 feet deep. We take 21S09, which initially bends south, rising over a slight ridge alongside the cut. In several dozen yards our road turns northwest and leads briefly up a ravine next to the ridge. Then we turn southwest onto *SNF Road 21S23* (7300/0.2), which nears a few gently sloped patchcuts amid the snow-encrusted conifers, curves across Peppermint Creek, and then ends in an area (7260/0.5) long proposed for commercial skiing.

Now we trace a *retired* extension of the *road* west, quickly reaching the former start of a south-trending logging road. (Some skiers may want to check out rumors of excellent skiing in the canyon to which this road leads. Although cliffs near the head of this canyon create quite an avalanche hazard, the canyon affords an alternate route up Slate Mountain that is better than the one described here when the local snow is compacted and less than 2 feet deep.)

We continue west from the junction, then enter a huge clearcut and shortly branch west again onto another *logging road.* This one is hard enough to find when it's free of snow; when it's buried, forget about finding it until you reach the clearcut's westernmost edge. There the road becomes distinct, and from there on we follow its corridor. It switchbacks up increasingly steep slopes, gaining breathtaking views of The Needles and the Sierra Crest, and presently forks north from yet *another road* (7600/0.4). We then round a knob and enter the canyon of

Peppermint Creek before descending somewhat in order to cross a tributary ravine. From there we take every old road that looks as if it will lead northwest and up the main canyon, a strategy that gets us through a series of junctions onto increasingly poor roads. Soon, and just before leaving the logging zone, our route becomes a *cross-country ski-route,* fords Peppermint Creek and starts switchbacking up south-facing slopes not far from the creek. On these slopes one will find the canyon's lowest, sparsest undergrowth, which assumes greatest importance when the local snowpack is thin.

After leaving the logging area, we switchback up and eventually reach a headwaters bowl of Peppermint Creek. Here skiers can choose between doing the herringbone step or the sidestep, or making skin-assisted zigzags while starting a steep 300-foot climb along a north-northeast-trending ravine. The usual strategy entails a little of each maneuver.

The climb brings us onto the crest of the Western Divide. Here we turn west after viewing Yokut Spire, a snow-capped volcanic monument in the foreground northeast of us, a precipitous Tule River canyon in the middle ground north of us and Jordan Peak, its lookout glinting, in the canyon's background. Now we ascend a lengthy, south-curving segment of crest while glimpsing exciting scenery in the east. Then we finish the climb atop wind-buffeted Slate Mountain (9302/2.6—see Trip 40).

From here the Slate Mountain Slopes extend northwest into an elongated bowl, granting the alpine skier the promised serenity and near-certainty of solitude for repeated breezy schussing. The open colonnade of red firs spread across this nearly brushless bowl offers shelter to any skiers who want to establish a base camp for any prolonged skiing. One easy excursion they could enjoy is the ascent of VABM Nelson (see the topo map) on the ridge west of the bowl. Metamorphic crags in bold relief against the snow intensify the landscape appeal from this viewpoint. At length we double back toward our cars, practicing turns in a speedy descent near Peppermint Creek on the way.

T58   Dome Rock Nordic Ski Tour

Ranking among the most captivating introductions to nordic skiing in the Southern Sierra, this tour culminates at Dome Rock, a granodiorite hemisphere with a 360° panorama. The basin viewed from Dome Rock is notched north and south by the Kern River canyon and rimmed in the west by the Western Divide, in the southwest by the Greenhorn Mountains and in the east by the Kern Plateau. This basin view seems to heighten by contrast the perpendicularity of the side-by-side, sky-high spires and domes—The Needles—that make up the northern horizon. There isn't another Sierran snow trip closer to Los Angeles involving such freedom from avalanche hazard, such beaten-track routefinding (beware of holiday snowmobilers) and so rewarding a destination for so little exertion.

Season   January through March

Distance   5.2 miles (8.4 km) round trip

Steep Upgrade   0.1 mile (0.2 km)

Elevation Gain and Loss   100 feet (30 m)

Exertion/Duration   easy/1 day

Skills   easy route-finding, beginner nordic skiing

Registration/Permits   none

Roadhead/Map   R50/M24

Canteens   1 quart

Description   Leaving the snowplowed stub (7190/0.0) of **TC Road MTN 107** a few dozen yards south of the Ponderosa Lodge, our course traces a mildly undulant, snowpacked segment of that road south. Young roadside conifers temporarily daubed with white and older ones behind them cast a fretwork of shadows especially beguiling when this tour is taken by moonlight. Unless the uppermost layer of snow is recent, the road is usually marked with numerous ski and snowmobile tracks, which help keep us on course wherever the road is obscured by drifts.

Early in our journey we meet northeast-bound SNF Road 21S06 (7140/0.6) where a corner of its sign protrudes from a snow hump. It leads independent nordic and alpine skiers toward the sheltered bowls and cleared runs situated alongside The Needles on the Needlerock Slopes. Afterward, where SNF Road 21S09 (7130/0.4) splits off to the west, we take leave of Trip 57 skiers. Moments later we glide across Peppermint Creek, which is sometimes encrusted with ice, and then while starting to kick up the

longest grade on this trip, we meet eastbound SNF Road 21S07 (7090/0.1), which gives access to excellent skiing downstream along Peppermint Creek.

Klister waxes or skins are often found appropriate for the upgrade ahead, and the delay to apply them sometimes increases the time of ascent to nearly 30 minutes. The grade relents where SNF Road 21S21 (7200/0.7) branches west, leading some alpine skiers up toward the heads of breezy runs near the Peppermint Heliport.

Meanwhile, we slog across a short, high fill and then, just before leaving the Peppermint Creek drainage through a drifted cut, diverge with skiers on Trip 59 and turn east onto narrow **SNF Road 21S69** (7200/0.1). It soon winds onto the crest of a hilly ridge, which guides us southeast whenever drifts conceal the road ahead. Usually less than 10 minutes after leaving the main road, we quickly work up the back side of Dome Rock and then take in the intensely bright swirl of colors displayed in the summit panorama (7221/0.7). Beware of venturing east or south off the level summit——the dome's initial, deceptively gentle slopes are sometimes slickened with ice. When the view can no longer hold us, we backtrack to our cars.

T59

Alpine Skiing
on Nobe Young Slopes

A slope for almost every capability and desired intensity of adventure can be found in the compact upper Nobe Young Creek drainage. Campsites facing the morning sun are readily found here, and easily reached and left via snowmobile-patronized but nonetheless dependably evident, straightforward and vista-packed roads.

Season   January through March

Distance   16.0 miles (25.7 km) round trip

Steep Upgrade   none

Elevation Gain and Loss   1510 feet (460 m)

Exertion/Duration   easy/3 days, moderate/2 days

Skills   easy route-finding, intermediate alpine skiing

Registration/Permits   Tulare County Sheriff's Department/USFS Campfire Permit

Roadhead/Maps   R50/M20, M24

Description

Southbound *TC Road MTN 107* Log

T58	Ponderosa stub	7190	0.0
	SNF Road 21S06	7140	0.6
	SNF Road 21S09	7130	0.4
	SNF Road 21S07	7090	0.1
	SNF Road 21S21	7200	0.7
	SNF Road 21S69	7200	0.1

While passing through the cut on Road MTN 107 just south of Road 21S69, we leave the Slate Mountain slopes and begin a descent by turns yielding, sticky and raspy toward Nobe Young Creek. In minutes we stride across Dome Creek and gain overviews of the drier south Western Divide drainages along with the row of ridge notches marking the Kern Canyon Fault. Then the roadside terrain grows precipitous where we traverse snow-shedding exposures of angular quartzite. Here the road's snow cover is sprinkled with reddish-gray rock fragments spilled from the cut's icicle-festooned slopes.

Then we arc across Horse Canyon, where cascades ensure roadside access to icy but not iced-up water. Some avalanche danger in the canyon, coupled with the hazard posed by an adjacent landslide—unpredictably active when saturated—nullify the appeal of lingering here. The sheltered slope crossed beyond the canyon lets us make tracks in haste. Afterward, on gentler slopes where a southern exposure sometimes makes for effortful slogging, the crossing of 3 consecutive creeks—Ice, Middle and Alder—offers scintillating ice sculpture and tingling cold water to distract us from our labors.

After crossing Alder Creek (which cascades closer to the road than the others), we cross a low divide and descend ½ mile across gentle, wooded slopes to meet westbound *SNF Road 22S03N* (6320/4.7) 100 yards short of Nobe Young Creek.

For curiosity-driven, adventuresome alpine skiers, this is where the fun begins, and their options are numerous. The recommended alternative is to work up Road 22S03N past several large, south-facing, stumpy patchcuts, skirt Nobe Young Meadow by and by, meet southbound SNF Road 22S72 (6610/1.0) and eventually cross Nobe Young Creek (6740/0.4). The road ends a few dozen yards from the creek in a vast logged zone of the Nobe Young Slopes, where given a snowpack at least 5 feet deep, one can enjoy repeated breezy schusses. John Harper mapped isohyetal contours in 1974 that indicate an average annual precipitation in this basin of 30–35 inches, most of which collects in winter as greatly inflated snowdrifts far exceeding the local stump heights. Base camps can be situated anywhere downstream along Nobe Young Creek, although near Nobe Young Meadow is best. Intermediate skiers will want to seek out runs starting from Road 22S72, while advanced skiers can work up a steep, retired section of Road 22S03N from Nobe Young Creek into the perched Mule Meadow bowl and onto the surrounding Last Chance Slopes.

In the first few days after intense snowstorms there is some danger of loose snow cascading onto the upper Nobe Young Slopes, and due caution should be exercised then, but there is consistently far less danger of avalanche along this tour than along the more popular tours in the High Sierra. Eventually we must return to our cars, so we begin to backtrack.

T60

Balch Park Snowshoe and Nordic Ski Tour

A good choice for the sequoia connoisseur, this tour of Mountain Home State Forest combines varying snow conditions, mild grades and easy route-finding with sight-seeing in proportions that have enticed novice snowshoers and nordic skiers seeking to improve their proficiency.

Once you start to explore the State Forest at its hushed, deserted, primitive best, the soothingness of the sequoia's endurance—especially apparent when these towering trees shed their snow earlier than their neighbors—can affect even the most by-the-book tourer. Other features include a unique spiral-grooved sequoia for naturalists to examine and a bevy of frozen ponds for would-be skaters to gaze at or cautiously try.

Season   January through March

Distance   15.4 miles (24.8 km), semiloop trip

Steep Upgrade   none

Elevation Gain and Loss   2000 feet (610 m)

Exertion/Duration   easy/3 days, moderate/2 days, strenuous/1 day

Skills   easy route-finding, novice nordic skiing

Registration/Permits   Tulare County Sheriff's Department/USFS-CDF Campfire Permit

Roadhead/Maps   R51/M28–M29, M38–M39

Description   Starting initially north from the Slick Rock switchback (5000/0.0), our gradually ascending course on a *TC Road MTN 220* overlaid with snowdrifts shortly weaves northeastward through ponderosa pines and Kellogg oaks usually only dusted with snow. Our trek's protracted first segment leads along a divide between forks of the Tule River, now and then touching its crest at swales overlooking (to the east) the deep, diverging canyons of 2 of these Tule River forks. Camping with the tacit approval of Sequoia National Forest authorities is especially practicable in these swales, because they intercept early morning light. Midway along this segment, in an especially broad swale, a sign pokes from an often-thin drift and notes the terminus of "Dunn Trail 30E16" (5300/1.4), which Trip 51 hikers ascend in a rain-shadow clime.

Much later, while oaks drop out of the forest regime, the segment gives way to another that cuts across slopes farther down from the ridgecrests and links a series of Bear Creek headwaters bowls in Mountain Home State Forest. (Camping is permitted only in designated campgrounds here.) We start traipsing up this crunchy-snow segment at the southern entrance to the 4590-acre State Forest, and early reach our first road fork of the trip, where a short, narrow road fork (5900/1.9) with pavement apparent in summer starts north toward the State Forest headquarters (closed in winter).

Beyond the fork, our course bends clockwise around a hill and enters the 2940-acre Mountain Home Grove, where loggers left only a few hundred giant sequoias standing amid the stumps of many more. Quite soon we touch the start of a linear, south-trending snow depression overlying the summertime Methuselah Group Campground road (6050/0.4). This semiloop road gives access to the vaunted Methuselah sequoia, reputedly the Forest's oldest.

Now our course winds past several logging roads that are usually well-hidden by snow and after a while enters the Balch Park bowl through an elongated saddle. The Summit Road comes in from the east and ends in a signed triangle junction (6370/0.7) here. Although we'll complete a loop through the State Forest on that road, our present course proceeds north, sticking to the county road.

Balch Park bowl has the first patch of snow en route that persists through mid-April and at other times offers a firm pack with a powdery surface. We glide across this surface, quickly entering Balch County Park, where a pair of fishing and swimming ponds lie covered with ice, flanking the road on both sides. (Only the western pond is visible from the road.) Large campgrounds charging $3 a night in summer, nothing in winter, lie alongside each of the ponds. The self-guided "Forestry Information Loop Trail" offers help to summertime visitors getting acquainted with the plants, history and management of the park and adjacent State Forest. Those impelled to delve into this region's checkered past will find Floyd Otter's *The Men of Mammoth Forest* enriching reading. Although out of print, that book can be found in some public libraries and also at the State Forest headquarters. Nevertheless, most of the artifacts that the book explains are concealed by snow when the skier or snowshoer passes this way, which is why much of the area's human history is omitted here in favor of wintertime natural phenomena.

The campgrounds (6350/0.2) mark the midpoint in our trek's Bear Creek bowls segment. North of this point, we shortly exit the county park and not long afterward loop around ice-coated Hedrick Pond, where logs were once stored for one in the region's succession of sawmills. Then, in a mild downgrade, we slog across more than a mile of often-tacky south- and west-facing slopes. Nearing the end of the Bear Creek bowls segment, we skirt the camouflaged Sunset Point Picnic Area, then arc across the Frazier Mill fork of Bear Creek to meet summertime-paved TC Roads MTN 296

(west) and **MTN 247** (northeast) in a signed **Y** intersection (6020/1.9). Thick snow slabs mantle roofs of nearby cabins remaining from the original 19th Century Mountain Home resort.

We turn sharply to start up MTN 247, then ascend its gentle gradient briefly and skirt Frazier Mill Campground (6120/0.3). The sequoias replaced by pines hereabouts were converted to fencing posts and stakes at the old Frazier Mill. Moments beyond the large southside campground, the northbound Bogus Meadow Trail (Trip 61) starts indistinguishably.

Soon in the midst of sparse, snow-decked sequoias, we work up a ¼-mile-long moderate grade, then trace the road where it grows faint in arcing northeast across an unfenced parcel of private land. The outline of a door may be visible in a sequoia trunk several dozen yards northwest of this short, faint stretch of road. This is the Hercules Tree, in which Jesse Hoskins took 5 years, 1897 to 1902, to carve a room. Russ Leadabrand reported in 1968 that Hoskins reckoned without the surviving tree's sap, which soon made the room too sticky to live in.

After returning to the State Forest, the road is obvious. It still leads northeast but now rises alongside a shallow draw. We presently cross a hummocky divide (6650/1.0) and then drop quickly east-southeast to meet the transverse Summit Road (6510/0.2). While some independent skiers turn north on this road to catch easy runs and superb run-outs on the Shake Camp Slopes, and while other skiers, ill-advised, head toward chronic avalanche danger on the nearby River Road, we turn south in ice-bejeweled mixed conifer forest, taking the **Summit Road.**

This road leads ½ mile across a steep, east-facing slope usually thick with drifting snow. Here and there drifts block the roadway, making progress tough for snowshoers. Then we pass through a gap in the divide, and re-enter the decimated sequoia grove (now thickened with other young conifers). Here we rise slightly to cross a transverse ridge and then descend gradually along the upper, west-facing slopes of a divide separating Tule River tributary watersheds. Shortly, while rounding the Balch Park bowl, we approach several saddles in the divide and meet a lateral logging road forking left through each. Our road bends sharply northwest at the last junction and quickly passes the signed "Oliver Twist Tree," a rare kind of sequoia mutant with spirally grooved bark, most common in the Mountain Home Grove, which redwood expert Richard J. Hartesveldt interpreted in 1975 as evidence for an exceptionally long isolation of this grove from others.

A few minutes of nearly effortless descending beyond "Oliver Twist" bring us to a signed triangle junction with **Road MTN 220** (6370/2.6). Here we turn south and then trace tracks we made earlier back to our cars (5000/4.4).

T61   Bogus Meadow Hike

The destination meadow may be "bogus," but the serenity of the sequoias that border this lotus-filled "meadow" is real and infectious.

Season   June through October

Distance   1.8 miles (2.9 km) round trip

Steep Upgrade   none

Elevation Gain and Loss   590 feet (180 m)

Exertion/Duration   easy/1 day

Skills   easy route-finding, Class 1 climbing

Permits   none

Roadhead/Map   R52/M38

Canteen   1 quart

Description   Our northbound adventure begins at a sign beside paved TC Road MTN 247 (6190/0.0) several dozen yards east of the entrance to Frazier Mill Campground. The **Bogus Meadow Trail** initially borders a tumbling brook by banks of fern and meadow lotus, then switchbacks up onto a nearby ridge and slants up along its north-northwest-trending crest. Sequoia stumps are evident in the midst of a post-logging-era stand of incense-cedar, sugar pine and white fir where manzanita, kit-kit-dizze and snow brush by turns hedge our path. Sequoias spared in the local late-19th-Century logging appear farther up the ridge, and herald a retired logging road (6690/0.8) that comes in from the east.

Our route turns west-northwest now to follow the roadbed away from the crest, and after we dip somewhat we reach the funnel-shaped clearing of Bogus Meadow (6640/0.1). Columbine, meadow lotus and stinging nettle jam this clearing—and what is a meadow with no room for grass? Bogus!

Our path leads across a seep by the "meadow's" tapered downslope tip and then, just a few paces beyond in the woods, branches at a triangular sign stenciled "G17."

The faint north branch, a retired road, leads to a cabin on private land while the southwest-trending path that starts here merely connects with a brush-choked road in a strip of Sequoia National Forest. The junction's best uses are for picknicking and for marking the point where backtracking to Frazier Mill Campground begins.

White fir

T62   Shake Camp Hike

This history-laden trip presents dramatic evidence of the contrast between those who survived in harmony with nature and those who disrupted it. Lacy brooks in early summer, dashes of motley color in fall and the Adam Tree—in any season the tallest in Mountain Home State Forest—add to this trip's value as an introduction to the sequoias.

Season   June through October

Distance   2.0 miles (3.2 km) loop trip

Steep Upgrade   0.1 mile (0.2 km)

Elevation Gain and Loss   420 feet (128 m)

Exertion/Duration   easy/1 day

Skills   easy route-finding, Class 1 climbing

Permits   none

Roadhead/Maps   R53/M38–M39

Canteen   1 quart

Description   Your tour of the Shake Camp vicinity starts at the parking lot (6460/0.0) on Summit Road just north of the signed entrance to Shake Camp Campground. You initially stroll north on **Summit Road,** signed for "Redwood Crossing," through banks of red-barked manzanita. Named in Spanish "little apple," manzanita grows laden with sour berries displaying the same range of colors as apples. In May and June a corps of bees and other insects fertilizes clusters of small, urn-shaped flowers, which then yield to the manzanita berries favored by foraging bears, foxes and some birds.

Almost instantly you touch a spur road starting west, and a few minutes later you turn north-northwest, leaving Summit Road, and begin ascending a moderate grade on **Long Meadow Trail 30E15** (6500/0.1). This short, ascending path segment leads through more exposed manzanita interspersed with islands of shade where sugar pine, white fir and mountain juniper shelter a low, pungent layer of kit-kit-dizze. The segment concludes as you skirt a concrete water tank, cut across a retired road, scrape through a subsequent patch of buckthorn and gooseberry and then touch the end of another roadbed. The course beyond nearly levels, then quickly encounters a cluster of Kellogg oaks and a signed junction with the **Shake Camp Loop Trail** (6710/0.3).

This path leads you initially west and rises through a few taxing zigzags while nearby scraggly oaks make room for incense-cedar and ponderosa pine. In minutes your course starts across sometimes hot, exposed, south-facing slopes, where the path luckily is level. A capped spring supplying water to the downslope Shake Camp Campground marks the end of the short open traverse, and precedes by moments your entrance into white fir/sequoia habitat. In late spring the littleleaf ceanothus that borders the conifers here becomes the only ceanothus in the State Forest to offer sprays with fragrant, tiny, powder-blue flowers.

Nearly 600 yards from the spring, we touch the apex of this hike next to a trailer-sized granite boulder signed "Indian Potholes." A rickety ladder leaned against the boulder in 1974, allowing visitors incapable of 3rd or 4th Class climbing to reach the deeply ground mortars atop the rock. Here in the 17th and a few preceding centuries Yaudanchi Indian women ground nuts to meal in relative safety while absorbing an inspiring panorama. Modern students of such "potholes" might expect to find water within a few hundred yards and, sure enough, after crossing a closed road (6810/0.7) just south of the boulder, the path leads 115 yards to a slender brook.

Dogwood lends a graceful form to the ford in all seasons, plus creamy white blossoms in early summer and flamboyantly colored leaves in fall. Here, too, is another denizen of moist places usually found near sequoia groves—the California hazelnut, a relative of the commercial filbert. According to Norman Weeden's *Survival Guide to Sierra Flora,* the hazelnut found ripening here in late summer and fall can be ground by those who would emulate Indians to make a high-protein bread.

Not far to the south you encounter another ford similarly garbed, and then you ascend a few yards to skirt the Eve sequoia, girdled by axe scars, a harbinger of the manmade devastation ahead. Not far beyond is the signed "Adam Tree"—at 240 feet the tallest one in the State Forest that escaped logging. A jaunt of several minutes more leads to the brink of the Bear Creek drainage, marked by a huge, exposed patch of silvering stumps. Although sequoias in the vicinity had been hacked down desultorily from 1886 until 1906, and although Thomas Hume (see Trip 92) bought what is now the State Forest in 1907, intending to protect the remaining sequoias, nothing compared to—or mitigated—the devastation that followed Hume's death in 1944. Floyd Otter, historian, interviewed Hume's agent Jack

Brattin, who was responsible for the devastation, and wrote in 1963 that the slaughter was a "last resort" meant to shock the state into buying Hume's Mountain Home holdings for the profit of Hume's successors. Brattin succeeded. Mountain Home State Forest was established in 1945.

Now your path skirts the clear-cut's edge, gradually descending east, and presently zigzags down to the side of an often-dry length of the brook crossed earlier. From there you pass under conifer cover and bypass Shake Camp Campground, quickly reaching your car in the Summit Road lot (6460/0.9).

T63   Moses Gulch Hike

Plummeting waters, towering trees, and dwarfing cliffs close to the San Joaquin Valley give the wilderness-threshold locale of this trip much of Mineral King's well-known appeal without its punishing access drive.

Season   June through October

Distance   5.7 miles (9.2 km), loop trip

Steep Upgrade   0.2 mile (0.3 km)

Elevation Gain and Loss   1200 feet (366 m)

Exertion/Duration   easy/1 day

Skills   easy route-finding, Class 1 climbing

Permits   none

Roadhead/Map   R54/M39

Description   A fallen giant sequoia athwart a terrace west of the North Fork of Middle Fork Tule River marks the start of our viewful jaunt. Our path, signed *"River Trail,"* begins in a large parking lot (5600/0.0) just south of the log, leads through a break in the log's middle, and then skirts some of the walk-in campsites of Moses Gulch Campground. Now the path traces the base of the river canyon's east-facing slopes, but after a while it zigzags momentarily up the slopes. These few zigzags put us onto a slanted, fallen sequoia, into which steps were carved for the novelty, and down which we walk toward its roots. Once there, we jump off the tree and over a brook where it plunges into a milky pool fringed with sword ferns.

Our path next winds from riverside terrace to bouldery floodplain to canyonside,

and eventually intertwines with a narrow network of paths serving the Japanese-garden-like Hidden Falls Campground. The river plummets into a chasm just east of the terraced, widely spaced campsites here, and several spur paths split off from our own to the chasm's brink while we progress. We shortly cross a parking lot (5930/0.9), then scramble east up an embankment and quickly reach the *River Road.* It leads several yards north, then bends southeast across the river on a sometimes submerged concrete slab, and afterward adjoins a small parking lot (5920/0.1) where Trip 64 begins.

Just across the road from the lot, we resume hiking the *River Trail* northwest at an identifying sign. Our path leads up the road bank and then, 40 yards from the road, branches northeast from a lateral to more walk-in campsites scattered amid sequoias. Quite soon we veer north-northwest, then ramble awhile up a mild grade across the main canyon's steep southwest-facing slopes. While we advance, thick stands of white fir, sugar pine, incense-cedar and sequoia provide plenty of shade. The base of one sequoia, west of the trail and nearly ½ mile from the road, partly envelopes a boulder the size of a small truck—bark extends over the rock as if it were part of the tree.

Then a lateral trail (6380/0.7) peels off to the northeast and weaves 0.2 mile up a steep slope to join the Eastside Trail. The River Trail, in the meantime, continues parallel to the cascading river while passing through a tobacco-brush patch and tracing the brink of a riverside bluff. In less than a dozen minutes, we zigzag down into a shallow ravine, and a bit later zigzag up to meet *Long Meadow Trail 30E15* (6590/0.4). While hikers on Trip 64 turn southeast here, we turn northwest, then stroll along this trail some 100 yards, passing a sequoia-shaded picnic site perched by one of the river's many falls. (Don't forget that camping outside of designated campgrounds in the state forest is illegal.)

We then ford the rock-strewn river at Redwood Crossing, where springtime torrents sometimes make a roped belay essential. The path quickly crosses a terrace west of the river, then bends south and starts a gradual ascent across steep, east-facing slopes. Sequoias drop out of the close-at-

Ferny dell on the North Fork of Middle Fork Tule River

hand forest while we progress, and it's not long before we momentarily leave the forest and cross an avalanche chute. Here on the flank of Moses Mountain, where a mishmash of metamorphic rocks is exposed, red penstemon decorates our ford of a snowmelt stream. Here, too, is the trip's first unlimited view of Formidable Crag and the immense west face of the Western Divide.

Not far beyond the chute, we leave the state forest's checkerboard lands and then alternate between state and national forest. Tree-posted signs, some of them easy to miss, mark the boundaries, and little more than a mile of sauntering (including more crossings of avalanche chutes) gets us past the last of these signs. Now beginning on our trip's final half, which lies inside the state forest, we shortly top a slight ridge, thus completing all of the trip's ascent, and then stroll down a mild grade to a signed fork with the Shake Camp Loop Trail (6710/1.7).

Beyond the fork, the Long Meadow Trail passes through the shade of oaks, then touches the end of a retired, west-trending road. There we start down a moderate grade through brush and trees, passing a concrete water tank midway to the Summit Road. Soon we turn northeast onto that road (6500/0.3) by a posted register (please sign in).

The Long Meadow Trail ends upon meeting *Summit Road,* so after signing a register posted next to the trailhead sign, we start northeast down the road. At first we stroll 120 yards, then pass a spur road departing southeast, and afterward turn east onto a short *side road* (6480/0.2), as a "Moses Gulch" sign directs. Beyond a 3-car lot where the driveable part of the road ends, we trace a retired section of road southeast. Soon we diverge from an eastbound lateral and start down a gentle grade. Our route leads through a forest of oaks and mixed conifers, and presently we touch a ridgecrest (6410/0.3), then leave the oaks and the retired road behind while hiking north on the *Moses Gulch Trail.*

This trail cuts across a lacework of kit-kit-dizze on an east-facing slope and occasionally passes remarkable views of the once-glaciated river valley north of the state forest. Midway along our traverse of the slope, we descend a section, 55 yards long, of an abandoned road, and then resume the sometimes steep trail. Kellogg oaks mingle with conifers (including giant sequoias) along Moses Gulch, which we soon cross, and there we start hiking a road that was built when parts of this forest were logged.

After 60 yards of walking on the road, we turn southeast to resume trail again. Then a descent of several minutes along the gulch puts us onto the dusty River Road (6070/0.6), which we hike northeast nearly 80 yards to regain the trail by a sign that identifies it. Starting downslope here, it shortly zigzags down into the gulch, where we skirt a seep spring. A sluggish creek issues from the spring, and white alders inhabit the gulch from here on down to the river. (In 1910

botanist Willis L. Jepson called the presence of alders by a stream proof that the stream doesn't dry up in summer.)

While we stride past the alders and nearby incense-cedars and sugar pines, we soon encounter the Moses Gulch Road (5800/0.3), onto which we turn east. The trail resumes in 35 yards, drops briefly southeast along Moses Gulch, then leaves the gulch and switchbacks down into the river canyon. After a while, we near the gulch again, and then our course turns north onto the **Moses Gulch Road** (5600/0.3) and slants down within earshot of the river. The road soon ends, and so does our ramble, in the lot beside Moses Gulch Campground (5600/0.1).

T64   Hidden Falls Hike

The North Fork of Middle Fork Tule River plunges through shadowy clefts with giant sequoias lining both banks. Erosion by the river has created a dramatic face-off between towering faces of pale and bronzy rock. With scenes such as these, the river generates much of the fascination to be found along this challenging trip today.

Season   June through October

Distance   8.1 miles (13.0 km) loop trip

Steep Upgrade   0.1 mile (0.2 km)

Elevation Gain and Loss   1860 feet (567 m)

Exertion/Duration   moderate/1 day

Skills   moderate route-finding, Class 1 climbing

Permits   none

Roadhead/Map   R55/M39

Description

Northwest-bound *River Trail* Log

T63	River Road	5920	0.0
	lateral to Eastside Tr	6380	0.7
	Long Meadow Tr 31E15	6590	0.4

From the River Trail we briefly hike the **Long Meadow Trail** southeast to a signed junction where we leave Trip 65 climbers and veer onto the **Eastside Trail** (6610/0.1). It rolls gently southeast through forest—leading us past a grassy spring, then rounding a nook with a transitory brook at the edge of sequoia habitat—before joining the lateral (6590/0.3) from the River Trail.

The ensuing dim trail through kit-kitdizze (the dominant ground cover along this trip) continues to roll southeast, crossing the corrugated slopes of the river's deep canyon. Formidable Crag soon appears to the east in a climber-luring vignette where our path crosses a ravine. Farther to the southeast, we enter Sequoia National Forest and then cross a stream that spills frothily over metamorphic rock in an avalanche chute. We advance even farther while Kellogg oaks and ponderosa pines join the trailside woods, and now and then view through portals in the forest the jumble of bronzy cliffs that make up a flank of Moses Mountain.

Eventually our course rounds a large, south-trending ridge, and shortly afterward joins the Galena Trail (6900/1.0), a shortcut from the River Road. We then rise on a mild grade, and shortly the path crosses a pair of chutes, the second of which holds a thicket of alder and willow graced with leopard lily and red penstemon. After stepping across a Galena Creek tributary amid the thicket, we cross a slope mantled with snow bush and manzanita, and presently round another ridge through a saddle. Here we pass a medium campsite (campsites are scarce on the Eastside Trail), and then we descend nearly 140 yards to the nearest water. This thready brook cascades in the thick of thimbleberry, meadow lotus, Bigelow sneezeweed and leopard lily where pine boughs usually cast plenty of shade. We ford the brook and then skid down a very steep 100-yard-long path segment, weaving amid chaparral. Our course then turns abruptly east while a lateral (6800/0.7) descends another 15 yards to a brookside medium campsite. A contouring jaunt through hanging gardens of wildflowers quickly puts us in an avalanche-scoured granite chute where Galena Creek slides and pools.

Quite soon after leaving the steppingstoned creek, the path abruptly gains 50 feet by weaving upslope, then turns parallel to the slope and rolls ½ mile southeast through conifers mingled with oaks. We then enter the Silver Creek drainage through a saddle in a divide and descend, steeply at times, via switchbacks and crossslope traverses into the Silver Creek recess. The Eastside Trail is sometimes overgrown but usually the path is obvious.

After descending ½ mile we cross Silver Creek in a slippery ravine often jammed with logs and other avalanche debris. Then our route contours across the creek's south bank, leaves its steep ravine, and encounters the last campsite for the next several miles. This medium campsite is situated on a slight, wooded ridge dividing the creek from a tributary to the south, and beyond it our path almost instantly drops into the tributary's ravine. The densely vegetated ford here precedes a long, moderate ascent across forested slopes to a signed junction with Griswold Trail 31E18 (6500/1.8). From here on, our route is much easier to follow.

Westbound *Griswold Trail 31E18* Log

T52	Eastside Trail	6500	0.0
	Wishon Trail 30E14	5290	1.1

Taking the **Wishon Trail** north, we shortly pass several mines with collapsed entrances, one of which, roughly 40 vertical feet downslope, nearly undermined the trail. Shortly we boulder-hop Silver Creek again, and then our course leads up the north bank and around a huge boulder onto a streamside terrace. Here we round an old

cabin's east side to resume the path in a short, moderate, westward ascent.

After the Wishon Trail leaves the canyon of Silver Creek, it contours across steep slopes bordering the North Fork of the Middle Fork Tule River. Our course presently leads across Galena Creek near picturesque sequoias, then continues through woods on a riverside terrace and shortly re-enters Mountain Home State Forest at an inconspicuous boundary. We then take a few strides farther up-canyon, ford the boulder-strewn stream, and later wind among mossy boulders up its west bank. Soon, after crossing a quasi-logged terrace, our route joins the **Moses Gulch road** (5600/1.1), where the Wishon Trail officially ends. Here the Moses Gulch Trail starts west-northwest, and from here we pace off a few hundred yards northwest on the road. It ends in a large parking lot (5600/0.1) walled in on the north by a giant sequoia that fell athwart the terrace. Although most of the Moses Gulch Campground is situated in conifers west of the lot (water is available there), a "River Trail" sign by a break in the fallen sequoia directs us north through the break.

Northwest-bound *River Trail* Log

T63	Moses Gulch Road	5600	0.0
	River Road	5930	0.9

Northbound *River Road* Log

	River Trail (south)	5930	0.0
	River Trail (north)	5920	0.1

T65   Moses Mountain Climb

Colorful—that's Moses Mountain! Few other peaks in Golden Trout Wilderness display great jumbled cliffs with so many shades of red, brown, yellow, green and white. No where else in this Wilderness but near the flanks of Moses Mountain do the orangish-barked giant sequoias flourish. No other streams showing blue, green and white are charged with as much rainfall each year as those on the flanks of Moses Mountain. No where else in this huge wilderness can experienced mountaineers reach so many subtle and lively colors so quickly from the San Joaquin Valley.

Season   June through October (avoid holiday weekends)

Distance   7.4 miles (11.9 km), round trip

Steep Upgrade   0.7 mile (1.1 km)

Elevation Gain and Loss   3450 feet (1052 m)

Exertion/Duration   moderate/1 day

Skills   moderate route-finding, Class 3 climbing (Class 4 and 5 pitches optional)

Permits   none

Roadhead/Maps   R55/M38–M39

Description

Northwest-bound *River Trail* Log

T63	River Road	5920	0.0
	lateral to Eastside Trail	6380	0.7
	Long Meadow		
	Trail 31E15	6590	0.4

Leaving hikers on Trip 63 at the end of the River Trail, we hike southeast on the **Long Meadow Trail** and quickly reach a signed junction with the Eastside Trail (6610/0.1). Here we part with hikers on Trip 64 while turning abruptly north. Then we encounter a Golden Trout Wilderness entrance sign and weave up-canyon past open patches of buckbrush. The trail presently fords a cascading temporary stream before overlooking the river again. Then we cut across Long Meadow, which is dotted with Bigelow sneezeweed flowers in season.

The mild upgrade continues up-canyon, sometimes leading by riverside bluffs, and we shortly pass through another meadow just before a river ford. After boulder-hopping the river, we start west on a **cross-country route,** (7180/1.2), doing some easy bushwhacking through thinning subalpine chaparral and forest. After we gain about 500 feet, we intercept a gully, which affords an easy Class 3 route up past timberline toward a Tule River divide. Soon after we climb from metamorphic to granitic rock, we turn south a few hundred feet below the ridgeline and then contour nearly ½ mile south, enjoying spectacular views. Then the ridgeline rises and so do we, scrambling up a parallel course. This brief stint of climbing gets us atop Moses Mountain (9331/1.4) where an airy panorama awaits.

Off to the west, the great sheer face of Dennison Peak stands in profile, while off to the east Formidable Crag is displayed against the Western Divide. Climbers inspired by the sight of so much rarely climbed rock will find more of the same close at hand on the flanks of Moses Mountain. "Moses," an old fisherman nicknamed for his age, was given a lasting memorial when Frank Knowles named the mountain for him during the 1870's, according to documents that historian Francis P. Farquhar disclosed in 1924.

After a suitable sojourn there, we backtrack to our cars.

T66   South Fork Bicycle Tour

Four distinct seasons a year, each affecting landscapes strikingly, plus consistent ease of access to the best of these landscapes: these are circumstances that set this trip above most others in the Sierra. Wintertime greenery contrasts with tall, snowy mountains; spring-colorful wildflowers make stippled patterns; ranch-gardens bloom in summer-morning balminess. All these entice bicyclists to the South Fork Kaweah River canyon. Finally, bold sashes of vivid fall colors there tie the seasons together within the scope of this package tour bounded by unfrequented, smoothly paved roads.

Season   all year

Distance   13.0 miles (20.9 km) round trip

Steep Upgrade   none

Elevation Gain and Loss   1180 feet (360 m)

Exertion/Duration   easy/1 day

Gears   1-speed conventional to 15-speed alpine

Permits   none

Roadhead/Maps   R56/M43, M50A

Canteen   1 quart

Description   The pavement of *TC Road MTN 347,* signed "Old Three Rivers Drive," begins on State Highway 198 just east of that road's South Fork Kaweah River bridge and a hundred yards west of an alternative roadhead, the lot of a Three Rivers general store. The county road leads southeast for a few dozen yards and then bends east, touching a loop of abandoned concrete—the former state highway and present Roadhead 56 (760/0.0), where Trip 66 begins. Our road aims at mottled Blossom Peak and leads us briefly through the midst of a thick assortment of willows, blackberry vines, sycamores, oaks and other water-loving plants, signs of a rich, moist soil beneath. Then the wild plants are either trimmed or replaced with domestic varieties while we pass among cottages. In the midst of these we cut east, away from the weeping-willow-lined road onto paved *Lane 347* (840/0.5), signed "Blossom *Drive.*"

Soon afterward, a church appears beside our lane, and then we turn south at a signed junction onto paved *TC Road MTN 348* (900/0.1). This road initially rolls across blue-oak-dotted grazing lands. Although a

subdivision-scarred hill mars views to the west, bicyclists tend to be more impressed with the lush assemblage of riverside plants ahead.

Our road soon turns east into a South Fork Canyon narrows where grapevines droop from boughs of sycamore, cottonwood, alder and black oak, spreading mounds along both sides of the road. A Blossom Peak slope is close in the north, and discerning geologists can trace the bottom of ancient ocean-floor sediments and later above-water volcanic rocks that have been compressed, twisted, melted, blended, restructured and invaded from beneath by molten granite. This bottom line records where the granite stopped rising and solidified. Of the rocks just above that line, the meticulous geologist Cordell Durrell wrote in 1941 that they were the most transformed ones yet exposed by erosion here.

Before long a roofless hut of granite boulders appears to the north by a dismembered flume, and shortly thereafter paved TC Road MTN 344A (950/0.9), signed "Heidi Drive," branches south toward a small subdivision. Then our road bridges two channels and crosses the wooded, inhabited, intervening island. The South Fork Canyon widens as we advance beyond the second bridge, and our road leads along the contact between riverside flats and steep slopes textured with metamorphic outcrops. Flaming fall colors adorning riverside trees to the east will remind transcontinental travelers of counterparts in New England. Elderberry bushes protrude from the roadside vines now and then, together with redbud shrubs and black walnut and wild fig trees, and vary the views from season to season so much that naturalists and photographers sometimes start planning repeat visits the first time they come here.

A spell of easy pedalling leads to a gated, southwest-bound fire-control road by signed "La Cuesta Ranch." The next ½ mile of road parallels a flume that currently serves that ranch. A bridge (1370/3.0) across the river constructed in 1959 marks the end of that road segment. Its recent emplacement and the bleached, rounded boulders prodigiously heaped by the water's edge remind us that floods periodically rip through this canyon, importing more fertile soil to flats such as the one we've just crossed.

A brief moderate pull amid the generally gradual upgrade presently interrupts our easy progress across an oak-dotted grazing terrace, and soon afterward we fork east from an equally wide paved road (1630/0.8) serving signed "Rancho Kawoia." Then our road bridges Cinnamon Creek, nurturer of an adjacent strip thick with sycamore, wild

fig, red alder, interior live oak, redbud, thimbleberry and spice bush, all in the coils of grapevines. The owner of nearby Cinnamon Creek Ranch, John T. Vincent, told me in 1977 that the creek was named for the cinnamon-colored bears that roam here from Sequoia National Park to feed on the thimbleberries.

Once beyond Cinnamon Creek Ranch, we might spot shetland ponies raised on a stock ranch south of the road. Our route presently bends south onto signposted *"MTN 319"* (1900/0.9), a short length of asphalt that skirts variegated residential gardens and is gated soon after bridging South Fork Kaweah River (1860/0.3). The primitive Grouse Valley Fire Control Road ascends from the gate toward Blue Ridge Lookout and though the land it crosses is private, its scenery is included in views that takers of Trip 49 enjoy. But at the gate we double back and later return to our cars.

T67   Garfield Grove Hike

The constant fascination found on this long-popular trip inspires hikers to keep coming back to study its landscapes through a camera lens, its rocks with geologic guides, its plants with botany books. There's so much to see and think about that it's easy to overlook the occasional presence of rattlesnakes and the lack of large-enough campsites en route. Near the end of this route the Sierra's sixth largest grove of giant sequoias stands by the scene of a violent landslide, and on the way there hikers can view massive cliffs, brooks in nooks, and an incredible assortment of showy flowering plants.

Season   May through November

Distance   6.8 miles (10.9 km) round trip

Steep Upgrade   none

Elevation Gain and Loss   2150 feet (655 m)

Exertion/Duration   moderate/1 day

Skills   easy route-finding, Class 1 climbing

Permits   none

Roadhead/Maps   R57/M44–M45

Description   According to averaged Wilderness Permit statistics for 1973–78, the South Fork trailheads received heavy use from backpackers and moderate use from

pack stock, with most of this use occurring in July and August on the South Fork Trail. The Park's travel pattern statistics for 1976, compiled by Gail Bennett, revealed that, surprisingly, only 72% of those intending to camp in the South Fork's canyon country entered via this trail. The rest evidently came from Mineral King to the northeast or from Mountain Home State Forest to the south, despite required car shuttles averaging 2½ hours one way. Additionally, while more than half the people starting their Park journey here intended to camp on the Hockett Plateau, they caused a mere 7% of the impact recorded there, which means that quotas for this trailhead will probably be large ones in the future. So if you're turned away from another hike, you're almost certain of getting on this one.

At a signed junction with SEKI Road 4–1 (3690/0.0), 50 yards west of its end, we start up *South Fork Trail 99,* which meanders south up a slight ridge in the shade of canyon live oaks. Quite soon it joins a dim, long-abandoned path (3740/0.2) from the west and turns southeast, starting its own mild cross-slope ascent of the South Fork Kaweah River canyon. In the early stage of this ascent, our sinuous course touches numerous nooks, some with splashy seasonal streams, where fern, laurel, holly, blackberry, wild ginger, miners lettuce, and kit-kit-dizze thrive in the shade of nutmeg, sycamore, Kellogg oak, incense-cedar and (later) ponderosa pine. The ridges we round between the nooks are thickly clothed in flannelbush, buckbrush, scrub oak, wild rose, twining brodiaea and wild cucumber, which sporadically part to allow views of Homers Nose on the northern horizon.

Midway along this lengthy stage, the river-loud shushing of hidden Big Spring reaches our ears. Shortly thereafter we boulder-hop a cascading Putnam Canyon brook. We conclude the early stage of the South Fork Trail's ascent by rounding Snowslide Canyon, a precipitous granite chute in which avalanche snow often lingers until early June. Although Snowslide Canyon discharges volumes of water each year in the form of snow or mush (its great landslide of 1876 is described in Trip 70) its creek often vanishes soon after snowmelt is complete. (The up-canyon chute offers access to Dennison Mountain for peakbaggers used to Class 2–3 scrambling.)

Just east of the avalanche-scoured swath, we stroll into the Garfield Grove of sequoias and there, in a smattering of sugar pines, skirt arcing boughs of dogwood and sprigs of hazelnut. This sprawling, 2220-acre grove—nearly as large as Giant Forest—ranks among the 6 largest groves in the Sierra. In 1902 the name "Garfield" was prefixed to this grove by the U.S. Geological Survey, in memory of James A. Garfield, twentieth President of the United States, assassinated 21 years earlier.

Shortly we reach a *lateral* (5840/3.2) departing downslope to an overused campsite that often has room for picnickers. Would-be campers should bear in mind that leveling or enlarging platforms on any slope in the Park destroys wilderness, is a misdemeanor and could earn them a stiff fine. During holiday weekends, large groups, for whom it would be especially hard to find a place to camp in the Garfield Grove, should continue up to Dennison Ridge or the Hockett Plateau.

A thready brook can be found a few dozen yards beyond the campsite turnoff on the main trail, but hikers in search of more sequoias will have to ascend the main trail at least ⅔ mile beyond the brook. While backpackers on Trip 68 continue on up the trail, everyone on Trip 67 should start backtracking to the cars at least a few hours before nightfall.

T68   Hockett Lakes Backpack

The first landscapes to be designated "Sequoia National Park" in 1890 were those centered at Hockett Lakes and the Garfield Grove of sequoias. This challenging trip touches an early trans-Sierra trail while leading past bold cliffs and vast meadows, roaring cascades and serene lakes, far-reaching panoramas and fascinating foregrounds. The dazzling scenery en route shows the wisdom of the Park's original sponsors in protecting this part of the Southern Sierra while its resources were still largely unknown.

Season   July through October

Distance   23.1 miles (37.2 km) semiloop trip

Steep Upgrade   0.3 mile (0.5 km)

Elevation Gain and Loss   5540 feet (1689 m)

Exertion/Duration   easy/4 days

Skills   moderate route-finding, Class 1 climbing

Permits   Wilderness Permit

Roadhead/Maps   R57/M44-M46

Description

Eastbound *South Fork Trail 99* Log

T67	SEKI Road 4–1	3690	0.0
	lateral	3740	0.2
	Snowslide Canyon		
	lateral	5840	3.2

Beyond the campsite lateral, the South Fork Trail leads up a stiff grade for nearly ⅔ mile before crossing a ridge. There it resumes a mild grade in the thick of the Garfield Grove sequoias. Interspersed among the sequoias are nutmeg and ponderosa pine, and the pine starts gradually gaining predominance while we advance east from the ridge. Our twisty path presently fords a brook spilling in scalloped cascades, and much later it rounds a ridge bristly with manzanita.

Several hundred yards after rounding the ridge, we turn west onto the path of *Summit Lake Wildroute 102* (7250/2.0) and shortly cross the ridge again amid chinquapin, snow bush and manzanita. After descending a gentle grade for a dozen minutes beyond the ridge, the path contours awhile past a pocket glade and mixed conifers including conspicuous sequoias. This section of path is an obstacle course, being partly blocked by blowdowns, sloughed off the slope and overlapped by brush. Despite the trail's unkempt condition, its steel culverts are still as shiny and as foreign to sequoia environs as when they were installed.

That section of path ends with a switchback. (Beware of an old dead-end trail departing straight ahead here.) Then we ascend slightly through shattered granite on a surprisingly wide, well-built path. Shortly thereafter, our course switchbacks, later skirts a churning spring and eventually gains Dennison Ridge (7540/1.5) in the Garfield

Grove's only camping zone, which sits astride a broad saddle.

Our path twists east, then leaves the saddle quite soon and continues to rise on a gentle grade while crossing the ridge's south flank. Most hikers will reach the first snowmelt creek, which slithers down a granite slab, some 20 minutes beyond the saddle. Here the path abruptly gains 50 feet to surmount the slab and cross the creek.

A bit farther on, we ford yet another snowmelt creek and then start weaving up a steep, slight ridge. The openness of this manzanita-mantled ridge permits a prospect of the great middle-ground canyon of the North Fork Tule River. Behind the canyon, in the southeast, rise the sheer folded flanks of Moses Mountain while, far away in the southwest, Lake Success glimmers near the vast San Joaquin Valley.

We presently zigzag up into a draw wooded with red fir and lodgepole pine, and later top a saddle set in a transverse ridge. Continuing to cross the flank of Dennison Ridge, we head northeast on a dim path and, after a spell, we approach the North Fork's headstream where it issues from Summit Meadow. Then we outflank the meadow through a sprawling camping zone where snowdrifts sometimes linger until early June, and presently we cross the rounded Tule-Kaweah divide. Now a short, contouring stroll through a red-fir corridor puts us at a signed junction with *Tuohy Trail 103* (9080/ 3.4).

Not surprisingly, the Park's special Wilderness Permit tallies for 1976 showed that everyone entering Sequoia National Park that year via the Tuohy Trail camped on the Hockett Plateau to the north, where they amounted to 12% of the year's visitors. Less detailed permit statistics averaged from 1973–78 revealed that moderate numbers of pack stock and of backpackers used this entrance each year, most of them coming in July and August from the state forest to the south.

Now we switchback northeast down the Tuohy Trail. Beyond 9 switchbacks of diminishing length, the course fords steppingstoned Tuohy Creek and then parallels spongy creek banks through which monkshood and cinquefoil flowers poke. Later our course forks northeast onto the *Tuohy Cutoff* (8530/1.2), which rolls at length across numerous gullies in lodgepole-pine-shaded terrain. Then we round a northwest-trending ridge and presently amble east-northeast across the largest of the short-grass South Fork Meadows. At length we cross a neck of the woods, ford the South Fork Kaweah River—a cold wade in early summer—and stroll north past an eastbound spur path (8530/1.6). Now, while we cross a second meadow, our path momentarily disappears, but we regain the path at the meadow's north edge and shortly meet Atwell Hockett Trail 90 (8550/0.2—see Trip 80) at one end of the South Fork Trail.

Here we turn west onto *South Fork Trail 99* and then ramble through a huge camping zone in the woods, by and by joining the signed Hockett Lakes Cutoff (8580/0.8) just a few minutes' stroll from the southernmost lake. (Camping is prohibited within 100 feet of the shore.) Beyond this justly popular lake, we stroll briefly southwest along its sometimes dry outlet stream and then zigzag down into a recess cut by the South Fork Kaweah River.

The ensuing stretch of trail encounters junction signs tacked to a lodgepole pine on the river's north bank, then fords to the river's south bank, where Tuohy Trail 103

(8230/0.9) starts southeast toward its namesake meadow and creek. John Tuohy's background—20 years of herding sheep in the watershed of the Kaweah River—made him the only practical idealist in the group that persuaded Congressman Vandever (see Trip 79) to introduce the Sequoia National Park bill in 1890. Historian Harold G. Schutt wrote in 1967 that while Tuohy's knowledge of the Sierra made him the one to choose land for the Park, he insisted along with the others that loggers and especially sheepherders should be excluded from it.

Our path then rolls over a rounded, north-trending ridge amid red firs, then passes the Ladybug Wildroute (8200/0.6—see Trip 70), an abandoned part of a trans-Sierra trail that a crew led by John B. Hockett built in 1862–64. We then traverse the headwall of the Garfield Creek canyon on a gradual southwest-trending descent, crossing quite a few brooks en route, the largest of which is Garfield Creek. Outlying sequoias of the Garfield Grove eventually come into view, and some time later we return to the Summit Lake Trail junction (7250/2.1). Our trek's final stage is a backtrack down the South Fork Trail to our cars (3690/5.4).

Hockett Lakes

T69

Cedar Creek Hike

When you think of sequoias, think of the South Fork Kaweah River. Although the river's drainage includes a generous portion of Sequoia National Park's most striking "front-country" features, admission to the South Fork canyon is free. This hike past the world's lowest sequoia to the South Fork Grove of giant sequoias can easily be done in a day. It leads you past channels swept by a wall of water just over 100 years ago, acquaints you with bronzy bedrock enclosing bluish-green pools, lets you feel the spume of cascades, and treats you to a heady view of a sheer dome named Homers Nose.

Season   March through December

Distance   5.8 miles (9.3 km) round trip

Steep Upgrade   none

Elevation Gain and Loss   1350 feet (411 m)

Exertion/Duration   easy/1 day

Skills   easy route-finding, Class 1 climbing

Permits   none

Roadhead/Maps   R57/M44–M45

Canteen   1 pint

Description   Embarking from a parking lot and corral at the signed end of SEKI Road 4–1 (3690/0.0), our path, the **Cahoon Trail,** leads 100 yards east to a high bridge, onto which we turn north to cross the South Fork Kaweah River. A wide, bouldery trail leads 50 yards north from the north bridge abutment, crossing a floodplain before turning east and rising onto a terrace. Now our path, deflected by clumps of laurel, flannelbush, kit-kit-dizze, buckbrush and blue witch, weaves in the shade of buckeye, canyon live oak and incense-cedar across the riverside terrace. Our sauntering shortly puts us at the start of the abandoned, north-trending Coffeepot Canyon Trail (3860/0.3), on which takers of Trip 71 depart.

Continuing east for some 100 yards from the junction, we cross the usually dry bed of Pigeon Creek and later veer east-northeast where a beaten use-trail (4000/0.2) leads toward the river. Our much diminished trail now slants up a moderate grade, crossing a few open slopes dappled with thistle, mariposa lily and larkspur. While doing so, it occasionally crosses ledges chipped from a mostly shaley metamorphic rock called flysch (defined in Trip 52).

Our path shortly curves north-northeast but still parallels the river; then, while continuing in the same direction, it enters the canyon of Squaw Creek. After looping across the creek, we return to the South Fork canyon and ascend eastward, passing numerous laterals and Ladybug Wildroute (4410/1.2), which leads to riverside Ladybug Camp and falls. Here we fork north, upslope.

From this fork our path leads up a steep but brief grade, and then turns *east* onto an older section of the Cahoon Trail. (Trees and brush have obscured this trail to the *west.*) Our trail shortly veers north in the river canyon, then crosses several grassy clearings that offer downslope views to the south-southeast of the world's lowest (not shortest) sequoia (enlarged upon in Trip 70). That tree's lone shaft extends high above the mixture of chaparral, broadleaf trees and conifers near the confluence of the South Fork Kaweah River and Garfield Creek.

The river canyon soon broadens, and while we progress up its side on a gentle ascent, mixed conifers close in to shelter scattered wild ginger and gooseberry amid miners lettuce, the dominant undergrowth. Shortly we saunter past pungent laurel and then ford Cedar Creek (5100/1.2) by log in the midst of a glen shaded by incense-cedars and South Fork Grove sequoias. The stock driveway beyond here, used by Forest Homer of Three Rivers to drive cattle up to his inholding at Cahoon Meadow, quickly forks south from an abandoned, mostly overgrown segment of the Cahoon Trail, and gives access to more of the sequoias reported to be in the South Fork Grove. After getting our fill of exploring or loafing, we double back to the cars.

T70   Hockett Meadows Snowshoe and Nordic/Alpine Ski Trek

Nearly 100 years ago, a mountainside liquified, then plummeted into the South Fork Kaweah River, planting what is today the world's lowest sequoia in the wake of its devastation. Although the wall of water released when the great landslide dam broke has not been equaled since, the river still surges in winter and spring through its headwaters and past the sequoia.

River fords separate this journey's 3 contrasting stages. A deep canyon embodies the first stage, containing the river, that sequoia and a tricky ford that assures trekkers of destination solitude. The second stage is a ridge ascent with the longest steep upgrade and most elevation gain to be found in this book's snow trips. Overcoming these obstacles brings trekkers up to the third stage: a high, wide and wild plateau ringed with outlooks, peaks, frozen lakes, clearings and slopes. The plateau's prodigious snowpack ranks among the Southern Sierra's thickest. Intensity, comprehensiveness and size make the challenge and opportunity that this trek's landscape offers nothing less than lavish.

Season   January through April

Distance   18.4 miles (29.6 km) round trip

Steep Upgrade   1.2 miles (1.9 km)

Elevation Gain and Loss   4970 feet (1515 m)

Exertion/Duration   easy/4 days, moderate/2 days

Skills   difficult route-finding, difficult nordic skiing

Registration/Permit   Sequoia National Park/Wilderness Permit

Roadhead/Maps   R57/M44–M46

Description

Eastbound *Cahoon Trail* Log

T69	SEKI Road 4–1	3690	0.0
	Coffeepot Canyon		
	Wildroute	3860	0.3
	Ladybug Wildroute	4410	1.4

The **Ladybug Wildroute,** an unmaintained trail, first descends slightly eastward from where the stock driveway forks directly upslope. Moments later, we pass a cluster of large riverside campsites shaded by oak and ponderosa pine, where we should start scanning the river for trees that have fallen across it. Now the path contours briefly across shelves of rust-stained quartzite inter-larded with schist. Then the trace ends abruptly at the abutment of a bridge that collapsed under the massive 1969 snowpack. Jim Carruth of the Park Service, who told of the bridge's demise in 1976, had the wreckage removed with dynamite, and because the path had long been abandoned, the bridge was never replaced.

The canyon narrows just upstream, and the chances of finding downed logs to assist belayed early-morning river crossings are usually better there. (Sometimes only gymnasts with life-jackets and wet-suits can make it across the river.)

A conical-crowned sequoia stands several dozen yards downstream from the abutment, near the confluence of Garfield Creek and the river. Drawing on his comprehensive knowledge of sequoias, Richard J. Hartesveldt wrote in 1975 that nowhere else has the sequoia naturally extended its range to such a low elevation. Hartesveldt reported that the sequoia's seed tumbled here from the Garfield Grove, and then sprouted in December of 1876. Floyd Otter told in 1963 how intense rain and snowmelt had turned the land to mush late one night that December. A mass of sopping soil and rock abruptly gave way along Dennison Ridge and plummeted down Snowslide Canyon, plucking sequoias from the Garfield Grove, pouring through Garfield Creek's defile, and finally damming the South Fork Kaweah River with debris from a swath 12 feet deep, ½ mile wide and 1½ miles long. The river downstream was dry for a day while the dam backed up runoff torrents. Then the dam's breaching that night sent a destructively huge surge of water down upon farming communities of the San Joaquin Valley.

Once on the river's east bank, we pick up the dim trail zigzagging steeply up an incipient divide between the river and Garfield Creek. The grade soon eases considerably for ¼ mile, where our ridge crosses an inclusion of less resistant marble. Beyond the edge of the marble inlay, the ridge is composed of granite, and in consequence rises steeply. Our path continues along it through exposed patches of snow bush and manzanita and widespread mats of kit-kit-dizze in the shade of mixed broadleaf-conifer forest, where snowdrifts often lurk. Old license plates halved diagonally and tacked high on trailside trees mark the route. Soon attaining the 6000-foot contour, our course starts veering away from the crest while ascending across southwest-facing slopes. Eventually, after hurdling many blowdowns, we outflank dome 7442, a bulge in the ridge.

Upon reaching a camping zone in a saddle just east of the dome, most snowshoers and some skiers will strap on their snowshoes or well-waxed skis because the snowpack ahead is usually continuous. The rising ridgecrest leads east from the saddle through snow-matted chinquapin patches and at length temporarily culminates in a viewsome hill. It signals our nearness to the South Fork Trail and marks the end of our prolonged ascent. Those who neglect to use skis or snowshoes from now on are in for lots of floundering.

Leaving the hill, we strike east onto the Mountaineer Slopes, dropping slightly into a swale with red fir often clad in dazzling snow. There, provided the drifts are not too deep, we find projecting metal signposts marking a junction with summertime **South Fork Trail 99** (8200/3.8). Our course then rolls over a rounded, southeast-trending ridge, veers southeast, encounters snow-draped lodgepole pines and then, upon reaching the South Fork Kaweah River, starts tracing riverside **Tuohy Trail 103** (8230/0.6). From here on, self-guidance is

the rule because none of the trees en route ahead has been either tagged or blazed.

Usually no more than 10 minutes elapse before we pick our way across converging Tuohy Creek, leaving the Mountaineer Slopes. These slopes tempt one with so many opportune, exhilarating runs that some skiers never advance beyond them.

Now we leave the trail (8260/0.2) while gradually arcing east on a **cross-country route,** ascending crackling snow near the rims of riverside bluffs and eventually crossing near-level terrain guided by the riverbank. After a spell of easy gliding while dodging tree-occupied wells in the snow of the Cyclone Slopes, we emerge into an exposed meadow heavily impasted with snow. Now tracking along the summertime Tuohy Cutoff, we glide east-northeast across the clearing, then search a neck of the woods for the most convenient, stable snow bridge spanning the South Fork Kaweah River (8520/1.3).

Our course beyond the ford quickly enters another, though smaller, clearing, follows its edge a few hundred yards north and then cuts through an isthmus of woods, crossing the license-plate-marked South Fork Trail (8550/0.2). (The license plates lead east and mark a route—the Atwell Hockett Trail—to Quinn Patrol Cabin, which snow surveyors use when gauging the depth and water content of the local snowpack. Other travelers will find the cabin securely barred and padlocked. Spirited ski trekkers content to camp outside the cabin will be rewarded with a cross-clearing vista of Quinn Peak, along with a central location for forays onto the Hidden Lake and Wet Meadows slopes, where the vistas, gradients and clearing configurations are as diverse as their insulation from grating mechanical intrusions is assured.)

Meanwhile, back on the Hockett plateau, our ski route continues north beyond the South Fork Trail, almost instantly cutting into the sprawling clearing of Sand Meadows. A snow-coated dune here offers the chance to make some playfully diverting slides. Over-the-shoulder views reveal the great exploratory and schussing potential of the Cyclone Slopes. Our course leads from the clearing's northernmost lobe (site of a summertime trail junction—8540/0.9) and makes a slight ⅓ mile descent north-northwest along the base of the Cahoon Slopes. We then veer alongside Whitman Creek and briefly ease down its banks to enter the Hockett Meadows clearing (8500/ 0.5). The opportunities to climb to viewpoints for jagged-horizon panoramas, to negotiate a melange of snow consistencies, to practice turns on reliably firm, powder-topped slopes, and to be absorbed in miles and miles of exhilarating runs with solitude almost a certainty make Hockett Meadows an enriching base camp for the most fastidious wintertime adventurer. The ranger station at its north end is usually unmanned, bereft of food, locked and a misdemeanor to enter while the snow is at its best. When time runs out—and it always happens too soon up here—we backtrack to the cars.

Nordic skiing

National Park Service

T71   Homers Nose Backpack

Although not the toughest pathfinder's puzzle possible in the Southern Sierra, this epitome of the "difficult" route-finding rating (see Chapter 4) is the hardest trip in this book, and should only be attempted by the most experienced and most physically fit of mountaineers. The scenic surprises along their way and the exciting climbing potential of the destination more than make up for the arduousness of this advance from foothill to alpine climes.

Season   June through October

Distance   14.6 miles (23.5 km) round trip

Steep Upgrade   0.4 mile (0.6 km)

Elevation Gain and Loss   6260 feet (1908 m)

Exertion/Duration   moderate/2 days

Skills   difficult route-finding, Class 1 climbing (Class 5 pitches optional)

Permit   Wilderness Permit

Roadhead/Maps   R57/M44–M45

Description   Embarking from a parking lot and corral at the signed end of SEKI Road 4–1 (3690/0.0), our path, the **Cahoon Trail,** leads 100 yards east to a high bridge, onto which we turn north to cross the South Fork Kaweah River, A wide, bouldery trail leads 50 yards north from the north bridge abutment, crossing a floodplain before turning east and rising onto a terrace. Now our path, deflected by clumps of laurel, flannelbush, kit-kit-dizze, buck brush and blue witch, weaves in the shade of buckeye, canyon live oak and incense-cedar across the riverside terrace. Our sauntering shortly puts us at the start of the abandoned **Coffeepot Canyon Trail** (3860/0.3), onto which we turn north. Beginning roughly 30 yards west of often-dry Pigeon Creek, the Coffeepot Canyon Trail offers the prospect of no streams or springs in its first and (often hottest) several miles. We initially switchback up a dim path, crashing through overlapping buckeye, canyon live oak, blackberry, buckbrush, flannelbush, pennyroyal, fern and—watch out—poison oak. (Mountaineer Jerry Keating followed the nearby Pigeon Creek bed up-canyon in 1973 and found it much freer of brush than the first 1.3 miles of trail.)

Soon entering Pigeon Creek canyon, our route twists north a few hundred yards upslope from the creek bed. Now our path is hidden by grass wherever we cross open slopes, but is easy to follow wherever it's shaded by live oaks. Small tree frogs inhabit the oaks, and sometimes create a sensation by leaping into the shirt collars of passersby. Mountain mahogany soon becomes the prevailing wayside shrub, and the disgusting cocoons of tent caterpillars have been known to dangle from its branches over the route. Numerous game tracks split off from or cross this first wildroute segment, compounding the pathfinder's difficulties. Eventually, the 5030-foot level is gained, and here the easily lost course switchbacks southwest, continuing up a moderate grade. We presently leave the shrubbery-lined corridors and cross open, south-facing slopes that sport some mariposa lilies, approaching the west rim of Pigeon Creek canyon.

Our route shortly touches the Pigeon Creek/Burnt Camp Creek divide just upslope from a flat, and turns north through the Kellogg oaks scattered along the divide, where misleading blazes abound. Many hikers who have descended this route in the last 20 years have found that this turn is the easiest part of the route to miss, so memorize its location.

The divide soon steepens while we ascend its grassy west shoulder away from the vanished trail, and then, where the divide undulates, we cross it through a swale. A blaze here directs us north-northeast, and after a few minutes' stroll we regain the path, which rises along the divide's east shoulder and often resembles a game track. It presently crosses a narrow, near-level length of the divide, where we encounter the trip's first stand of ponderosa pines, and then it veers away from the divide, rolling mildly toward the northwest.

We soon cross a muddy seep near the head

of Burnt Camp Creek's canyon, then bushwhack briefly and cross yet another divide, where we enter the Bennett Creek watershed. Then we stroll north in the welcome shade of nutmeg, white fir, sugar pine, incense-cedar and ponderosa pine while gooseberry, kit-kit-dizze, thimbleberry, and laurel border the trail by turns. At length we skirt an overturned stock trough, then cross Bennett Creek on a log at the lip of a reflective, cascade-fed pool. Creekside Surprise Camp (5750/3.5) offers a pleasant bit of civilization: a table, firepit and several large campsites, some of which can be found not far downstream.

North of the campsites, the path rises briefly up a steep bank, then switchbacks several hundred yards up a minor ridge and subsequently weaves northwest, continuing through the woods. Along the northwestward traverse we encounter 2 seasonal streams, one of which drops into a glen, striking a midway ledge and spurting out in a horsetail fall. At length we switchback to cross a major southwest-trending ridge at a swale, then stroll along the ridge's west flank for nearly a dozen minutes before meeting *Salt Creek Ridge Wildroute 95* (6700/1.1) at a cairn.

(The Coffeepot Canyon Wildroute continues north ¼ mile to Salt Creek Ridge, where it joins an unkempt northwest-trending path leading out of the Park to the Case Mountain Grove of sequoias. As Francis P. Farquhar reported in 1924, the place name stemmed from a 19th Century resident logger, Bill Case, who is rumored to have reduced some sequoias to shakes before sledding them to market, hauled by horse, mule, burro and steer. In 1978 State Forester Glen Moran confirmed that logging of the privately owned sequoias here had resumed that year.)

For now, we take the Salt Creek Ridge Wildroute southeast from the junction. Initially a path but soon becoming less, our route recrosses the same ridge we just crossed down the slope, then undulates to and beyond a ford of a snowmelt tributary, crossing slopes laden with ponderosa and sugar pine. At length we resume a moderate grade, then switchback upslope (sometimes quite steeply), exercising quite a bit of the pathfinder's art. Afterward, our course advances up Salt Creek Ridge, shuttling between north- and south-facing slopes. After some forging through prickly snow bush on these slopes, a final short stint of climbing steep, pathless duff gets us through a stand of red fir and beyond to the rounded, barren tip of Homers Nose (9050/2.4).

A rousing assortment of Class 5 routes on the sheer south faces of this granite dome and its eastern twin show climbers that although Homers Nose was named for the nose of Joseph Homer it's not to be sneezed at. After climbing the dome's face or viewing its summit panorama, we backtrack to the cars.

Surprise Camp

T72   Mineral King Ski Trek

*Beginning in a grove of the world's fastest-growing trees—
sequoias—this trek negotiates a canyon with scalloped headwalls down
which plunge resounding stepladder falls. Sawtooth Peak with its clean,
bold outlines and beckoning backward slant then appears on the facing
eastern horizon in an inspiring massif. Couloirs and bowls among the
peaks at Mineral King entice the proficient alpine skier to brave the
demanding runs they afford, and then venture beyond the Mineral King
horizon into the High Sierran vastness. But almost anyone can reach the
best viewpoints on the Mineral King valley floor.*

Season   January through April

Distance   17.8 miles (28.6 km) round trip

Steep Upgrade   none

Elevation Gain and Loss   2230 feet (680 m)

Exertion/Duration   easy/2 days

Skills   easy route-finding, novice nordic
and alpine skiing

Registration/Permits   Sequoia National
Park/none

Roadhead/Maps   R58/M50B–M52

Description   (This is not only the trip most
frequented by nordic and alpine skiers but
also one on which snowmobiles are likely to
be seen.) Although it can start lower or
higher, depending on the coldness and wet-
ness of the current winter's storms, our trek
usually begins at Redwood Creek (5710/0.0)
where paved *TC Road MTN 375* runs between 2 sentinel sequoias. These giants mark
our entrance to the Atwell Grove which,
geographer John Harper reported in 1974,
contains 1267 mature sequoias spread across
1434 acres of land. The findings of Richard
J. Hartesveldt and other sequoia researchers, published in 1975, include their theory
that no other tree in the world has grown as
quickly as the giant sequoia.

Our road winds eastward from Redwood
Creek, climbing moderately in its first mile
while passing through snow-dusted
incense-cedars and Jeffrey pines. Downslope
views scattered along this first mile reveal the
drier climes of a chaparral belt close at hand.
Eventually the snow thickens around the increasingly prevalent conifers, and our gradient eases.

We presently track across Atwell Creek
and then skirt the Atwell Mill Ranger Station

(6500/2.7—unmanned and locked in winter)
while sequoias become prominent. (See Trip
73 for details of the sequoia logging that
once took place here.) Shortly we pass the
start of the Atwell Redwood Trail (often
concealed by snow), then skirt an elongated
campground and advance just less than a
mile farther to slide between 2 rows of cabins, and afterward pass under a "Cabin
Cove" sign suspended between 2 road-
flanking trees.

More cabins appear ½ mile beyond the
sign in the outskirts of unincorporated Silver
City (6935/1.6), where a resort is sometimes
kept open throughout the winter. Again we
ascend in earnest, crossing the first in a series
of active avalanche chutes on precipitous
slopes in sight of the river's stepladdering
falls. The falls herald our nearness to Faculty
Flats and the Mineral King valley beyond.

Shortly beyond the last avalanche chute,
we finish most of this trip's ascent and start
to thread rows of snow-caked cottages at
Faculty Flats just upslope from the river.
The Cold Springs Campground road
(7500/2.4) soon branches south, crossing the
river by bridge en route to a shade-dappled
campground, where digging through snow
can uncover a few of Mineral King's public
latrines.

Then we ski by a few outlying cabins just
before reaching a clearing in which stands
the wintertime-padlocked Mineral King
Guard Station, often the first recipient of
early-morning sunlight. The stark stems of
deciduous cottonwoods, alders and aspens
border our road's riverside flank while we
kick on beyond the station, soon crossing the
toe of a south-facing avalanche swath—the

Gary Kenwood

White Chief, Eagle, Mosquito bowls near Mineral King make for risky but thrilling alpine skiing

first in a convergent series. Then our road rises and rounds a hill on which a huge, snow-flecked boulder is perched, where we gain the affecting view of Sawtooth Peak described in the "Features" section. Beyond, we encounter cabins clustered about a canopied Forest Service interpretative display. It marks the start of the summertime Sawtooth Pass Trail (7800/0.9), and stands a few dozen yards northeast of the only other outhouse in the Mineral King area.

Now in Mineral King valley, we advance toward braided Black Wolf Falls, where Monarch Creek tumbles into the valley. Moments later, the road turns southeast along with the valley, then bridges the boisterous creek. Farewell Gap is visible now in the climactic view of the trip.

Then skiers skirt one last cluster of cabins and momentarily go straight ahead through a fork onto a narrower *pack station road* (7830/0.2—the divergent county road bridges the river just beyond here). Rambling onward beyond the fork, we cross the

last of the convergent avalanche swaths at the foot of Potato Patch Ridge and then, after stepping over a gate beside mounds concealing a pack station, saunter across a creek spilling west from Chihuahua Bowl. The valley-floor clearing continues at length until we ford Crystal Creek, the course of which periodically chutes snow across our ski-route. Then we encounter a conifer enclave near the aspens of Aspen Flat (7930/1.1), a suitable base camp for skiers exploring surrounding high cirques and couloirs.

David Beck's *Ski Tours in California*, published in 1972 but now out of print, described difficult alpine skiing and ski-mountaineering routes from here to Tulare Peak, Farewell Gap and the White Chief crest. Because Beck worked as a snow surveyor here for several years in the late 1960's, his published guidance is well worth seeking at public libraries.

From Aspen Flat we eventually backtrack to our cars.

T73   Sequoiaside Falls Hike

Newcomers to Mineral King—especially groups of supervised children—could hardly do better than to take this trip first. Sequoia groves saved from the sawmill, an emerald-pooled gorge bedecked with ferns and framing a cataract, the presence of Indian potholes, and a vignette of the peak that ranks as the most eye-catching in Mineral King impress hikers here with the diversity of offerings in the Mineral King area. This trip's mild workout at elevations conducive to acclimatization, plus its position midway on the tortuous drive to Mineral King, confirm its appeal. This trip also offers you a chance to test your pathfinding skills on a short, obscure, blowdown-littered wildroute.

Season   June through October

Distance   3.5 miles (5.6 km) semiloop trip

Steep Upgrade   none

Elevation Gain and Loss   790 feet (241 m)

Exertion/Duration   easy/1 day

Skills   easy route-finding, Class 1 climbing

Permits   USNPS Entrance Permit

Roadhead/Map   R59/M51

Canteen   1 pint

Description   Our jaunt begins in a parking lot (6540/0.0) east of Atwell Mill Campground and leads downslope, west, on **SEKI Road 5–3** through the campground itself. Soon bearing left (west) through 2 consecutive forks in the road, we saunter along in the deep shade of sequoias, incense-cedars and white firs, presently leaving the road by a "trail to Hockett" sign (6480/0.2).

The **Atwell Hockett Trail** starts west here as a wide, well-beaten path, and quickly leads us over a slight ridge. Manzanita clumps occupy a ridgetop clearing which might date back to 1879, when—according to Russ Leadabrand—the completion of the Mineral King road allowed lumbermen Collins and Redfield to start the desultory toppling and milling of sequoias and other conifers here. It wasn't long before the operation passed into A.J. Atwell's hands, which advanced the logging more vigorously. A mill built here at Atwell's behest reduced the sequoias to shingles, grape stakes and posts—without profit. The mill shut down in 1888 after 2 years of operation, and in 1890 most of the land adjoining Atwell's passed into U.S. Army protection as Sequoia National Park. Captain J.H. Dorst, the first Park Superin-

tendent, was so incensed when logging resumed on Atwell's land in 1891 that he and his troops illegally seized the mill, temporarily shutting it down. Nevertheless, by 1898 the mill was active again, furnishing board for the 30,000-foot roadside flume that shunts some East Fork Kaweah water from Oak Grove to generate power in Hammond.

Despite the early revulsion and consequent clamor of conservationists for government purchase and protection of the remaining sequoias, the threat of logging wasn't banished till 1920, when private philanthropy intervened. D.E. Skinner bought the property and had it transferred to National Park Service jurisdiction in 1920, Leadabrand wrote in 1968. There was some attempt to commemorate Skinner by changing the name of the sequoia grove here to his, but the Park Service preferred the name Atwell, and so today the grove with its 600 sequoias honors a man who long ago tried to despoil it!

Now we drop quickly west from the ridge and then, upon meeting a lateral (6410/0.2) leading northwest toward a private road, turn south beside a meadow. Long grass parting about an old iron flywheel here reveals the sawmill site. The main trail leaves the meadowy cove in 70 yards and then descends gradually southeast into the canyon of the East Fork Kaweah River. Moments later, a short lateral (6390/0.1) signed "Indian Potholes" starts southwest. The pitted slab that it leads to demonstrates the nutgrinder's preference for picturesque vistas and proximity to water—Atwell Creek is a few dozen yards to the west.

Beyond the pothole junction, our path descends amid kit-kit-dizze and the sugar pine that supplants sequoias in most of the landscapes ahead. We soon step across an intermittent cascading brook that surfaces near the campground's privies not far upslope from here. Then we coast more than ½ mile farther and cross Skinner Creek where it spills and splashes among mossy boulders. A few minutes' walk from there gets us to a signed junction we'll be returning to shortly—that with the Sawtooth View Trail (6080/0.7).

Takers of Trips 73–75 continue descending while the distance-muted hiss of the river grows to a roar. We soon spy the river, emerald-pooled in a gorge, and then we traverse a man-made ledge that Mike Hill, Hockett Backcountry Ranger 1973–76, attributed to sledge hammer-wielding construction crews. Sprightly wildflowers and ferns adorn niches interspersed in the gorge's cliffs, and while admiring them we quickly come to a burly log bridge spanning the gorge. We cross it in sight of the head of the gorge, where the East Fork Kaweah River tumbles in a striking but nameless sequoia-side fall. At the bridge's southern abutment (5920/0.3), a lateral forks east toward a few of the sequoias composing the East Fork Grove. They stand near a bouldery picnic site just upstream from the falls. Consider the numerous cabins discharging pollutants upstream, and chlorinate the water you scoop from the river before drinking it. Now, while backpackers on Trips 74 and 75 advance southwest on the Atwell-Hockett Trail, we retreat to the Sawtooth View Trail junction (6080/0.3).

The *Sawtooth View Wildroute,* now unmaintained, zigzags northeast from the junction through an aromatic, ankle-high shroud of the seemingly ubiquitous kit-kit-dizze. A thick overhead conifer canopy subdues what light strikes our path, which is often blocked by blowdowns and sometimes crossed by game tracks. After 6 zigzags we catch the vignette most emblematic of Mineral King, in which Sawtooth Peak, a skyscraping, leaning, wedge-like massif some 6 miles to the east-southeast, is framed in the midst of a ponderosa-pine colonnade standing in low manzanita. We then alternately zigzag beside and ascend the crease of a ravine too densely wooded to have been recorded by contour-line map plotters. The path shortly leads

past an engraved "BLM Cadastral [property] Survey Post," then touches a tagged Park boundary and fades away. Follow the tree-mounted boundary tags 50 yards north from that point to reach *TC Road MTN 375* (6750/0.9) at the Park's signed Cabin Cove entrance. (Here we have the option of hiking the road east to the hot showers, cafe and store at Silver City, which would add 1.2 miles round trip to our hike.)

Our course descends the dusty road west from the entrance, still in the shade of dense conifers but now with chinquapin clumps at hand. Less than 15 minutes later we round a usually dry ravine, then stroll nearly 25 yards farther, watching the northern bank to catch the start of the unmaintained Cabin Cove Cut-off (6560/0.4). Hikers who revel in tracing dim trails on their own can start northwest on this one while the rest of us stroll west along the road's edge. In doing so, we soon cross Skinner Creek again, and shortly afterward—just as pavement begins on the main road—we turn south onto SEKI Road 5-3 (6564/0.4). The lot with our cars lies a few steps away from the junction.

T74   Ansel Lake Backpack

A granite gorge lined with ferns and flowers is this trip's first attraction. Sequoias tower near the brink of the gorge, its width is spanned by a burly log bridge, a cataract rubs its rocky depths, and the gorge has a string of emerald pools. Yet this gorge is a mere harbinger of the other treats along this journey to an alpine lake.

Season   July through October

Distance   23.0 miles (37.0 km) round trip

Steep Upgrade   0.2 mile (0.3 km)

Elevation Gain and Loss   5200 feet (1585 m)

Exertion/Duration   easy/4 days

Skills   Mod. route-finding, Class 2 climbing

Permits   Wilderness Permit

Roadhead/Maps   R59/M46–M47, M50B–M51

Description

Westbound *SEKI Road 5–3* Log

T73	Backpackers' parking lot	6540	0.0
	Atwell Hockett Trail 90	6480	0.2

Southbound *Atwell Hockett Trail 90* Log

SEKI Road 5–3	6480	0.0
Atwell Mill lateral	6410	0.2
Indian Potholes Trail	6390	0.1
Sawtooth View Trail	6080	0.7
East Fork Kaweah River	5920	0.3

Statistics derived from Wilderness Permits and compiled by the National Park Service in 1973–78 indicate that this trail received heavy use from backpackers and moderate use from packstock, with most of both uses occurring in August, averaging 4 visitors a group and 4 days a visit. The 1976 Park travel pattern and influence study showed that more than 99% of the people using this trail who complied with the permit requirement intended to go no farther than the Hockett Meadows area, and that, once there, these people were responsible for ¼ of all wear and tear to campsites, trails, stream banks and lake shores. (The remaining ¾ of the wear and tear was mainly due to the much greater use of the Tar Gap Trail.)

At the East Fork Kaweah River bridge, Trips 74 and 75 begin a stage on which few day-hikers venture. There the Atwell Hockett Trail turns southwest and begins a mild ascent to Hockett Meadows across the 940-acre East Fork Grove of giant sequoias. Only a dozen or so of the grove's 353 sequoias that Phillip W. Rundel tallied in 1969 can be seen along the trail, but even though they're partly obscured by white firs and sugar pines, these sequoias usually manage, by dint of their hugeness, ancientness, orangeness and shagginess to retain a high place in visitors' memories after this trip is over.

After a mile, our course fords a trickling fork of Deer Creek and shortly afterward leads across boulder-studded Deer Creek itself. This ford lies on the slick brink of a granite bluff where the creek spills in a lacy fall. From there, backpackers quickly advance to the long switchbacks the path makes while ascending a ridge next to Deer Creek. Kellogg oaks mingle with the woods here, contributing dazzling gold and crimson leaves that set off the surrounding greenery when autumn frosts arrive.

We presently cross a transitory brook where dogwood displays its distinctive blossoms in May and June. After roving 1.1 miles from Deer Creek, we leave the far-flung East Fork Grove at an outpost of sequoias. At length our course crosses exposed granite slabs and eventually rounds a divide into the Horse Creek watershed. Large groups of backpackers with ample water in their bottles can take advantage of the roomy, nearly flat camping area just down the ridge from here. (The nearest water—a snowmelt trickle— wets a creekbed 0.7 mile to the southeast on the trail.)

The steady upgrade continues while we make a lengthy traverse of the furrowed, southwest-facing slopes beyond the divide. Early in this traverse we ford the transitory stream, and then after passing through manzanita alternating with mixed conifers, we work upward into a belt of red fir and chinquapin, eventually fording stride-wide, signed "Clover Creek."

In the second half of this traverse, we

quickly reach a bog beside signed "Corner Creek." Mountain bluebells and willows embellish both the bog and the adjacent ford of the boulder-strewn, cascading creek. Our route presently ends the traverse by linking up with the Tar Gap Trail (8550/6.2) and then, only a few dozen yards later, forks southeast amid lodgepole pines onto inconspicuous, abandoned *Horse Creek Trail 92.* Evelyn-Lake-bound backpackers leave us at this fork, veering south on the Atwell Hockett Trail.

Our path now weaves up through the gradually inclined, glaciated valley of Horse Creek, soon entering a sprawling camping area, the westernmost part of which gets the earliest sunlight. Our course shortly advances through small, gritty barrens, then leads over a typical recessional moraine. This cross-valley dike of rounded boulders and finely ground rocks was left in a long prehistoric cold spell when intense storms stalled the melting of the Horse Creek glacier. Because a glacier acts as a conveyor belt for rocks that it plucks at its head and flanks, this refuse is dumped at its snout—spread evenly when the glacier is shrinking fast, but usually left in elongated heaps like the one we see here. Past an ensuing flat, we cruise upvalley through lodgepole pines, which now and then are graced with garlands of labrador tea. After a lengthy, meandering ascent, we leave the camping area and then cross a bog-spawning fork of Horse Creek while tracing the dim path with the help of triangular blazes. Our course then turns south across a Horse Creek ford, which we can boulder-hop across. Just past the ford, we meet a spur path departing west toward more campsites, and afterward our course veers east while skirting debris at the toe of an avalanche track.

The valley beyond starts a stepladdering phase, incorporating alternating risers and steps in a pattern determined by the spacing of cracks in the granite beneath. Glaciers quarried rocks from along the cracks readily, but skimmed over the least cracked bedrock, leaving us a series of moderate ascents, the first of which we now zigzag up. Our course shortly roams across a terrace near the base of chutes that scallop a ridge in the south. Camping zones occupy this terrace on both sides of Horse Creek, which we soon leap across at a ford. Here, western white pine

finds a niche in the woods, as corn lily does at the edge of the creek, but lodgepole pine continues to offer most of the shade en route. Now the path grows increasingly dim and rocky while guiding us up increasingly steep risers, zigzagging often. At length we reach a timberline bench much better suited for camping than the shores of Ansel Lake. A pair of tarns embellish a hidden part of the bench, drawing campers in search of seclusion. Another advantage of this camping zone is that firewood and wind screens, nearly absent at Ansel Lake, are amply available here.

*   *   *   *   *

A cross-country excursion involving some scrambling over hunks of granite contours northwest from this bench, then veers north near a camping zone beside an island-dotted tarn. Eventually that route rises to a giddying crest overlooking cirques in which the Eagle and Mosquito lakes are nestled. During the late 1960's and early '70's, officials of the Forest Service and Walt Disney Productions envisioned a sandwich bar capping this crest, linked by an aerial tramway across Eagle Lake to other tourist facilities they'd planned to build in Mineral King. The Forest Service reluctantly shelved the project in response to political pressure in 1978, and before the year was over, Congress had voted to add Mineral King valley to Sequoia National Park.

*   *   *   *   *

Now our path dwindles to a ducked *cross-country route,* which zigzags up polished slabs near Horse Creek and shortly touches the outlet of Ansel Lake (10,500/3.8). Flanked in part by boggy sod, in part by slabs and shattered rock, Ansel Lake occupies part of a thin-rimmed bowl that was scooped into the side of Falcon Peak. This is the spot where the Horse Creek glacier originated, and later retreated to before vanishing altogether. From here, we backtrack to our cars.

T75   Evelyn Lake Backpack

In this combination of a distinct path and a pathless route, each scene along the way could stop hikers in their tracks if they weren't aware that more striking scenery lay ahead. Giant sequoias stand by the brinks of waterfalls and fern-decked gorges. One cascade after another is bordered by gorgeous wildflowers. Meadows where herds of deer congregate extend far away from the trail. A vast plateau appears, backed by sheer granitic and volcanic mountains. These views and more make even backtracking from the Evelyn Lake area exhilarating.

Season   July through October

Distance   24.8 miles (39.9 km) semiloop trip

Steep Upgrade   0.1 mile (0.2 km)

Elevation Gain and Loss   4510 feet (1375 m)

Exertion/Duration   moderate/3 days

Skills   moderate route-finding, Class 2 climbing

Permits   Wilderness Permit

Roadhead/Maps   R59/M45–M46, M50A–M51

Description

Westbound *SEKI Road 5–3* Log

T73	Backpackers' parking lot	6540	0.0
	Atwell Hockett Trail 90	6480	0.2

Southbound *Atwell Hockett Trail 90* Log

	SEKI Road 5–3	6480	0.0
	Atwell Mill lateral	6410	0.2
	Indian Potholes lateral	6390	0.1
	Sawtooth View Trail	6080	0.7
	East Fork Kaweah River	5920	0.3
T74	Tar Gap Tr and		
	Horse Cr Tr	8550	6.2

The Atwell Hockett Trail continues southeast beyond the Horse Creek Trail junction, passes through lodgepole-pine shade over a hill, crosses a capacious camping zone and soon afterward fords boulder-studded, signed "Horse Creek." A path (8540/0.3) from the east soon connects with our own, and then we stroll across a bridged bog. Then our course is deflected west to round a ridge that separates the glacier-carved Horse Creek valley from the Whitman Creek watershed. Prolonged strolling through red firs and increasing numbers of lodgepole pines puts us at a signed junction

with *Evelyn Lake Trail 96*(8500/1.3) by a trail register (please sign in). Trip 80 trekkers join our route here, and while some hikers detour 160 yards south into Hockett Meadows to the ranger station there, eventually everyone on our trip takes the Evelyn Lake Trail northwest.

We initially stroll parallel to Whitman Creek, early crossing a camping zone, soon cutting across a pasture and eventually fording signed "Whitman Creek." Just a few steps beyond the ford, the long abandoned, largely overgrown Eden Grove Trail forks north, and then our path roves west to a leap-across ford of a meadow-banked creek. Then our course zigzags gradually upslope, and presently veers west (right) through a signed fork with the Cahoon Trail (8730/1.5), on which we will return.

We then weave and zigzag over the eastern flank of Cahoon "Rock" (really a mountain), and take in a panorama encompassing the Hockett plateau and the glacier-carved peaks behind it. Vandever Mountain, near Mineral King, shows through a gap in the east, and its reddish gray schist (a metamorphosed volcanic rock) contrasts strongly with its surroundings of off-white granite.

Shortly returning to the shade of red fir, lodgepole pine and western white pine, we step past pussypaws, pinemat manzanita and chinquapin. Most hikers can take this junction-to-lake section of trail in less than 1¼ hours, and those in search of a campsite will find two viewful camping zones not far from water along the way. A sheer-sided dome hiding Homers Nose shows in westward vignettes on the final descent.

After reaching the fir-green water of Evelyn Lake (8700/1.5), we start on a *cross-*

country route around to the lake's forested west shore, and then zigzag south in a brief, steep ascent toward Cahoon Rock. (A path laid out by the Boy Scouts parallels this cross-country route, but Dean Cambre, the Hockett Ranger in 1978, called it poorly designed and not worth finding.)

Then our route tops a broad, gently inclined ridge and follows it southwest through a camping zone, soon connecting with the *Cahoon Trail* (9270/0.7) just a few steps from Cahoon "Rock." The lookout that long stood unused here, preempted by fire-watch aircraft, was moved north to Yosemite National Park in 1977. Pat Quinn, who supplied the information, dynamited the lookout's foundations that year. With the lookout gone, the panorama is more breathtaking than ever.

Now we take the Cahoon Trail east, soon switchbacking down past more ground-hugging shrubbery into a wooded vale. The path descends gently along the vale, soon zigzags into an adjoining dell, then cuts through the dell's long, meadowy strip. Then we parallel the meadow while descending, and eventually return to the signed *Evelyn Lake Trail* (8730/1.0). Our trip's final stage involves backtracking on the Evelyn Lake and *Atwell Hockett trails* to Atwell Mill Campground, from where Road 5–3 leads us west to the backpackers' parking lot (6540/10.8).

Alpine tarn above Hockett Plateau

Dave McCoard

T76   Paradise Peak Hike

Although the Paradise Peak vicinity won't be termed "paradise" by everyone who visits it, it does include the world's highest (not tallest) sequoia, a panorama that validates the name "Great Western Divide" and an alluring alternate destination for Mineral King weekenders who want to escape its crowds.

Season   June through October

Distance   9.2 miles (14.8 km) round trip

Steep Upgrade   none

Elevation Gain and Loss   2860 feet (872 m)

Exertion/Duration   strenuous/1 day

Skills   easy route-finding, Class 1 climbing

Permits   NPS Entrance Receipt

Roadhead/Maps   R59/M50B–M51

Description   The onset of our trip, indicated by a sign beside paved TC Road MTN 375 (6510/0.0), involves ascending northeast on *Atwell Redwood Trail 83*. Nutmeg shortly drops out of the surrounding mixed-conifer forest while we take 6 zigzags in stride, and then meet an abandoned, though signed, lateral to Cabin Cove (6880/0.5).

Here our path turns abruptly northwest, and in several minutes it leads us amid open manzanita and then across a ravine carrying a sluggish trickle of water. Sequoias of the Atwell Grove start to dominate the trailside scenery here. In just over 100 yards, we switchback near one sequoia that toppled during the mid-1970's, smashing into a dozen splintery segments and strewing the slope with chips and limbs. The debris blocks

our view of Atwell Creek, the only reliable water en route.

Several ensuing short zigzags guide us into a patch ringed with sparse hazelnut that contains an exuberant melange of lupine, pinedrops, currant, false solomons seal, and leopard lily. Beyond this small clearing, the path switchbacks up onto open slopes mottled with snow bush and manzanita, eventually entering red-fir forest at a saddle set in a divide.

Here we diverge from backpackers taking Trip 77 and start west on signed *Paradise Peak Trail 82* (8430/2.5), which initially rises along the divide past northward vignettes of Alta Peak, plus southeastward vistas including, nearby, the world's highest (not tallest) sequoia and the distant Great Western Divide. Our course presently leaves the divide and weaves up through the semi-open forest on the east and south flanks of Paradise Peak to its westernmost rockpile, the summit (9362/1.6). A lookout was once maintained here, but it was dynamited when abandoned during the mid-1950's, and only scattered bits of wreckage remain. After taking in sweeping views of the High Sierra, we backtrack to the cars.

Richard C. Burns, NPS

Getting the picture

T77

Backpacking Down the Middle Fork's Canyon

Backpackers who tolerate ascending but love descending will find this trip tailor-made for them. It combines a quick, stiff ascent past vignettes of Mineral King and the world's highest sequoia with a long descent down Sequoia National Park's deepest canyon. For trekkers in search of solitude, this trip traverses some steep, rarely trod trails. But going places propelled by gravity, even in solitude, isn't enough for some backpackers. For them, this trek links several large groves of giant sequoias, bridges a chasm backdropped by jagged peaks, approaches seething white water often, and ends between spires and domes that rival those in Yosemite.

Season June through October

Distance 19.8 miles (31.9 km) shuttle trip

Steep Upgrade 0.3 mile (0.5 km)

Elevation Gain and Loss 3070 feet (936 m), 6280 feet (1914 m)

Exertion/Duration easy/4 days

Skills easy route-finding, Class 2 climbing

Permits Wilderness Permit

Roadheads/Maps R59, R63/M51, M56A–M56B

Description

Northbound *Atwell Redwood Trail 83* **Log**

T76	TC Road MTN 375	6510	0.0
	Cabin Cove Trail	6880	0.5
	Paradise Peak Trail 82	8430	2.5

We leave the start of the Paradise Peak Trail at a saddle on the East Fork/Middle Fork divide, and zigzag north amid red firs, descending into the Castle Creek watershed. Shortly the zigzags abate, and we skirt a sometimes boggy patch garnished with asters, lupines, currants, corn lilies, mountain bluebells and ranger's buttons. These colorful wildflowers, supplemented with ferns, will reappear in scattered nooks along the next few miles of trail.

Beyond the bog we skirt a small meadow, then ford a step-across tributary mistakenly signed "Castle Creek" and soon afterward find destination and mileage signs where the abandoned, limb-littered Castle Creek Trail (7930/0.7) starts northwest. (By 1978, this path had become so thoroughly sloughed away, covered with blowdowns and over-

grown that only a dogged pioneer would want to go where it led.)

Now our course ascends gradually while twisting at length from nook to nook, crossing cascades in a few of the nooks. Along the way we catch occasional vignettes of Alta Peak in the north and the Castle Rocks in the west. Then lodgepole pine filters into the forest and we skirt Bigelow-sneezeweed-flecked Little Sand Meadow (8080/1.7), which indeed does show very little sand. Not far beyond the meadow, the path starts a gradually steepening descent north, parallel to the Castle Creek/Cliff Creek divide. We presently zigzag down a ravine, and where the ravine swerves northwest, we veer northeast, soon crossing the divide at a saddle.

Vistas observed during the ensuing eastward descent reveal the immensity and cliffiness of the Great Western Divide ahead. Losing 1630 feet in 1.4 miles on a dusty path bordered by kit-kit-dizze, we eventually drop across slopes wooded with incense-cedar and Kellogg oak, and then approach the descent's end, Cliff Creek. Once near its banks, we cross a sequoia-sheltered terrace and then ford the creek. It can usually be boulder-hopped, but when snowmelt turns it into a torrent, the safest way across is by log or, if logs can't be found, by wading it at dawn. The use of a rope and belaying tactics can make this ford less dangerous then.

After crossing the creek (5570/2.9) and its bouldery floodplain, the path guides us briefly north across a terrace abutting the creek, and then inclines up a steep grade in the midst of ponderosa pines. We shortly step onto less-steep terrain, later pass the

rarely occupied Redwood Meadow Ranger
Station and then turn north at a sign onto
Timber Gap Trail 84 (6040/0.7).

Our course leads between the station and a
barn with a corral while bits of Redwood
Meadow can be glimpsed in the east, beyond
the barn. The path shortly outflanks the
meadow, then touches a camping zone before crossing a sluggish, sometimes polluted
stream. A few steps beyond, we turn northwest onto signed **Middle Fork Kaweah Trail
70** (6000/0.3) among shaggy-barked shanks
of giant sequoias. Our new course soon
leaves the grove and descends a moderate
grade through 9 switchbacks. Patches of
open manzanita mingled with stands of
sugar pine mark our progress into the Middle Fork canyon before we boulder-hop
Eagle Scout Creek—another ford deemed
hazardous when snowmelt amplifies the
creek's force.

A terrace lies next to the creek's north
bank just downstream from the ford, and
here we meet a lateral leading west-
southwest to a camping zone. Our path turns
abruptly northeast at the fork and mounts a
slight ridge dividing the creek from the
Middle Fork Kaweah River. Quite soon we
fork north from signed, northeast-trending
Bearpaw Trail 71 (5520/0.7).

From the junction we stride briskly down
toward the roaring river, then cross the
chasm containing it on a surprisingly
battered steel bridge. Part of the Great
Western Divide beautifies the up-canyon
vista from this bridge. Our course begins a
mild westward ascent at the bridge, and
shortly leads past greater eastward views of
the Great Western Divide. Then the route
contours around a wooded ridge that juts
into the canyon, skirts a smattering of wild
ginger amid mixed conifers and shortly
meets the signed Little Bearpaw Trail
(5680/0.9), which starts east-northeast toward its namesake meadow.

From here on down the Middle Fork canyon, we alternate between wooded recesses
and brushy ridges while pounding the twisty
Middle Fork Kaweah Trail and making a
mild descent. In the larger recesses,
streamlets spill across our path, and we
round one such recess soon after leaving the
junction. Afterward, the path zigzags down
into another large recess, and later crosses
an undergrowth-free wooded terrace that

overlooks Buck Creek.

A high steel-girder bridge is moored to the
terrace, spanning the boulder-bordered
creek in the midst of its sand-bottomed
pools. Then a short, arduous ascent of a
live-oak-laden slope puts us at the start of the
north-trending Sevenmile Hill Trail (5060/
1.8), signed "closed/unmaintained." Some 50
yards southwest of the fork, a dead-end path
branches east from our trail, which then contours west awhile in the Middle Fork canyon,
crossing a slender stream en route. Now the
gradual descent resumes through sometimes
hot and sunlit brush, and at length we stroll
across steppingstoned Mehrten Creek. After
sauntering a few minutes beyond the creek,
we pass the Castle Creek Trail (4720/2.2),
and from there proceed on down the main
canyon.

Westbound *Middle Fork Kaweah Trail 70* Log

T82	Castle Creek Trail	4680	0.0
	Crescent Creek Trail	3530	4.5
	SEKI Road 12–1	3300	0.4

Cascades on the Middle Fork Kaweah River

Robert Badaracco, National Park Service

T78   Running Through the Sierra's Most Controversial Valley

What was it about Mineral King that inspired a decade of intense national debate? Come, run, and see for yourself!

Season   July through October

Distance   6.4 miles (10.3 km) round trip

Steep Upgrade   none

Elevation Gain and Loss   680 feet (207 m)

Exertion/Duration   strenuous/1.5 hours

Skills   easy route-finding, Class 2 climbing

Permits   none

Roadhead/Maps   R60/M51–M52

Description   (Taking this run is an excellent way to acclimatize for hikes to the heights above Mineral King.) Our run starts by a parking lot just southwest of the Mineral King Ranger Station on paved TC Road MTN 375 (7500/0.0). First jogging southwest on the country road, we turn south within minutes onto the pavement of the Cold Spring Campground road, which immediately bridges the East Fork Kaweah River. The bridge leads into the campground, and right away our route turns east onto the *east campground road* (7490/ 0.1). This road's design is a figure 8 course, and we follow its northernmost segments while passing the campsites it serves. Campsite 6 (7500/0.1) marks the start of *Iron Spring Trail,* on which we jog up-canyon.

Almost warmed up, we hustle up the path's gentle grade, watching for walkers ahead and noting the showier plants that we pass. After 100 yards of skirting thimbleberry, corn lily, lupine and columbine patches, we pass a spur path leading north to the river and start jogging through some aspen groves. Shortly we rise above the river, briefly tracing an abandoned 1880's mining road. Not far away lie pits and mounds that mark a few of Mineral King's old silver, lead and garnet mines, none of which repaid the cost of their mining.

We shortly run over a terrace where numerous aspens were snapped off or bent when avalanches swept in from the south in the winter of 1969. Here we skirt the riverbank's brink several times, observing the river bed's bright orange-brown lining. This is residue from an upstream soda spring, but not the one that we're running to.

Then Sawtooth Peak on the Great Western Divide looms above Black Wolf Falls in the east, and while glancing at that uniquely bold peak, we fork east, away from a path that becomes overgrown. While it leads southeast to Iron Spring, a soda spring in a large, mushy meadow, our path cuts across a drier part of the meadow and soon connects with the *Sunny Point road* (7780/0.7).

Starting in a small stand of red fir, our road passes through the Sunny Point Campground, which was retired in 1977. Now the road winds southeast, soon merging with the muddy spur trail to Iron Spring and later threading rows of cabins. It ends in a historic ore-milling site owned since 1963 by Walt Disney Productions, and there we turn north onto paved *Road MTN 375* (7830/0.5). It bridges the river quite soon at an often-photographed viewpoint of strikingly V-shaped Farewell Gap. In minutes we reach the *pack station road* (7830/0.1) just south of the "alpine village" that Disney Productions first proposed in 1965. Their plans, endorsed by the Forest Service, situated in the village a 5-story hotel, numerous restaurants and stores, swimming pools, skating rinks, tennis courts, a golf course and stations for tramways and ski lifts that were to fan out toward the nearby national park. After a lengthy political battle, the Forest Service shelved the project in 1978; and, later that year, Congress voted to transfer Mineral King valley to Sequoia National Park, securing its protection.

Reflecting on the controversy, we jog southeast from the junction on the pack station road, which leads parallel to the river. Immediately we pass a sign: "road closed/ parking reserved for pack station customers," and later we skirt the pack station itself toward a locked gate (7890/0.3) barring our road.

Outflanking the gate on a trail, we then lope on the road farther across the Mineral King valley floor, soon passing the westward exit (7910/0.2) for Mid-Valley Trail travelers. It's possible to surprise deer as we go, for many does raise their fawns in the valley.

After a while, we boulder-hop Crystal Creek, and then stick to the closed road where Franklin Pass Trail 31E09 (7930/0.9)

starts southeast. Our course next weaves through a stand of aspens and black cottonwoods at Aspen Flat, and we bear southeast through several road forks (this once was a campground) until our road ends in a loop (8000/0.2).

Until the mid-1960's, the main **trail** to Franklin Pass began here, and now we jog up this abandoned path's gentle grade while brushing past sagebrush. After 200 yards, brush overlaps the old trail, and we cut west from it slowing to a walk while following a **cross-country route.** In just a few yards we start treading up the river's west shore, reaching the destination soda spring (8140/ 0.3) quite soon. Here we double back toward our cars.

T79   Silver Lake Backpack

This trek encompasses most of the charms of Mineral King—including a well-stocked laboratory for geologists, botanists, sketchers, painters and photographers.

Season   July through October

Distance   25.0 miles (40.2 km) semiloop trip

Steep Upgrade   0.9 mile (1.4 km)

Elevation Gain and Loss   7130 feet (2173 m)

Exertion/Duration   moderate/3 days, strenuous/2 days

Skills   easy route-finding, Class 2 climbing (Class 3–5 pitches optional)

Permits   Wilderness Permit

Roadhead/Maps   R61/M47–M48, M52

Description

Northbound *TC Road MTN 375* Log

T78	Sunny Point road	7830	0.0
	pack station road	7810	0.1

Southeast-bound *pack station road* Log

TC Road MTN 375	7830	0.0
pack sta (gate		
across pack sta rd)	7890	0.3
Mid-Valley Trail	7890	0.2
Franklin Pass Tr	7930	1.1

The **Franklin Pass Trail,** which we take, forks east from the retired segment of the

pack station road at a trail register posted beside a mileage and destination sign. Our course quickly veers southeast from the sign through sagebrush, and a short part of it is muddied by runoff from a spring. Passing willows and cow parsnip, we outflank the aspens of Aspen Flat, stroll through a bunch of black cottonwoods and soon start across drier slopes. There we intercept westward views in which cataracts lace lichen-blackened phyllite cliffs in white relief. Our course now cuts through a medley of manzanita and snow bush spread with lone, hunched mountain junipers. The slate chips and fractured sandstone that now clink underfoot complete the coloristic ensemble with a streaky reddish brown while, directly ahead, groves of foxtail pines accent the **V** shape of steeply rising Farewell Canyon.

We presently boulder-hop Franklin Creek at the lip of one of its many plunge pools, then rise past a nearby small campsite and afterward zig and zag up a slope through silky corn lilies and other spring-watered wildflowers. Beyond 12 hairpin turns, our course resumes its southeastward tack before leading briefly through a red-fir corridor. Then we cut across slopes of a cleft in which a cascading headstream alternates between surface and underground flow. We presently round a divergent ravine in sight of a medium campsite perched on the ravine's partitioning ridge. Subsequently, our track zigzags up through an alpine mishmash of greenery in which blue gentian, blue flax and mountain bluebells vie for the most zesty blues.

This stint of zigzaggery quickly leads to the signed start of the *Farewell Coyote Trail* (9300/2.1), which continues our ascent southeast to the **V** of Farewell Gap with a segment of straightaway. Soon after glimpsing inlays of gleaming white marble in nearby Farewell Canyon, we join a dim, unkempt track that once descended the verdant west flank of the canyon.

Now we advance up-canyon, briefly close to its wash, encountering a spring in a marble alcove before switchbacking 13 times up through a sprinkling of foxtail pines to a lucky northwestward outlook on Mineral King that will set photographers reaching for their cameras. Then, while we stroll up 9 final switchbacks, geologists can find fascination aplenty in the contrasting metamorphism of Tulare Peak's underwater deposits and in Vandever Mountain's volcanic rocks. Vandever Mountain, incongruously estranged from the nearby National Park, was named in homage to Congressman William Vandever. In an 1890 legislative session, with 1 year left to serve and only 3 to live, Vandever introduced the bills that established Yosemite, Sequoia and General Grant (now enlarged as Kings Canyon) national parks.

Of more immediate concern is the 2-part question, where am I, and where do I go from here? Our bemused ambling has led us to Farewell Gap (10,650/2.6), which, though it ranks among the Sierra's most distinctive, conspicuous passes, is often so fiercely windy that few hikers can absorb its panorama for long. Instead, they start a southeast descent, bearing in mind that shortcutting switchbacks, even via old trails, is a misdemeanor along this ranger-patrolled trail.

Transferring from Sequoia National Park to Sequoia National Forest and Golden Trout Wilderness at the gap, we dip into the Little Kern River's glaciated headwaters valley via 10 switchbacks. A spattering of ephemeral color from larkspur, wallflower, wild onion, Douglas phlox, forget-me-not,

Indian paintbrush and mountain bluebells beautifies the herbaceous greenery here.

Then the descent continues on a traverse of intermittently sodden slopes, presently intercepting 2 creeks, the second of which drains overflow from the Bullfrog Lakes. Subsequent striding of 58 yards gets us to the signed eastside turnoff of Bullfrog Lakes Trail 31E05 (9910/1.4), where a discretionary detour to the lakes starts.

*   *   *   *   *

The Bullfrog Lakes path initially weaves steeply up amid sparse foxtail pines over hornfelses. These rocks—once thin-bedded sandstone and siltstone—have been metamorphosed to the point of breaking irregularly, unlike slate. We shortly approach an outcropping extension of Mineral King's slate and phyllites and then switchback away from the creek where it tumbles over and slickens this vivid vermillion rock. The small set of ensuing zigzags leads to a timberline bench on which a large campsite is perched. Here we progress from sand flat to soggy meadow before making a yards-long final ascent beside the willow-lined Bullfrog Lakes creek to the lower of the 2 lakes (10,680/0.6). At least 3 medium campsites can be found between boulders near this granite-bound lake's north and east shores. After sating any exploratory urges, we backtrack to the Farewell Coyote Trail.

*   *   *   *   *

Resuming the down-valley trek on the Farewell Coyote Trail, we soon switchback down to the valley floor west of 2 large campsites flanking the Little Kern River near its confluence with the Bullfrog Lakes creek. The valley floor is at first fairly level, but shortly beyond several large campsites perched among foxtail pines it slants downward. A short path links most of the campsites with a river ford and our eastbank trail.

Soon descending on a bias across southwest-facing slopes, we veer away from the river past bunchy corn lily, a shooting-star-garlanded spring, snow bush and sagebrush mats, an avalanche track and a sporadic recurrence of woods. Midway along this traverse, we corner through a pair of switchbacks, then cross a thin brook and afterward meet a signed west-trending segment of Wet Meadows Trail 31E11 (9040/1.7).

Our course now descends somewhat farther southeast fords a step-across creek, and then rises on clinky slate. Presently it passes a waterless medium campsite near a strikingly bold snag and afterward rounds a near-level length of the Little Kern River/Shotgun Creek divide. We cross the divide at a red-fir-clad swale where Lion Meadows Trail 32E02 (9140/0.8) starts downslope, and later catch views of Class 4 to 5 pitches on impressive upslope bluffs. The southward panorama we get while traversing brushy clearings here emphasizes the spaciousness of the Little Kern Basin.

We presently steel ourselves for a taxing ascent and then start northeast at a signed fork up slippery, exceedingly steep **Shotgun Pass Wildroute 32E01** (8970/0.7). This rarely maintained path initially twists upslope a few dozen yards west of Shotgun Creek, which remains hidden while we cut through a low layer rife with labrador tea, snow bush, manzanita, chinquapin and willow, plumed here

and there by bracken fern.

Zigzagging only sporadically now, the path cuts across the first in a series of meadows. Then it traverses the base of steep east-facing slopes, outflanking 2 of the meadows and a small campsite between them. Shortly we get our first vista of Shotgun Pass through the gunsight **V** formed by 2 blond snags, then advance nearly 500 yards to skirt a spring fringed with flourishing wild onion, corn lily, larkspur and other ephemeral floral sparklers. Beyond the spring we briefly clamber up ledges of a granite outcrop, afterward cross a rivulet flanked by a showy array of flowers, weave awhile up a steep wooded slope and finally cross the lip of a bowl containing Silver Lake (10,500/1.4). This popular, campsite-ringed lake offers room for 28 sleepers a night, an estimate made by Barbara Rose in the 1977 USFS campsite inventory.

Now we boulder-hop Shotgun Creek where it issues from this exceptional lake, then pace off some 50 yards and fork north-northeast from a better-defined lakeshore lateral near a "Silver Lake"—signed pine. Then our course leads diagonally up a moderate grade on a forested slope,

Shotgun Pass panorama extends beyond Silver Lake and Little Kern Basin to the Kern Plateau and the Greenhorn Mountains

bearing north after 150 yards where a lateral to large, bench-perched campsite departs northwest. The ensuing main trail soon becomes distinct, then rises above timberline and tilts steeply up loose, gritty slopes. The southern panorama during this ascent encompasses Silver Lake and the Little Kern basin. After traversing a network of ledges garnished with monkey flower and primrose, our course leads across the Great Western Divide at Shotgun Pass (11,380/0.5), going into Sequoia National Park in sight of peak-packed alpine terrain, including Mount Whitney.

Of the backpackers who obtained a permit to cross this pass into the Park from 1973 to 1978, the average annual total was moderate, occurring mostly in August and consisting on the average of 2-person groups who planned to stay there 3 days. Park Scientist David J. Parsons' 1976 use statistics revealed that, while nearly ⅓ of those using this entrance intended to reach the Big Five Lakes, almost ⅔ were taking our semiloop trip. Furthermore, his figures showed that no one entering the Park this way added substantially to the fraying of Park terrain.

At once our path makes a gentle descent north-northwest across bouldery slabs, then turns northeast to run down the first slight ridge north of the pass. After a spell of moderate descending, we bear north on an often faint trace and gradually diverge from the ridge to cross a timberline bench. Here our trace skirts a large campsite sheltered by foxtail pines, and beyond it we weave downslope beside a brook past sprigs of red heather. Zigzags complete this quick descent, which yields to a northeastward stroll at a large campsite where the steepened slope terminates. The stroll consumes 220 yards of a path that often resemble a dry watercourse. Then we cross a broad meadow laced with meandering stream channels, maintaining a bearing of north-northeast. In crossing this meadow, one can indulge in sidelong glances at Florence Peak's pyramidal wall towering in the west. Although the faint path disappears in the meadow, we resume it at the meadow's north edge while heading toward Mount Kaweah. Our course continues north-northeast across a lodgepole-pine-forested bench and presently roves down a short, steep slope, guided by triangular blazes. The path disappears for the last time

just shy of a meadow bisected by Rattlesnake Creek, and from there we briefly outflank the meadow, passing near several large campsites. Then we boulder-hop Rattlesnake Creek and almost instantly turn west onto *Rattlesnake Creek Trail 107* (10,240/1.7). An engraved metal "Shotgun Pass" sign marks the spot.

The next mile of mild ascent takes us past sundry creekside campsites. Its procession of labrador tea, red heather, wild onion and shooting star ends in a willowy meadow that floors a sheer-walled cirque.

A set of 19 rocky zigzags then leads north amid slabs to a northeast-trending series of switchbacks. These presently guide us to a High Sierran outlook where a northwest-trending ridge adjoins a spire. Then we trudge up along the ridge, eventually crossing the Great Western Divide at a nick signed "Franklin Pass" (12,000/2.1).

Ranking among the most heavily used entrances to the National Park's backcountry, Franklin Pass was the entrance that an average of nearly 1500 people a year (1973–78) declared their intention of using when applying for Wilderness Permits. Most of these people entered in August, and those who entered in 1976 stayed an average of 4 days in groups averaging 4 people. More than half of them stayed in the Rattlesnake Creek watershed, causing 42% of the impact recorded there. Nearly a quarter of the backpackers passing through Funston Meadow and almost a sixth of those camping at Big Five Lakes entered here as well. Parsons, who was responsible for the statistics from which these conclusions were drawn, said that such knowledge helps the Park Service to devise daily entrance quotas designed to reflect the capacity of backcountry destinations, replacing the arbitrary quotas that were imposed in the early 1970's.

The final stage in our trek—a descent to Mineral King—starts as we descend briefly south the slight grade of the *Franklin Pass Trail*. We then make a prolonged traverse northwest just downslope from the crest. This traverse treats us to a stunning panorama. Here the wine-red hornfelses and streaky white marble of Tulare Peak abut the creamy granite of Florence Peak in the sheer headwall of a cirque containing the Mine Dump Rock Glacier and the lapis-lazuli-blue Franklin Lakes. Bruce Rogers of the US Geological Survey asserted in 1976 that this rock-mantled glacier is the southernmost active body of ice in the United States.

The tediously gradual downgrade continues through 12 switchbacks and past a midway spring. Then, at the bottom of the switchbacks, a lateral from a cluster of large, bench-perched campsites in the southeast joins our path. Beyond that sometimes blocked lateral, our descent continues near the largest, lowest and most visited of the Franklin Lakes. This length of trail skirts several small campsites, then leaves the woods, touches 2 springs and passes upslope from the lower lake's dam. Built of native rock masonry in 1904–5, this dam holds back some spring snowmelt runoff till Southern

California Edison Company employees open its valves in late summer. This storage gives their downstream turbines a small buffer against drought.

We then switchback down near a popular bunch of campsites lacking privacy, and much later zigzag down slopes of marble past an old silver mine and a nearby spring to a boulder-hop ford of Franklin Creek. Past a small, exposed, creekside campsite, we cross a few wildflower-spangled nooks, then zigzag downslope and later skirt century-old mining prospects in a stand of silver pine and red fir. Then our route rounds a metamorphic rock ridge and eventually meets the *Farewell Coyote Trail* (9300/4.5). To end our journey, we now trace its first stage in reverse to the cars (7830/3.8).

T80   Mineral King Backpack

Mineral King! The name evoked rockbound wealth to 19th Century prospectors and recreational wealth to 20th Century industrialists. For today's backpackers, it conjures up mountains wealthy with rarefied air, multiform water, jagged landscapes and vastnesses where camping is limited only by imagination and prudence. This trip's scenery offers a wealth of persuasion that hard-won refreshment of mind, body and spirit is the ideal use of Mineral King.

Season   July through October

Distance   31.2 miles (50.2 km) loop trip

Steep Upgrade   0.2 mile (0.3 km)

Elevation Gain and Loss   5500 feet (1676 m)

Exertion/Duration   easy/6 days

Skills   easy route-finding, Class 1 climbing

Permits   Wilderness Permit

Roadhead/Maps   R61/M46–M47, M51–M52

Description

Northbound *TC Road MTN 375* Log

T78	Sunny Point road	7830	0.0
	pack station road	7830	0.1

Southeast-bound *pack station road* Log

TC Road MTN 375	7830	0.0
pack sta (gate across our rd.)	7890	0.3
Mid-Valley Trail	7890	0.2
Franklin Pass Tr	7930	1.1

Southeast-bound *Franklin Pass Tr* Log

T79	Closed Rd & Soda Sp Tr	7930	0.0
	Farewell Coyote Trail	9300	2.1

Southeast-bound *Farewell Coyote Trail* Log

Franklin Pass Trail	9300	0.0
Farewell Gap	10,650	2.6
Bullfrog Lake Trail 31E05	9910	1.4
Wet Meadow Trail 31E11	9040	1.7

Our trip begins a unique part upon starting west-northwest on the **Wet Meadow Trail** at an acute-angle junction with the Farewell Coyote Trail. A gradual descent begins immediately and leads us through pungent, thick chinquapin, willow, fern, columbine, wallflower, leopard lily, mountain bluebells, scarlet penstemon and Indian paintbrush. Shortly we meet an old, abandoned link of the Farewell Coyote Trail, which gives access to a pair of small campsites several hundred yards northwest in a grove of red firs.

We turn abruptly southeast at the fork, then saunter down-canyon through sagebrush and mountain juniper. Shortly a lateral forks southwest toward Broder Cabin, now merely several tiers of notched logs standing in a group of large campsites perched upslope from the far side of the river.

Beyond the lateral junction, red fir and lodgepole pine shortly join the juniper in sparse stands that become more dense where the nearby river churns through a gorge. In minutes we zigzag downslope past a few small, perched campsites while our canyon veers to run nearly straight south. Our course then drops onto a riverside flat, and skirts several large campsites. There we presently fork southwest from a short, south-trending trail (8420/1.0) to a medium campsite. This trail once followed the riverbank south to connect with the Little Kern Trail but, as USFS Ranger Bob Werner explained in 1974, after a flood partly obliterated the trail in 1966, it was abandoned.

Our path, meanwhile, leads a few feet to a wade-across ford. Although the river is usually quite placid here, it plummets from a resistant ledge of metamorphic rock just downstream. When snowmelt torrents swell its strength, look for an upstream blowdown to cross on.

Once on the west bank, we turn south-southwest along the river, pass its often sunny cascade, then briefly resume the descent. Later, the river is seen bending southeast past scalloped slopes beyond where our path starts slanting up out of the canyon.

Our ascent initially leads us across slopes laden with snow bush and manzanita and intermittently graced with mariposa lilies. The upgrade soon becomes moderate and guides us steadily through red firs, only to be interrupted where we step gingerly in crossing a bog redolent with wild onions. Presently the path grows gullied and rocky for a few hundred feet, then crosses fizzing Wet Meadows creek and improves while ascending the creek bank south. Soon we attain a broad, forested flat and veer west past 4 small campsites and one large one.

Newlywed Wildroute 31E13 (8930/1.6) starts south from signs posted just beyond these campsites, while our path swerves southwest, passing a medium campsite in a few yards and a cluster of large ones soon afterward. The large campsites, collectively labelled Deadman Camp, flank a clearing with corn lily, monkey flower and shooting star where a rain gauge and a snow pillow stand.

USFS technician Floyd Gililland said in 1976 that a "snow pillow" constantly measures the wintertime snowpack's water content and radios measurements to a distant office. This device, enclosed here by a barbed-wire fence, offers the California Department of Water Resources a means of predicting how much water the Southern Sierra will provide each year for quenching our thirsts and growing our crops. Gililland said that the snow pillow is more efficient than conventional snow surveys.

The trail beyond this apparatus switchbacks up an open manzanita slope, then starts to outflank Wet Meadows on forested slopes where snowdrifts commonly linger till July. Lodgepole pine starts to displace red fir as we trudge ½ mile beyond the switchbacks, and several spur paths diverge north toward numerous large campsites. Shortly thereafter, we skirt a signed lobe of Wet Meadows, then gradually rise southwest while crossing a few intermittent brooks, presently reaching the signed "Pitt Brothers Cabin." Two large campsites occupy the flat in front of the cabin, which will probably be demolished soon, now that it stands inside Golden Trout Wilderness. Then our course passes another cluster of large campsites and afterward zigzags a short distance upslope to top the Western Divide.

Here at the signed "Wet Meadows Entrance" to Sequoia National Park, the Wet Meadows Trail turns north upon touching the end of Summit Lake Trail 102 (9840/2.0). Wilderness Permit statistics for 1973–78 supplied by Gail Bennett of the USNPS indicate that most of the light stock and moderate backpacker use this entrance received occurred in July. The Park's backcountry travel figures for 1976 show that although nearly 95% of the people using this entrance were taking this trip (the remainder went west to Garfield Grove), they were far outnumbered that year by backpackers headed for Hockett Meadows from the Atwell Mill and Cold Springs campgrounds. Consequently, future backpackers turned away from other Park entrances can probably get in here.

An easy stroll north from the junction along the mildly undulating Western Divide shortly brings us to a signed junction with north-trending Blossom Lakes Trail 104 (9850/0.6). This short path leads to the lowest lake in the Blossom Lakes chain, where campsites are often crowded. Superior though hard-to-reach campsites in the midst of the upper lakes are rarely used.

Wet Meadows Trail 100 turns southwest at the junction, leads down a moderate grade on a ridge and soon joins a lateral (9610/0.3) from the Summit Lake Trail that comes in from the southeast. Just a bit farther downslope, we stroll across a mile-long ridgetop camping zone before resuming the moderate descent into a lodgepole-pine dominion. Switchbacks presently ease the protracted grade and eventually we ford Hunter Creek. Then our path leads a few dozen yards along the west creek bank to merge with signed *Atwell Hockett Trail 90* (8640/2.4).

This path leads us northwest, rarely straying more than 100 yards from the South Fork Kaweah River, and cuts through a grassy nap sprinkled with brittle red heather sprigs. We soon ramble into a large camping zone near South Fork Meadows, then stroll across a lobe of the meadows and afterward fork northwest from an 0.3-mile-long lateral to the Tuohy Cutoff (8550/0.9). Our course then proceeds to an isthmus of woods separating the South Fork Meadows to the south from Sand Meadows to the north. Here the Atwell Hockett Trail turns north through a signed junction (8550/0.3) with the southeast-trending Tuohy Cutoff and the west-trending South Fork Trail.

Now we track across granite grit just inside the lodgepole-pine cover from sprawling Sand Meadows, presently passing the sand dune for which these barrens were named. Shortly our course meets signed, southeast-trending Hockett Lakes Cutoff (8500/0.9) near the north tip of Sand Meadows. Then the path roams north through the forest, outflanking part of Hockett Meadows in several dozen minutes before turning northeast into the meadow and bridging Whitman Creek.

The flagpole of Hockett Ranger Station (8500/1.0) confronts backpackers approaching northeast from the bridge, and a flag's presence signifies the ranger's readiness to render emergency services. The flag usually flies from 8 a.m. to 5 p.m. from June through early September when the ranger is not out on patrol.

The Atwell Hockett Trail turns abruptly northwest several dozen yards short of the station, then veers north, crosses a sluggish creek, and quickly returns to the woods. Here it links with signed Evelyn Lake Trail 96 (8500/0.1), which departs to the northwest.

Northbound *Atwell Hockett Trail* Log

T75	Evelyn Lake Trail	8500	0.0
	Horse Cr & Tar Gap Tr	8550	1.6

We take *Tar Gap Trail 91*, which outflanks the ridge containing Tar Gap but does not lead to the gap itself. Our path starts north-northwest from its offset junction with the Horse Creek and Atwell Hockett trails. The Tar Gap Trail begins its long, twisty undulations with a compact, mild ascent while red firs bit-by-bit supersede lodgepole pines. At signed "Corner Creek" a ford awaits us, preceding a longer descending amble to the braided effervescence of signed "Clover Creek" at another ford. Clover Creek is erratically hedged, not only with wild onion, which brandishes short-lived magenta flowers, but also with mountain bluebell, whose edible rootstock nurtures a May-through-August efflorescence.

A subsequent 0.3-mile stroll intersects a thready, transitory brook midway and leads to a brook with banks filagreed by leopard lily and columbine. Shortly we cross a ledge hammered from sloping granite slabs, catching a glimpse of Homers Nose on the west-southwestern horizon. Our course beyond the slabs leads across strips of open manzanita splotchy with clumps of snow bush, and at length rounds a divide marked by a house-tall boulder, entering the watershed of the East Fork Kaweah River.

In less than 10 minutes we skirt a spring issuing from a boulder's base, and 0.4 mile later, while glimpsing Paradise Peak to the north, we gingerly tread across Deer Creek. Our foreground for the next 150 yards is jammed with corn lilies, thimbleberries, swamp whiteheads and goldenrods. We then progress 1000 yards to another display where lupine, larkspur, leopard lily, rangers buttons, Indian paintbrush and Richardsons geraniums bracket a spring-fed trickle embellished with bracken fern.

Beyond the creek we shortly catch fugitive vistas of Sawtooth Peak—the peak emblematic of Mineral King. Presently we cross a few additional intermittent creeks and later gain an upslope view of a stark, conical peak.

Some 20 minutes of brisk pacing lead beyond to Fowler Creek, named for Tom Fowler, a flamboyant Irish-emigrant entrepreneur who took control of Mineral King mining in 1878. He renewed enthusiasm for mining there after the original investors had pulled out, declaring its silver too costly to extract. Under Fowler's direction, mines on Empire Mountain near Timber Gap (which can be seen from just ahead on the Tar Gap Trail) were enlarged and connected via tramway with a mill being built on the valley floor. He quickly learned the hard way that the first investors were right, and retired from mining, bankrupt; but he soon returned to power by representing Mineral King and part of the San Joaquin Valley in the state legislature.

We soon reach the Timber Gap vista, then ramble a bit farther past chinquapin clumps in assorted sizes, presently boulder-hop signed "Mineral Creek" and subsequently cross a slight ridge toward recessed Mosquito Creek. Several zigzags lead into the recess, where we cross the creek and then turn abruptly north upon meeting the abandoned Mosquito Lakes Trail (7920/7.3).

After we negotiate a gullied, bouldery segment of trail, our route zigzags a few hundred yards to the northeast, passing a register midway and afterward connecting with the Cold Spring Campground road (7500/0.5) near the east end of the campground. This road now guides us east-northeast for some 300 yards while linking campground parking slots. Then it joins a road from the west next to a "Tar Gap Trail" sign (7490/0.1). The main road turns north toward the main Mineral King road here, but we proceed straight ahead onto the east campground road.

Eastbound *east campground road* Log

T78	campground road	7490	0.0
	Iron Spring Trail	7500	0.1

Eastbound *Iron Spring Trail* Log

east campground road	7500	0.0
Sunny Point road	7800	0.7

Southeast-bound *Sunny Point road* Log

Iron Spring Trail	7800	0.0
TC Road MTN 375	7830	0.3

For the nimble and sure-footed only

Beverly Steveson

T81   Marble Falls Trail Hike

Brilliantly colorful landscapes of a region steeped in history make this easy canyon ascent stimulating to photographers, geologists, botanists and anthropologists; and relaxing to sunbathers and other refugees from the city. But while the waterfall destination is delightful almost any time of the year, it's certainly not perfect; hikers en route to it should keep an eye peeled for rattlesnakes and poison oak; and hikers should not even try to get to it on holiday weekends in early summer. Then this canyon is too beautiful for its own good, attracting more visitors than it can take.

Season   all year

Distance   6.4 miles (10.3 km) round trip

Steep Upgrade   0.1 mile (0.2 km)

Elevation Gain and Loss   1400 feet (427 m)

Exertion/Duration   moderate/1 day

Skills   easy route-finding, Class 1 climbing (Class 4 pitches optional)

Permits   USNPS Entrance Receipt

Roadhead/Map   R62/M55

Description   Our outing begins on **SEKI Road 11–2** (2150/0.0) just north of the loop road through Potwisha Campground, a site with a considerable past. John R. White (who was Park Superintendent for 24 years) and Samuel J. Pusateri wrote in 1949 that the misspelling "Potwisha" commemorates the Patwisha tribe of Yokuts Indians. Anthropologist A. L. Kroeber asserted in 1925 that the Patwisha tribe was made up of migrants from east of the Sierra who wintered here. The Patwishas, he said, summered at Eshom Valley and Mineral King from the 9th or 10th to the 19th Century. White and Pusateri ignored his findings completely. Instead, they reported that the Patwishas' place was taken by a forerunner of the Southern California Edison Company. It established a camp here in 1911 for the men constructing a hydroelectric complex that included the nearby aqueduct. Later, 1933–40, workers of the federal Civilian Conservation Corps were dispatched to projects throughout the Park from a camp located here. If the CCC didn't build the trail that we're about to hike, it certainly kept it passable.

For now, we stroll 75 yards beyond the gate on Road 11–2, then veer north where a road branches northwest toward a gauging station on the shrubbery-screened Marble Fork Kaweah River. ("Kaweah" was the name of the Patwisha Indians' neighboring tribe.) Our road soon crosses the concrete-lined aqueduct on a diagonal bridge and then meets **Marble Falls Trail 76** (2180/0.2) at a trailhead sign opposite an aqueduct-control gate.

We turn southwest onto the path, zigzag briefly upslope, and then trace a twisting course generally north in the thick of chamise, yucca, yerba santa and flannelbush. Continuing a mild ascent, we presently cross a thin brook flanked by dogwood and sycamore, and later touch colorful outcrops of schist, a metamorphosed volcanic rock whose story is told in Chapter 1. Although our path winds through Deep Canyon high upslope from the river, the river's hiss can still be heard, and its cascades and plunge pools can sometimes be seen.

Shortly we enter an oak woodland that includes sharp-needled nutmeg trees, and there our path becomes bordered by kit-kit-dizze. Poison oak crops up sporadically beside the path (watch out!) while we advance farther up-canyon, and then a brook cascades down white marble steps, crossing our path beside balconied ferns. The path leads 10 yards beyond the stream to a bench carved from a steep slope (camping is prohibited here).

Now our route turns directly upslope and, after a taxing but quick ascent, we start contouring northwest on the path. After a while it leads within sight of a wide, spumy fall where the river plunges from a ledge of dazzlingly white marble. The path ends 30 yards north of the fall on a ledge (3560/3.0) overlooking the river.

A short, easy scramble down from the trail puts us on slabs near the brink of the fall, which is not the "Marble Falls" for which the trail was named. Marble Falls, which can be seen from the Generals Highway, is located nearly a mile up-canyon, and only mountaineers equipped for 4th Class climbing can reach it. Those who stay at the slabs will find them ideal for sunbathing, and will probably term the nearby fall "satisfying enough." The sun sets in early afternoon here, and while there's still enough light to see, everyone backtracks to the cars.

T82　　Mehrten Creek Backpack

Castle Rocks, a group of fins and spires, and Moro Rock, a dome, bracket part of the 7000-foot-deep Middle Fork Kaweah River canyon, and dominate views along this up-canyon trip. The low elevation of the route ensures that it can be traveled all year, and even though its first several miles can grow uncomfortably warm in summer, numerous streams and shady recesses are scattered along the way, and short optional hikes from the destination campsites give access to bathing and fishing pools. Experienced hikers with only a day to enjoy the cliff-and-cascade scenery here can also take this trip even though they will have to move fast.

Season　all year

Distance　9.9 miles (15.9 km) round trip

Steep Upgrade　0.1 mile (0.2 km)

Elevation Gain and Loss　1700 feet (518 m)

Exertion/Duration　easy/2 days

Skills　easy route-finding, Class 1 climbing (Class 3–5 pitches optional)

Permits　Wilderness Permit

Roadhead/Maps　R63/M56A–M56B

Description　(The Castle Rocks, which loom southeast of this trailhead, rival the greatest rock-climbing challenges of Yosemite and, increasingly, climbers attempt to reach them. Most climbers start on the abandoned Castle Rocks Trail at Potwisha Campground, not far from here, only to find that it ranks among the most sloughed away, blowdown-riddled, overgrown paths in the Park, and that few other trails are more overgrown with poison oak. The Paradise Peak approach—via Trip 76—is best, unless you want to climb Castle Rock Spire, of which Fred Beckey warned it was extremely difficult to find when approaching from Paradise Peak. The defenses of Castle Rock Spire rank among the greatest challenges facing rockclimbers in the Sierra.)

The records of travel patterns that Park Scientist David J. Parsons incorporated in Wilderness Permit statistics for 1973–78 show that although the Middle Fork Kaweah Trail got heavy use from backpackers (mostly in May) and light use from pack stock (mostly in August), this path was not used as an avenue to the High Sierra. Future hikers should not expect to find solitude in campsites along it during spring weekends.

We embark on our jaunt at the end of SEKI Road 12–2 (3300/0.0), where a trailhead sign stands just west of the Moro Creek Corral. Our course leads east through the corral's 2 barbed-wire stock gates (please close), and then connects with *Middle Fork Kaweah Trail 70*. It starts twisting up-canyon by curving into a recess and fording stepping-stoned Moro Creek. Beyond the creek's hedge of shrubbery and trees, we stroll up a mild grade, soon pass through another stock gate, and then cross the wake of a 1969 controlled burn (see Trip 90), which chamise and buckbrush have already covered with thickets.

Then our course rounds the first of many slight ridges jutting into the Middle Fork canyon, and soon afterward it forks north from the abandoned Crescent Creek Trail (3530/0.4). This largely overgrown path initially follows a powerline. Although this trail once led up to Crescent Meadow, hikers attempting to trace it have become lost, and some have even had to be rescued.

National Park Service

**Middle Fork Kaweah Trail
seen across from Castle Rock Spire**

into the river at a much lower level. Only climbers adept at rappelling and Class 4–5 climbing can safely reach the river from here.

The trail ascends the creek's short east bank, then crosses an oak-sheltered bench, zigzags briefly upslope and resumes its sinuous eastward course. At length we walk into one of the larger recesses, where a purling brook crosses our path through a stand of incense-cedar. On the outskirts of the stand we pass thimbleberries and Kellogg oaks, then resume the mild ascent through chaparral and presently meet the signed but abandoned *Castle Creek Trail* (4680/4.5). Here we veer southeast, starting down the Castle Creek Trail through woods. Quite soon our route reaches a delightful camping zone (4640/0.1) and then crosses Mehrten Creek.

Mehrten Creek is cold, and scarcely large enough to bathe in, which prompts some hikers to don day packs and head for larger streams. They have 2 streams with 2 different access routes to choose from. They can descend the Castle Creek Trail 0.9 mile to the river, crawling through brush at times, or they can backtrack to the Middle Fork Kaweah Trail, then follow it east for 2.4 miles to Buck Creek. Whatever they decide, they should allow themselves plenty of time to backtrack to their cars.

Soon after leaving the fork, we ford a creek in a nook with laurel and poison oak shaded by sycamore and canyon live oak. The path next makes a protracted traverse of convoluted, chaparral-clad slopes that often become quite hot by mid-morning in summer. Sporadic views of Castle Rocks and the Great Western Divide compensate for the trail's exposure until our canyon narrows, approaching the canyon of Panther Creek. At the edge of that canyon, our path abruptly drops more than 100 feet, and then we make a boulder ford of the creek itself. Panther Creek plunges over a ledge just downstream from the ford, and then flows

T83   Sunset Rock Hike

This brief, well-shaded journey starts in view of a gorge seething with white water and later delivers hikers to an outlook from which interlocking distant ridges occasionally form profiles in brilliant sunsets. Among the options available midway along this trip are explorations among the sequoias of Giant Forest, including jaunts to a store, a cafeteria and a campfire-talk amphitheatre.

Season   May through October

Distance   5.0 miles (8.0 km) round trip

Steep Upgrade   none

Elevation Gain and Loss   1260 feet (384 m)

Exertion/Duration   easy/1 day

Skills   easy route-finding, Class 1 climbing

Permits   USNPS Entrance Receipt

Roadhead/Map   R64/M55

Canteen   1 quart

Description   *Marble Fork Trail 57* starts northeast by the eastern abutment (5140/0.0) of an old bridge on SEKI Road 13–1 spanning a Marble Fork Kaweah River gorge. With emerald pools among echoing rapids spottily visible to our left, we stroll some 20 yards up-canyon through white fir, black oak, hazelnut, gooseberry and aromatic kit-kit-dizze before an unmaintained path forks north toward the river's slabby shores. The ensuing zigzags lead up past ferny nooks that showcase thimbleberries, and presently skirt the incense-cedar and slender-branched dogwood that take the place of oaks. Quite soon, at a zigzag near recessed Little Deer Creek, we embark on a series of elevation-gaining traverses joined by occasional switchbacks.

Manzanita puts in an appearance before the traverses take us on to north-facing slopes, where a dense forest's shade and occasional lingering snowdrifts keep ground-cover growth to a minimum. A ford of an intermittent brook precedes the last switchback (6200/2.0), where an east-trending path signed "Caution/End of Maintained Trail" begins. A lengthy final traverse puts us in the midst of sugar pines on rolling terrain, and ends at a junction (6380/0.4) where a north-westward vista reveals Sunset Rock.

A wide, beaten path now leads a few yards down to the rock (6365/0.1) and there gives way to a barren expanse of exfoliating, pothole-pocked Giant Forest granodiorite. The rock's position allows us to catch interleaved western ridge profiles in bold relief at sunset—hence the name. Now we can double back to our cars either immediately or later, for trails beckon that give quick access to the sequoias, campfire-talk amphitheatre, lodge, store and cafeteria at Giant Forest.

T84   Crystal Cave Hike

Everyone who has ever had a yen to explore secret passages, or to find out what inhabits the surface above and beyond such passages can do so at Crystal Cave. Here the National Park Service provides visitor and environmental protection, plus passive and active interpretation, to ensure that its guests leave the delicate beauty of Crystal Cave and its approach route just as they found it, returning to their cars well-informed.

Season   Mid-June through August

Distance   1.7 miles (2.7 km) semiloop trip

Steep Upgrade   0.1 mile (0.2 km)

Elevation Gain and Loss   410 feet (125 m)

Exertion/Duration   easy/¼ day

Skills   easy route-finding, Class 1 climbing

Permit   cave-tour tickets 50¢ each

Roadhead/Map   R65/M55

Canteens   none

Description   *Crystal Cave Trail 56,* a paved, designated nature trail, begins beside a trailhead sign next to the doughnut-shaped parking lot (4920/0.0) where SEKI Road 13–1 ends. Leaflets discussing plants, animals and rocks commonly seen by the trail ahead can be picked up at a dispenser that stands in tandem with the trailhead sign. The leaflets are free to borrow, or 10¢ to buy (leave a dime in the dispenser), and their descriptions add depth to, rather than repeat, information in this book. Still another sign advises that you bring a jacket or sweater, because temperatures inside the cave are nearly always close to 50°F.

Our path starts north in Kellogg-oak shade, descending a sometimes-steep grade via stairs alternating with ramps. Quite soon our course skirts a sign that interprets a nearby outcrop of marble, and then we cross dry slopes interrupted by moist nooks. A variety of oaks clothe the slopes while Jeffrey and ponderosa pines, incense-cedar, white fir, dogwood and California nutmeg congregate in the nooks and canyons. Bleeding heart, sweet shrub, California hazelnut and—watch it!—poison oak thrive near these often-cool recesses.

The trail presently bridges Cascade Creek in the midst of bigleaf maple and white alder. Ivylike wild ginger soon flanks the trail as we approach a drinking fountain, an in-

terpretative display and shady benches. These artifacts are situated just off the trail and west of a kiosk (4540/0.6) where 50¢ tickets for guided tours of Crystal Cave are sold. Visitors group to enter the cave's wrought-iron "spider web" gate (just north of the kiosk) every half-hour from 9 a.m. to 4 p.m. during weekends from Memorial Day to Labor Day, and during weekdays from late June through August. (Tour guide Milo

Fantastic formations in Crystal Cave

National Park Service

Jenkins told me in 1977 that the early morning and noon tours are usually the least crowded.)

Although Crystal Cave may have been found by Indians long ago, no one of this century knew of the cave until C. M. Webster and A. C. Medley spotted it in 1918. (They had been fishing in Cascade Creek, which is now closed to fishing.) Although the Park managers had wanted to open the cave to the public then, they had to wait until the late 1930's before the money and manpower to build the trails and other needed facilities became available. The construction, mostly done by the Civilian Conservation Corps, was completed in time for the Memorial Day weekend of 1940, when the public was first allowed inside the cave.

In 1966 geologist Arthur L. Lange described how the cave was probably formed. Between 1.8 million and 10 thousand years ago, when the local yearly rainfall was nearly twice what it is today, and glaciers had expanded across the Sierra, water soaked down through the ground, dissolved molecules that turned it acidic, then saturated this pod of calcium-rich limestone and began dissolving it. Later, the glaciers melted, and the runoff cut into caves like this one, flushed away their debris, and enlarged them. Then the runoff receded inside the cave, and water seeping down through the limestone overlying the cave dissolved some of it. When the water dripped into the cave, the dissolved molecules resolidified, forming "draperies", spires and upside-down pinnacles on the cave's roof and floor. Today, while you walk the cave's 0.4-mile-long semiloop trail, your guide can point out evidence of these stages in the cave's creation.

The sensuous sheen of the cave formations makes some visitors want to feel them, but if you get the urge, STOP! Touch any growing formation, and the oil from your skin will not only keep it from growing but also will make it decay. Since caves are the most easily damaged features in the Southern Sierra, the Park Service and groups of responsible cavers, such as the National Speleological Society (address in Chapter 2), give out the locations of the region's "wilderness caves" only to cavers of proven ability who practice cave conservation.

After returning to the portal of this relatively civilized cave, we backtrack to the cars.

T85   Moro Rock Hike/Climb

Moro Rock juts abruptly like a fin from the plateau of Giant Forest into the snaggletooth-peak-surrounded Middle Fork Kaweah River canyon. It affords climbers immense walls of exfoliating granodiorite where no route except the path has yet been found to be easier than 5th Class. Moro Rock has a fascination for trail-borne tourists also, and it is one attraction their mass visitations are not likely to wear out. Its fascination stems from the violence of the earth-shaping forces (lightning, floods, earthquakes, rockfalls) that have been at work here. Such violent forces can still act at any minute, making the stairs and railings on Moro Rock seem like a fragile illusion of security instead of a taming of nature.

Season May through November (avoid holiday weekends)

Distance 0.4 miles (0.6 km)

Steep Upgrade negligible (except for climbers)

Elevation Gain and Loss 420 feet (128 m)

Exertion/Duration easy/1/12 day

Skills easy route-finding, Class 1 climbing (Class 5 pitches optional)

Permits USNPS Entrance Receipt

Roadhead/Map R66/M56A

Canteen 1 pint

Description At the start of *Moro Rock Trail 65* south of the Moro Rock Loop road (6430/0.0), climbers are offered 4 choices. They can choose to descend at first along the western base of the rock's facade, to which access is brushy—especially strenuous for those burdened with heavy climbing gear. Or, if they're very ambitious and want to attempt the rock's extremely steep eastern flank, they can descend southeast, initially through a brush-poor forest, and trace the chute in which Moro Creek surfaces. The easiest 5th Class climbing routes run along the spine of the rock parallel to the dynamited, stairway-interspersed trail. It's railings enclose a route so easy and versatile that just about any kind of footwear—or no shoes at all—can be used to climb it.

A sign by the trailhead warns of the severe lightning hazard when thunderstorms visit Moro Rock. Vic Vierra, a ranger stationed here several years ago, recalled in 1976 that some tourists who had run out to the rock to catch better views of a violent lightning display caught the lightning itself in one strike. The bolt, said Vierra, arced from point to point on their bodies, scorching their skin and disintegrating their clothes but missing their hearts. Transformed into a surging ground current, the discharge ran down the trail, blasting concrete from the reinforcing rods inside it and killing the only man who had taken refuge under an overhang.

Taking the hint, we venture south on the trail when lightning is unlikely, ascending past increasingly rare showy wildflowers, manzanita, Kellogg oak, white fir, and sugar pine wherever they cling to the rock. The rock's flanks rapidly steepen, soon forcing our course to switchback up across the rock's spine and then start ascending its western flank. In minutes we emerge on a long, narrow summit platform (6725/0.2) enclosed by railings. The convoluted Great Western Divide on the distant eastern skyline is the product of an ongoing contest between mountain building and forces of erosion. Closer to and southeast of us, the fins, spires, domes and other projections collectively labeled "Castle Rocks" are a result of the same force that shaped Moro Rock—the contraction of molten granodiorite as it cooled, forming master joints. The less jointed the monolith, the more it resisted erosion, and that is why Moro Rock gained the supermacy over its setting that it enjoys today.

After gazing at the results—restraining ourselves from dropping or throwing things because flying debris can hurt hidden downslope climbers—we double back toward our cars. Most climbers who scaled the rock's faces will follow our exit route.

The Great Western Divide from Moro Rock

Richard C. Burns, NPS

T86   Drum Valley Bicycle Tour

Among the many people drawn to this trip by its all-season usability, by the provocative transformations that its scenery undergoes, by the long coasting descents it offers, are aspiring geologists who find in the jumble of rocks en route as much of a workout for their minds as the trip's upgrades give their muscles.

Season   all year

Distance   28.5 miles (45.9 km) loop trip

Steep Upgrade   none

Elevation Gain and Loss   2190 feet (668 m)

Exertion/Duration   moderate/1 day

Gears   10-speed conventional to 15-speed alpine

Permits   none

Roadhead/Maps   R67/M53–M54, M57A–M57B

Description   We mount bikes at the intersection (420/0.0) of Road 152 and Avenue 416, both paved, and set off eastward on *Avenue 416*, which is distinguished by a dashed centerline. It guides us directly through a patchwork of citrus orchards through which dark, erosion-resistant outcrops of the olivine gabbro composing Stokes Mountain gain prominence now and then in the south. After a mile of easy sight-seeing, in which we pass a couple of white farm houses, marked by tall palms like so many other survivors of early San Joaquin Valley settlement, we cross the signed "Friant Kern Canal" and begin touching minor spur roads at quarter-mile intervals. Avocado groves mingle with citrus on this side of the canal.

At the fourth crossroads past the canal our guiding centerline curves sharply north onto *Road 168* (470/2.0). Its course is straight for ¾ mile and then it bends northeast at the base of a granite hill. Soon after passing the bend and an adjacent spur road to a turkey ranch, we gear down and make a taxing ascent amid Sierra foothills. Our road soon narrows, dispensing with shoulders, and shortly reveals 19th Century origins in the mortarless masonry of its downslope retaining walls. The ascent presently grows less wearying while we advance across private cattle pastures studded with blue oaks. Eventually we top a rolling watershed divide where the spring wildflowers that commonly flourish in grazing country abound in season.

Then our route briefly allows coasting while intersecting an assemblage of private roads. The coasting temporarily ends where we cross intermittent, sycamore-lined Moore Creek, but soon afterward it begins again. Quite soon our road curls across a steep-sided gulch, then heads through a series of minor ups and downs and at length merges with *State Highway 245* (1260/6.4).

Roadcuts along the state highway segment that we're about to ride show soils derived from a melange of granite, mica schist, severely metamorphosed clays, carbonates, lava and pumice, each of which forms outcrops where markedly concentrated. Diversified soils foster not only a great variety of plants and animals but also a delicate landscape appeal.

The state highway northeast of the junction briefly ascends to a gap in the Grapevine Creek/Cottonwood Creek divide, then undulates slightly and presently leads parallel to intermittent Cottonwood Creek past a windmill to a bridge. Cottonwoods, sycamores and black oaks line the creek bed, both all-at-once and by turns, but abundant blue oaks always abut them. After bridging the creek, our route passes under high-tension lines, skirts Auckland Ranch and meanders up canyon, eventually rising away from the streambed up west-facing slopes.

Shortly before the canyon expands on leaving the strip of metamorphic rocks, we branch north onto a narrow paved *road* (1470/4.3) signed "DIA 152." This road's first few hundred yards slant down to a grapevine-festooned bridge across Cottonwood Creek. A gentle ascent over granitic rock in basinlike Slickrock Canyon ensues, and the cyclist making it follows the border between cleared sheep-grazing land to the north and thick chaparral to the south. Our road presently narrows where a deceptively similar ranch road (1500/1.1) forks north, and an instant beyond the fork we bump over a cattle guard. Cattle frequently drift across the road in the ranch we've just entered, depositing extra hazards for the bicyclist to avoid.

Slickrock Canyon presently narrows, and there our road makes a brief, stiff ascent and then winds, contouring out of the canyon. Quite soon we enter Drum Valley, pause to gauge its dimensions and then quickly ride on, repelled by a hideous quarry of marble marring the valley's southern rim.

Soon our course starts to undulate west across the valley, crossing another cattle guard before spanning Bull Creek in mid-valley. Beyond the sometimes subterranean water indicated by willows here, we soon meet California Department of Forestry (CDF) fire road T1 (1770/4.4), signed "Baker Cutoff," which starts north under a locked gate. Shortly thereafter, our road aims directly at Buttonwillow Peak in the west, and we pedal easily toward the high-tension lines athwart its face, soon nearing it on the outskirts of a cacophonous turkey ranch. (Drum Valley has been associated with fowl or foul livestock since Andrew Drumm was the resident hog-raiser, probably—wrote historian Harold G. Schutt in 1976—during the 1850's.) Upon cycling under the lines, we turn abruptly to outflank the peak and shortly depart Drum Valley through a gap between that peak and Corn Jack Peak to its south. The steel meshwork of a power station disfigures the westward view from here.

A few minutes' ride takes us past the station and down an ensuing, oak-bordered grade into the Sand Creek watershed. This truncated mile of free-wheeling descent is flanked in the north near its midpoint by the boarded-up Drum Valley schoolhouse, and ends where our road passes over Sand Creek. In making the subsequent brief, stiff ascent, we cross adjacent inclusions of ancient clayey pool and watercourse beds, erupted andesite fragments and—the oldest rocks found on this trip—undersea basalt-flow slabs; all metamorphosed beyond recognition except to practiced geologists. The upgrade abates where roadcuts again reveal granite, and quite soon an off-limits CDF fire road signed "T1" is met in the gap of a drainage divide (1840/3.0).

Now we speed into Long Valley, where many blue oaks and much brush has been cleared to enlarge the pasture for stock. Some trees were left to shade the road, as we

A family sport

Beverly Steveson

soon find out with relief. Tides of color sweep this district when wildflowers bloom in spring. After skirting a picturesque windmill, the road then tops a mild rise and begins to descend the Negro Creek watershed. This long descent past sycamore dells and glimmering pools along the occasionally surfacing creek is soon interrupted for most cyclists, who pause to admire the domesticated redwood and colorful garden of a roadside ranch. Later in the descent, the San Joaquin Valley figures in ever-more-encompassing views while we skew out of the Negro Creek drainage, traverse a hodgepodge of foothills above Long Creek,

and then pass through another breached divide and shoot southwest past the western exit of signed, paved Johnson Drive 156 (590/5.5).

By and by, our course nearly levels where we rush past one more turkey ranch. Then we skirt citrus groves, round one last hill, cross the wide, tantalizing but off-limits Friant-Kern Canal and pedal a final mile south. In this ultimate segment of our trip, our route's designation switches from "Drive" to *"Road" 152* while crossing rural roads before it reaches our cars near the crossroads of Avenue 416 (420/1.8).

T87   Dunlap Bicycle Tour

From springs among towering sequoias in Kings Canyon National Park down through mazy foothill topography, Mill Creek gathers water from slopes of granitic, metamorphic, volcanic and sedimentary rocks just south of the Kings River watershed. The descent of Mill Creek eases midway to the San Joaquin Valley, its canyon becoming a valley of distantly audible turkey ranches and a stockman's settlement, Dunlap. A ridge of resistant, rusty metamorphic rocks, defining the valley's south edge is breached by a branch of Mill Creek in which recurrent floods have scoured a lustrous spillway, exposing streaked metamorphic slabs and illustrating a passage along this trip's circuit of lightly traveled roads. Bicyclists wheeling along this circuit will find the most picturesque of oaks—the valley white oak—nurtured up-canyon from the breach by underground waters percolating toward Mill Creek. They'll also find a wealth of diversely thought-provoking plants where metamorphic soils touch exfoliating, disintegrating granite en route. If they're at all alert to the subtle beauties fostered by Mill Creek, bicyclists who finish this ride feeling stimulated attribute the feeling not only to the swooping descents they have made but also to the natural processes they've been privileged to glimpse.

Season   all year

Distance   9.3 miles (15.0 km) loop trip

Steep Upgrade   none

Elevation Gain and Loss   850 feet (259 m)

Exertion/Duration   easy/1 day

Gears   3-speed conventional to 15-speed alpine

Permits   none

Roadhead/Map   R68/M62A

Canteens   1 quart

Description   This easy adventure begins on the pavement of *Dunlap Road* in front of the Dunlap Post Office (1900/0.0). From here we pedal west on the road, skirting a profusion of water-loving plants which shortly part to either side of an incongruous pair of decrepit, long-abandoned gasoline pumps. The road beyond there enters horse-raising country and finds a triangle junction with southbound, paved *Ruth Hill Road* (1880/0.2) just as a tantalizing scene with Dunlap Road curving into a portal overarched by oaks becomes visible in the west.

Since that road leads to no better scenes, but only to speeding traffic on State Highway 180, we take Ruth Hill Road now, cross the intermittent stream, and ease quite soon across a bridge spanning the creek itself. Valley white oaks, with great rounded crowns, outwardly arching and far-flung boughs, and secure trunks knurly with wedges of bark begin to supplant stringy-barked blue oaks as our roadside companions. Redbuds dash steeping slopes by the road with scattered masses of red-purple blossoms from late winter through spring, and herald our entry into the breached ridge of metamorphic rock described in the "Features" section.

We presently leave the short canyon and push pedals west up a brief grade to an elongated triangle junction, where we leave the Ruth Hill Road (2200/1.6). **Sans Baker Road,** signed at the junction and paved beyond it, leads south, crossing an open, unnamed valley and passing between Baker Ranch buildings situated in the middle of it. Shortly, upon outflanking foothills just south of the valley, we leave the ranch pastures behind. Again white oaks shade our road, which soon comes in sight of a private graveyard and then bridges the Mill Creek tributary that we paralleled back in the breach. Scooting beyond it, we cycle up another short grade onto chaparral-cloaked west-facing slopes and then turn sharply north at a fork onto signed, paved, center-striped **Sand Creek Road** (2220/1.3).

We now negotiate an easy grade across exposed slopes, noting scrub oak and interior live oak amid roadside brush, and rounding some exfoliating granite slabs ½ mile from the fork. The mildly sinuous road from the slabs cuts across north-facing slopes, encountering lone cottonwoods near clumps of laurel and elderberry in the gulches it crosses. We eventually ascend through a grove of buckeye trees, catch over-the-shoulder views west toward Baker Ranch and then end the last significant upgrade on Trip 87 by crossing a pass.

Next our road crosses a small, open pasture cupped in a hanging valley, which we soon leave through what geographers call a "water gap"—a notch through which runoff also exits the valley. A panorama of Dunlap's valley backed by McKenzie Ridge, apparent as far east as the headwaters of Mill Creek, is then revealed while we contour across reddish-brown rocks of a metamorphic scarp. Dogwood, laurel and wild raspberries appear at surprisingly low elevations in nooks found along this contouring section of road. A chuckling sound emanating from hundreds of turkeys bred in the valley we overlook may cause us to pause and listen while taking in the view. Bicyclists who allow themselves a day to complete Trip 87 have plenty of time for such dawdling, for all that remains of the trip now is a few minutes more of relaxing contouring and then a brisk descent to Dunlap.

That descent starts where Sand Creek Road, rerouted in the last 20 years, abruptly veers downward from stranded traces of its former contouring alignment and joins signed, paved Dunlap Road (2530/3.1). Sand Creek Road was among the first routes of access to Sierra summer retreats to be built in the 19th Century: the mortarless masonry that buttresses its downslope edge attests to its age.

Dunlap Road now leads us northeast, down a grade just downslope from the last contouring section of Sand Creek Road. Brakeless racing is hazardous on this segment of road because of the sand and gravel that sometimes get washed onto its surface and because of the sharp bend near the base of its grade. That bend introduces us to the many Dunlap valley ranches, and a few minutes beyond the bend, we're reacquainted with Mill Creek where it's bridged. Not far beyond the bridge, we bypass a signed Fresno County road-maintenance yard and then traverse pastures studded with blue oaks to reach a signed junction (1990/2.6) with Millwood Road. (More ambitious bicyclists fork east onto this stripeless, narrower pavement early in Trip 88.)

Dunlap Road turns west at the junction, touches the grounds of Dunlap Elementary School in ¼ mile and then descends slightly into a gulch to find Dunlap's inn and post office (1900/0.5) side-by-side just off to the north. Here at our cars our bike trip concludes.

T88   Miramonte Bicycle Tour

This fine trip is certain to be a selection of bicyclists out to keep in shape during the temperate seasons of the year. It traverses a puzzlelike landscape where canyons were inlaid rectangularly, where most plants found in Sierra foothills mingle shadily, vividly and instructively; where streams tumble refreshingly; and where a long, swooping descent ends the trip effortlessly.

Season   all year

Distance   20.7 miles (33.3 km) semiloop trip

Steep Upgrade   0.1 mile (0.2 km)

Elevation Gain and Loss   2630 feet (802 m)

Exertion/Duration   moderate/1 day

Gears   5-speed conventional to 15-speed alpine

Permits   none

Roadhead/Maps   R68/M57C—M58, M62A—M62B

Description   Eager to get underway, we mount our bikes at the Dunlap post office (1900/0.0), move out onto paved *Dunlap Road* and pedal steadily east up its mild grade, soon passing between a church and an elementary school. Then our course leads straight ahead onto the signed but stripeless and narrower pavement of *Millwood Road* (1990/0.5), where Dunlap Road forks southeast.

We'll roll in on that road toward the end of this trip, but for now we rove east amid straggly blue oaks and fenced stock ranches. Our road approaches the foothills past several hidden cattle-watering reservoirs and then turns up a moderate grade, beginning an ascent most comfortably done during a cool spell or early morning. Working our pedals up the grade, we rise among bunches of the California buckeye tree—unique in shedding its leaves after blossoming in May and June—and an abundance of buck brush, yerba santa, flannelbush and other chaparral flora. Bulging granite slabs appear where the soil mantle has crumbled away on the opposite side of Milk Ranch Canyon, and over-the-shoulder views showing how far we've ascended from Dunlap's valley are also available.

Quite soon we round the recessed and polished granitic bed of an intermittent creek, and then as our road nears the Milk Ranch Canyon watercourse, we might wonder why it and so many other canyons nearby are straight, and why, where they do turn, they turn 90°. When the Sierra Nevada rose to its present height, its granitic rock was cracked along rectangular lines in far-flung places. Acids from surface soils and organic decay seeped down into these cracks, rotting the rock along them, and the rotten rock was later worn away. The runoff from rain and melted snow enlarged the cracks, eventually forming canyons. Magma from under the earth's crust rose along some of these cracks and surfaced as a basalt (lava) flow that quickly spread several miles northwest. Filling an ancestral Milk Ranch Canyon, this olivine basalt became so resistant to erosion that millions of years later its surface could still be named Stony Flat. We'll inspect that feature presently.

Soon our road's grade momentarily eases while we skirt the alders of intermittent Milk Ranch Canyon creek and scoot past a trail's creek-spanning suspension bridge, abundantly signed "KEEP OUT!" Then we pass by a small downslope reservoir and a few isolated ranches before gearing down for another stiff climb, still within sight of buckeye and familiar chaparral but now among scattered Jeffrey pine, redbud and elderberry. Soon we observe a roadcut ahead, traversing diagonally upward above bulging granite slabs. That's a segment of Todd-Eymann Road, separated from us by Milk Ranch Canyon, which turns northeast here, tracing an ill-defined fracture in the bedrock.

We presently fork southeast onto signed, paved *Todd-Eymann Road* (3480/4.7) and then coast 100 yards down to an old concrete bridge that crosses Milk Ranch Canyon creek. The small, shady grove of mountain

California buckeye flower, leaves, fruit

alder, Oregon ash, black walnut and incense-cedar that graces this roadside, plus our earlier glimpse of the ascending road just ahead, makes the urge to pause for liquids or food nearly irresistible.

Resuming our pedalling upward before we relax too much, we soon pass above the slabs while watching for cars on a narrower section of road. Runoff from slopes above sometimes leaves pebbles and grit strewn across, making it slippery for bicyclists taking this trip in reverse (not recommended). Our road rounds a watershed divide near the slabs, permits views of small reservoirs to the southwest at Johnson Flat, and rises toward the banks of a seasonal southeast-trending creek. Silk tassel and Brewers oak join the roadside chaparral retinue before we enter an environment too moist for chaparral. Here, while still climbing, we benefit from a canopy of Kellogg-oak and Jeffrey-pine boughs and cycle past masses of wild blackberries that the roadside stream occasionally threads.

We presently pass photogenic reservoirs paired near the source of the creek, and separated from one another by buildings of the Todd Ranch. Our ascent continues beyond the ranch entrance and soon we find ourselves looking north across Stony Flat, which has recently been cleared of most brush by its owners. An electrical transformer station is the next landmark, just up the road, and less than 100 yards beyond that, a ridgetop sawmill can be spied to the south. Shortly thereafter, we leave the volcanic crest rising east from Stony Flat and freewheel into Sequoia National Forest and ½ mile down to the Cedarbrook Picnic Area (4120/3.5), a charming, appropriate spot by Mill Creek at which to snack or lunch.

Sheltered by incense-cedar, big leaf maple, white fir, mountain alder and the seldom-seen California nutmeg, the picnic table is situated several dozen yards from the road on the creek's east bank and is reached by a signed path that starts where the road bridges the creek. Upstream from the picnic table, the creek is lined with cabins, and so it is probably polluted. Some bicyclists may prefer to press on to Pinehurst in hopes that the store there will be open when they arrive; eventually even those who have stopped for lunch will follow their example.

The Todd-Eymann Road undulates south from Mill Creek, soon merging with a gated, paved road from the northwest signed "Cedars"; it leads to the private cabins along Mill Creek mentioned earlier. Midway along the undulating segment of road, we go through a cluster of cabins beside slopes shrouded just above the ground by lacy kit-kit-dizze. Somewhat later, the road bends around a great wild blackberry patch where, according to local legend, the men of

Pinehurst once cleared paths through the brambles to let local women pick the berries—a quaint custom, but one no longer practiced here.

The undulating road segment ends a few minutes' ride from the blackberry patch and then, at a junction (4110/0.9) signed "Cedarbrook 1", we start descending *State Highway 245*. Almost instantly we pass the Pinehurst Lodge and cafe, and moments later encounter a store with gas pumps in front, where we may want to celebrate having disposed of the worst grades this trip has to offer. If this store is closed, there is always a chance that the one a few miles ahead at Miramonte will still be open.

Just a few yards from the market, we start around a hairpin turn and then pause midway to consider whether we need any of the services offered just off to the west at Pinehurst Ranger Station (4060/0.2), headquarters for the Hume Lake District of Sequoia National Forest. (See the "Organizational Resources" section of Chapter 2 for the services and the hours in which they are offered.)

Our state highway, frequented by motorists only on holiday weekends, slopes down a few hundred yards from the ranger station, skirts a cafe signed "Loggers Point Inn" and then leads us past a state-highway-maintenance outpost. Then we coast down a short gulch, and minutes after leaving it we cross a saddle and briefly contour across the one watershed on this trip that does not connect with the Kings River—Badger Creek, a feeder of the distant Kaweah River.

Then we ride straight ahead onto signed, paved *Dunlap Road* (3790/1.3) just as the state highway starts dropping southeast. Our road quickly crosses back into the Mill Creek watershed and descends circuitously across slopes checkered with Kellogg oak, white oak, blue oak and manzanita. Cabins are scattered at random across these slopes until we start wheeling beside another forested Mill Creek tributary, where the cabins proliferate at the outskirts of Miramonte. The tributary quickly leads us to Deer Crossing, our road's bridge over Mill Creek, marked by the generous shade of a valley white oak. Willows occasionally bracket this lively, permanent creek now while our road slants down beside it, and the elongated grove of ponderosa pines, interior live oaks, mountain alders and black walnuts we coast through by the creek parts at one point, allowing a glimpse of cavelike shelves in the opposite bluffs. Then we pass a general store with gas pumps in front by the Miramonte post office (3110/3.0). Requests for canteen refills should be addressed to the store manager, for this is your last source of clean water until you return to Dunlap.

Spottily paved Brookside Drive begins by the store and offers independent bikers with tough tires a quiet, pastoral alternative to the next few miles of Dunlap Road. Cyclists with sew-up tires or lightweight frames should stick to the described route, which leads briefly west from the store, bridges Mill Creek, forks with Orchard Drive (3080/0.1—signed "Miramonte Conservation Camp") and then gently descends the Mill Creek drainage opposite steeper Brookside Road. While the creek drops northwest away from us, Brewers oak, flannelbush, buckeye, redbud, yerba santa and buckbrush signal our return to low elevations, where the

familiar valley of Dunlap can be glimpsed. Spinning our wheels faster now, we quickly note another entrance to the state Department of Forestry's conservation camp, a penal facility, and afterward pass through a swale from which those who pause can see Redwood Mountain in the national park to the east. Shortly thereafter a junction with southbound, signed "Sundew Lane" precedes one in which signed "Brookside Drive" (2600/2.8) returns self-guiding cyclists to our road from the north.

Mill Creek is again relatively close at hand, and as it makes another of its fracture-determined right-angle turns, a few hundred yards from the Brookside Drive junction, incoming Trip 87 cyclists on Sand Creek Road (2530/0.6) join us in swooping down Dunlap Road.

Northwest-bound *Dunlap Road* Log

T87	Sand Creek Road	2530	0.0
	Millwood Road	1990	2.6
	Dunlap post office	1900	0.5

T89   Badger Bicycle Tour

This tour, a few enjoyable hours long, offers a change of pace and scenery for bicyclists tired of seeing the nearby national parks on foot. Because the narrow, shoulderless, oft-traveled Park roads are uncongenial to bicycle touring, the need of visitors drawn there for a variety of experiences is in part met by this foothill tour, with its views of distant Park features, its serene rural settings, its isolated fruit stands and its old-fashioned stores. A variety of additional alternatives to the usual Park excursion can be discovered during a visit to the Forest Service's Hume Lake District headquarters at the start of this trip.

Season   all year (avoid holiday weekends)

Distance   12.5 miles (20.1 km) loop trip

Steep Upgrade   none

Elevation Gain and Loss   1280 feet (390 m)

Exertion/Duration   easy/1 day

Gears   5-speed conventional to 15-speed alpine

Permits   none

Roadhead/Map   R69/M58

Canteen   1 quart

Description

Southbound *State Hwy 245* Log

T88	Pinehurst Ranger Station	4060	0.0
	Dunlap Road	3790	1.3

After the state highway forks southeast from Dunlap Road, it switchbacks downslope through a triple-deck canopy consisting of ankle-high kit-kit-dizze, waist-high manzanita, flannelbush and cascara buckthorn, and the overhead crowns of buckeye, black and interior live oak, and ponderosa and Jeffrey pine. The switchbacks soon end and we start coasting down a gentle grade beside a runoff fork of Badger Creek, which initially leads past some incense-cedars and black walnuts en route to oak-dominated scenery. We presently leave the fork, climb slightly, enter Tulare County and then crest a swale to begin a rousing descent toward Badger.

Quite early in the descent, passersby note a signed fire-control outpost (3170/3.5) of the California Department of Forestry, where one can refill canteens with water after asking for permission. Next, you skirt motel-like buildings belonging to Synanon and spy the long asphalt airstrip that that organization recently bulldozed across meadows in nearby Badger Creek valley. Then you drop past a telephone-relay station to wheel by a motel heralding the main junction (3030/1.3) and community of Badger to finish the mild descent. Resident Beverly Barton told the author in 1977 that a teamster who was named "Old Badger" for his birthplace, Wisconsin, the Badger State, made his living here during the 1870's and then left the town part of his nickname.

The "Hartland" signed pavement of county **road MTN 465** leads us southeast from Badger junction and almost instantly bridges the usually scant flow of Badger Creek. Then our road makes a casual 10-minute ascent while skirting scattered houses, and forks beside the Sierra Elementary schoolhouse (3300/1.0), a structure of nostalgic design. Here we can choose either to start north up signed, paved Drive 254 without delay, or to make a quick detour northeast along Road MTN 465 to buy snacks or get water at the Sierra Glen general store and relax at adjacent picnic tables. The detour ends with an easy ascent back up the road to this junction.

Drive 254 north of the junction initially offers a long-running eastward panorama that is less inspiring in its Dry Valley foreground—except when the redbuds assembled there bloom—than for its scenically varied background, an exceptional juxtaposition of Big Baldy's domelike face and sequoia crowns on Redwood Mountain. Swiveling our heads to catch the view every so often, we pedal along the rolling, mildly rising Dry Creek/Badger Creek divide, even-

tually passing an orchard. Owners of the signed "Sunrise Ranch" tend the orchard and, on weekends from September through December, sell home-made apple cider, apples, pears and honey to passersby.

More than a mile beyond that ranch, we enjoy a brief respite from the exposed ascent in a grove of black oaks, and then, entering Fresno County, we grind past several ranches, one with a small orchard and one signed as a "private game refuge." According to Sandy Carlton, a USFS recreation advisor at Pinehurst, the sign empowers California Department of Fish and Game wardens to patrol the property in hunting season and cite any hunters they catch inside. (See Trip 90 for the story behind the signs.)

The lengthy ridgecrest ascent ends just short of the Sequoia National Forest boundary, which our road crosses while ascending across corrugated, southwest-facing slopes. Elderberry, yerba santa, flannelbush, manzanita and scrub oak provide a thick and thorny ground cover here, through which Kellogg oaks sporadically poke. The drab San Joaquin Valley is in view until we round a hill and approach the end of our upgrade in the shade of incense-cedars and Jeffrey and ponderosa pines.

That shade temporarily ends just before we turn west onto signed **State Highway 245** (4260/4.6), midway in that road's descending hairpin turn. Quite soon we scoot by cabins clustered in the shady cove of Etheda Springs, and then a relaxing 5-minute ride leads us past merging Todd-Eymann Road (4110/0.6—see Trip 88) and through the Pinehurst commercial enclave to our cars in front of the Pinehurst Ranger Station (4060/0.2).

T90   Eshom Valley Bicycle Tour

*Side-by-side Eshom and Dry valleys offer inquisitive bicyclists views
that even skeptics would term sublime, in addition to settings of provocative and important events in wild-turkey propagation, fire-ecology dis-
coveries and Sierra Indian sufferings. Lightly trafficked roads of cared-
for asphalt link these valleys in a variety-packed loop.*

Season   April through November

Distance   21.7 miles (34.9 km) loop trip

Steep Upgrade   none

Elevation Gain and Loss   2450 feet (747 m)

Exertion/Duration   easy/2 days, moderate/
1 day

Gears   10-speed conventional to 15-speed
alpine

Permits   none

Roadhead/Map   R70/M59

Description   The Sierra Glen general store
(3190/0.0), where our outing begins, stands
just east of paved TC Road MTN 465. An
imported Chinese elm shades the store, from
the Badger post office in back to the gas
pumps and road in front. Supplementary
shade for a nearby phone booth and picnic
tables is supplied by groups of camphor and
mulberry trees. Just north of the store, the
worn, unstriped asphalt of **TC Road MTN
469,** signed for "Hartland," begins and directs us southeast. Almost instantly we pass a
trailer court with laundromat and commercial fishing ponds, and then our road switchbacks downslope amid thick layers of scrub
oak, buckbrush, redbud and other chaparral
associates. Our road lets us gently down to a
Dry Creek bridge, where we breach lines of
live, black and white oaks and Jeffrey pines.

A "Hyde Ranch/Wildlife Development/No
Trespassing/USDA" sign on a gate just
northeast of the bridge got its message explained in 1978 by Mike Jeffries of the US
Soil Conservation Service. In 1968, said Jeffries, wild turkeys were introduced here and
in nearby drainages to give future hunters
and wild predators more diverse game to
pursue. One local resident paid to have his
birds distributed and periodically checked,
neighboring ranchers agreed to accept and
assist his birds until they could fend for
themselves, and the project was made possible through the advice and coordination of
state and federal range and wildlife managers. While some ranches have already allowed hunters back onto their property,
most maintain signs such as the one we see
here beside Dry Creek.

A few hundred yards beyond the sign
along our fence-bordered road, the contrasting sign of a ranch to the south notes "We
regret that we cannot let you hunt today."
Jeffries also mentioned that quiet, alert
bicyclists stand a good chance of spying some
turkeys in exposed brush near this road.

Switching to looser gears, we pedal up out
of Dry Valley past a sometimes-dry reservoir
before crossing a gap into Eshom Valley. A
delightful difference in vegetation is immediately apparent. Kellogg oaks begin to
shelter the road and to dot adjacent cow
pastures. Beneath the oak boughs, bitter
cherry clings to roadcuts, and solitary
domestic plum trees stand by the road's
north shoulder. A conspicuous "University
of California Demonstration Range" sign
here arouses the curiosity of passersby.

Prompted by inquiries, University Farm
Advisor Bob Miller explained in 1978 that
research on effects of the widespread controlled burning of brush during the 1950's
was conducted at this Eshom Valley ranch.
The statewide burning program, he said,
was sponsored by organized livestock ranchers and was implemented mostly on their
ranches to increase feed for their stock.
While federal, state and county fire-control
officials tended to the safety and effective-
ness of the burns, UC farm advisors gave the
ranchers the benefit of their leadership and
their ongoing investigation of postburn seed-
ing, sprouting and grazing of grasses and
naturally fertilizing plants. Improved
wildlife habitat and increased runoff for
drinking and irrigation were claimed to be
among the program's benefits to the public
at large.

But, Miller went on to say, fires sometimes got out of control, occasionally during a burn but often a day or two after firemen had returned to their stations, thinking the fire was out. Toward the end of that decade, the McGee Fire left a swath of devastation across Sequoia National Forest from its west boundary to Highway 180 at Cherry Gap, 12 miles north of here. Because that fire initially touched a controlled burn scar that a rancher had made a few days before, state and federal fire-fighters sued that rancher for more than $1 million in damage and suppression costs. The government suit, unsuccessful because it was based on circumstantial evidence, caused the controlled-burning concept to go out of favor until late in the 1960s.

The National Park Service recognized then that total fire suppression let chaparral age until it would no longer send out sprouts on which wildlife fed, becoming instead thick, dying, volatile patches. The managers of Sequoia-Kings Canyon National Park also saw the arboreal competitors of giant sequoias, formerly kept in check by fire, crowding out young sequoias. Richard J.

Hartesveldt, with other Park researchers, discovered that the sequoia's seedlings failed to survive because fires were prevented from sweeping the floors of the groves. Consequently, the Park Service took the lead in rejuvenating sequoia groves and chaparral with trial-and-error but usually restrained applications of fire (see Trip 93).

Now that computer predictions increase the control that managers exercise over such fires (and now that the bill for getaway fires is shared among US taxpayers), officials of nearby National Forests are slowly regaining their confidence in the controlled-burning concept. To Farm Advisor Bob Miller, the "Demonstration Range" sign in Eshom Valley is a nostalgic reminder of early directions in 20th Century man's attempts to understand the ecological necessity of fire.

Shortly after we pass the sign indicating the demonstration range, as we pedal down a slight gradient, a gated road signed "Shadequarter Mountain Lookout Road T3F/Not A Public Road" joins ours from the southeast. Then we leave the shade of Kellogg oaks and approach a long row of poplars that line paved TC Road MTN 468.

Reservoir lures cyclists into northern Eshom Valley

Dave Liggett

Once reached (3360/4.2), this road, public despite its "no trespassing" sign, can lead inquisitive, detouring cyclists north-northeast into historic Eshom Valley.

*   *   *   *   *

The Lombardy poplars that line the first few hundred yards of **Road MTN 468** separate the pasture we had been riding beside from the long-grass matting along Eshom Creek to the east. Beyond the poplars, our road becomes dappled with the shade of ponderosa pines and valley white oaks that fringe the valley's matting of grass on the west. The cyclist hasn't been riding this road more than 10 minutes before a paved road (3360/0.6), signed "MTN 461" and apparently used more than MTN 468, branches northeast. Because tax-maintained MTN 461 leads only to a ranch headquarters, we veer northwest at the fork and then ride farther up the serene valley.

Eshom Creek has gashed the valley's thick topsoil, revealing its richness here in cross section. Soon we ascend out of sight from the gash, loop around a private, sometimes dry reservoir, crossing buck-brush-bristly slopes, and finally note our pavement widening to include room for more than a dozen parked cars by signposted "Eshom Valley Cemetery" (3450/1.1). Here, overlooking the valley in a ponderosa-pine colonnade, we pause to recall the Waksachi tribe of Shoshone Indians and the Caucasians who wrenched this valley away from them more than 100 years ago.

The Waksachi, wrote ethnologist A. L. Kroeber in 1925, were the first human emigrants here, having left settlements near the eastern Sierra several hundred years before John P. Eshom, cattleman-homesteader, arrived from across the continent in the middle of the 19th Century. Historian Harold G. Schutt publicized the ensuing racial friction in 1952, writing that in the summer of 1866 J. H. Harrel also arrived with his cattle. With him were Elizabeth Bacon, his young racist sister-in-law, and James Breckenridge, Harrel's foreman, Elizabeth's suitor and, it would seem, her pawn. The old Waksachi chief Cho-o-po was gathering acorns when Breckenridge met and beat him and ordered his tribe out of the valley. That

night, when the chief and his sons confronted Breckenridge at his cabin, demanding an explanation, Breckenridge shot the chief and was in turn shot by the chief's eldest son. A few years later (wrote eyewitness Enos Barton in 1953), Indians from across the Sierra foothills—some resentful of similar incidents, some belligerent, some mystical, some convivial, some coerced into attendance—converged on Eshom Valley to join in a great "ghost dance." Although the dance promotors had assured them that their dead would return to help banish usurping Caucasians and restore peace and prosperity in the ritual's finale, the Indian dead were not resurrected. The Indians disbanded, their resistance nearly broken, and they were relegated to reservations.

Backtrack from the cemetery to Road MTN 469.

*   *   *   *   *

Beyond the Eshom Valley junction, county **road MTN 469** leads southeast across barely declivitous grassland. It soon affords a far-reaching view of the Great Western Divide and intervening spires and ridges captivatingly framed by close-at-hand poplars, Kellogg oaks and white oaks. Less striking but no less inspiring variations on this view recur in our journey's next few miles, where cyclists ascend strenuously and need every inspiration available. Before this ascent begins, however, the road bridges Eshom Creek, and early in the ascent we meet a gated road signed "John Tarbell's Pocket" while reluctantly leaving Eshom Valley. Then chaparral gives way to pine-oak woodland, several cattleguards are bumped across, Sequoia National Forest is entered and a spur road signed "Camp David Wurthman BSA" is found before the upgrade abates. Moments beyond the Boy Scout road, we observe the southeastward departure of TC Road MTN 466 (4180/3.7), signed "Cherry Flat Road," a harbinger of the easy riding ahead.

A thick roadside stand of incense-cedar, ponderosa pine, black oak and white fir is wreathed at the base with kit-kit-dizze where we wheel a few minutes north from the junction. Then our road bridges Eshom Creek and runs alongside its bracketing alders for more than a mile before entering Hartland

(4390/1.5), a religious retreat. Badger old-timer Beverly Barton declared in 1977 that the name "Hartland" commemorated Eshom's son-in-law, Bill Hart, who homesteaded here. A phone booth and gas pumps stand outside the main dining hall.

The main road spans Eshom Creek quite soon, then skirts the northernmost cabin of Hartland, recrosses the creek after ⅓ mile, and quickly gains the Eshom Creek/Dry Creek divide amid clumps of gray-green manzanita. Now we traverse the outskirts of a camping zone while ascending the lengthy, slightly rolling divide to a signed junction with paved Road MTN 465 (4840/2.6). Pleasantly wooded Eshom Creek Campground is situated less than a mile northeast on this road, and cyclists either taking Trip 90 in 2 leisurely days or needing canteens refilled will find the detour to there rewarding.

Eventually, after checking their brakes, everyone takes *Road MTN 465* southwest from the ridgecrest junction, swooping at first down a twisty traverse of corrugated slopes. Soon we trade forest for chaparral and switchback down toward Dry Valley, drab except when its masses of redbud blossom in flaming hues. We presently leave Sequoia National Forest at an unmarked boundary and then scoot down a final few switchbacks to a small apple orchard near Dry Creek.

Blackberry vines have overrun a creekside picnic table and the railings of our road's creek-spanning bridge. The leaves of nearby black walnuts become flakes of bright yellow in fall to accent the willows and alders adjoining the creek. Now our road rises slightly as we ride southeast for more than a mile, to where the store-side junction of Sierra Glen (3190/6.3) marks the conclusion of our trip.

T91   Hume Lake Bicycle Tour

This trip lets bicyclists choose between lake swimming and pothole bathing, between views dominated up close by flaring lakeshores or chuting streams and panoramas highlighting distant ragged horizons. This trip also displays examples of the logging depredations that inspired the formation and later the expansion of Sequoia-Kings Canyon National Parks. The demonstration makes this trip a must for any who might tend to take the Parkscape for granted. The package is tied with a final descent that rivals the most exhilarating one anywhere.

Season   June through October

Distance   22.2 miles (35.7 km) round trip

Steep Upgrade   0.1 mile (0.2 km)

Elevation Gain and Loss   2090 feet (637 m)

Exertion/Duration   easy/2 days, moderate/1 day

Gears   5-speed conventional to 15-speed alpine

Permits   USFS Campfire Permit for easy riders

Roadhead/Map   R72/M64

Description   Our subalpine journey begins in front of a burly log cabin that a flagpole marks as the Hume Guard Station (5270/0.0), and we initially coast down paved *SNF*

Road 13S24 amid Jeffrey pines. In yards, our course bends southwest onto an oblique paved road, and moments later we exit east on a narrower strip of pavement (5240/0.1). A locked gate athwart this road near its start calls for the lifting of bicycles over it with the tacit approval of the U.S. Forest Service. A brief jaunt northeast from there on an increasingly primitive road gets us to an abutment of the multiple-arch dam impounding Hume Lake.

Interesting but not unforgettable, the dam, its cement in protruding corners crumbling, confronts a mass of downstream willows. You can readily imagine the narrow-gauge railway bridge that existed across the face of the dam because its jutting supports are still visible, but to restore in imagination the industry that was rampant locally years ago when the dam was completed, you'll need guidance from the exhaustive research, engaging narrative and revealing photos in Hank Johnston's *They Felled The Redwoods.*

Johnston describes the Sierra in the grip of engineers and loggers of the Industrial Revolution, and tells how in 1890 a 54-mile-long flume was completed from Sanger, a San Joaquin Valley mill town and railroad depot, to operations near newly impounded Sequoia Lake, in the first major watershed west of here. Leaving devastation in its wake, the logging operation crept eastward across intervening Converse Basin and by 1908 had temporarily settled here in the Tenmile Creek watershed. Under the auspices of millionaire Thomas Hume, the Sanger flume was re-routed through the Kings River gorge, up precipitous slopes by Tenmile Creek and through a large mill to the nearby Hume Dam. Intended to back water up as a log-storage lake, the 677-foot-long dam, although engineered by John S. Eastman, was adapted from a design first proposed in Spain, back in 1736. To Eastman's credit, the Hume Lake Dam was the first multiple-arch dam built in the United States and the prototype for dams constructed later elsewhere in the Sierra at Florence Lake, Gem Lake and Lake Eleanor. The flume—at 59 miles, the world's longest—along with the mill and dam were in service by the autumn of 1909, and a company town was erected where the USFS guard station and campground are now situated.

The railroad spanning the dam soon expanded its reach with a main line along Tenmile Creek and spurs to wherever sequoias inhabited that and adjacent eastern drainages. But despite the prodigious rate of logging the operation had always sustained, its expenses continued to eat up not only its profits but also its backers' investments. Disabling mill fires curtailed logging here by the start of World War I. The great flume was partly dismantled for lumber, partly consumed in a widlfire at the onset of the Depression. The logged land was bought by the Forest Service and its rehabilitation begun in 1935. The rails were scrapped and melted for forging weapons in World War II. The railroad ties, mill foundations and subtler ar-

tifacts can still be found in far-flung locations by patient searchers armed with a copy of Hank Johnston's book. The vigorous forest that shades our way throughout the rest of this trip has grown up since the thorough logging ceased, but is still being cut piecemeal under Forest Service direction.

After a while, we backtrack to the end of the guard-station spur, Road 13S24 (5250/ 0.1), and then, rather than take it, head north for a few dozen yards on a divergent paved road. Paved **SNF Road 13S43** then emerges from 85-unit Hume Lake Campground—where camping near swimming beaches costs $3 a night—and absorbs our road, guiding us a few minutes farther north. This upslope grade ends where we turn southwest at a signed junction onto paved **SNF Road 13S09** (5350/0.2).

After we skirt the campground, SNF Road 13S42 (5320/0.8) presently leaves our road heading north to a gate, and eventually we drop slightly to meet a stanchion-closed end of the campground road. Moments later, our road is flanked by the A-frame headquarters of an interdenominational Christian conference that controls most of the cabins we'll skirt just ahead in the south-shore community of Hume.

Hank Johnston's book tells of Swede Gustaf Anderson, who homesteaded 480 acres here in the early 1880's. Anderson's store and saloon were often thronged with loggers when the Hume Lake operation was bustling, but since 1946, when the property changed hands, its expanded facilities—no saloon now—have often teemed with Christians whenever their churches have sponsored retreats. Just south of the A-frame, a dock protrudes into a picturesque, lawn-bordered Hume Lake inlet, and just across the road to the west, a store (5220/0.5) caters to passersby from May through October.

Our road next bridges the inlet creek, then skirts a fenced lakeside swimming pool—a Christian camp property—before rolling slightly around a point between lakeview cabins and audibly lapping waters. An inlet we soon pump beside is shortly pinched shut by converging shores where Tenmile Creek bounces in from a potholed, granite-slab spillway. A lakehead overlook parking lot by the road here is sometimes equipped with a chemical toilet, while across the main road, a sign points out "access to

Where multiple arches dam Hume Lake, a narrow-gauge logging railroad once crossed

lots 19–23, 36–49" up incipient SNF Road 13S40 (5220/1.0). This inferior road leads to Aspen Hollow Campground, where groups of 25–50 can reserve space when their spokesmen phone Pinehurst Ranger Station. (Logger Flat Group Campground, upstream along Tenmile Creek, allows organizers a choice of sites.) The sun-warmed water of and the slabs beside Tenmile Creek draw bathers and sunbathers to its shore.

Now our road arcs across a creek-spanning bridge and there, upon meeting SNF Road 13S06 (5220/0.1), turns south in the bed of the vanished main logging railway line. Then, while making our way up-canyon, we briefly touch reddish soils derived from an upslope basalt flow (see Chapter 1 and Trip 88 for its probable origin and history). Granitic roadside soils reappear momentarily, and the cyclist who glances west across the foreground manzanita and the willow-banked creek can spot the mortarless masonry that retains the downslope fill of a parallel railway bed. Incense-cedars and ponderosa and Jeffrey pines thrive on the slope split by the bed, a tribute to the tendency of east-facing slopes to retain snow and absorbed snowmelt.

Quite soon, narrow SNF Road 13S05 (5370/0.5), signed with the understatement

"not recommended for trailers" departs obliquely north, tracing a railway bed engineered solely for transporting felled Kings Canyon sequoias to mill earlier this century. Wherever the rails were laid across trestles, the current road rolls steeply and sometimes slopes sideways toward the brinks of cliffs.

Then our road crosses a gulch on fill, cuts through an adjacent small ridge and veers southeast from the start of SNF Road 13S37 (5380/0.2), which leads to Logger Flat Group Campground. Our gradual ascent presently forks with the inferior Landslide Campsite road (5750/1.1), then loops around a bowl, early bridging Landslide Creek and ending not much later in a cut through the bowl's rim. That rim extends ¼ mile north to include unseen Lava Butte. SNF Closed Road 13S33 leads hikers toward upper Landslide Creek from a junction (5970/0.9) signed "free wood area—permits required" just beyond the road-cut rim.

From there our road briefly descends to bridge Tenmile Creek amid the multiple spur roads of signed Tenmile Creek Campground (5790/0.5). The off-road-vehicle tracks that radiate from this 15-table campground and the many unimproved campsites that ring it suggest that recreational use here is intense during holiday weekends. Beyond the campsite, our road cuts through a slight ridge, connects with offset roads (5790/0.3) to the Bearskin Meadow Diabetic Camp (north) and an USFS work center (south). Then we swing past a meadow fringed with ponderosa pines and subsequently grind pedals up to a signed junction with SNF Road 13S02 (6000/0.8).

The ascent continues, although more gradually, while the main road arcs east, then rounds a ridge and leads south within sight of pooling, chuting Tenmile Creek. Shortly after the chutes appear, a rough spur road leads off to a popular creekside camping zone. Soon our road veers away from the creek, skirts a private meadow bordered by fluttering quaking aspens, meets laterals to meadow-side Bauman's Cow Camp and then switchbacks upslope on moister soils where fir and chinquapin flourish. Over-the-shoulder views including the jagged north rim of Kings Canyon are occasionally available while the cyclist makes

his way up past displays of gooseberry, currant, whitethorn, snow bush and tobacco brush. Eastward outlooks on the commanding finger of Buck Rock are interspersed among the fir. Midway on the final rise from the switchbacks, we pass the signed exit of primitive SNF Road 13S45 (6740/3.3), and later, at the top of the rise, we go south through a triangle intersection (6900/0.7) with SNF Roads 14S42 (west—jeeps only) and 14S02 (east—paved). Cyclists desiring a more adventuresome workout can extend this trip to 2 or more days by tracing the pavement east from this junction across Burton Pass to voluminous Boulder Creek. Our road, meanwhile, leads alongside the signed log-storage apparatus of the Quail Flat Reloading Station and quickly ends at a signed junction with the oft-driven pavement of the Generals Highway (6900/0.1). From here we backtrack to our cars, enjoying spectacular views in a brisk descent.

Religious-camp dock at peaceful Hume Lake

T92   Park Ridge Nordic Ski Trek

This High Sierran threshold tour offers more than vistas of shafts of rock and of living wood, plus remote, ragged horizons. It also offers some of the addictive skiing exhilaration needed to reach those horizons. Skiers enjoying these advantages here also get to test the 1973 contention of ski instructors Lito Tejada-Flores and Allen Steck that snow is most skiable in morning hours on southeast-facing slopes, at noon on north-facing slopes and in late afternoon on west-facing slopes.

Season   January through March

Distance   6.8 miles (10.9 km), shuttle trip

Steep Upgrade   0.3 mile (0.5 km)

Elevation Gain and Loss   1240 feet (378 m)

Exertion/Duration   easy/1 day

Skills   easy route-finding, novice nordic skiing

Permits   USNPS Entrance Receipt

Roadheads/Maps   R71–R73/M63–M64

Description   Our ridgecrest romp starts at Quail Flat (6900/0.0), which is sometimes as far east as snowplows get on the Generals Highway. Here we leave the obvious north-trending channel of incipient SNF Road 13S09 to skiers with only a few hours for recreation. While they descend the Bearskin Slopes into dells of the upper Tenmile Creek drainage, we track over usually hidden *SNF Road 14S42* west-northwest from the flat up a gently inclined segment of the Kings-Kaweah divide. En route we cross sundry clearings—both man-made and natural ones—where Buck Rock and the High Sierra draw attention in vignettes to the east. After ⅓ mile, our road contours briefly west from the ridge, then rises through logger-thinned red-fir forest up the first ravine it meets. The road shortly narrows beside Bacon Meadow (7100/0.8)—a small, snow-slabbed clearing that we quickly pass before reaching a saddle in the divide. There we turn abruptly southwest, leaving the road on the cross-country *King's Rim Ski-route*. Although skiers with adequate map-and-compass skills can depart northward to hummocky flats and fluted slopes (breezy runs for the alpine skier), we stick to the divide. A brief, steep ascent precedes ¼ mile of south-trending advance in which we skirt east of the crest twice to avoid west-facing cliffs. Then the ridge peaks and we start traversing ½ mile of mildly rolling crest.

The crest then dips across SNF Road 14S36 and along the edge of a clearcut to a swale, from which it rises steeply on the far side toward Peak 7646. Leaving the crest at the swale, we swoop north-northeast, descending onto the Bearskin Slopes. Quite soon our route starts to follow Road 14S36 down a forested ravine. Shortly we enter a bowl and turn west onto yet another road, continuing west onto *SNF Road 14S37* (7200/1.4) within minutes. Moments later, we cross a slight divide, then leave 14S37 on a *cross-country route,* touch Log Corral Meadow and finally ascend a subsequent moderate slope over logging debris. Not far up the slope we step onto the shelf of *SEKI Road 24–12* (7360/0.3) at the tagged boundary of Kings Canyon National Park.

This road now guides us northwest through unspoiled forest, then crosses north-trending Park Ridge through a saddle (7400/0.5). The southwestward vignettes of Grant Grove and the San Joaquin Valley that this saddle affords usually reveal the ebb and swell of wintertime valley fog among sequoia crowns.

Our course leaves the road here, starting north on the *Point-of-View Trail,* guided by conspicuous metal tags posted on trees at intervals. Soon we gain 200 feet of elevation in a taxing ascent, then stick to the ridge while the trail contours across steep manzanita slopes to the west. When reviewing plans for this book, Grant Grove Ranger Bob White warned of some avalanche hazard on these exposed slopes, although 2 years earlier, in 1976, Paul Spivey, a long-time resident of nearby Wilsonia, had said that the longest of these slopes was a ski run with a rope tow during the 1940's. Today, Point of View (7761/0.5), at the head of this exposed slope, offers us a panorama extending across San Joaquin Valley fog to the distant Coast Ranges.

Park Ridge rolls beyond Point of View and our course follows its crest, momentarily rejoining the trail and in time reaching Panorama Point, where much of the serrated skyline and deeply cleft drainage of the Kings River is exhilaratingly visible. The tagged route turns west here and shortly connects with paved *SEKI Road 24–10* (7360/1.3) where the road makes a looping switchback.

In the concluding part of our trip, well-shaded Road 24–10 offers a brisk descent through mixed conifers via 6 banked switchbacks—a run that often is at its best in the early afternoon. At length we slide south past a southeast lateral leading to government trailers at Cedar Springs.

Shortly, while scooting along a subsequent ravine, we pass just downslope from a few snow-caked Park maintenance buildings and then meet a road (6580/1.8) branching northwest toward the Sierra's second largest

sequoia, the 267-foot-tall General Grant Tree. Quite often this tree's high limbs are snow-free while surrounding incense-cedars and white firs are heavily loaded with snow. Try to be here when the sun strikes the orangish-brown sequoia bark, making a vivid contrast between the bark and the bluish shadows on nearby snow. Although some road segments along the optional detour to the General Grant Tree are plowed, the forest flanking the plowed corridor is usually open enough to permit skiing parallel to the road. This detour is so enticing that all but the most pressed-for-time skiers will add its round-trip distance of 2.0 miles and elevation gain of 250 feet to the Trip 92 totals.

But sooner or later most everyone takes *SEKI Road 24–10*, which branches southwest from the utility junction. On it, they quickly kick past drift-covered lodge cabins and a store in a stretch of level going. Then they find the lot (6590/0.2) where their shuttle cars are parked, sandwiched between a visitor center and a restaurant-gift shop.

T93   Hiking around Redwood Canyon

Most newcomers to Sequoia-Kings Canyon National Parks make a point of visiting the General Sherman Tree, the world's largest living thing, but how many have an inkling that the Hart Tree is the tallest of the world's 4 largest sequoias? Despite the prestige of the Hart Tree, throngs of tourists won't be beating the path to its foot. Nor will they crawl through the path's 2 tunnel logs, nor will they stroll through a nearly pure stand of sequoias at the Sugarbowl. Why? Because the hike there is a strenuous one. It's only for the physically fit. Families in that select group are especially likely to find this trip a thorough pleasure and challenge.

Season June through October

Distance 9.2 miles (14.8 km) loop trip

Steep Upgrade none

Elevation Gain and Loss 2120 feet (646 m)

Exertion/Duration strenuous/1 day

Skills easy route-finding, Class 1 climbing

Permits USNPS Entrance Receipt

Roadhead/Maps R74/M60, M64

Description We start south up the *"Sugarbowl Trail"* (so signed) at a trailhead parking lot in Redwood Saddle (6200/0.0),

where other signs prohibit taking pets, firearms or vehicles on the trails of Kings Canyon National Park. Here we enter the 4425-acre Redwood Mountain Grove, with more than 65,000 sequoias the rival of Giant Forest as the Sierra's largest grove. Sequoia research is still going on, as a "Research Area/Ecology of Sequoias/Do Not Disturb" sign just up the trail attests. District Ranger Bob White warned in 1978 that "Prescription burning" (see Trip 90) is conducted here, too, and at any time in September or early October each year, visitors might be barred from this trip for their own protection by federal fire managers.

Our path first leads up a gradual grade under boughs of sequoias, white firs and sugar pines along the crest of Redwood Mountain. Most people will reach a west-trending spur path (6440/0.3) signed "Burnt Grove 50 yards" in less than 25 minutes—it leads to a tangle of abandoned trails, faint logging scars and recently cut firebreaks.

Our path, meanwhile, rolls south on the crest and presently crosses some firebreaks that look confusingly like trails. The ridge soon rises mildly and our path leads along its east shoulder. Later we intercept a south-eastward vista of Big Baldy's sheer granite facade, and pass now and then through plots in which the Park Service has burned the undergrowth. We subsequently switchback leisurely downslope, crisscrossing part of the crest just south of the apex of Redwood Mountain.

After our short, switchbacking stint, we crawl through a long, low tunnel (6700/1.9) that runs the length of a fallen sequoia, then stroll several hundred yards through the Sugarbowl group of sequoias and cross the Redwood Mountain crest for the last time. Beyond a "3 Miles"-marked post misplaced here at the 2.6-mile mark, we make a few lengthy switchbacks northeast down a moderate grade across corrugated slopes, sighting the shining Buck Rock Lookout (Trip 96) in the northeast quite early, and crossing an overscorched patch of "prescription burned" forest midway.

Sometimes the errors in managing fires are caused not by ignorance but by economic and political pressures. Park research technician George Lester said that in 1977, one of the driest years on record, managers had to risk burning this plot when a fire could have done more harm than good, or else face losing fire-management money for the following years. The fire they lit killed quite a few trees, but did not escape the firebreaks that had been cut to contain it. Although research toward better prescription burning goes on nearby even now, only your representative in Congress can make sure that it is applied effectively. Tell him that you're interested.

The path eventually bridges a gully in which a seasonal stream is hedged by thimbleberries and tiger lilies. Then, while the downgrade abates and trailside slopes become gentler, we amble some distance up Redwood Canyon past nooks decked with fern, dogwood and hazelnut to the signed *Redwood Canyon Trail* (5480/2.0), a closed jeep road on which we now turn southeast.

Several minutes of striding suffice to put us beside the usually dry wash of Redwood Creek, and then we branch southeast onto the signed *"Hart Tree Trail"* (5470/0.1), which crosses the wash without delay. It shortly slants up a moderate grade across the east side of Redwood Canyon, and presently passes just downslope from the signed "Fallen Goliath" sequoia. The ascent continues, and after we pass a seep spring garnished with meadow lotus, our course weaves directly upslope. In the meantime, white fir debuts in the midst of the conifers that continue to shade us.

Not long after passing the Fallen Goliath, our course ascends via mostly gradual, sometimes steep grades into the East Fork Redwood Creek drainage, crossing 2 sliding seasonal brooks en route. At length we stroll by the signed "Hart Tree" (6240/1.8) which, R. J. Hartesveldt and other sequoia researchers reported in 1975, was the world's tallest and fourth bulkiest *Sequoiadendron giganteum* when measured in 1931. Taking into account Hartesveldt's theory that the sequoia is the world's fastest growing·tree, the Hart Tree has probably long since exceeded its measured height of 277.9 feet.

An ensuing switchback leads down to a boulder-hop ford of the East Fork, which on rare occasions dries up. Resuming the gradual ascent, we then rove a few dozen minutes before crawling nearly 20 yards through a tunnel log (6280/0.6) in a gathering of sequoias. Much later, we polish off most of the ascent and cross sometimes-dry Buena Vista Creek at the downslope tip of Hart Meadow (6420/0.6).

Several hundred yards later, our path winds just north of open granodiorite slabs into which Yokut Indians ground potholes while pulverizing acorns. Like most Indian potholes in the Southern Sierra, this one commands a sweeping view of its surroundings. We skirt a lone mountain juniper wedged in the slabs and then descend past an intermittent creeklet on a long, twisty, sometimes zigzagging course into northern Redwood Canyon. After a spell, our path leads past shake-sided, signed "Pierce Cabin," which was built when desultory logging took place before Redwood Canyon received the protection of park status in 1940. We then ford a transitory brook, undulate across several slight ridges and presently cross a headwaters section of Redwood Creek that usually flows. It is wrongly signed "Bartons Creek."

Not much remains at signed "Bartons Post Camp" beside the creek. When interviewed

in Sierra Glen in 1977, Beverly Barton recalled having forged the jeep road down Redwood Canyon to serve a remote tungsten mine that he had sporadically dug.

Our journey's final mild ascent, which usually takes less than 30 minutes, joins the **Redwood Canyon Trail** (6080/1.6) midway and then switchbacks up to the Redwood Saddle parking lot (6200/0.3), where our cars await.

Mule deer shows size of giant Sequoia trunk

Bill Jones, National Park Service

T94   Big Baldy Run/Climb
Nordic Ski Trek

Versatile is the word for this crestline traverse of Big Baldy Ridge. The intensely photogenic scenery here draws adventurers any time of the year. Runners getting a workout here will find inspiration to come back in winter and try their hand at nordic skiing, or to come back with ropes as practiced climbers and tackle the bluffs that abut the crest. They might find fascination in art, photography, botany or geology here, for Big Baldy is rich in such opportunities, and can arouse an urge to return again and again.

Seasons   May through November (running and climbing) December through April (skiing)

Distance   5.6 miles (9.0 km) round trip

Steep Upgrade   none (except for climbers)

Elevation Gain and Loss   1000 feet (305 m)

Exertion/Duration   variable/1 hour to 1 day

Skills   easy route-finding, Class 2 climbing (Class 5 pitches optional), novice nordic skiing

Roadhead/Map   R75/M60

Permits   none

Description   The Big Baldy trailhead beside Generals Highway (7580/0.0) is signed for the *"Big Baldy Ski Touring Trail,"* a wintertime route that occasionally deviates from, and will be described concurrently with, our *summertime trail* ahead. (Climbers will probably use the trail to reach challenging rocks indicated in this description, but they should resort to their own imagination to find routes up these rocks.) Firs shade the combined routes where they lead as one trail from the highway south along Big Baldy Ridge past large granodiorite boulders and scattered clumps of snow bush and chinquapin. After 270 yards, the ski-route—marked by brown sequoia cones painted on yellow metal triangles—forks south from our route while we lope southwest. The routes have diverged to skirt, one on each side, hill 7878, underlain by a massive wedge of hornfels, schist and less metamorphosed, grainier, purer volcanic rocks identified by Donald C. Ross in 1958. While skiers skip to the ski-route description below, we enter Kings Canyon National Park near the fork. We then cross the hill's west side, noting currant bushes close by and catching vistas of Kings Canyon in the north, Redwood Mountain sequoia profiles in the west and, beyond the sequoias, the San Joaquin Valley. We regain the ridgecrest quite soon, joining the ski-route there (having skipped the following ski-route description).

*   *   *   *   *

The *ski-route* ascends gradually south from the fork, crossing the snow-laden Big Chimney Slopes. Skiers soon zigzag upslope while outflanking hill 7878 and, minutes later, contour to join the summertime trail.

*   *   *   *   *

The *summer and winter routes* coincide for the next 650 yards of crestline travel, in which we find nosegays of pentstemon along with some ponderosa pines in the red-fir forest. Then our path again splits southwest from the *ski-route,* which makes a short, mild, direct ascent south. In the meantime, running the *trail,* we soon round a jutting transverse ridge and from there get a southward glimpse of the sheer, fluted facade of Big Baldy (excellent climbing terrain). Now the path contours briefly southeast to the crest and there rejoins the ski-route.

Again the *summer and winter routes* coincide in tracing the crest, this time for a mile, and transfer from metasedimentary to granitic terrain, while views of Redwood Canyon in the west gradually earn the right to be called spectacular. A few western white pines put in an appearance at the end of that mile, where runners and climbers again split with skiers. Beyond the junction, the *footpath* quickly zigzags up onto a wedge of exfoliating Big Baldy granite, then touches the summit benchmark (8211/2.2). There it affords a jagged-horizon panorama encompassing much of the High Sierra, the San Joaquin Valley and the Coast Ranges. A precipice brink within arm's reach makes the view from Big Baldy thrilling in any season, but sometimes in winter the summit block is unapproachably iced in. From there, our path traces 100 yards of knife-edge ridge crest southward, then zigzags down below timberline and rejoins the ski-route.

*   *   *   *   *

Skiers at the trail's first zigzag north of Big Baldy should start sliding south-southeast on a *ski-route* which bypasses the summit talus by staying just below timberline. Usually not more than 5 minutes elapse before their marked course merges with the summertime path.

*   *   *   *   *

All together now, we follow the triangle-marked **all-season route** south along the wooded ridgecrest for 560 yards, then slow while crossing northwest-facing talus slopes amid chinquapin and finally climb a few zigzags to attain Overlook 8168 (8168/0.7). In views from this southern tip of Big Baldy Ridge, the domes, "campanile" and "martello tower" assembled at Chimney Rock, in the southeast, beguile climbers (see Trip 99), while successive ridge profiles recede into the southern haze. Closer to our overlook, fine 4th and 5th class routes abound. Eventually we backtrack to our cars.

T95   Big Meadows Nordic Ski Tour

The nordic ski trip with the deepest, most powdery, least avalanche-prone snowpack in this book is also the one most likely to persuade novices that nordic skiing is for them, the one apt to be most popular with San Joaquin Valley collegiate ski groups and the one with the least motorized disturbance of its route. This trip is the one.

Season   January through April

Distance   6.5 miles (10.5 km) semiloop

Steep Upgrade   none

Elevation Gain and Loss   450 feet (137 m)

Exertion/Duration   easy/1 day

Skills   moderate route-finding, novice nordic skiing

Permits   none

Roadhead/Maps   R75/M60, M64–65

Description   We get underway by toting skis northeast on the **Generals Highway** from the small Big Baldy Ridge turnout (7580/0.0), unless recent heavy snowfall has closed the highway at Quail Flat. (Sequoia Park Ranger John Chew observed in 1978 that the highway from that flat to here is not plowed until most other post-storm maintenance chores have been done. If you find the road closed at Quail Flat when you arrive, add 6 miles and 680 feet elevation gain to the totals for this trip.) A short jaunt from Big Baldy Ridge gets us to the signed junction where paved but not plowed **SNF Road 14S11** (7600/0.2) starts north.

Once mounted on skis, we clack up this road's overburden of snow, usually guided by multiple snowmobile tracks and watching for triangular red-fir-mounted tour markers. Quite soon our route and the road diverge, and we enter territory that the Forest Service declared off limits to snowmobilers in 1977. Our **cross-country route** leads parallel to the road for nearly ⅓ mile and then veers northeast, away from the road on the mildly undulating Kings-Kaweah divide. The divide segment we'll trace ahead hardly seems obtrusive enough to separate 2 such important rivers.

Shortly we start on this tour's loop by arcing southeast along the crest from the point where the end of the loop (7640/0.8) comes in from the east. Chimney Rock is prominent (although its spectacular side remains hidden) in southward views from a pair of clearings that consecutively straddle our crest beyond the junction. More impressive in these views is the vast, thick layer of fog in the San Joaquin Valley beyond Chimney Rock that gives some skiers a sense of being insulated from civilization.

Now our crest seems more the rim of a southern declivity than a divide because the remarkably planar tableland to the northeast slants away from the crest almost imperceptibly. Our "rim" soon curves east, heralding a crossing of a drift-concealed jeep road (7640/0.9). This road connects Road 14S11 to the north with SNF Road 14S18A to the south and crosses our ski-route twice en route, affording independent ski-skiers a means of assembling their own circuits from parts of this trip and Trip 97. (The option of following one of the many ski-routes signed by the staff of the nearby Montecito-Sequoia Lodge is also available.)

Now we ski up a jeep road that all but disappears when snowbound. Our crest at length rises somewhat and its Jeffrey-pine forest at times allows northward vistas of Big

Meadows. Then, upon meeting SNF Road 14S03 (7840/1.5) just northeast of the course of Trip 97, we turn abruptly northwest and begin a quick and delightfully breezy run down across the Big Meadows Slopes to an arm of Big Meadows itself. Geographer John Harper indicated in 1974 that this region receives an average precipitation exceeding 50 inches a year, virtually assuring us that the Big Meadows Slopes snowpack will be at least 20 feet deep during the local skiing season.

Our course now leads straight north-northwest inside this long, thin, evenly surfaced clearing, presently enters a greater clearing, and then veers westward, hugging the forest's edge. This maneuver leads us up another long, thin arm of the meadow, beyond which our course, at first rolling somewhat, strikes west across the pine tableland. (This is an excellent place to acquire and practice map-and-compass route-finding skills—the route is poorly marked.)

After a prolonged stint of direct, fairly monotonous travel, we cross the barely discernible transverse jeep track (7640/1.8) mentioned earlier, then leave the Big Meadows Slopes for crunchier snow, shortly returning to the crest we tracked earlier. Here we complete the Big Meadows loop (7640/0.3) and start to backtrack out to the cars (7580/1.0).

T96   Buck Rock Hike/Climb

Self-propelled takers of Trips 91–93 and 95–96 sometimes catch sight of the lookout-capped stack of Buck Rock and are eventually drawn there expecting the invigoration of lofty footing to augment the exhilaration of viewing an alpine panorama. Buck Rock does not disappoint them. Others whose summertime pleasure expands in proportion to the number of bare, chisled peaks they can log will count Buck Rock as the best— certainly the most accessible–attraction in this book north of Moro Rock.

Season   June through October

Distance   0.4 mile (0.6 km) round trip

Steep Upgrade   0.1 mile (0.1 km)

Elevation Gain and Loss   210 feet (64 m)

Exertion/Duration   easy/1/12 day

Skills   easy route-finding, Class 1 climbing, Class 5 pitches optional

Permits   none

Roadhead/Map   R76/M64

Canteens   1 pint

Description   The route to Buck Rock begins on *SNF Closed Road 13S04B* where it forks north from SNF Road 13S04 (8350/0.0). We stroll north along the spur road a few yards, then bypass the locked gate across it and trace it for an additional 300 yards through red-fir forest interspersed with chinquapin clumps. Buck Rock looms directly north of the swale (8340/0.1) where our road ends, and if a car is parked in the swale, the hidden lookout capping the rock is open for visiting, but only from 9 to 7.

While climbers scan the seamy "stack" for challenging 5th Class routes, most visitors elect to climb it via the Class 1 trail. *Buck Rock Trail 29E09* starts north from the swale, zigzags, and then follows several gulf-bridging flights of giddying stairs. Midway up the stairs we encounter a gate which bars farther progress from November through late May, and also ensures the lookout employee's privacy during the night. Shortly thereafter, we top the "stack" and take in the immense sweep of landscape visible from the lookout (8500/0.1). At length we backtrack to the road junction beside which our cars are parked.

T97

Lower Shell Mountain Nordic Ski Tour

A snowpack ranking among the Sierra's deepest keeps the dominant south- and west-facing slopes that this trek explores skiable, and a Forest Service exclusion of snowmobiles from these slopes protects their serenity. The guidance of roads which are also tagged conspicuously as ski trails makes the delightful vistas en route unmistakably accessible. A wide range of snow conditions makes this an ideal trip for giving waxes and waxing techniques a trial.

Season   January through March

Distance   8.5 miles (13.7 km) semiloop trip

Steep Upgrade   none

Elevation Gain and Loss   1190 feet (363 m)

Exertion/Duration   moderate/1 day

Skills   easy route-finding, novice nordic skiing

Permits   none

Roadhead/Maps   R77/M60M61, M65

Description   Our tour begins on *SNF Closed Road 14S18* where it starts southeast from the Generals Highway (7270/0.0), and while warming up we track over a low, rounded ridge, then slide down a gradual grade roughly parallel to that highway. Quite early in this descent through artificially thinned forest on slightly corrugated terrain we pass northbound SNF Road 14S18A (7260/0.2) in a gulch. Midway down the descent, SNF Road 14S18B (7150/0.5), another dead-end logging spur, departs to the northeast. We then crunch across a fork of Woodward Creek and begin a gradual, roundabout ascent in territory favored by ski-touring patrons of the nearby Montecito Sequoia Lodge. As we loop around a ridge, we catch vignettes of Chimney Rock and Pine Ridge on the southern horizon, and then we progress up a northeast-trending gulch, soon touching the start of another short, deadend spur—southeast-bound SNF Road 14S32 (7210/1.2).

Still working at ascending, we shortly branch east onto *SNF Road 14S60* (7450/0.5), starting the loop part of this trip. Our course almost instantly leads south across the gulch and then rambles a mile across a west-facing slope, catching more southward vistas. The road then rounds a slight bouldery ridge, winds up a ravine, crests a high, bouldery

gap, and then nearly levels in crossing the least icy slope on this tour.

For most skiers, the ascent concludes less than 20 minutes beyond the boulders. Upon crossing the Stony Creek/Woodward Creek divide, our course starts a gradual descent, instantly passing a negligible spur road (8000/2.1). Now we slip briefly downslope, round a slight ridge, briefly traverse a barely noticeable part of the Kings-Kaweah Divide and then meet northeast-bound SNF Road 14S03 (7840/0.8). This road connects with the Big Meadows Ski Trail in several dozen yards, allowing unorthodox skiers to graft parts of both trips together. From the fork we arc southwest onto *Road 14S58* and resume our descent, soon kicking across a flat cove and then veering south for a few minutes' run to tracks we made earlier at the junction with Road 14S60 (7450/0.8), where the loop ends and backtracking to the cars begins with 2.4 miles of skiing left.

T98   Chimney Slopes Ski Tour

A whopping average yearly precipitation exceeding 50 inches ensures that snow on the compact Chimney Slopes will be skiable long after snow in most other parts of the Southern Sierra has turned to slush or has disappeared. Beginners out to discover what nordic skiing is all about have found this acquainting tour across the lower Chimney Slopes worth more than the relaxation it offers.

Season   January through April

Distance   8.6 miles (13.8 km) semiloop

Steep Upgrade   none

Elevation Gain and Loss   675 feet (206 m)

Exertion/Duration   easy/1 day

Skills   easy route-finding, intermediate nordic skiing

Permits   none

Roadhead/Maps   R78/M60–M61

Description   From a sign by the Generals Highway (7025/0.0), snow-caked **SNF Road 14S29** winds diagonally (southwest) downslope, and on it we begin near-level going within a few hundred yards. Then we cross Woodward Creek, usually muffled beneath a cover of snow, and start across the Chimney Slopes, moving from snow-garnished Jeffrey pines to snow-capped red firs. Shortly we round a slight, southeast-trending ridge on what is usually a slightly yielding snow surface and presently meet SNF Road 14S56 (6950/0.5) coming in from the southeast. (We'll return to here on that road later.)

Our course beyond stays on Road 14S29, traversing alternating strips of selectively logged and patchcut red firs where logging debris had been cloaked by snow. Shortly we touch the northbound spur of SNF "Closed" Road 14S55A (7010/0.6)—the first of 2 tracks giving access to upslope alpine skiing possibilities. The near-level going continues past overlooks upon a Beartrap Meadow organizational camp, soon afterward crosses a depressed, tumbling, transitory stream emanating from Big Baldy and, several hundred yards later, connects with the second upslope road—SNF "Closed" Road 14S33 (7080/1.3). Minutes later, we kick across an effervescent, ice-flanked fork of Woodward Creek and then turn east where a stubby road (7100/0.8) branches southeast to a viewless saddle.

Intermittently negotiating places where snow has filled the road's niche, restoring the original slope, we now speed down a road segment called the Otter's Slide, which rounds a hill, then switchbacks before reaching the shelf of **Road 14S56** (6560/0.9). Here we can start to take that road north toward the cars either immediately or after taking a side trip south to a viewful point at the head of the North Fork Kaweah River.

To reach that point, we turn south onto 14S56 at the oblique junction and shortly round an east-trending ridge, gliding down the weaving road's gradual grade. At length our course leaves the Chimney Slopes, then passes through Jeffrey pines randomly mingled with oak and crosses the level-crested part of a southeast-trending ridge. Then the road turns, briefly aligns its crackly, uneven snow cover with the ridge, and afterward ends in a ridgecrest swale (6500/1.1) just short of a dinky dome. Skiers who cautiously near its slick summit can survey the gorge in which Stony and Dorst creeks merge to become the North Fork Kaweah River. Snowy Muir Grove sequoia crowns accentuate the southeastern horizon. From here we backtrack to the junction (6560/1.1) and there start to swoop downslope, northward—still on 14S56 but once again on the Chimney Slopes. Quite soon we cross a Woodward Creek fork that we crossed earlier. Leaving the creek just downstream from the hump of a snow-plastered private cabin, we start up the road's mild grade across a succession of logger-cleared plots onto increasingly gentle, rolling slopes. Shortly we meet west-trending spur roads A (6710/0.8) and B (6830/0.6). Eventually our road winds to a junction with **Road 14S29** (6950/0.4), marked with our earlier ski tracks. Now we backtrack quite briefly northeast to reach our cars on Generals Highway (7025/0.5).

T99   Chimney Rock Climb

An imposing array of tall, long-faced domes and spires cluster about Chimney Rock, known for its knobby granite, inspiring views and easy accessibility.

Season   June through October

Distance   0.8 mile (1.3 km) round trip

Steep Upgrade   0.4 mile (0.6 km)

Elevation Gain and Loss   620 feet (189 m)

Exertion/Duration   easy 1/5day

Skills   easy route-finding, Class 2 climbing (Class 3–5 pitches optional)

Permits   none

Roadhead/Map   R79/M60

Description   The ***Chimney Peak Wildroute*** starts northwest as a jeep road from a spur of SNF Road 14S29 (7100/0.0) in a broad, red-fir-forested saddle. After ascending moderately for 325 yards, the jeep road narrows to trail width beside a row of adjoining cylindrical concrete tanks, each with its own peaked roof. Beyond the tanks, the steeply ascending path at first zigzags amid chinquapin clumps. Then it leads diagonally upslope to a junction (7530/0.3) just short of a visible shoulder on the southeast ridge emanating from Chimney Rock.

*   *   *   *   *

The obvious path leading southwest from here is the one of most interest to climbers. It crosses the ridgecrest in 30 yards, then weaves down a brief, steep stretch in a manzanita-packed col and exits west via a short granite ledge. The ledge adjoins a timbered swale between a tall campanile-like spire and a martello-tower-topped hidden precipice. After the climb, the path of access provides the best exit.

*   *   *   *   *

Most novice climbers will prefer taking the dim northwest-trending path from the junction. Climbing up its grit, they thread chinquapin and Brewers oak patches, now and then passing near ponderosa pines while taking care not to get sidetracked on game trails

or in diverging corridors in the shrubbery. The sparsely ducked route turns south after 135 yards and quickly leads to rough, broken slabs up which one clambers to attain Chimney Rock (7711/0.1).

The "campanile" and "martello tower" stand in the southern foreground, separated from us by a gulf, while an array of snaggletoothed Sierra peaks form the eastern horizon. In due time we backtrack to our cars.

Chimney Rock and its campanile point to the Great Western Divide

T100 Hiking through the Muir Sequoias

This path, heavily beaten as far as the Muir Grove of giant sequoias, offers surprising vistas to those who hike its seldom-trod final segment beyond the grove's representatives of the sequoia's many ages. However, because of numerous trail-obstructing blowdowns, including massive sequoias, the Park Service is now letting this final segment return to nature.

Season   June through October (avoid holiday weekends)

Distance   5.8 miles (9.3 km) round trip

Steep Upgrade   none

Elevation Gain and Loss   850 feet (259 m)

Exertion/Duration   easy/1 day

Skills   easy route-finding, Class 1 climbing

Permits   USNPS Entrance Receipt

Roadhead/Map   R80/M61

Canteen   1 quart

Description   *"Muir Grove Trail,"* so signed at the westernmost point in Dorst Creek Campground (6690/0.0), initially makes a mild descent west through a white fir/sugar pine stand interspersed with chinquapin clumps. Shortly we skirt a pocket meadow and then touch the start of a north-trending path (6620/0.1) to pools along Dorst Creek.

We soon reach a step-across slab ford of a part-time brook and afterward switchback up to a clearing astride a north-trending ridge. A broad bulge of isolated quartz monzonite 50 yards north of the trail here offers a view of Muir Grove sequoia crowns profiled in the west.

Beyond the outlook our course contours for ½ mile. Then hazelnut and dogwood signal the presence of a permanent brook, and after we step across that brook we begin a 15-minute hike up a gradual grade. Then we top a broad saddle (6840/1.6) where some of the 327 Muir Grove sequoias subsist, absorbing noise in their shaggy red bark and imbuing visitors with the peace of the sequoia's apparent timelessness.

Now the path narrows, indicating that most visitors start backtracking here. We advance for a few moments, then touch a spur path leading south. Only 80 yards long, it ends in a semicircle of sequoia shanks. Our path, meanwhile, zigzags in a westward descent across deep, rich, deeply-shaded loam.

Thimbleberry, horsetail, dogwood and fern adorn a tiny brook where we step across it 300 feet lower than the Muir Grove saddle. More of this vegetation, along with a nearby hidden but audible creek, marks the onset of a gradual descent across northwest-facing slopes. Several shallow ravines lie athwart our path in this traverse, which presently leads to a thick-trunked, fallen ponderosa pine blocking the trail. A sign engraved with "warning/end of trail" has been tacked to the fallen tree, which a scrambler's trail bypasses just up the slope. A few moments later, the hiker finds an exposed corner where downcanyon views toward the North Fork Kaweah River appear. Here the deep forest yields startlingly to oak woodland on west-facing slopes of rotten granite and quartz monzonite. To the north-northwest, across the canyon, Chimney Rock and the "campanile," "martello tower" and domes clustered about it stand in eye-catching supremacy. Park Service naturalists call our position "Valley View," no doubt because when haze clears away, agricultural cross-hatching in the San Joaquin Valley can be discerned in the western distance, (6320/1.2).

Our path, once called the "Black Oak Trail," used to extend beyond this viewpoint, rounding Pine Ridge to the south and eventually ending near Crystal Cave. Many years of official neglect and subsequent abandonment have erased most of that lengthy trail segment, so all but the hardiest explorer will have nowhere to go from here except back along our footprints to the cars.

Sources and Recommended Reading

(Entries marked * are esoteric, and most readers will need to refer to specialized dictionaries in order to understand them.)

Cultural History

Farquhar, Francis P., *History of the Sierra Nevada*. Berkeley: University of California, 1965.

————, "Place Names of the High Sierra." Sierra Club Bulletin 11 (4), 12 (1) and 12 (2).

Johnston, Hank, *They Felled the Redwoods*. Costa Mesa: Trans-Anglo, 1966.

Los Tulares, the newsletter of the Tulare County Historical Society, 1950–78.

Powers, Bob, *North Fork Country*. Los Angeles: Westernlore Press, 1974.

Guidance

Jenkins, J. C., *Self-Propelled in the Southern Sierra, Volume One: The Sierra Crest and the Kern Plateau*. Berkeley: Wilderness, 1978.

Roper, Steve, *The Climber's Guide to the High Sierra*. San Francisco: Sierra Club, 1976.

Oberhansley, F.M., *Crystal Cave*. Three Rivers: Sequoia Natural History Association, 1977.

Sequoia Natural History Association. "Cascade Creek Trail Guide."

————,"Moro Rock."

Winnett, Thomas, *Sierra South*. Berkeley: Wilderness, 1975.

Natural History

American Geological Institute, *Dictionary of Geological Terms*, rev. ed. Garden City: Doubleday/Anchor, 1976.

Axelrod, Daniel I., "History of the Coniferous Forests, California and Nevada." University of California Publications in Botany 70 (1), 1976.

*————. and William S. Ting, *Early Pleistocene Floras from the Chagoopa Surface, Southern Sierra Nevada, California*. University of California Publications in the Geological Sciences 39 (2): 119–194, 1961.

*Christensen, M.N., "Structure of Metamorphic Rocks at Mineral King, California." University of California Publications in the Geological Sciences, 42 (4): 159–198, 1963.

————,"Late Cenozoic Crustal Movements in the Sierra Nevada of California." Geological Society of America Bulletin 77 (2): 163–182, 1966.

Dott, Jr., Robert H. and Roger L. Batten, *Evolution of the Earth*, 2nd ed. New York: McGraw-Hill, 1976.

*Durrell, Cordell, "Geology of the Sierra Nevada Northeast of Visalia, Tulare County, California." California Journal of Mines and Geology 39 (2): 153–168, 1943.

Fritsche, A. Eugene, "Miocene Paleogeography of California" in Late Mesozoic and Cenozoic Sedimentation and Tectonics in California. (SJGS Short Course Notes) Bakersfield: San Joaquin Geological Society, 1977, pp. 109–119.

Griffin, James R. and William B. Critchfield, *The Distribution of Forest Trees in California*. (Research Paper PSW–82.) Washington: US Forest Service, 1972.

Harper, John L., *The Southern Sierra Nevada of California: A Regional Plan for Integrated Recreational Development*. Ann Arbor: Xerox University Microfilms International, 1974.

Hartesveldt, Richard J., H. Thomas Harvey, Howard S. Shellhammer and Ronald E. Stecker, *The Giant Sequoia of the Sierra Nevada*. Washington: National Park Service, 1975.

Hill, Mary, *Geology of the Sierra Nevada* (California Natural History Guide 37). Berkeley: University of California, 1975.

Leasure, John A., *et al.*, *Little Kern Environmental Statement*. Washington: US Forest Service, 1977.

————, *Mineral King Environmental Statement* Washington: US Forest Service, 1976.

Oakeshott, Gordon B., *California's Changing Landscape*, 2nd ed. New York: McGraw-Hill, 1978.

Ross, Donald C., *Igneous and Metamorphic Rocks of Parts of Sequoia and Kings Canyon National Parks, California*. San Francisco: California Division of Mines, 1958.

Sudworth, George B., *Forest Trees of the Pacific Slope*. New York: Dover, 1967.

Thompson, Steven, and Mary Thompson, *Wild Food Plants of the Sierra*. Berkeley: Wilderness, 1972.

Twisselmann, Ernest C., *A Flora of Kern County, California*. San Francisco: Wasmann Journal of Biology, 1967.

*Saleeby, J.B., "Fieldtrip Guide to the Kings-Kaweah Suture, Southwestern Sierra Nevada Foothills, California." Geological Society of America, Cordilleran Section, 73rd Annual Meeting, 1977.

*_____,W. D. Sharp, S. E. Goodin and C. Busby, "Mesozoic Paleogeographic Evolution of the Southern Sierra Nevada" in Howell, D., ed., *Mesozoic Paleogeography of the Western United States*. Los Angeles: Pacific Section, Society of Economic Paleontologists and Mineralogists, 1978.

Storer, Tracy I., and Robert L. Usinger, *Sierra Nevada Natural History*. Berkeley: University of California, 1971.

*Stewart, J. H., C. H. Stevens, A. E. Fritsche, eds., *Paleozoic Paleogeography of the Western United States*. Los Angeles: Pacific Section, Society of Economic Paleontologists and Mineralogists, 1977.

Watts, Tom, *California Tree Finder*. Berkeley: Nature Study Guild, 1963.

Weeden, Norman, *Survival Handbook to Sierra Flora*. (Self-published; sold through Wilderness Press.) 1975.

Prater, Gene, *Snowshoeing*. Seattle: The Mountaineers, 1974.

Robbins, Royal, *Basic Rockcraft*. Glendale: La Siesta, 1971.

Sloane, Eugene A., *Complete Book of Bicycling*. New York: Trident, 1970.

Steck, Allen and Lito Tejada-Flores, *Wilderness Skiing*. San Francisco and New York: Sierra Club, 1973.

Uman, Martin A., *Lightning*. New York: McGraw-Hill, 1969.

US Forest Service and US Ski Assn., *Winter Recreation Safety Guide*. Washington: US Government Printing Office, 1976. $0.90.

Winnett, Thomas, *Backpacking Basics*. Berkeley: Wilderness, 1979.

Skills for Self-Propelled Sports

DeLong, Fred, *DeLong's Guide to Bikes and Bicycling: the art and science*. Radnor, Pennsylvania: Chilton, 1974.

Editors of *Runner's World* magazine, *The Complete Runner*. Mountain View: World, 1974.

Fear, Gene, *Surviving the Unexpected Wilderness Emergency*. Tacoma: Survival Education, 1975.

Ferber, Peggy, ed., *Mountaineering: The Freedom of the Hills*, 3rd ed. Seattle: The Mountaineers, 1974.

Fletcher, Colin, *The New Complete Walker*. New York: Afred A. Knopf, 1976.

Halliday, William R., *American Caves and Caving*, New York: Harper and Row, 1974.

Manning, Harvey, *Backpacking: One Step at a Time*. New York: Vintage Books, 1975.

Mitchell, Dick, *Mountaineering First Aid*. Seattle: The Mountaineers, 1972.

Part 3: Maps

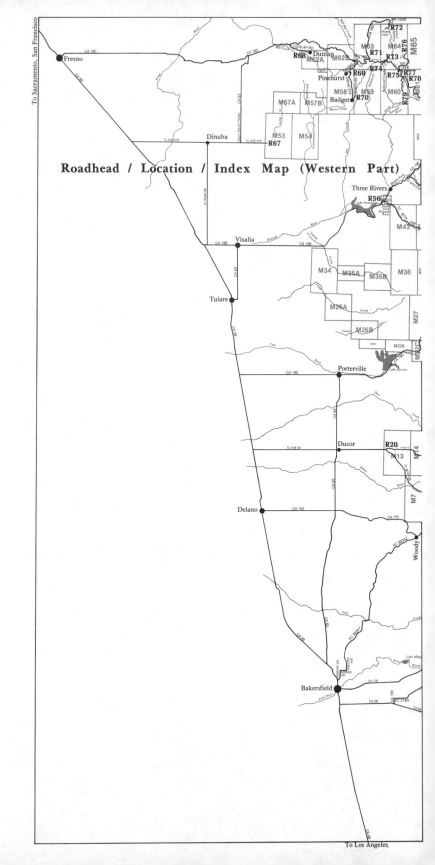

Roadhead / Location / Index Map (Western Part)

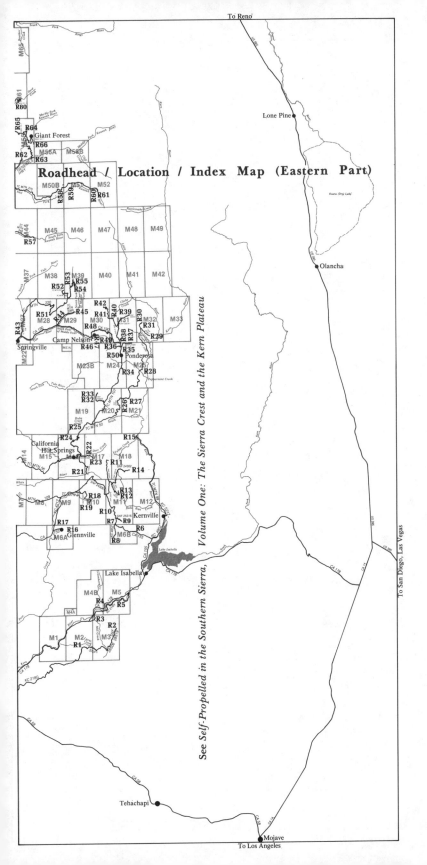

Roadhead / Location / Index Map (Eastern Part)

To Reno

Lone Pine

Owens (Dry) Lake

Olancha

See Self-Propelled in the Southern Sierra, Volume One: The Sierra Crest and the Kern Plateau

To San Diego, Las Vegas

R80

R65
R64
Giant Forest
R66
M56A   M56B
R62
R63

M50B   M52
R58   M51
R59   R60   R61

M45   M46   M47   M48   M49
R57

M37   M38   M39   M40   M41   M42
R52   R53
R54   R55

R42   R51   R45   R41   R40   R39   R30
M28   M29   M30   R48   R31   M32   M33
R43   M31   R38   R37   R29
Springville   Camp Nelson   R46   R49   R36   R35
R50   Ponderosa   M24   M25
M23B   R34   R28
Peppermint Creek

R33   R27
R32   R26
M19   M20   M21
R25   R24

California
Hot Springs   R22   R15
M15   M16   M17   M18
R23   R11
R21   R14

R18   R13
R12
M9   M10   M11   M12
R19   R10
R7   R9   Kernville
R17   R16   R6
Glennville   M6B
M6A   R8

Lake Isabella
Lake Isabella

M4B   M5
M4A   R4
R5

M1   M2   M3   R3
R1   R2

Tehachapi

Mojave
To Los Angeles

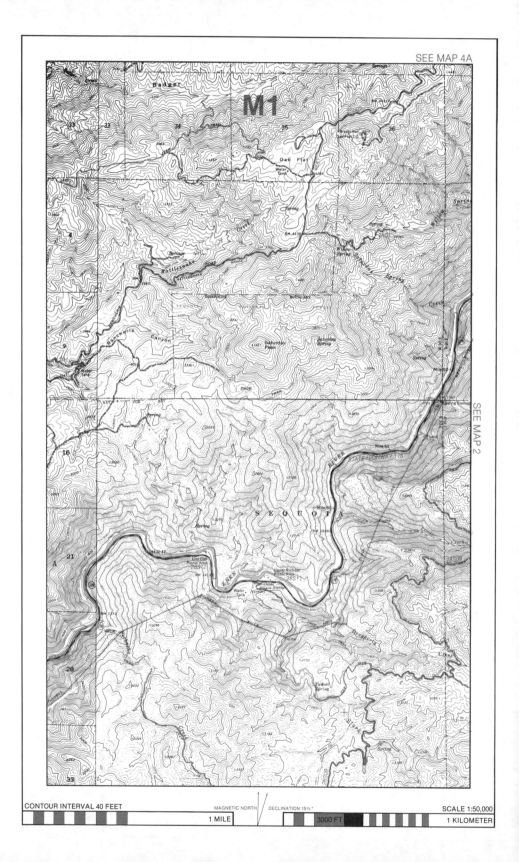

M1

CONTOUR INTERVAL 40 FEET

MAGNETIC NORTH

DECLINATION 15½°

SCALE 1:50,000

1 MILE

3000 FT

1 KILOMETER

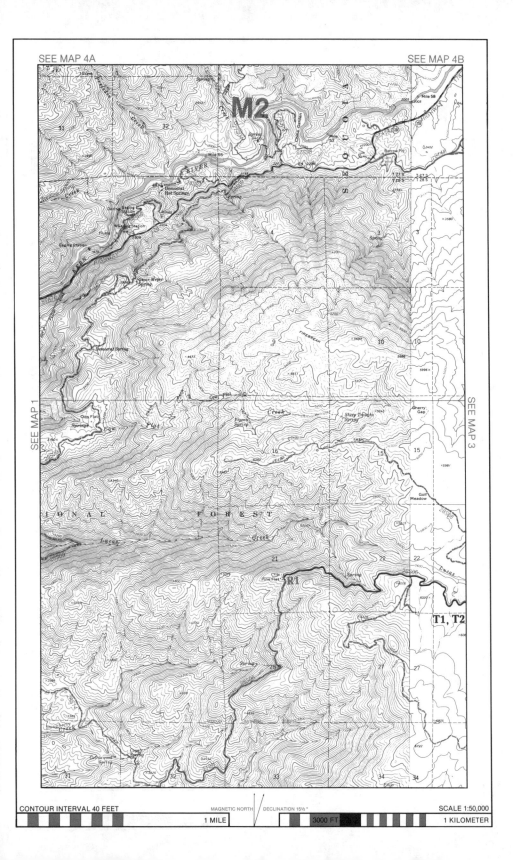

M2

R1

T1, T2

CONTOUR INTERVAL 40 FEET

MAGNETIC NORTH DECLINATION 15½°

SCALE 1:50,000

1 MILE

3000 FT

1 KILOMETER

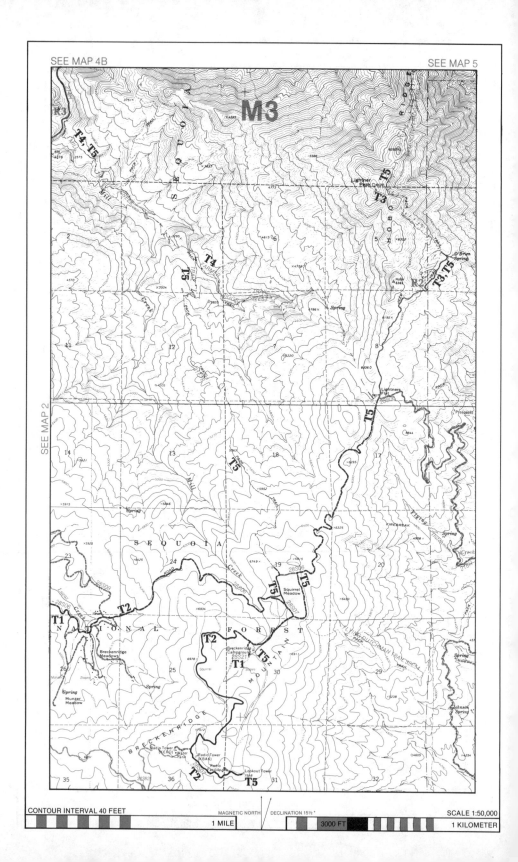

CONTOUR INTERVAL 40 FEET

MAGNETIC NORTH   DECLINATION 15½°

1 MILE

3000 FT

SCALE 1:50,000

1 KILOMETER

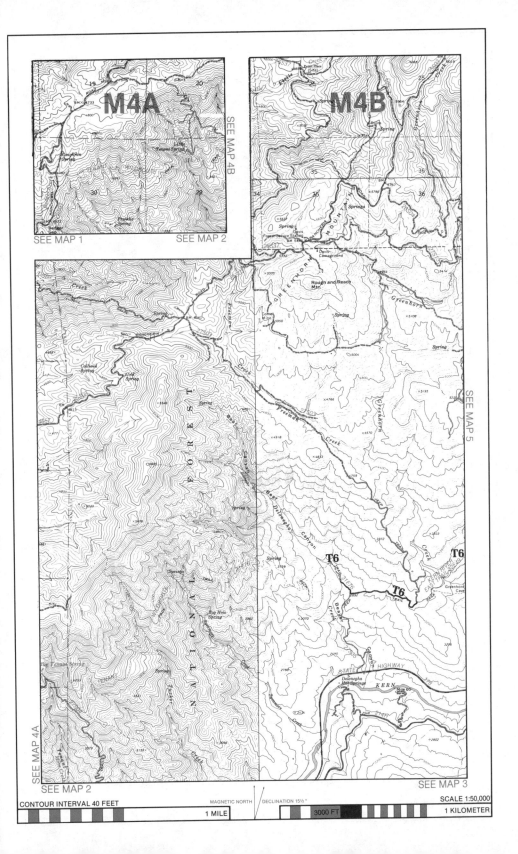

SEE MAP 4B

SEE MAP 1

SEE MAP 2

M4A

M4B

SEE MAP 5

SEE MAP 4A

SEE MAP 2

SEE MAP 3

CONTOUR INTERVAL 40 FEET

MAGNETIC NORTH

DECLINATION 15½°

SCALE 1:50,000

1 MILE

3000 FT

1 KILOMETER

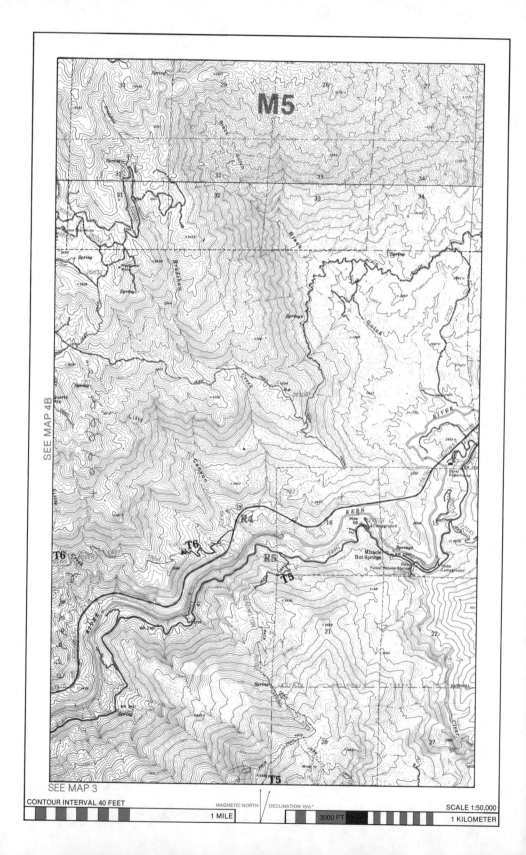

SEE MAP 4B

SEE MAP 3

CONTOUR INTERVAL 40 FEET

MAGNETIC NORTH DECLINATION 15½ °

1 MILE

3000 FT

SCALE 1:50,000

1 KILOMETER

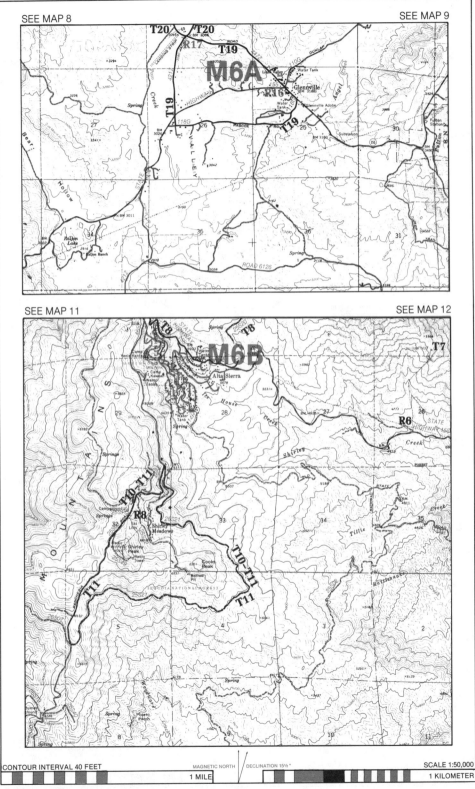

M6A

M6B

CONTOUR INTERVAL 40 FEET

MAGNETIC NORTH   DECLINATION 15½°

1 MILE

SCALE 1:50,000

1 KILOMETER

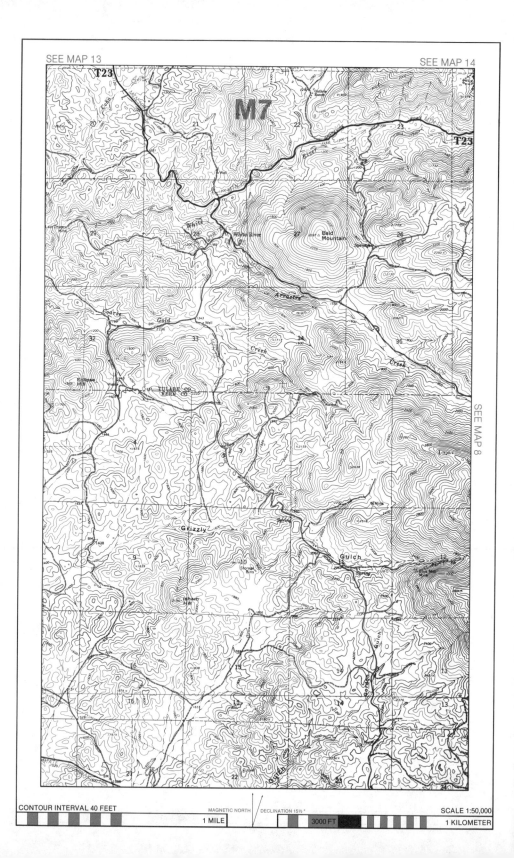

SEE MAP 8

CONTOUR INTERVAL 40 FEET

MAGNETIC NORTH DECLINATION 15½°

1 MILE

3000 FT

SCALE 1:50,000

1 KILOMETER

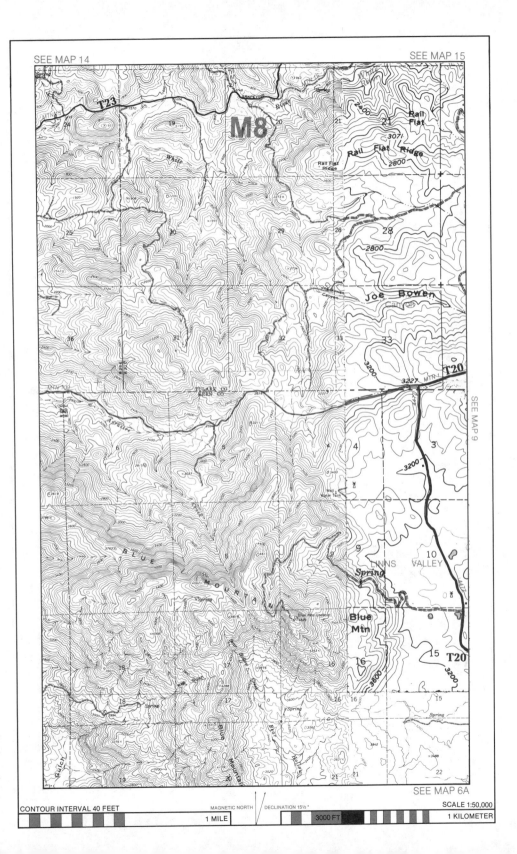

M8

SEE MAP 9
SEE MAP 6A

CONTOUR INTERVAL 40 FEET

MAGNETIC NORTH

1 MILE

DECLINATION 15½°

3000 FT

SCALE 1:50,000

1 KILOMETER

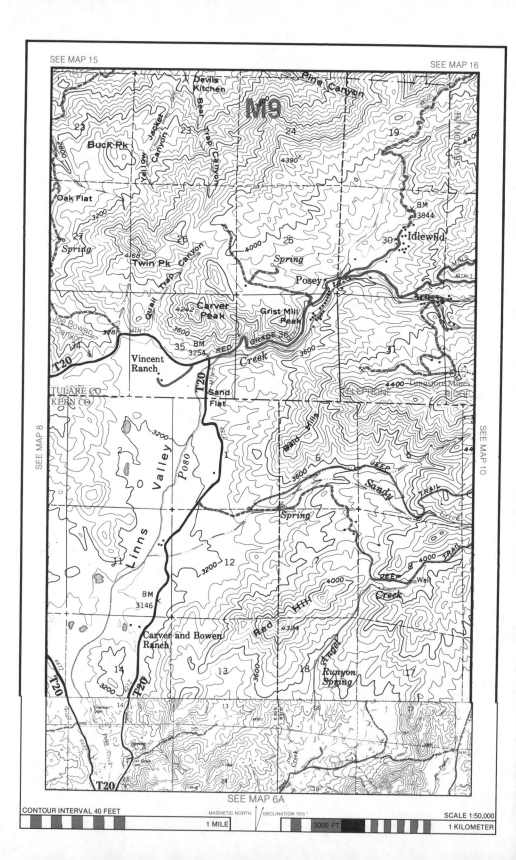

CONTOUR INTERVAL 40 FEET

MAGNETIC NORTH / DECLINATION 15½°

1 MILE

3000 FT

1 KILOMETER

SCALE 1:50,000

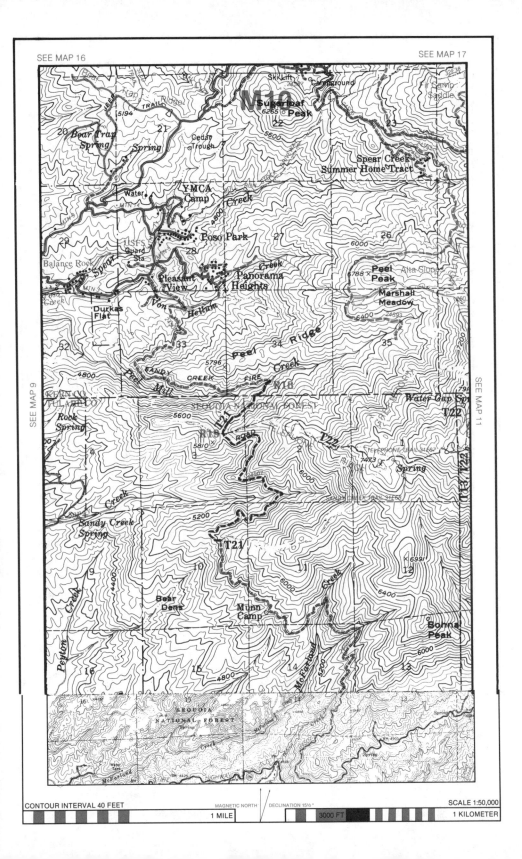

SEE MAP 9
SEE MAP 11

M10

Bear Trap
Spring

Spring

Cedar
Trough

Sugarloaf
Peak
6265

Ski Lift
Campground

Camp
Saddle

Spear Creek
Summer Home Tract

YMCA
Camp

Creek

Water

Poso Park

USFS
Guard
Sta

Balance Rock

Spear

Pleasant
View

Panorama
Heights

Creek

Peel
Peak
6788 x

Alta Slope

Marshall
Meadow

Durkes
Flat

Von   Helium

Peel   Ridge

5796

Peel   Creek

KERN CO.
TULARE CO.

SANDY   CREEK   FIRE

Mill

4800

Rock
Spring

5600

SEQUOIA NATIONAL FOREST

M18

R19
5810 x

agap

T22

Water Gap Sp
T22

TELEPHONE TRAIL

7473 x

Spring

Sandy Creek
Spring

Creek

5200

6000

T21

10

11

6991

12

Bear
Dens

Munn
Camp

6400

Bonna
Peak

6000

Peyton

Creek

16

15

4800

14

McFarland

5200

13

16

SEQUOIA
NATIONAL FOREST

15

4898

13

Spring

Spring

Creek

Spring

BM 490

McFarland

MAGNETIC NORTH

DECLINATION 15½°

1 MILE

3000 FT

1 KILOMETER

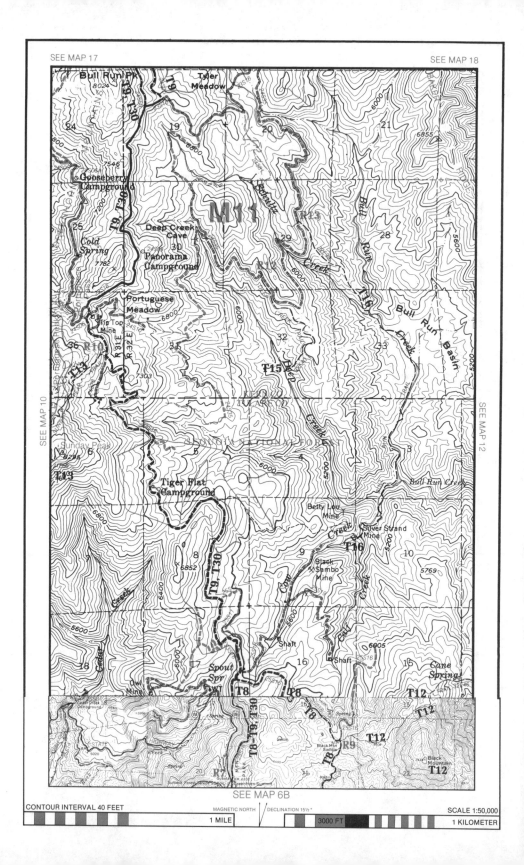

SEE MAP 10

SEE MAP 12

SEE MAP 6B

CONTOUR INTERVAL 40 FEET

MAGNETIC NORTH

DECLINATION 15½°

SCALE 1:50,000

1 MILE

3000 FT

1 KILOMETER

SEE MAP 18

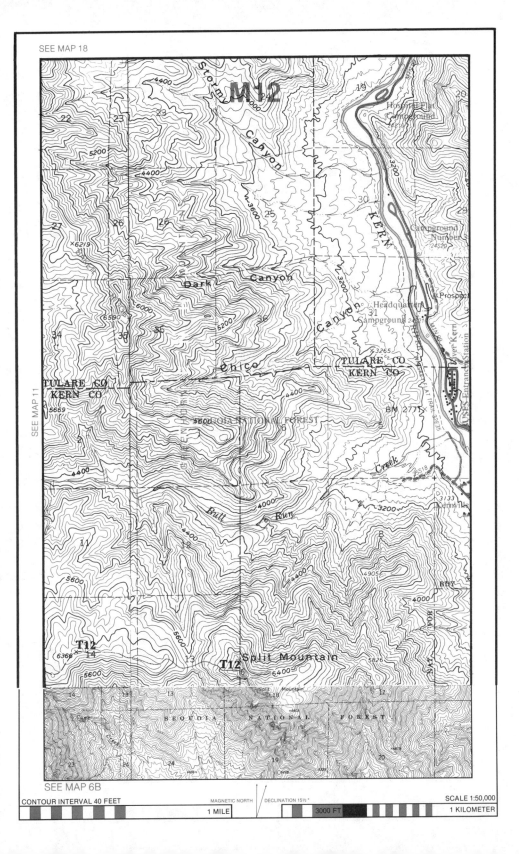

SEE MAP 11

SEE MAP 6B

CONTOUR INTERVAL 40 FEET

MAGNETIC NORTH DECLINATION 15½°

SCALE 1:50,000

1 MILE

3000 FT

1 KILOMETER

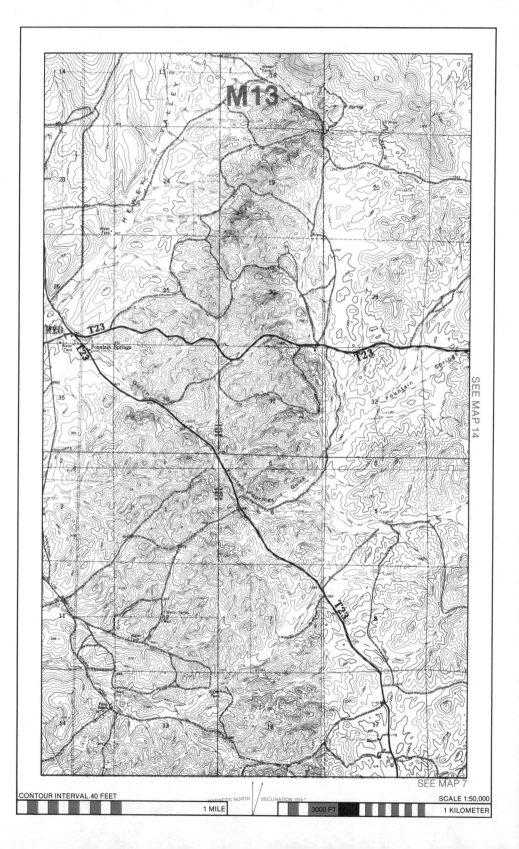

SEE MAP 14

SEE MAP 7

CONTOUR INTERVAL 40 FEET

MAGNETIC NORTH   DECLINATION 15½°

3000 FT

1 MILE

1 KILOMETER

SCALE 1:50,000

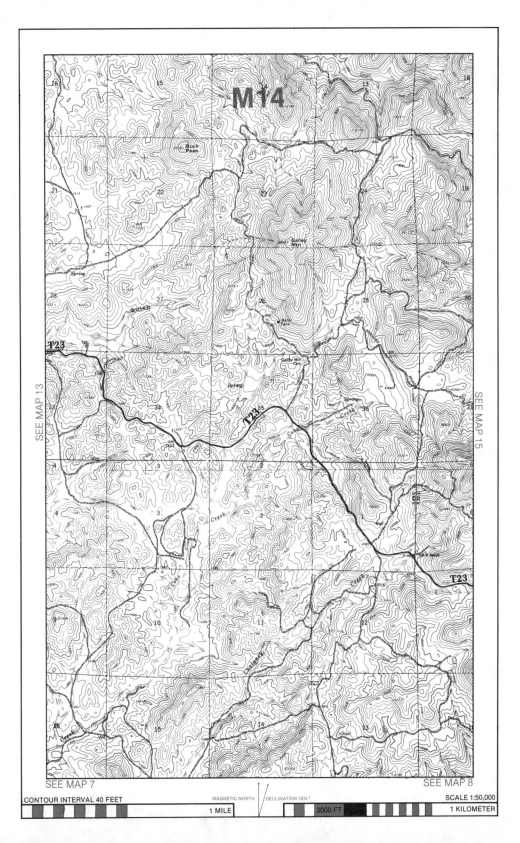

SEE MAP 13

SEE MAP 15

SEE MAP 7

SEE MAP 8

CONTOUR INTERVAL 40 FEET

MAGNETIC NORTH

DECLINATION 15½°

SCALE 1:50,000

1 MILE

3000 FT

1 KILOMETER

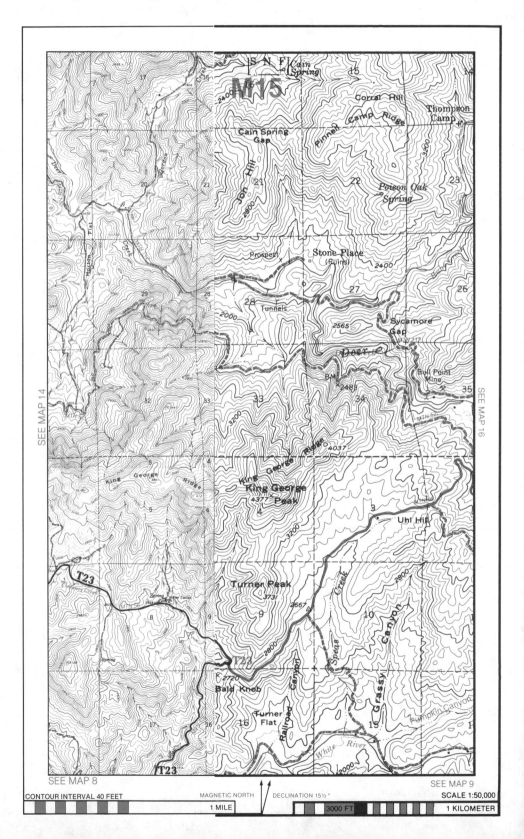

M15

S N F Cain Spring

Corral Hill

Thompson Camp

Cain Spring Gap

Pinnell Camp Ridge

Jon Hill

Poison Oak Spring

Prospect

Stone Place (Ruins)

Tunnels

Sycamore Gap

Deer

Bull Point Mine

King George Ridge

King George Peak

Uhl Hill

Turner Peak

Bald Knob

Turner Flat

Railroad Canyon

Grassy Canyon

Pumpkin Canyon

White River

CONTOUR INTERVAL 40 FEET

MAGNETIC NORTH   DECLINATION 15½°

SCALE 1:50,000

1 MILE

3000 FT

1 KILOMETER

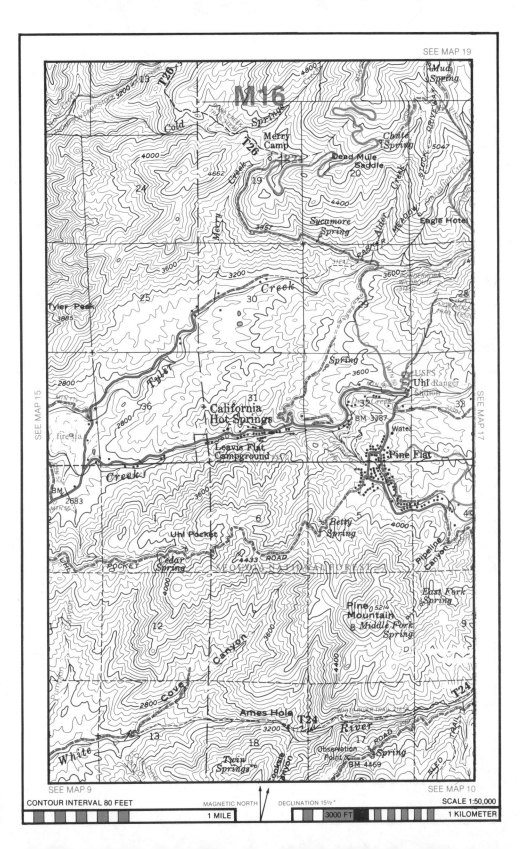

M16

Mud
Spring

Cold

Merry
Camp

Chute
Spring

Dead Mule
Saddle

5047

Sucamore
Spring

Eagle Hotel

Tyler Peak
3885

Creek

Spring

USFS
Uhl Ranger
Station

California
Hot Springs

BM 3387

Water

Leavis Flat
Campground

Pine Flat

BM
2683

Uhl Pocket

Betty
Spring

4000

Cedar
Spring

4433 ROAD

SEQUOIA NATIONAL FOREST

East Fork
Spring

Pine
Mountain
5214

Middle Fork
Spring

Cove

Ames Hole

River

Spring

Twin
Springs

Observation
Point

BM 4469

CONTOUR INTERVAL 80 FEET

MAGNETIC NORTH

DECLINATION 15½°

SCALE 1:50,000

1 MILE

3000 FT

1 KILOMETER

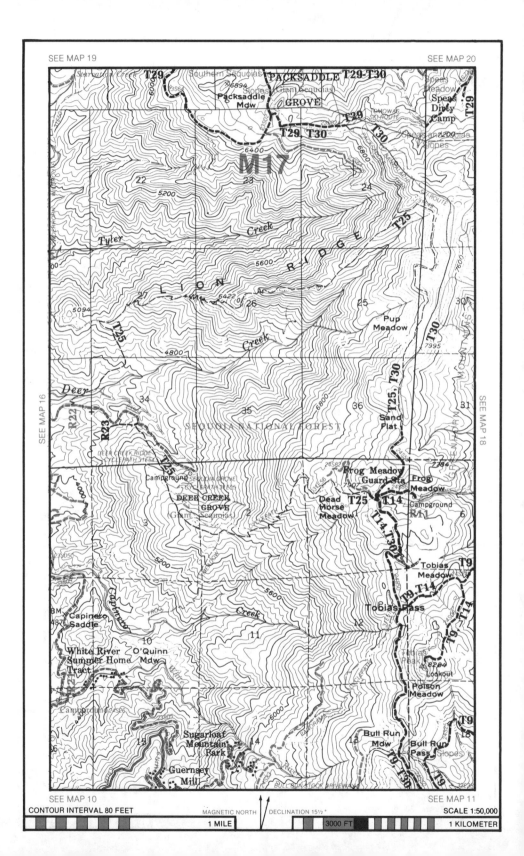

CONTOUR INTERVAL 80 FEET

MAGNETIC NORTH   DECLINATION 15½°

SCALE 1:50,000

1 MILE   3000 FT   1 KILOMETER

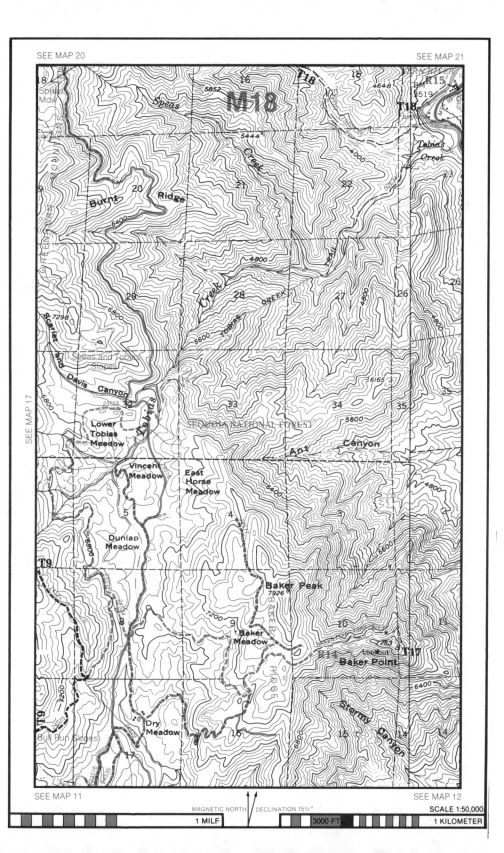

MAGNETIC NORTH | DECLINATION 15½°

SCALE 1:50,000

1 MILE

3000 FT

1 KILOMETER

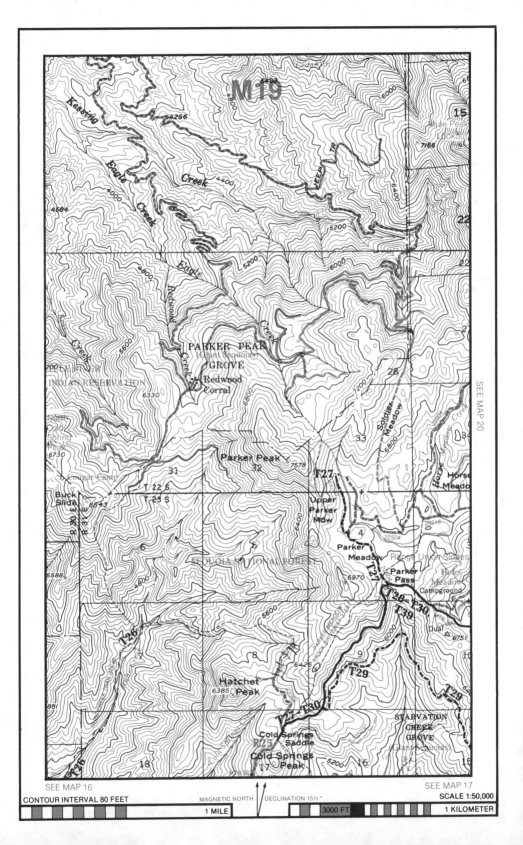

SEE MAP 20

SEE MAP 16

SEE MAP 17

CONTOUR INTERVAL 80 FEET

MAGNETIC NORTH   DECLINATION 15½ °

SCALE 1:50,000

1 MILE   3000 FT   1 KILOMETER

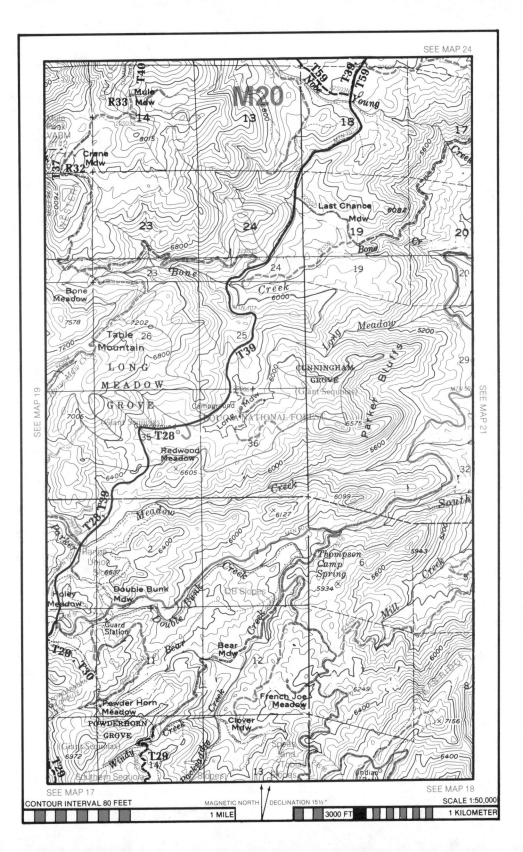

SEE MAP 19

SEE MAP 21

CONTOUR INTERVAL 80 FEET

MAGNETIC NORTH   DECLINATION 15½°

SCALE 1:50,000

1 MILE   3000 FT   1 KILOMETER

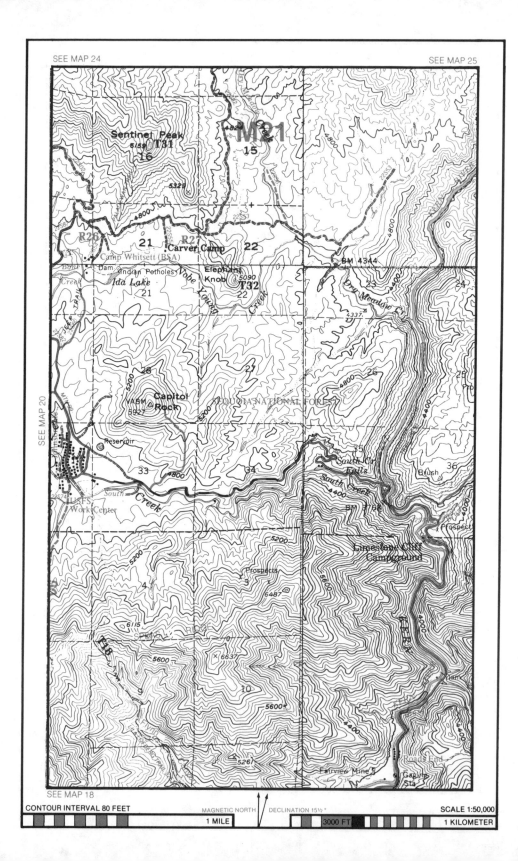

SEE MAP 20

CONTOUR INTERVAL 80 FEET

MAGNETIC NORTH   DECLINATION 15½°

SCALE 1:50,000

1 MILE

3000 FT

1 KILOMETER

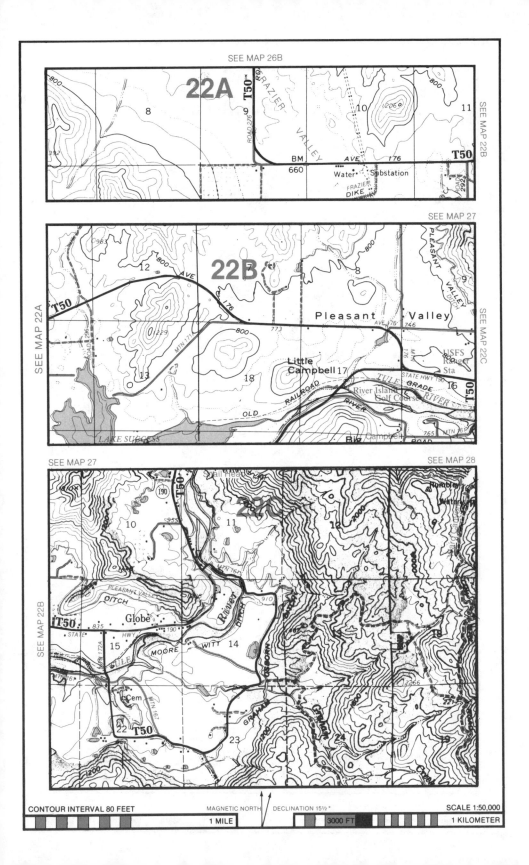

SEE MAP 26B

22A

SEE MAP 22B

T50

ROAD 276

8

FRAZIER VALLEY

10

1206

11

BM

AVE

176

660

Water • Substation

FRAZIER DIKE

292

T50

SEE MAP 27

SEE MAP 22A

SEE MAP 22C

22B

T50

12

AVE

983

176

7

8

PLEASANT VALLEY DITCH

9

800

Pleasant Valley

773

AVE 176

746

ROAD 294

229

MTN 171

800

13

18

Little Campbell

17

RAILROAD

OLD

STATE HWY 190

USFS Ranger Sta

16

T50

TULE

GRADE

RIVER

River Island Golf Course

765

MTN 167

LAKE SUCCESS

Big Campbell

ROAD

SEE MAP 27

SEE MAP 28

SEE MAP 22B

Trail Head

190

T50

955

Rumble

Waterfall

22C

10

11

12

9

2000

MTN 167

PLEASANT VALLEY DITCH

T50

835

Globe

STATE

HWY

190

172A

15

TULE

MOORE

WITT

River

OSBORN

DITCH

910

14

GRAHAM OSBORN

18

266

77

Cem

MTN 167

22

T50

23

GRAHAM

24

19

1200

CONTOUR INTERVAL 80 FEET

MAGNETIC NORTH

DECLINATION 15½°

SCALE 1:50,000

1 MILE

3000 FT

1 KILOMETER

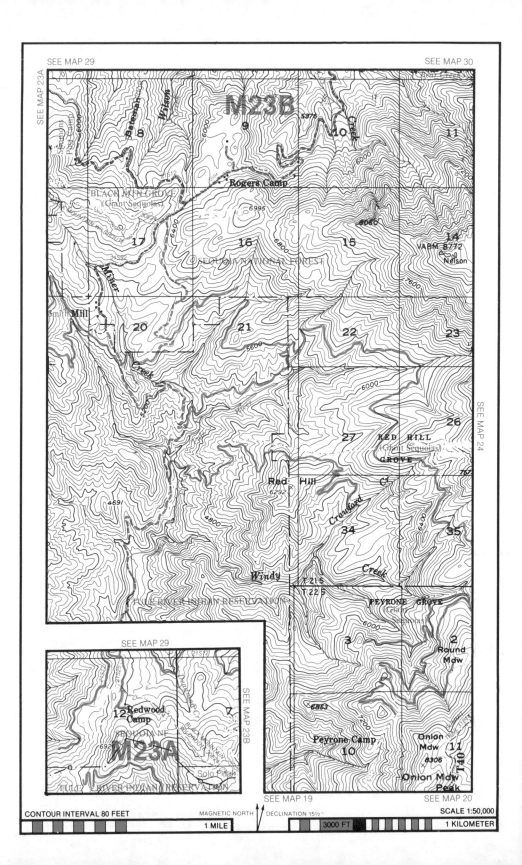

SEE MAP 23A

M23B

SEE MAP 23A

8
9
10
11

Rogers Camp

BLACK MTN GROVE
(Giant Sequoias)

SEQUOIA NATIONAL FOREST

17
16
15
14
VABM 8772
Nelson

Smith Mill

20
21
22
23

Creek

27
26

RED HILL
(Giant Sequoias)
GROVE

Red Hill
6292

Crawford

34
35

Windy
T 21 S
T 22 S

Creek

TULE RIVER INDIAN RESERVATION

PEYRONE GROVE
(Giant
Sequoias)

3
2
Round
Mdw

6853

Peyrone Camp
10

Onion
Mdw 11
8306

Onion Mdw
Peak

SEE MAP 29

SEE MAP 23B

12 Redwood
Camp

M23A

Solo Peak

TULE RIVER INDIAN RESERVATION

SEE MAP 24

CONTOUR INTERVAL 80 FEET

MAGNETIC NORTH   DECLINATION 15½°

SCALE 1:50,000

1 MILE   3000 FT   1 KILOMETER

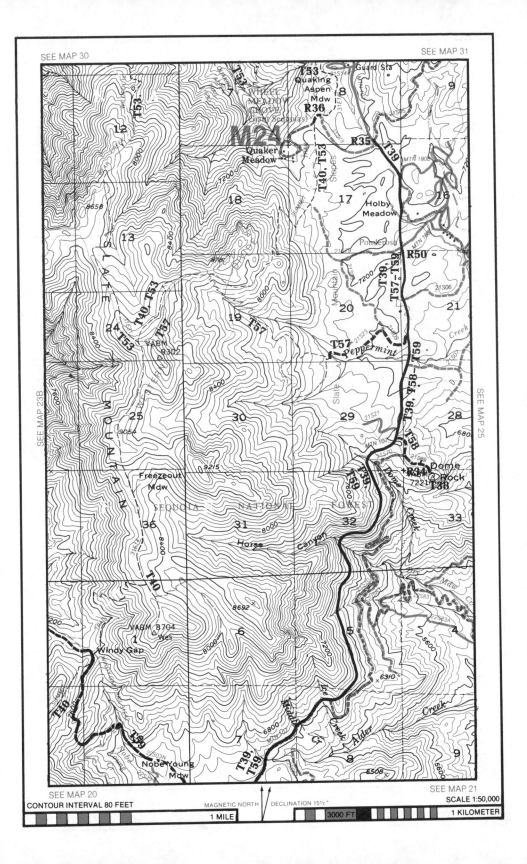

SEE MAP 23B

SEE MAP 25

CONTOUR INTERVAL 80 FEET

MAGNETIC NORTH   DECLINATION 15½°

SCALE 1:50,000

1 MILE

3000 FT

1 KILOMETER

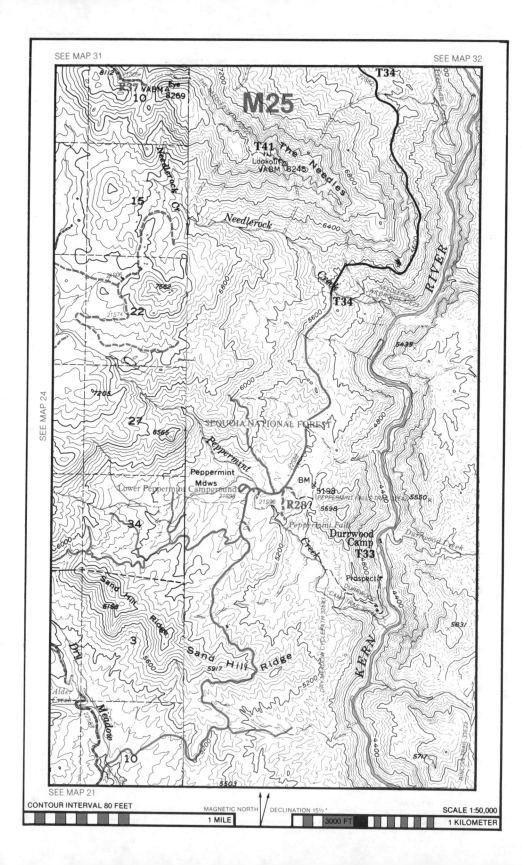

M25

T34

F37 VABM
10   Eye
          8269

T41 The Needles
Lookout
VABM 8245

Needlerock

Needlerock Cr.

15

7562

22
21574

27
8565

7205

SEQUOIA NATIONAL FOREST

Peppermint

Peppermint
Mdws
Lower Peppermint Campground
21898

34

21896
R28

3

Sand

Dry

Sand Hill Ridge
5917

Alder
Creek

Meadow

10

Creek

T34

T34

RIVER

5435

BM
5198
5698

PEPPERMINT FALLS TRAIL

5550

Peppermint Falls

Durrwood
Camp
T33

Prospect

DURRWOOD
CAMP TRAIL

Durrwood Creek

KERN

DRY MEADOW CYCLE PATH 32E33

5831

5717

RINCON TRAIL 35E23

CONTOUR INTERVAL 80 FEET

MAGNETIC NORTH   DECLINATION 15½°

1 MILE   3000 FT

SCALE 1:50,000

1 KILOMETER

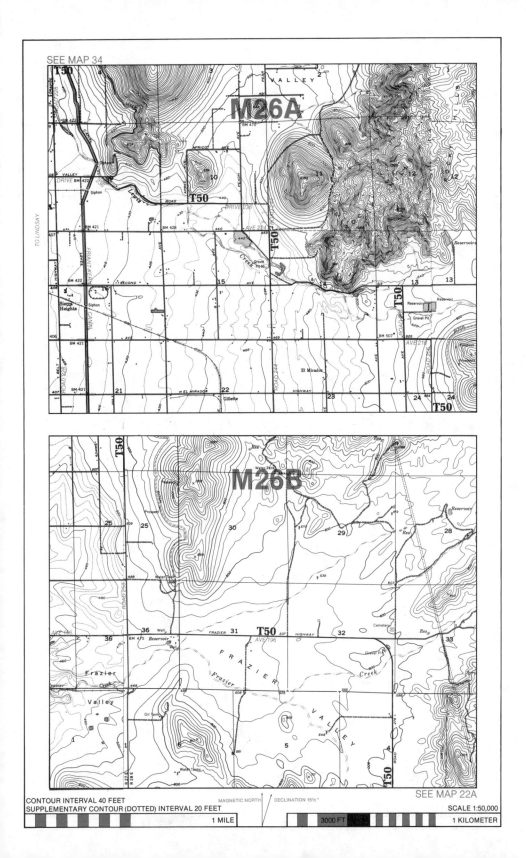

M26A

M26B

SEE MAP 22A

CONTOUR INTERVAL 40 FEET
SUPPLEMENTARY CONTOUR (DOTTED) INTERVAL 20 FEET

MAGNETIC NORTH   DECLINATION 15½°

SCALE 1:50,000

1 MILE

3000 FT

1 KILOMETER

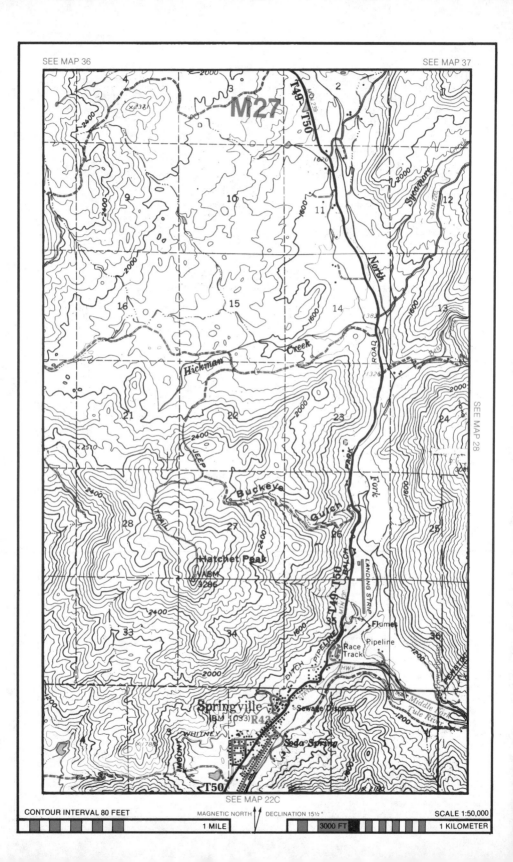

SEE MAP 28

CONTOUR INTERVAL 80 FEET

MAGNETIC NORTH   DECLINATION 15½°

SCALE 1:50,000

1 MILE

3000 FT

1 KILOMETER

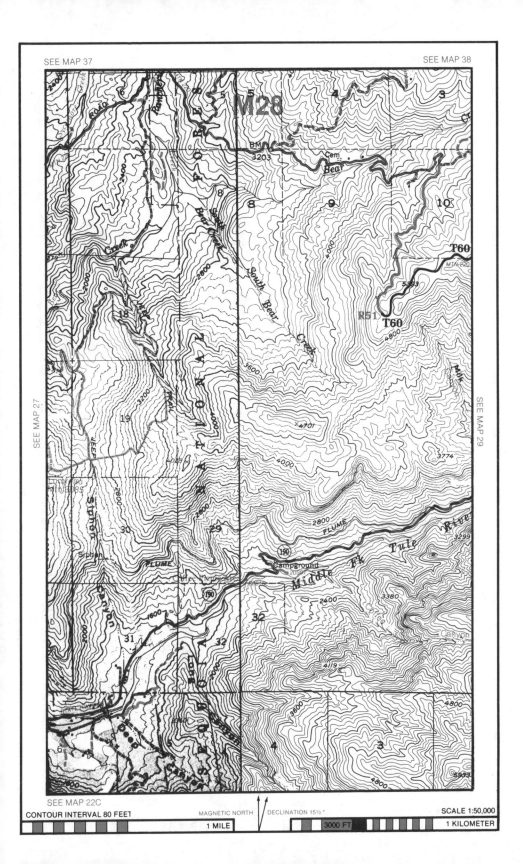

M28

CONTOUR INTERVAL 80 FEET

MAGNETIC NORTH   DECLINATION 15½°

SCALE 1:50,000

1 MILE

3000 FT

1 KILOMETER

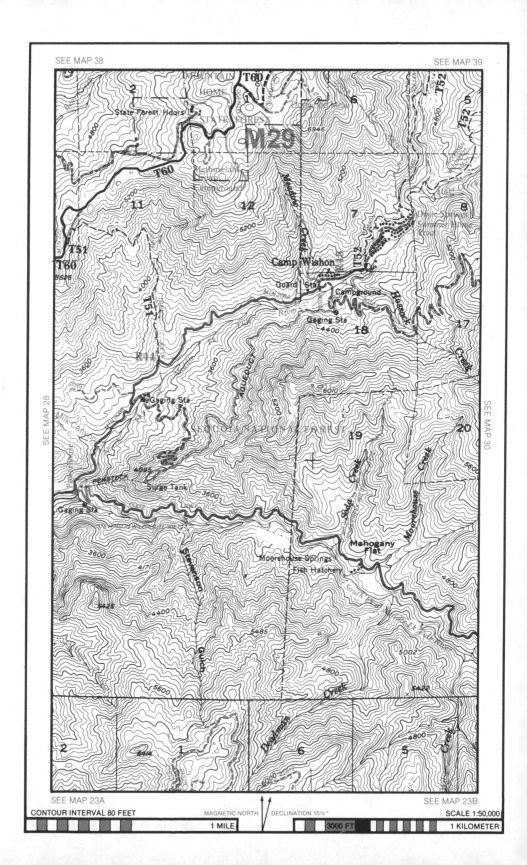

CONTOUR INTERVAL 80 FEET

MAGNETIC NORTH   DECLINATION 15½°

SCALE 1:50,000

1 MILE   3000 FT   1 KILOMETER

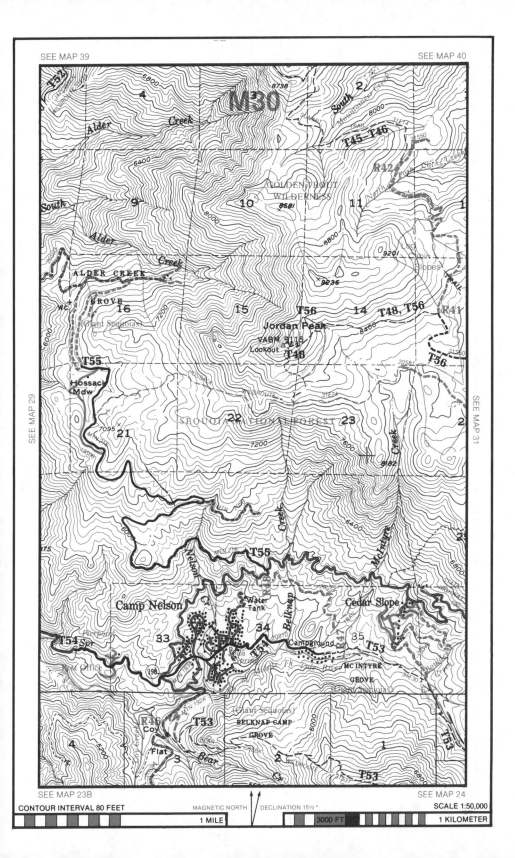

CONTOUR INTERVAL 80 FEET   MAGNETIC NORTH   DECLINATION 15½°   SCALE 1:50,000

1 MILE   3000 FT   1 KILOMETER

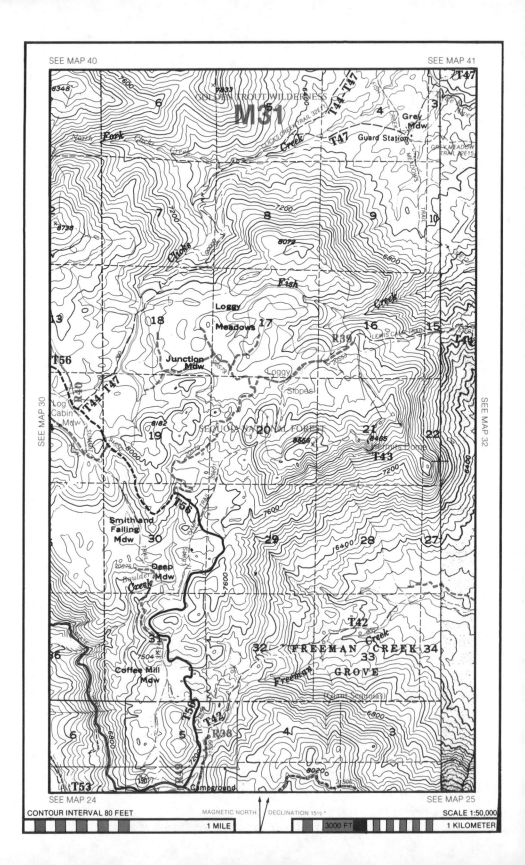

CONTOUR INTERVAL 80 FEET

MAGNETIC NORTH DECLINATION 15½°

SCALE 1:50,000

1 MILE   3000 FT   1 KILOMETER

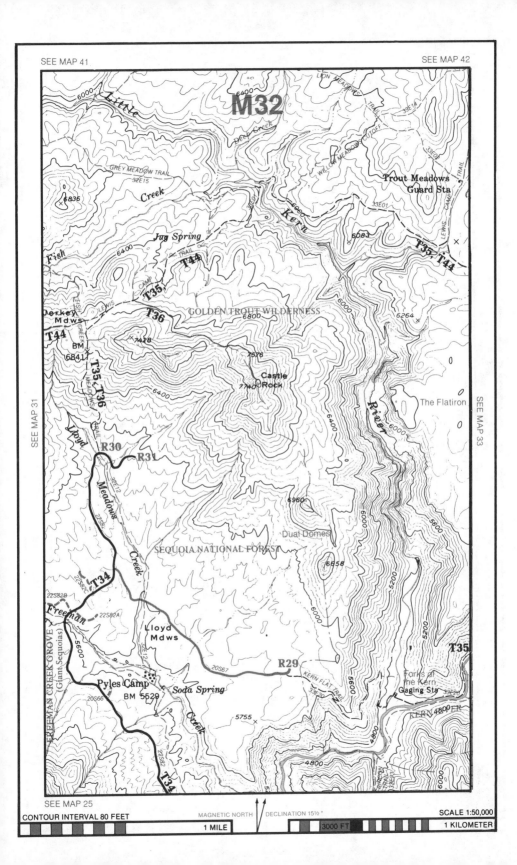

M32

SEE MAP 31

SEE MAP 33

Trout Meadows
Guard Sta

GOLDEN TROUT WILDERNESS

Castle
Rock

The Flatiron

Dual Domes

SEQUOIA NATIONAL FOREST

Donkey
Mdws

Jug Spring

Freeman

FREEMAN CREEK GROVE
(Giant Sequoias)

Lloyd
Mdws

Pyles Camp
BM 5529

Soda Spring

Forks of
the Kern
Gaging Sta

T34

T35, T44

T35

T36

T44

T35, T36

T34

T35

R30

R31

R29

CONTOUR INTERVAL 80 FEET

MAGNETIC NORTH   DECLINATION 15½°

1 MILE

3000 FT   1 KILOMETER

SCALE 1:50,000

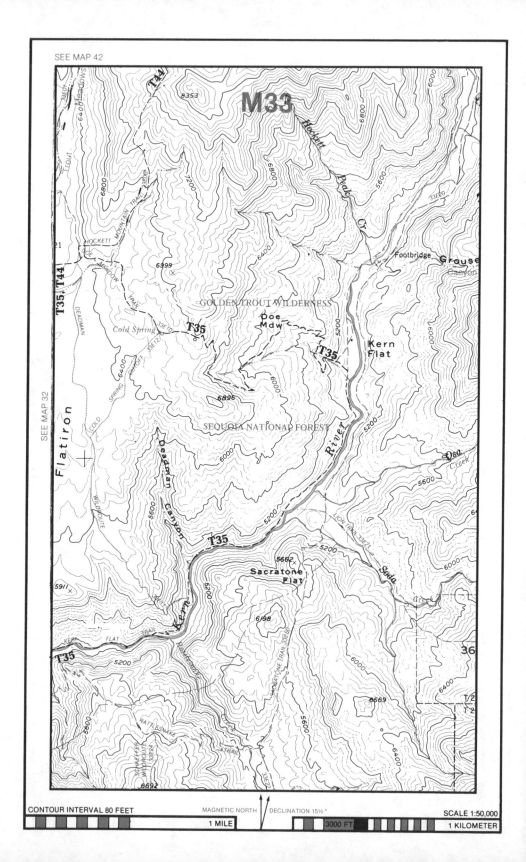

SEE MAP 42

SEE MAP 32

M33

8353

T44

Hockett Peak Cr.

6000

6800

5600

Trout

6400 Meadows

3360

3360

Footbridge Grouse
Canyon

HOCKETT

MOUNTAIN TRAIL 33E06

6800

7200

6400

6800

5200

6000

T35, T441

6999

X

GOLDEN TROUT WILDERNESS

Doe
Mdw

Kern
Flat

Cold Spring

33E12

T35

T35

SPRING CUTOFF 33E12

5600

5896

SEQUOIA NATIONAL FOREST

6000

River

5200

Osa
Creek

COLD

5600

DEADMAN

Flatiron

6000

5600

6000

Deadman Canyon

WILDROUTE

5600

5200

LION TRAIL 33E21

6000

T35

5662

X

Sacratone
Flat

5200

Soda

Creek

5911

X

6198

Kern

Kern

Trail

5200

KERN FLAT

RATTLESNAKE

TRAIL

6669

6400

36

T35

5200

5600

SCHAEFFER WILDROUTE

33E24

SACRATONE TRAIL 33E50

5600

5200

TRAIL

33E50

5600

6400

6000

6692

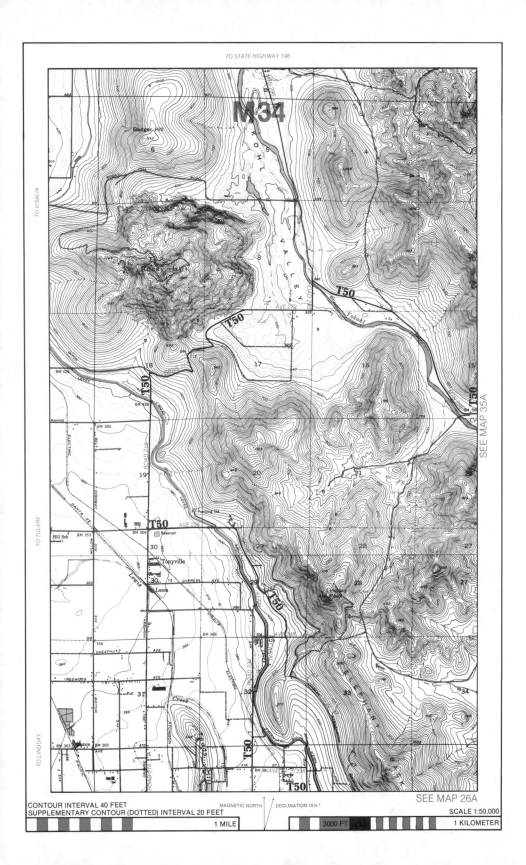

M 34

TO VISALIA

TO TULARE

TO LINDSAY

SEE MAP 35A

SEE MAP 26A

CONTOUR INTERVAL 40 FEET
SUPPLEMENTARY CONTOUR (DOTTED) INTERVAL 20 FEET

MAGNETIC NORTH   DECLINATION 15½°

SCALE 1:50,000

1 MILE   3000 FT   1 KILOMETER

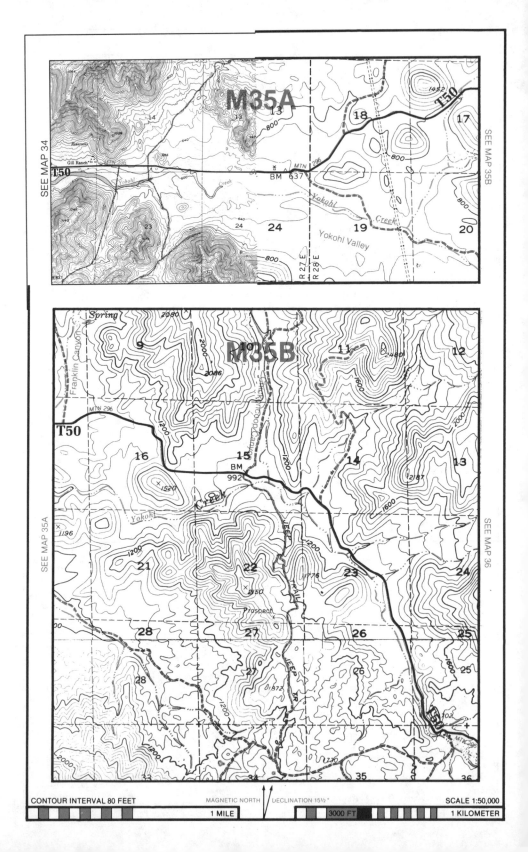

CONTOUR INTERVAL 80 FEET   MAGNETIC NORTH   DECLINATION 15½°   SCALE 1:50,000

1 MILE   3000 FT   1 KILOMETER

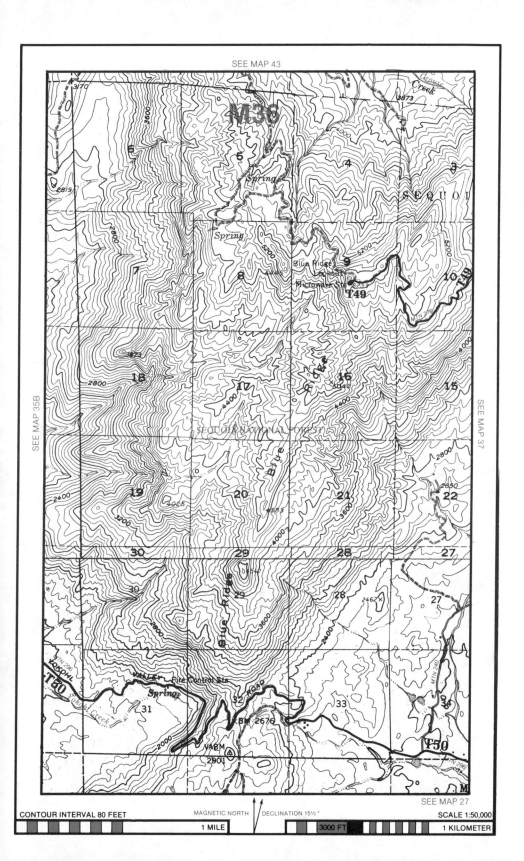

SEE MAP 35B

SEE MAP 37

CONTOUR INTERVAL 80 FEET

MAGNETIC NORTH   DECLINATION 15½°

SCALE 1:50,000

1 MILE   3000 FT   1 KILOMETER

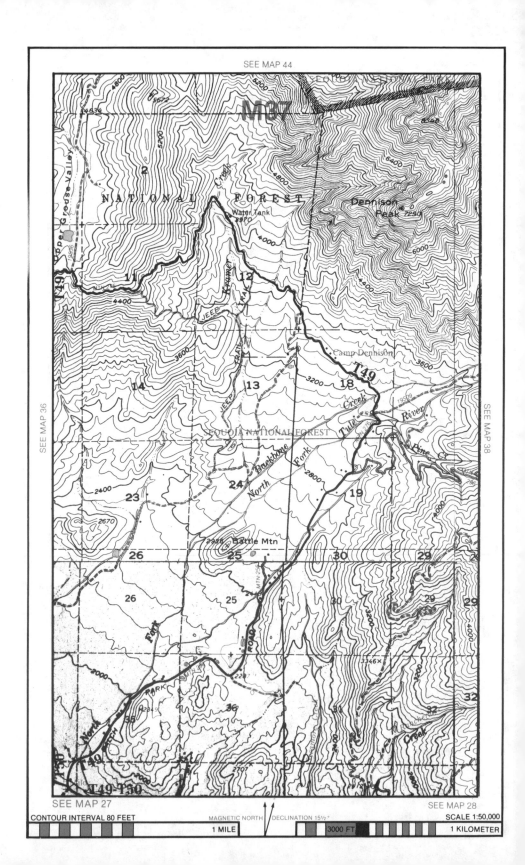

SEE MAP 36

SEE MAP 38

CONTOUR INTERVAL 80 FEET

MAGNETIC NORTH | DECLINATION 15½°

SCALE 1:50,000

1 MILE

3000 FT

1 KILOMETER

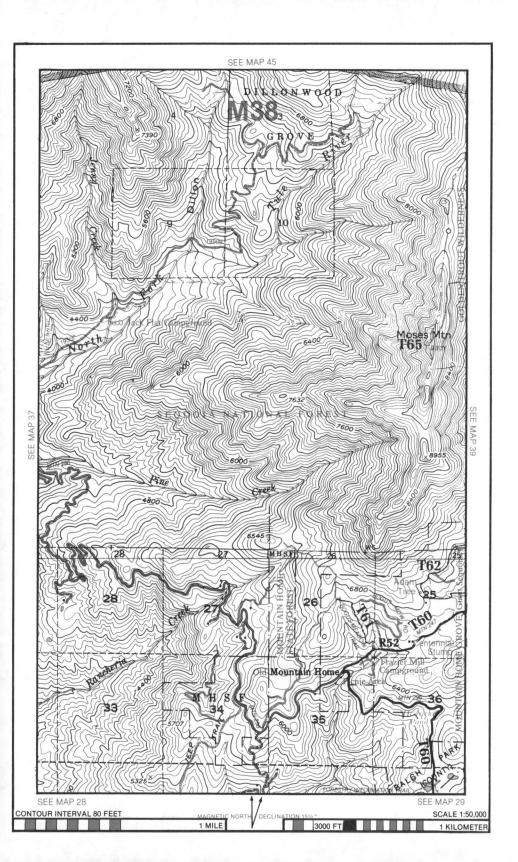

SEE MAP 37

SEE MAP 39

DILLONWOOD GROVE

M38

Tule River

Moses Mtn
T65

SEQUOIA NATIONAL FOREST

Pine Creek

Jack Flat Campground

North

T62

Adam
Tree

T61

T60

R52

Centennial
Stump

Frazier Mill
Campground

MOUNTAIN HOME STATE FOREST

Old Mountain Home

M H S F

Rancheria

DEEP TRAIL

Balch
Park

MOUNTAIN HOME GROVE

Hidden Falls Campground

FORESTRY INFORMATION TRAIL

CONTOUR INTERVAL 80 FEET

MAGNETIC NORTH DECLINATION 15½°

SCALE 1:50,000

1 MILE

3000 FT

1 KILOMETER

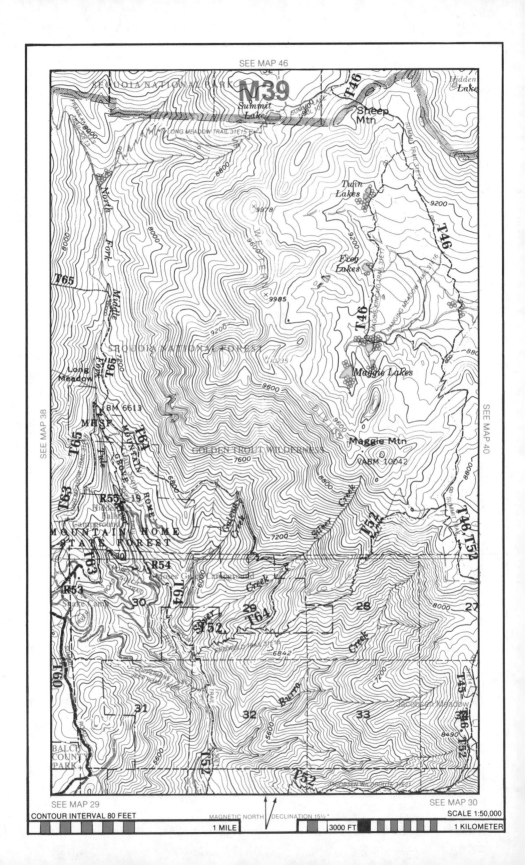

M39

Hidden
Lake

Summit
Lake

Sheep
Mtn

T46

Twin
Lakes

9200

Frog
Lakes

T46

Maggie Lakes

Long
Meadow

BM 6613

MHSP

Maggie Mtn

VABM 10042

GOLDEN TROUT WILDERNESS

7600

SEQUOIA NATIONAL FOREST

T65

R55

MOUNTAIN HOME
STATE FOREST

R54

R53

R52

T63

T64

T60

T45

T46, T52

31

32

33

Jacobsen Meadow

BALCH
COUNTY
PARK

CONTOUR INTERVAL 80 FEET   MAGNETIC NORTH DECLINATION 15½°   SCALE 1:50,000

1 MILE   3000 FT   1 KILOMETER

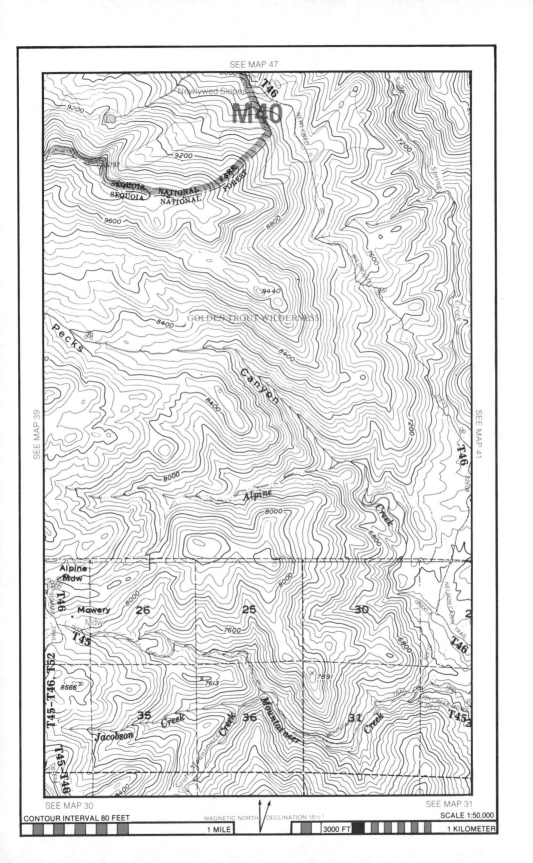

Newlywed Slopes

M40

9200

9297

SEQUOIA NATIONAL FOREST
SEQUOIA NATIONAL

9600

9200

7200

Springs

8800

9440

GOLDEN TROUT WILDERNESS

Pecks

8400

8400

Canyon

8400

7600

8000

Alpine

8000

Creek

7200

Creek

6800

T46

T46

Alpine
Mdw

8000

Mowery
Mdw

26   25   30   2

7600

6800

T45

T46

NELSON CBRN

8566

7613   7591

35   Creek   36   Mountaineer   31   Creek   T45

Jacobson

South Mountaineer Creek

8400

CONTOUR INTERVAL 80 FEET

MAGNETIC NORTH / DECLINATION 15½°

SCALE 1:50,000

1 MILE   3000 FT   1 KILOMETER

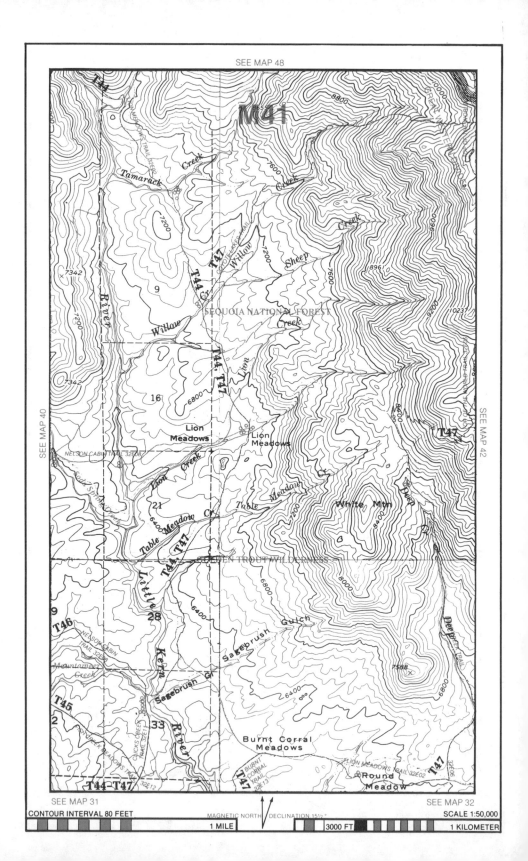

M41

CONTOUR INTERVAL 80 FEET

MAGNETIC NORTH DECLINATION 15½°

SCALE 1:50,000

1 MILE   3000 FT   1 KILOMETER

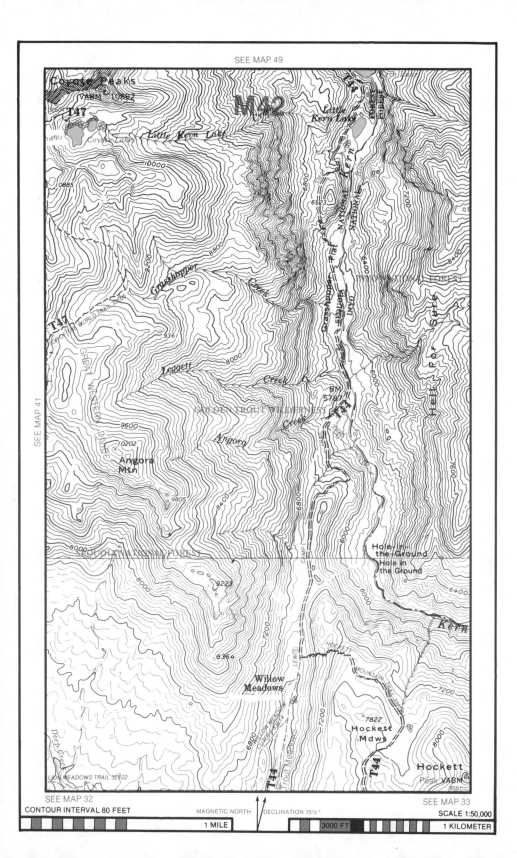

SEE MAP 41

CONTOUR INTERVAL 80 FEET

MAGNETIC NORTH   DECLINATION 15½°

SCALE 1:50,000

1 MILE   3000 FT   1 KILOMETER

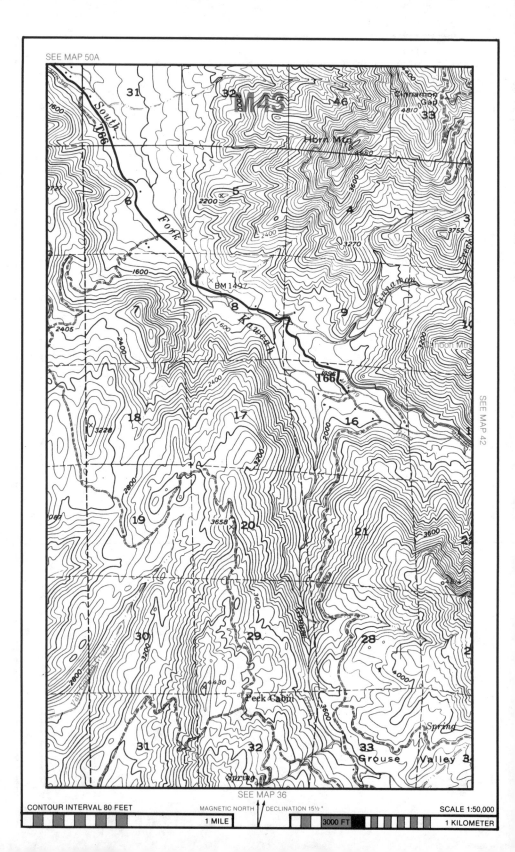

SEE MAP 50A

SEE MAP 42

SEE MAP 36

CONTOUR INTERVAL 80 FEET

MAGNETIC NORTH | DECLINATION 15½°

SCALE 1:50,000

1 MILE

3000 FT

1 KILOMETER

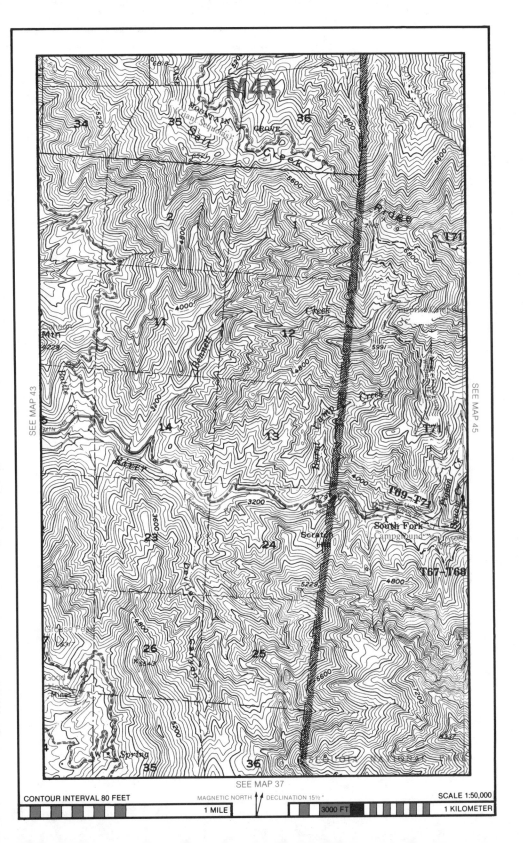

SEE MAP 43

SEE MAP 45

SEE MAP 37

CONTOUR INTERVAL 80 FEET

MAGNETIC NORTH DECLINATION 15½°

SCALE 1:50,000

1 MILE

3000 FT

1 KILOMETER

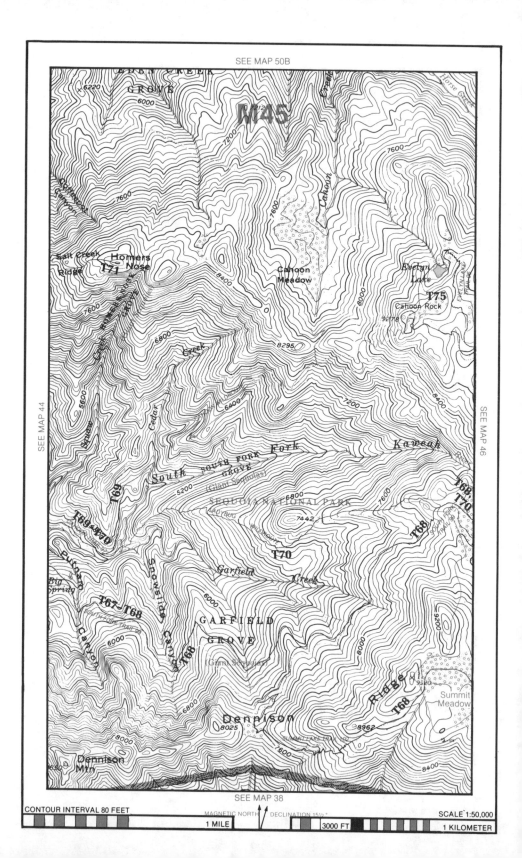

M45

GROVE

Horse Creek

7600

Cahoon

Cahoon
Meadow

Evelyn
Lake

T75
Cahoon Rock
9278

8295

8000

8400

Kaweah

South Fork Fork

South Fork
GROVE
(Giant Sequoias)

T69

T68
T70

5200

SEQUOIA NATIONAL PARK

8800

7442

7600

T68

T69-T70

T70

9200

Snowslide Canyon

Garfield Creek

Eureka

Big
Spring

T67-T68

GARFIELD

GROVE
(Giant Sequoias)

Canyon

T68

Ridge T68

9320

Summit
Meadow

8025

8962

Dennison

Dennison
Mtn

8000

8400

CONTOUR INTERVAL 80 FEET

MAGNETIC NORTH   DECLINATION 15½°

1 MILE   3000 FT   1 KILOMETER

SCALE 1:50,000

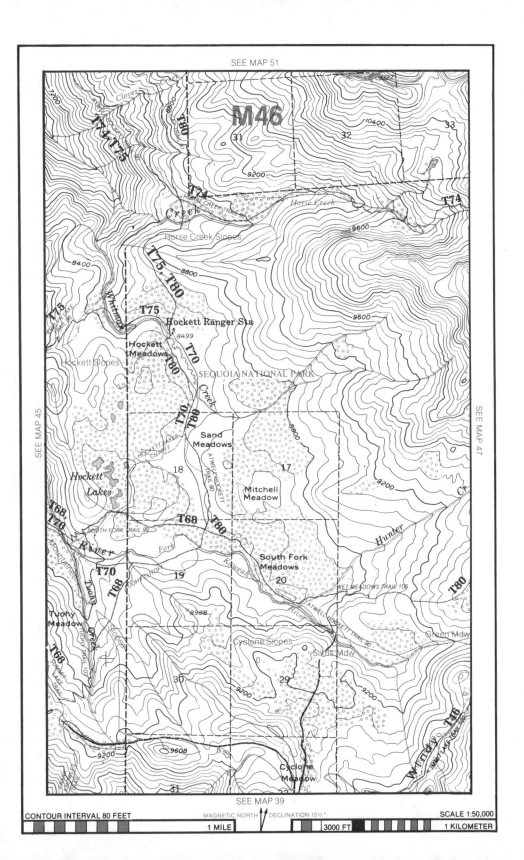

M46

SEE MAP 45

SEE MAP 47

Clover

Creek

Horse Creek

Creek

Horse Creek Slopes

HORSE CREEK TRAIL

Whitman

T74·T75

T80

31

32

33

T74

T74

T75·T80

T75

T80

T75

Hockett Ranger Sta

Hockett
Meadows

Hockett Slopes

SEQUOIA NATIONAL PARK

T70

T80

T70

T80

Sand
Meadows

ATWELL·HOCKETT TRAIL 90

HOCKETT LAKES CUTOFF

18

17

Hockett
Lakes

Mitchell
Meadow

T68·
T70

T68

T80

SOUTH FORK TRAIL 99

River

Fork

South Fork
Meadows

Kaweah

Hunter

Ct

T80

T70

T68

Middle Fork

19

20

Kaweah

River

ATWELL·HOCKETT TRAIL 90

WET MEADOWS TRAIL 100

Tuohy
Meadow

Twin Creek Slopes

TUOHY TRAIL 101

8988

Cyclone Slopes

Slins Mdw

Green Mdw

T68

SUMMIT TRAIL

30

29

W TUOHY

T46

9608

Cyclone
Meadow

TWIN LAKE TRAIL 106

31

8400

8800

9200

9200

9600

9600

9200

9200

10400

8800

8800

9200

9200

8499

2200

CONTOUR INTERVAL 80 FEET

MAGNETIC NORTH   DECLINATION 15½°

SCALE 1:50,000

1 MILE   3000 FT   1 KILOMETER

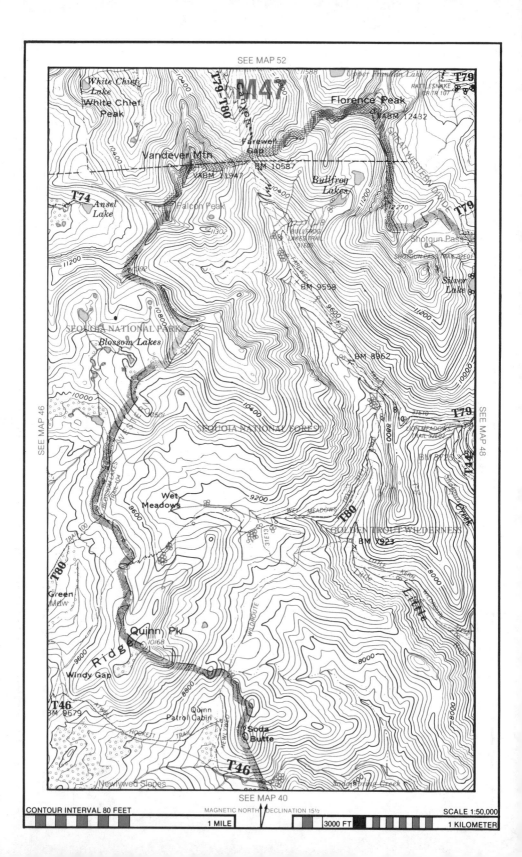

M47

White Chief
Lake
White Chief
Peak

Florence Peak
VABM 12432

T79

RATTLESNAKE
TR (TR 107)

Farewell
Gap

Vandever Mtn
VABM 11947

BM 10587

T74   Ansel
Lake

Falcon Peak

Bullfrog
Lakes

12270

T79

Shotgun Pass

11302

SHOTGUN PASS TR (TR 201)

Silver
Lake

11200

BULLFROG
LAKES TRAIL

BM 9558

11200

BM 8962

SEQUOIA NATIONAL PARK

Blossom Lakes

SEQUOIA NATIONAL FOREST

10500

10000

T79

FRANKLIN MEADOWS
TRAIL (TR 80)

BM

SEE MAP 46

SEE MAP 48

Wet
Meadows

9200

WET   MEADOWS

T80

GOLDEN TROUT WILDERNESS

BM 7923

Green
Mdw

Little

Kern

River

Kern

8000

T80

Quinn Pk
10168

8000

Ridge

Windy Gap

9600

T46
BM 9679

Quinn
Patrol Cabin

HOCKETT   TRAIL

Soda
Butte

Newlywed Slopes

T46

CONTOUR INTERVAL 80 FEET   MAGNETIC NORTH DECLINATION 15½   SCALE 1:50,000

1 MILE   3000 FT   1 KILOMETER

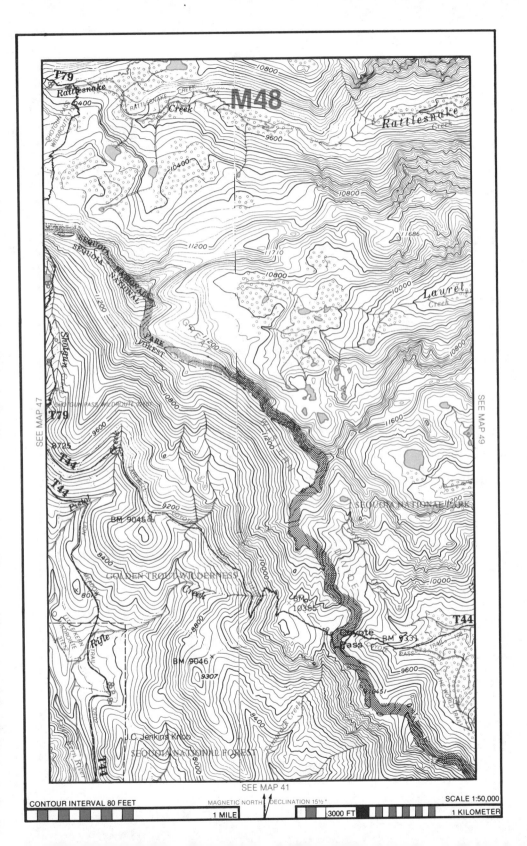

SEE MAP 47

SEE MAP 49

SEE MAP 41

CONTOUR INTERVAL 80 FEET

MAGNETIC NORTH DECLINATION 15½°

SCALE 1:50,000

1 MILE   3000 FT   1 KILOMETER

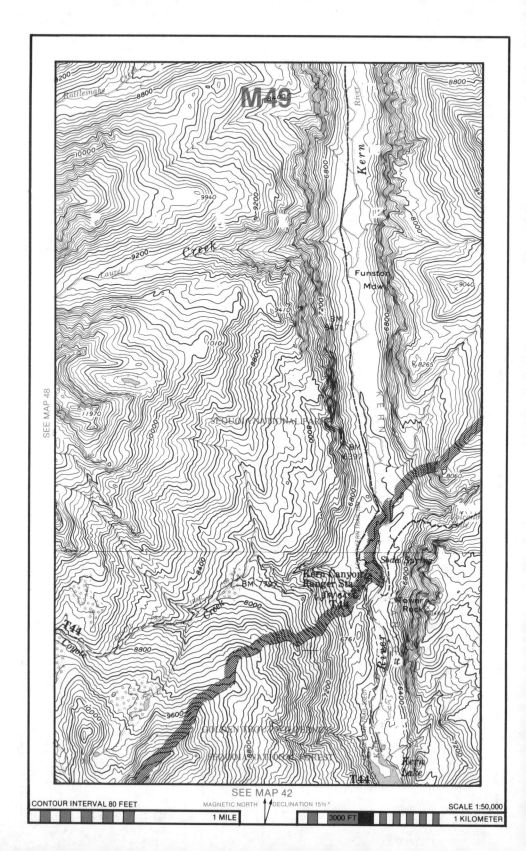

SEE MAP 42

CONTOUR INTERVAL 80 FEET

MAGNETIC NORTH   DECLINATION 15½°

SCALE 1:50,000

1 MILE

3000 FT

1 KILOMETER

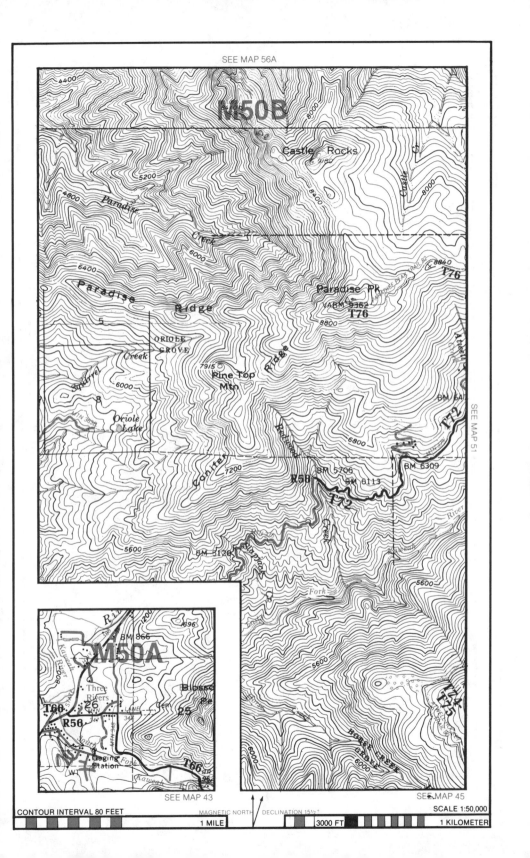

M50B

Castle Rocks

Paradise Creek

Paradise Ridge

Paradise Pk
VABM 9362
T76

T76

ORIOLE GROVE

Squirrel Creek

Pine Top Mtn
7915

Oriole Lake

Conifer Creek

BM 5706
R58
BM 6113

T72

BM 6309

Kaweah River

BM 5128

Redwood Creek

HORSE CREEK GROVE

M50A
BM 866
Three Rivers
T60
R50
Gaging Station

SEE MAP 43

SEE MAP 51

SEE MAP 45

CONTOUR INTERVAL 80 FEET

MAGNETIC NORTH   DECLINATION 15½°

1 MILE   3000 FT   1 KILOMETER

SCALE 1:50,000

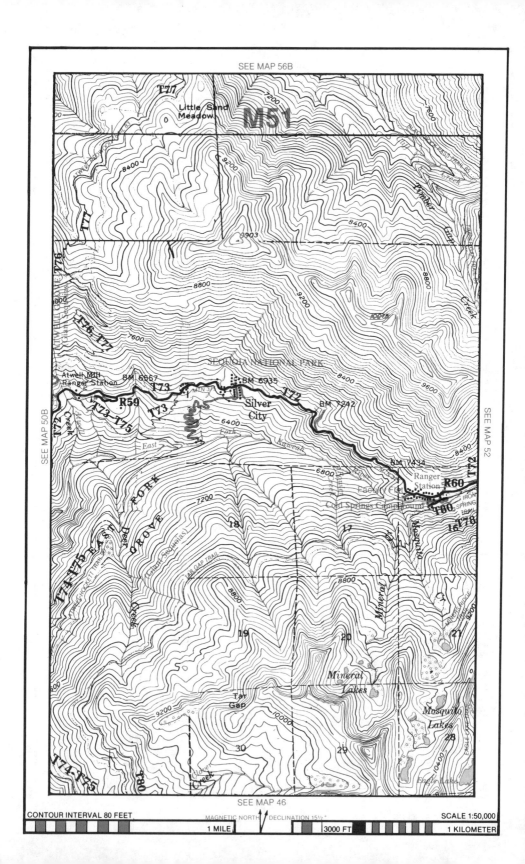

SEE MAP 50B

SEE MAP 52

CONTOUR INTERVAL 80 FEET

MAGNETIC NORTH DECLINATION 15½°

SCALE 1:50,000

1 MILE

3000 FT

1 KILOMETER

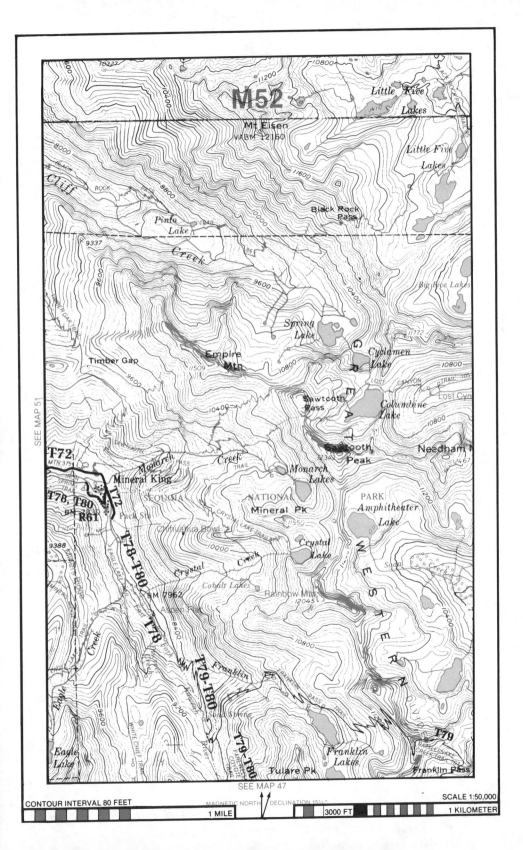

M52

Mt Eisen
VABM 12180

Little Five Lakes

Little Five Lakes

CLIFF

BLACK ROCK

Pinto Lake

Black Rock Pass

Creek

9337

Big Five Lakes

9600

Spring Lake

Cyclamen Lake

10800

Timber Gap

Empire Mtn
11509

Sawtooth Pass

GREAT

Columbine Lake

Lost Cyn

10800

LOST CANYON TRAIL

9600

10400

10800

10400

SEE MAP 51

T72
MTN 375

Monarch PASS

Creek TRAIL

Sawtooth Peak
12343

Needham

Mineral King

12467

T78 T80
BM 885 R61

T72

SEQUOIA

Mineral Pk
11550

Monarch Lakes

PARK
Amphitheater Lake

11200

9388

T78-T80

Pack Stn

Chihuahua Bowl

CRYSTAL LAKE TRAIL

Crystal Lake

WESTERN

9000

Soda Creek

T78

Crystal Creek

10000

BM 7962

Cobalt Lakes

Rainbow Mtn
12045

10400

T78

EAGLE LAKE TRAIL

8400

10800

Eagle Creek

T79-T80

Franklin Pk

FRANKLIN PASS TRAIL

T79

9600

Soda Spring

9200

WHITE CHIEF TRAIL

FARCWELL COYOTE TRAIL

T79-T80

Franklin Lakes

RATTLESNAKE CREEK TRAIL

Eagle Lake

Tulare Pk

Franklin Pass

SEE MAP 47

CONTOUR INTERVAL 80 FEET

MAGNETIC NORTH   DECLINATION 15½°

SCALE 1:50,000

1 MILE   3000 FT   1 KILOMETER

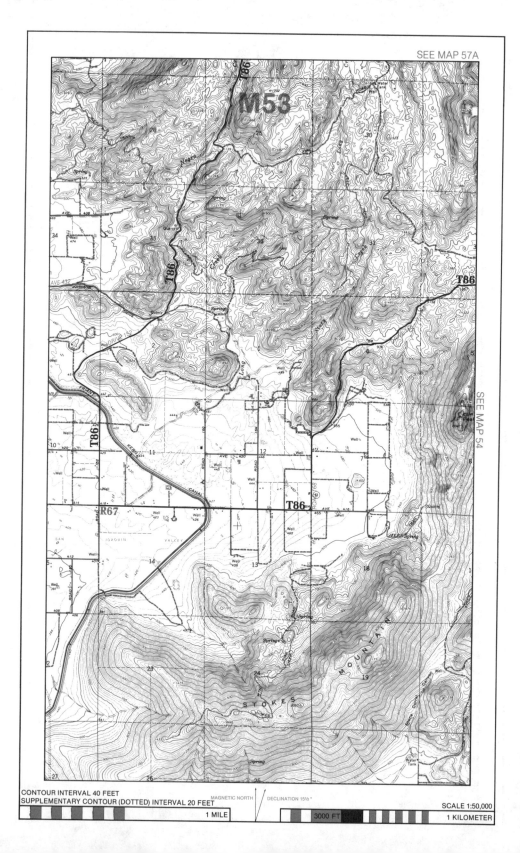

SEE MAP 54

CONTOUR INTERVAL 40 FEET
SUPPLEMENTARY CONTOUR (DOTTED) INTERVAL 20 FEET

MAGNETIC NORTH

DECLINATION 15½ °

SCALE 1:50,000

1 MILE

3000 FT

1 KILOMETER

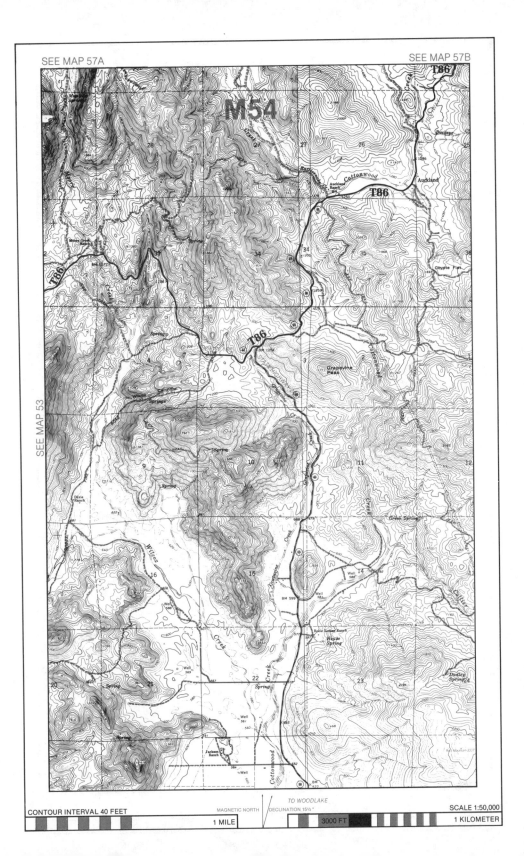

M54

T86

CONTOUR INTERVAL 40 FEET

MAGNETIC NORTH

TO WOODLAKE

DECLINATION 15½°

1 MILE

3000 FT

SCALE 1:50,000

1 KILOMETER

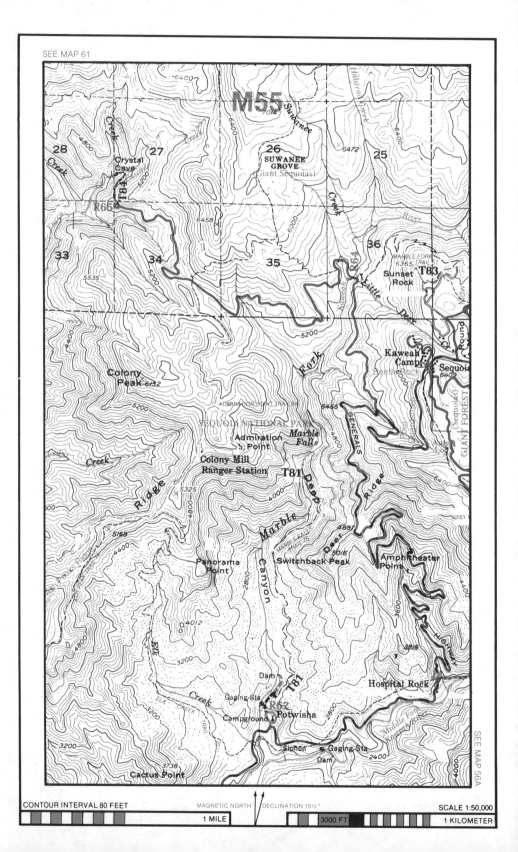

M55

28   27

Crystal
Cave

26
SUWANEE
GROVE
(Giant Sequoias)

25

33   34

35

36

Sunset
Rock

T83

Colony
Peak

Kaweah
Camp

Sequoia

GIANT FOREST (Sequoias)

SEQUOIA NATIONAL PARK

Admiration
Point

Marble
Falls

Colony Mill
Ranger Station

T81

Panorama
Point

Switchback Peak

Amphitheater
Point

Marble   Canyon

Dam

T81

Hospital Rock

Gaging Sta

R62

Potwisha

Campground

Siphon   Gaging Sta
Dam

Cactus Point

CONTOUR INTERVAL 80 FEET   MAGNETIC NORTH DECLINATION 15½°   SCALE 1:50,000

1 MILE   3000 FT   1 KILOMETER

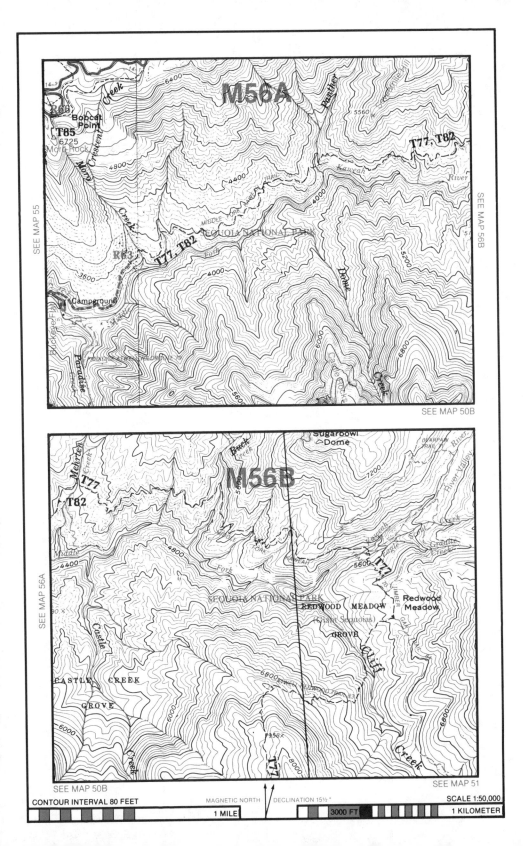

M56A

SEE MAP 55

SEE MAP 56B

Bobcat Point
T85
6725
Moro Rock

R63

Campground

SEQUOIA NATIONAL PARK

T77, T82

T77, T82

Kaweah

River

SEE MAP 50B

M56B

Sugarbowl
Dome

BEARPAW
TRAIL

SEE MAP 56A

Mehrten
Creek
T77
T82

Buck
Creek

River
Valley

Middle
4400

SEQUOIA NATIONAL PARK

REDWOOD MEADOW
(Giant Sequoias)
GROVE

Redwood
Meadow

T77

CASTLE CREEK
GROVE

Castle
Creek

7958 x

SEE MAP 50B

SEE MAP 51

CONTOUR INTERVAL 80 FEET

MAGNETIC NORTH   DECLINATION 15½°

SCALE 1:50,000

1 MILE

3000 FT

1 KILOMETER

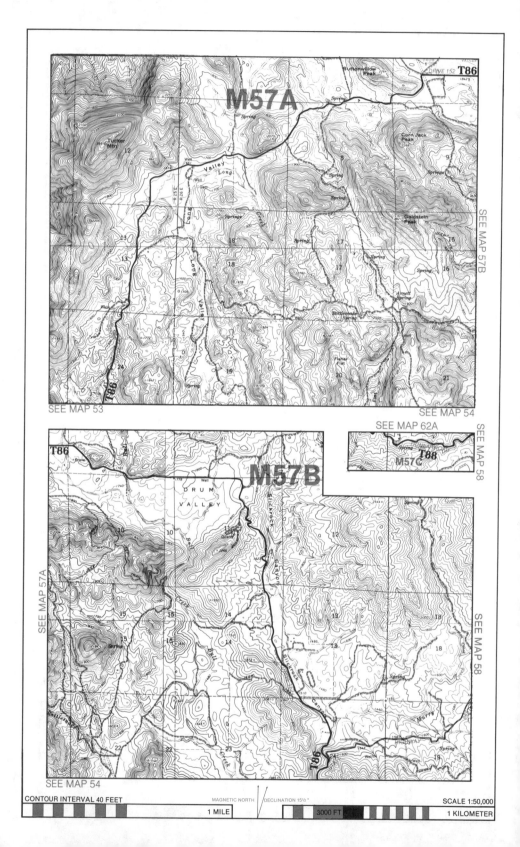

SEE MAP 53

SEE MAP 54

SEE MAP 62A

SEE MAP 58

SEE MAP 57A

SEE MAP 58

SEE MAP 54

M57A

M57B

M57C

T86

T88

CONTOUR INTERVAL 40 FEET

MAGNETIC NORTH

DECLINATION 15½°

SCALE 1:50,000

1 MILE

3000 FT

1 KILOMETER

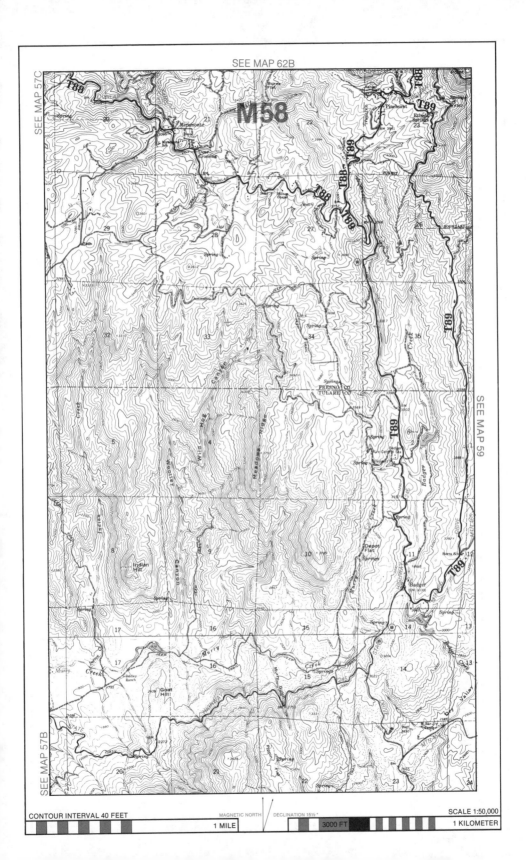

SEE MAP 62B

SEE MAP 57C

SEE MAP 59

SEE MAP 57B

M58

CONTOUR INTERVAL 40 FEET

MAGNETIC NORTH

DECLINATION 15½°

SCALE 1:50,000

1 MILE

3000 FT

1 KILOMETER

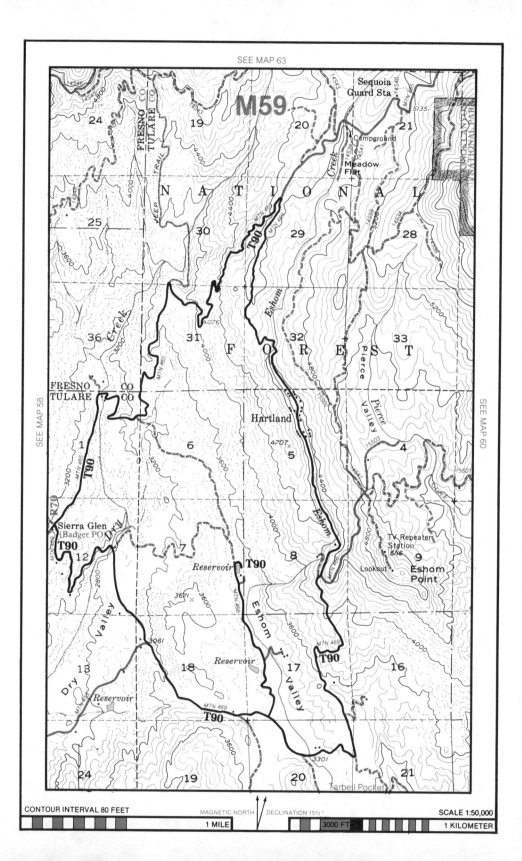

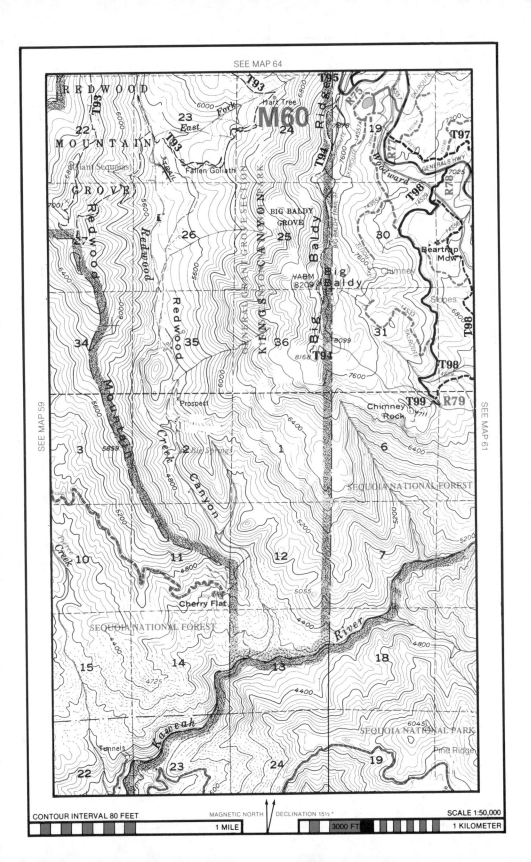

SEE MAP 59

SEE MAP 61

CONTOUR INTERVAL 80 FEET

MAGNETIC NORTH   DECLINATION 15½ °

1 MILE

3000 FT

1 KILOMETER

SCALE 1:50,000

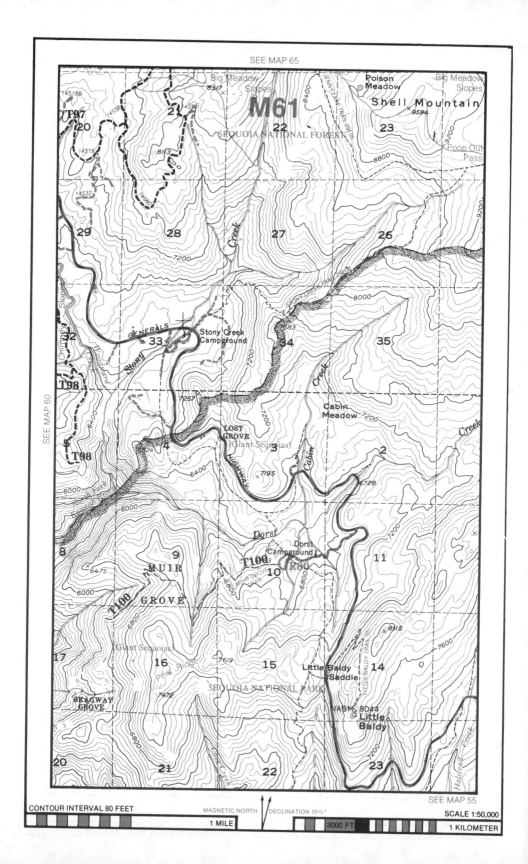

M61

SEQUOIA NATIONAL FOREST

Big Meadow Slopes

Poison Meadow

Big Meadow Slopes

Shell Mountain
9594

Poop Out Pass

T97
20

21

22

23

29

28

27

26

GENERALS

Stony Creek Campground

33

34

35

T98

SEE MAP 60

LOST GROVE
(Giant Sequoias)

Cabin Meadow

5

T98

4

3

2

8

9

MUIR

GROVE

Dorst

Dorst Campground

T100

R80

10

11

17

16

Pine Ridge

15

Little Baldy Saddle

14

Giant Sequoias

SKAGWAY GROVE

SEQUOIA NATIONAL PARK

VABM 8044 Little Baldy

20

21

22

23

CONTOUR INTERVAL 80 FEET

MAGNETIC NORTH

DECLINATION 15½°

SCALE 1:50,000

1 MILE

3000 FT

1 KILOMETER

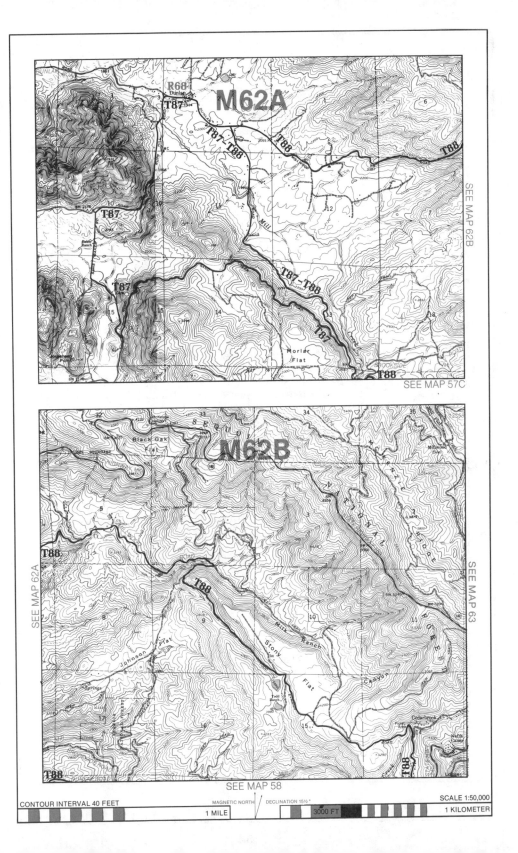

SEE MAP 62B

SEE MAP 57C

SEE MAP 62A

SEE MAP 63

SEE MAP 58

M62A

M62B

CONTOUR INTERVAL 40 FEET

MAGNETIC NORTH / DECLINATION 15½°

SCALE 1:50,000

1 MILE

3000 FT

1 KILOMETER

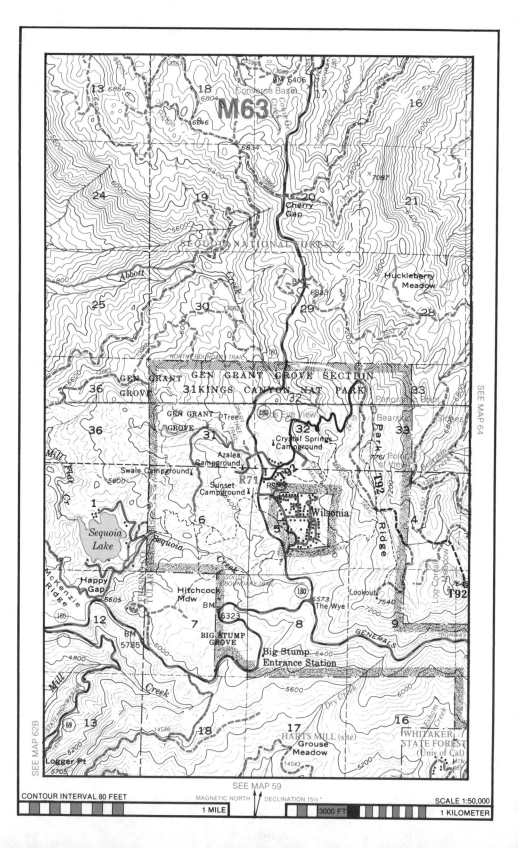

SEE MAP 64

SEE MAP 62B

SEE MAP 59

CONTOUR INTERVAL 80 FEET

MAGNETIC NORTH   DECLINATION 15½°

SCALE 1:50,000

1 MILE   3000 FT   1 KILOMETER

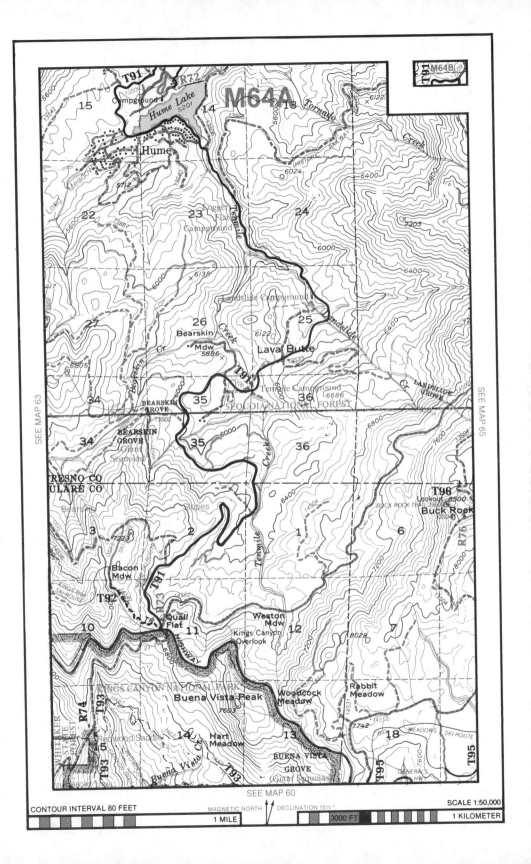

CONTOUR INTERVAL 80 FEET

MAGNETIC NORTH DECLINATION 15½°

1 MILE 3000 FT 1 KILOMETER

SCALE 1:50,000

SEE MAP 60

SEE MAP 63

SEE MAP 65

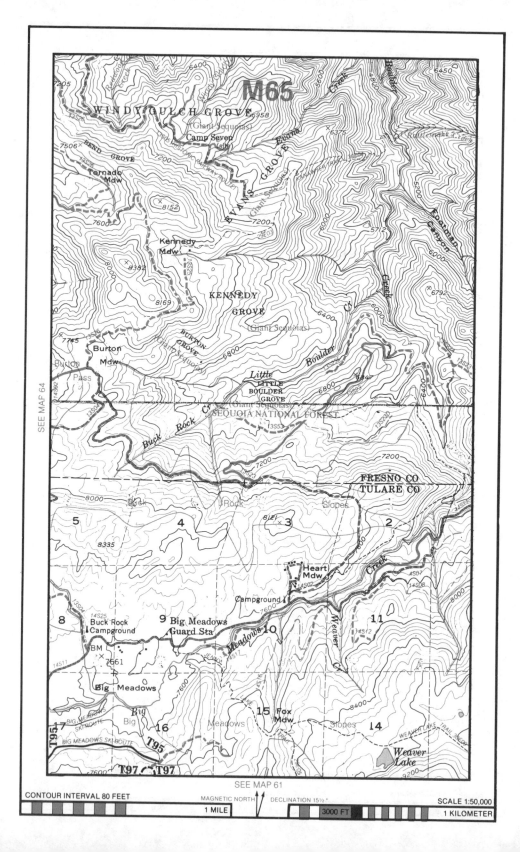

CONTOUR INTERVAL 80 FEET

MAGNETIC NORTH DECLINATION 15½°

SCALE 1:50,000

1 MILE

3000 FT

1 KILOMETER

SEE MAP 61

Index

Index

Index